W9-AVS-674

VÁMONOS

VÁMONOS

LIBRO DE ESPAÑOL

FERNANDO AUSIN GÓMEZ

RASSIAS CENTER AT DARTMOUTH COLLEGE

SERGIO INESTROSA

ENDICOTT COLLEGE

 BookStudio

VÁMONOS: Libro de español
Copyright © 2020 by Fernando Ausin Gómez, Sergio Inestrosa

First published in United States by BookStudio
2741 Kraft Lane, Missouri Valley, Iowa 51555

www.mybookstudio.com

Produced by BookStudio
Cover image by David Inestroza

All rights reserved. No part of this publication may be reproduced, stored in a retrieval system, or transmitted in any form or by any means electronic, mechanical, photocopy, recording, or otherwise—other than for "fair use" as brief quotations embodied in articles and reviews—without prior written permission of the publisher.

Paperback ISBN: 978-1-952891-01-4

For Library of Congress Cataloging-in-Publication Data for this title, visit http://www.loc.gov/help/contact-general.html.

To John Rassias' memory,
to our friend Jeff Wheeler,
and to all our students

Table of Contents

Prefacio

Vámonos is a complete introductory program that teaches the basic structures and vocabulary of the Spanish language and culture. This book serves as a great pedagogical tool to teach and learn Spanish. Based on real life scenarios that include many colloquial expressions, we infuse drama to help students participate didactically as actors of the different characters in the book.

The basis of this book stems from the French book *Le Français: Depart-Arrivée* by John Rassias and Jacqueline de La Chapelle Skubly, and from our own teaching experiences at the Accelerated Language Programs (ALPs) at Dartmouth College. It is through these two instances that the late Professor Rassias' influence permeates to create this comprehensive textbook.

Rationale

"You must speak a language to learn it—not learn a language to speak it" was Professor Rassias' main motto behind foreign language education and the basis for his internationally acclaimed Rassias Method®. This textbook relies heavily on this philosophy by offering creative tools for instructors to teach the language, and the necessary resources for students to practice speaking Spanish in contextualized opportunities.

It is based on a variety of real-life examples to easily identify with people from the Spanish-speaking world. Since communication occurs through an understanding of the language and how it works in a structural and cultural context, this textbook provides many possibilities for substantive thought and dramatic action. Students can identify with what Spanish-speaking people do when they speak, what they read, what inspires them, what bothers them, and what amuses them. It's a delicate mix of grammar, comprehension, vocabulary, fluency, and accent.

Each chapter, except **the preliminary chapter** begins with an **escenario**, each **escenario** is reinforced by the many exercises that appear throughout the chapter. Each exercise has been properly contextualized. We firmly believe that language is best grasped and registered when the use of senses and emotions are fully present. Communicating face-to-face then changes from a challenging or tedious encounter to a stimulating, entertaining and fun opportunity to perfect the language. Mutual respect, cooperation and engagement between instructors and students are key for these learning situations to occur.

Each **escenario** serves as an introduction to the core vocabulary and structure to be learned in the ensuing chapter. It also paves the way for further character development and relating to the various subjects presented. The **Notas culturales** further develop pertinent information about the subjects. The **Vocabulario ilustrado** and its accompanying exercises continue to construct the vocabulary.

Each chapter introduces new grammatical structures in the five

Apuntes gramaticales. Each grammar point is then reinforced by a sequence of exercises that invite either repetition, reflective responses, or creative answers.

These preparatory steps lead to more detailed activities provided by the carefully constructed **Trabajos prácticos**, the personalized **Preguntas** to answer among classmates, the multipurpose **Micrologues**, the practically designed **Lecturas** (which include many literary texts). All of these culminating activities encourage students to combine the chapter vocabulary and grammar in new ways to achieve a variety of purposes and prepare the students to perform at the intermediate and advanced levels of foreign language proficiency.

Finally, the **Vocabulario** section at the end of each chapter will further help students to check their mastery of the learned vocabulary.

Structure of the book
The book has 16 chapters. Besides those chapters, the book also has a **Capítulo preliminar**, a **Capitulo Informativo**, and two anexos.

The **Capítulo preliminar** presents practical Spanish expressions that may be put to use immediately, the correct usage of the Spanish alphabet, helpful hints on determining the gender of nouns, and other basics.

Beginning in **Capítulo 2**, at least one **Micrologue** appears in every chapter. These brief, culturally oriented passages may be used to develop auditory comprehension, dictation, and discussion skills.

The **Capítulo informativo**, contains eight optional grammar points. In the **Mundo de habla hispana**, reading passages on the history of the Spanish language and its evolution from the Middle Ages until today. A very important part of this segment is **El español en los Estados Unidos**, a historical perspective.

A Special Note to the Students

An exciting adventure awaits you. Because language influences the ways in which we think and perceive, studying languages gives us insight into how we view the world. As you study Spanish, your insight will expand as you learn to perceive the world through the eyes and the language of another culture. To acquire another language is essentially to acquire another worldview.

Learning another language means developing competence in five areas:

Grammar. Grammar provides an organized approach to learning a language. This textbook teaches grammar through dialogues, explanations, and exercises. Grammar is something taught inductively (by presenting examples of a structure before explaining it) and sometimes deductively (by explaining how a structure works and then presenting examples). To ensure that you will readily understand the explanations, we urge you to familiarize yourself with the **Glosario de términos gramaticales** in the **Apéndice** section, and to consult it every time you are puzzled by a particular term.

Comprehension. Comprehension of spoken Spanish may be developed relatively easily if you are alert in class, practice the **escenarios** thoroughly, and use the language laboratory. You will develop reading comprehension as you work on the various reading selections and activities.

Vocabulary. You will acquire vocabulary through the active use of words you learn in each chapter. You will quickly forget new words if you do not use them. Therefore, this text presents practical vocabulary in meaningful contexts.

Fluency. Many students mistakenly equate fluency with rapid speech and thus try to perform the miracle of speaking a foreign language as rapidly as a native speaker. In reality fluency is the ability to express your thoughts and feelings clearly, without stumbling too often. It is totally unrelated to the number of words spoken per minute. The drills and exercises in this book are designed to help you acquire fluency. To further aid fluency, do not attempt to visualize a word when you hear it, but get into the habit of "just gist" learning: try to grasp the general sense of words and sentences, rather than trying to decode word-for-word equivalencies.

Accent. You can cultivate as accurate an accent as possible by imitating the pronunciation of your instructor or any native speakers that you may know. Do not expect to develop "perfect" pronunciation, for there is no such thing!

The best advice we can give you about how to learn Spanish is to have the courage to allow yourself to make as many mistakes as necessary. Mistakes allow learning to take place and people speaking to each other allows communication to happen. Therefore, in order to learn to communicate in Spanish, you must begin speaking right from the first day of class. Make learning Spanish a productive experience — and most importantly — have fun!

CAPÍTULO PRELIMINAR

En este capítulo...

You will be introduced to the Spanish language. You will learn to use the Spanish alphabet, and become familiar with phonetic symbols. This will help you to pronounce new words. You will learn about the accents in Spanish, and will receive some instruction about gender, and the use of articles. You will also learn the present progressive form, a brief introduction to the reflexive verb **llamarse**, and the use of the verb **haber** ("hay") to express there is/there are. Along the way, you will learn several practical expressions so that you can begin speaking Spanish immediately. **!Vámonos!**

EL ALFABETO

El alfabeto o el abecedario (y su pronunciación fonética)

There are 27 letters in the Spanish alphabet. Their names are pronounced as indicated below. The phonetic transcriptions use the signs of the phonetic pronunciation.

Written	Phonetic sound	Written	Phonetic sound
a	a	ñ	éñe
b	bé	o	o
c	sé	p	pé
d	dé	q	kú
e	é	r	érre/ere
f	éfe	s	ése
g	gé	t	té
h	hache	u	ú
i	i	v	vé
j	jóta	w	doble vé/doble u
k	ka	x	équis
l	éle	y	yé/ i griega
m	éme	z	zéta
n	éne		

Follow the **interactive link to** help you with your pronunciation:

INTERACTIVE LINK

bookstudio.pro/9gq

Note that even though Spanish is a very phonetic language, some letters change their sounds when used with a vowel. See the following examples:

a. The letter h is silent in Spanish:

¡hola!	"ola"
hoy	"oy"
hombre	"ombre"

The only time when the "h" has a light sound is when is followed by the vowels "-ue" like in: hueso, huevo, huérfano, ahuecar.

b. The sound of the letter *c* is pronounced like a *k or q* before in most contexts, but it is pronounced the same as *z* or s (in Latin América) when followed by the vowels —*e* and —*i* :

casa	"kasa"	cena	"zena/sena"
coche	"koche"	cine	"zine/sine"
cuna	"kuna/quna"		

Note that words that have the double vowels —**ua** use the letter **c**: cuatro, cuarto; and words that have the double vowel —**ue** or –**ui** uses the letter q: quince, que, quien.

c. The letter "r" has a strong sound at the beginning of the word and soft after; then if you need to make a strong sound you need to use double "rr":

   ratón (trilled sound)
   pero (flapped sound)
   perro (strong sound)

d. In Spanish there is no difference between the sound of the letters "b" and "v". In México there is a tendency to pronounce both as b:

vocal	"bocal"
burro	"burro"
vuelvo	buelbo

e. In Spanish we use the letter "q" with vowels —**ue**, and —**ui** and we use the letter "c" with –ua:

"que"   "cuarto"

"quince"   "cuaderno"

f. Be aware that the "y" may have a sound of "i" when used alone or "y" in company of a vowel:

Yolanda **y** su esposo van a comprar el mandado.

Yo vivo en México.   I live in México.

g. In many Latin American countries the pronunciations of "ll" and "y" are similar or even identical. They may be pronounced like English *y*, or *j* (as in "job") or even *zh* (as in "plea*s*ure") or *sh* (as in "fish"), especially in areas such as Buenos Aires, Argentina.

h. In Mexico the letter x may sound as j like in the expression México (Méjico) and as s in words of nahuatl (Aztec) origin, such as Xochimilco.

i. The letter **z** in Latin American countries sounds like s, but in Spain sounds as "th" in the word thing:

        zapato   "sapato"

        zorro   "sorro"

        azul   "asul"

EJERCICIOS PRÁCTICOS

☺ ☺[1]

Use the Spanish alphabet to spell your first name and your last name. If your name has either a double vowel or a double consonant, you can simply say **doble** and then name the vowel or consonant.

Remember that not all Spanish speakers share the same pronunciation, just as not all English speakers pronounce their language in the same way.

---

[1] ☺ ☺ "Perform this exercise orally".

✎ "Write out this exercise".

Correct pronunciation should never become an obsession at the expense of speaking freely. Listen carefully to your professor, the CDs, online resources, and whenever you have the opportunity, to native speakers.

To pronounce anything, to communicate anything, you must first open your mouth. Therefore, rule number one for pronunciation and communication is to OPEN YOUR MOUTH AND SPEAK! Repetition is also crucial if you are to acquire a new language. Rule number two: PRACTICE, PRACTICE, PRACTICE! Rule number three: Don't be shy!

ACENTOS[2]

There are 4 types of words in Spanish according to the syllable that is stressed:

1. **Palabras agudas: canción, país, café, Lulú, José. Las palabras agudas** are stressed on the last syllable, and need an accent mark (tilde) if they end with the consonants **n/s** or any vowel.

   Note that all the verbs in infinitive are **palabras agudas**, and are not accentuated except for the verbs that end in –oír or –eír: oír, desoír, reír, sonreír, freír.

2. **Palabras graves: cama, árbol, difícil, lápiz, libro. Las palabras graves**, also called **llanas**, are stressed on the second to the last syllable, and need an accent mark if they <u>do not</u> end with the consonants *n/s* or a vowel. In terms of accentuation we can say that Spanish is a "grave" language, as easily 70% of Spanish words are **graves**. But that doesn't mean we are serious all the time! ☺

3. **Palabras esdrújulas: México, pájaro, película, obstáculo, máscara, estómago, cáscara, oxígeno, fósforo, hígado. Las palabras esdrújulas** are those that have a stress on the third to last syllable. All **palabras esdrújulas** have an accent mark no matter how the word ends.

---

[2] It is important to understand that the "acentos" never switched places, once you learn the stressed syllable it will remain invariable forever.

You can practice more at the **interactive link**:

INTERACTIVE LINK

bookstudio.pro/6z1

4. **Palabras sobresdrújulas: véndeselo, cómpresela, llévaselos. Las palabras sobresdrújulas** are those that are stressed on the fourth to last syllable, and they always require an accent mark. In general, these words are positive commands (either formal or informal) and they are not very common.

5. A diphthong consists of two vowel sounds together in one syllable. Spanish diphthongs combine either one strong vowel (**a, e, o**) with a weak one (**i, u**), or they pair two weak vowels together. Consider the words **veinte, siete, farmacia, democracia,** and **ciudad**; these words do not carry an accent mark because their diphthongs form a single syllable; also in some cases the tilde is over a strong vowel, in those cases there is no separation of syllables either; consider this examples: **canción, pasión, luciérnaga.** If, however, a pairing of vowels is broken down into two syllables, an accent mark (tilde/acento) is used to indicate this separation. If the pairing involves a strong and a weak vowel, place the accent mark on the weaker vowel, as in the following words: **filosofía, raíz, maíz, Raúl, baúl, laúd, día, río, biología**.

6. On some occasions you may find a triphthong, where words have a weak vowel added to a diphthong: continuáis, cambiáis; in those cases the tilde or acento is over the strong vowel.

7. Spanish also uses an accent mark to determine the proper usage of palabras homófonas (homophonous words), that is, words pronounced and spelled the same way as another word, but that have a different meaning. The Spanish language uses this type of accent for the word with the less-commonly used meaning. The following are very common examples: **te** (pronoun), **té** (tea), **de** (preposition) and **dé** (present subjunctive of the verb dar), **el** (article), **él** (personal pronoun).

8. All interrogative words have a written accent mark in Spanish: ¿cómo?, ¿cuándo?, ¿qué?, ¿cuál?, etc.

9. **Diéresis** (diaeresis) (**ü**). On rare occasions in Spanish you will find words that require the use of a diaeresis. This symbol emphasizes the pronunciation of the vowel **u**, and only two type of syllables can have a diaeresis: —**gue** or —**gui** like in the words: **pingüino, cigüeña, güero, lingüística.**

Note that not all words with the syllable —**gue** or —**gui** need diaeresis like the word guerra, guerrilla, guía, guisado, águila.

GÉNERO Y NÚMERO

1. In Spanish, all nouns have a gender, masculine or feminine, and they can be either singular or plural:
   MASCULINE SINGULAR: perro, coche, libro, cuchillo, país, mexicano.
   FEMININE SINGULAR: casa, cuchara, servilleta, chica, ciudad, paz, acción.

2. The plural is formed by adding —**s** to nouns that end in a vowel and —**es** to nouns that end in a consonant:
   MASCULINE PLURAL: perros, libros, lápices, peces, árboles, países.
   FEMININE PLURAL: casas, vacas, chicas, ciudades, luces, acciones.

   Note that if the noun ends in –z you will have to change the "z" to a "c" and continue to follow the rules for consonants. For example: the plural of **lápiz** becomes **lápices.**

3. The best way to remember a word's gender is to memorize it when you study the word, although there are some general tendencies, explained below. **Gender never changes.**

4. If masculine and feminine nouns are referred to collectively, they take the masculine form: **Los** abuelos (that includes el abuelo y la abuela)

5. Although there are exceptions, nouns with the following endings are usually **FEMININE:**

a. Most nouns ending in -**a**: puerta, toalla, chica, taza, casa, idea, cama, loma, toma, bufanda, agua.

Exceptions: día, sofá, papá, mapa, cura (priest), vodka, planeta, panda, tranvía, nirvana, puma, cometa, gorila, insecticida, pesticida (and all other chemicals ending in —cida) and most nouns ending in —ma (when they come from the Greek language and are masculine in Greek): problema, tema, poema, idioma, clima, trauma, sistema, aroma, cisma, diploma, dilema, lema, programa, prisma, fantasma, fonema, enigma, estigma, esquema, síntoma.

b. Nouns ending in **—ción, —sión, —gión**: nación, canción, inflación, prisión, presión, división, religión, legión.

c. Nouns ending in **—red** and **—dad**: pared, red, amistad, libertad, igualdad, genialidad, ciudad.

d. Some nouns ending in **—z** are feminine: faz, tez, vejez, gravidez, niñez, raíz, cruz, luz.
   Exceptions: lápiz, pez, arroz, jazz, maíz, disfraz, avestruz.

e. Nouns ending in **—sis**: tesis, crisis, dosis or **—itis**: sinusitis, poliomielitis,

f. Some nouns can be masculine or feminine depending on the article that is being used: el policía (a male officer) la policía (the entity, or a female officer), el modelo, la modelo, el dentista, la dentista, el atleta, la atleta, el artista, la artista, el huésped, la huésped, el presidente, la presidenta, el cura (*the priest*) la cura (*the cure*), el capital (*money*) la capital (*capital city*), el guía (*the guide*) la guía (*telephone book or female guide*), el dentista, (*male dentist*) la dentista (*female dentist*), el estudiante (male student) la estudiante (female student), el editorial (*the editorial*) la editorial (*the publishing house*), el orden (*sequence*) la orden (*religious order, command*), el papa (*the pope*) la papa (*potato*) etc.

6. Although there are exceptions, nouns with the following endings are usually **MASCULINE:**

a. **Words ending in —o:**
   plato, vaso, escritorio, carro, lapicero, muchacho.

   Exceptions: una mano, una foto (fotografía), una moto (motocicleta), libido, nao, polio (poliomielitis), porno (pornografía), radio (radio station).

b. Nouns ending in **consonants:**

—l: árbol, apóstol, ángel, capital (amount of money) with some exceptions like: sal, cárcel, capital (as a capital city), miel, piel, cal.

—n: balcón, bandolón, camión, andén, camisón, fisgón, campeón, refrán, pan, varón with some exceptions like: imagen, unión, razón, orden (command, religious group)

—r: borrador, marcador, profesor, proyector, pastor, castor, calor, color with some exceptions like: mujer, flor, labor, azúcar[3].

Words ending in consonants other than —l, —n, or —r are rare, like the words ending in —j: reloj, boj, carcaj, or in —t like debut.

But most often those words are of foreign origin that now are used in Spanish, such as clímax, fax, módem, pub, and boom.

c. **Compound** nouns are masculine:
paraguas, abrelatas, sacapuntas, lavaplatos, tocadiscos, portaaviones, rascacielos, parabrisas, sacacorchos, quitamanchas, etc.

d. Names of rivers, lakes, oceans and mountains are all masculine: el (río) Amazonas, el Paraná, el Usumacinta, el océano Pacífico, el Atlántico, el lago Titicaca, los Alpes, los Andes, los Pirineos, etc.

7. The gender of nouns ending in **—e** is difficult to determine; it is simpler to learn them one by one.
Feminine: clase, leche, noche, servidumbre, costumbre (and all words ending in —umbre: cumbre, lumbre, muchedumbre).
Masculine: coche, bache, broche, tache, acné, lente, trípode, traje (and all words ending in **—aje:** equipaje, pasaje, hospedaje, personaje and words ending in **—ambre** like: alambre, enjambre, calambre). But do not forget hambre is feminine.

8. Nouns ending in **—u** or **—i** (weak vowels) are not very common in Spanish. Here you have two masculine examples: **rubí, iglú.**

9. Nouns ending in **—y** are not very common and can be either masculine: **buey, carey, rey**, or feminine: **ley, grey.**

---

[3] Azúcar, in general, is a feminine noun in latin America but is masculine in Spain. Both forms are accepted.

10. Masculine nouns ending in **—o** are transformed into feminine nouns by changing the **—o** to **—a**: abuelo/abuela; amigo/amig**a**; gato/gat**a**; candidato/candidat**a**.

11. Masculine nouns ending in **–r** are transformed into feminine nouns by adding an **—a** to the **–r**: profesor/profeso**ra**.

12. For some animals (like elefante, serpiente, ballena, mosquito, mosca,) their gender is completely arbitrary and in general the word hembra (*female*) or macho (*male*) is used after the noun: el elefante hembra, la ballena macho.

13. Some nouns have different forms for masculine or feminine: actor is masculine, actriz is feminine, caballo is masculine, yegua is feminine, rey is masculine, reina is feminine, yerno is masculine, nuera is feminine, padre is masculine, madre is feminine, marido is masculine, esposa is feminine, carnero is masculine, oveja is feminine, toro is masculine, vaca is feminine, etc.

ARTÍCULOS DEFINIDOS E INDEFINIDOS

A. El artículo definido

1. The definite article **el, la, los, las** ("the" in English) indicates that the noun it accompanies refers to something specific. In general, the definite article used with masculine singular nouns is **el**, while the definite article used with feminine singular nouns is **la**:

MASCULINE SINGULAR	FEMININE SINGULAR
el avión	la azafata
el cuchillo	la comida
el vaso	la película
el plato	la taza
el piloto	la servilleta
el estudiante	la cuchara
el menú	la bandeja

Some feminine words that start with a stressed "a" like **agua**, are used with the masculine singular article[4] **el** or **un** for ease of pronunciation (to avoid cacophony): **el** agua. Other examples of feminine nouns that follow a similar pattern are: **área, águila, arma, arpa, hada, hampa, arca**.

2. Definite articles and nouns also have number: they may be singular, as in the examples above (section 1) or they may be plural. A noun ending in a simple vowel has an **—s** when plural or **—es** if a noun ends in a consonant:

MASCULINE PLURAL	FEMININE PLURAL
los menús	las azafatas
los cuchillos	las comidas
los vasos	las películas
los platos	las tazas
los pilotos	las servilletas
los estudiantes	las cucharas
los aviones	las bandejas

Note that feminine nouns which take the definite article "**el**" in the singular form do *not* use the masculine plural article; rather, they retain the feminine plural article **las**: **las hadas**, **las águilas**, **las armas, las aguas**.

Note also that compound nouns like paraguas, parabrisas, abrelatas, sacacorchos or nouns borrowed from Greek like *tesis* do not change when they are used as plural.

Note also that a singular noun ending in an unstressed vowel + **s** does not undergo any change in the plural form:

el virus	los virus
el campus	los campus
el lunes	los lunes[5]
la tesis	las tesis
la crisis	las crisis
la dosis	las dosis

---

[4] This rule only applies for articles. For instance, you use the feminine demonstrative adjective or the adjective mucha: "**Esta** agua está fría". "Ella bebe mucha agua". Both sentences are fine.

[5] All the days of the week follow the same pattern, with the exception of **sábado**, and **domingo**; el sábado/los sábados, el domingo/los domingos.

B. El artículo indefinido

1. The Spanish indefinite articles are **un, una, unos, unas** (a, an, one, or some in English)

MASCULINE SINGULAR
un pasajero
un estudiante
un señor
un piloto
un policía
un avión
un país

FEMININE SINGULAR
una pasajera
una estudiante
una señora
una azafata
una mujer
una flor
una silla

MASCULINE PLURAL
unos pasajeros
unos estudiantes
unos señores
unos políticos
unos policías
unos aviones
unos países

FEMININE PLURAL
unas pasajeras
unas estudiantes
unas señoras
unas azafatas
unas mujeres
unas flores
unas sillas

2. The indefinite article indicates that the noun it accompanies is referred to in a nonspecific sense. Note the different meanings of the indefinite and definite articles in the following sentences:

INDEFINITE ARTICLE
En los aviones por lo general hay **un** piloto y **un** copiloto.
Airplanes in general have **a** pilot and **a** copilot.

DEFINITE ARTICLE
En el avión de Thomas y John, **el** piloto se llama Jorge y **el** copiloto se llama Jesús.
In Thomas and John's airplane, **the** pilot's name is Jorge and **the** copilot's name is Jesús.

3. As a general rule, in Spanish, place an article in front of all nouns. There are some common exceptions to this general rule (you will study this in the Facultative Chapter). One of those exceptions is that Spanish does not place articles after the verb "jugar", bailar, or escuchar:

Ellos juegan fútbol.   They play soccer.
Nosotros bailamos salsa.   We dance salsa.
Ella escucha música.   She listens to music.

4. Spanish do not use articles in front of proper nouns (the names of peoples or countries):

Yolanda vive en Puebla.   Yolanda lives in Puebla.
México es un país hermoso.   Mexico is a gorgeous country.

Note that Latin Americans put the definitive article in front of some countries like Ecuador, Perú and Argentina. It is better not to use the article:

(La) Argentina es un país grande.   Argentina is a large country.

LOS PRONOMBRES PERSONALES[6]

SPANISH PRONOUNS	ENGLISH PRONOUNS	USAGE
yo	I	First-person singular:

Used when the subject is the speaker.

| tú | you | Second-person singular: |

Used among friends or equals, by adults to address children, and generally by children to address their parents[7]; sometimes used in arguments to indicate scorn. In general, one does not use this form when speaking to older people, strangers or people in a higher position in the social scale.

| vos | you | Second-person singular: |

---

[6] In Spanish, the use of the personal pronouns is optional since they are understood from the verb conjugations. Sometimes Spanish speakers use them to emphasize the subject.

[7] In some places like Guatemala, and Costa Rica it is normal for children to refer to their parents using **usted** instead of **tú**. In Colombia, the **usted** form is generally/often used not only with family members but also with friends.

Used among friends or equals, by adults to address children in countries like Argentina, Uruguay, Bolivia and Central America. In general, one does not use this form when speaking to older people, strangers or people in a higher position in the social scale.

usted[8]   you   Second-person singular:
Used to refer an unfamiliar person, an older person or a person who can be considered to be in a higher social position.

él he/it   Third-person singular:
Used to indicate a male person or a noun whose gender is masculine.

ella   she/it   Third-person singular:
Used to indicate a female person or noun whose gender is feminine.

uno   one   Third-person singular:
Used to indicate an indefinite person.

nosotros   we   First-person plural:
Used to refer to oneself and one or more other persons.

vosotros[9]   you   Second-person plural:
Used to address several people at one time in a very informal way. In cases in which you would use **tú** to address each person individually, use **vosotros** for the plural only when you are in Spain.

ustedes[10]   you   Second-person plural:
Used to address several persons at one time either in a formal or informal way, regardless of whether you would use **usted** or **tú** to address each individually, use **ustedes** for the plural form.

ellos   they   Third-person plural:

---

[8] In many countries the youth are not using the formal form, and they prefer to use tú or vos depending the country that they live in.

[9] This form is never used in Latin American countries.

[10] In Latin America this pronoun can be either formal or informal, depending on the context or the situation.

Used to indicate two or more masculine persons or things, or two or more persons or things of mixed gender.

ellas   they   Third-person plural:
Used to indicate two or more feminine persons or things.

Unos   some   Third-person plural:
Used to indicate two or more unspecific persons.

EL VERBO LLAMARSE

1. Spanish uses the reflexive form of the verb **llamar** (to call) to say one's name[11]. You will learn more about reflexive constructions in **Chapter Seven**, but for the moment it is important to learn the use of the verb **llamarse** (to call oneself).

2. In Spanish, there are two types of verbs from the perspective of conjugation:

a. **Verbos transitivos**. A transitive verb is one that affects or refers to another noun separate from the one that is performing the action in the sentence. For example, "Llamar" (to call): El hombre **llama** a su esposa.

b. **Verbos pronominales**. A pronominal verb is identified in Spanish by the suffix **se** that is attached to the infinitive, and is conjugated by placing a pronominal pronoun in front of the verb, for example, "**vestirse**" (to dress oneself): Ella **se** viste rápido. She dresses **herself** quickly.

3. The reflexive pronouns are:
me (for yo)   **nos** (for nosotros)
te (for tú)   **os** (for vosotros)
se (for él, ella and usted, uno)   **se** (for ellos, ellas, ustedes, unos)

Ex.: ¿Cómo **se llama** usted?
   Yo **me llamo** Sergio.
   Ella **se llama** Carolina.

---

[11] You can also use the verb **ser**, as you will learn in Chapter One.

EJERCICIOS PRÁCTICOS

☺ ☺

A. Practice the form llamarse in class.
(Yo)[12] me llamo (instructor's name).

    1.   ¿Cómo se llama usted? (formal)
        (Yo) me llamo _____.

    2.   ¿Cómo te llamas tú? (informal)
        (Yo) me llamo _____.

    3.   ¿Cómo te llamás vos[13]? (informal Argentina, Uruguay, Central America)
        (Yo) me llamo _____.

    4.   Él se llama (name of a male student)
        Él se llama _____.

    5.   ¿Cómo se llama la estudiante?
        Ella se llama _____. (name of a female student)

☺ ☺

B. One student begins the round robin: **Yo me llamo _____.** That student turns to the next student and asks: **¿Cómo se llama usted?** The second student answers: **Me llamo _____.** Then the first student reports to the professor: **Él/Ella se llama _____.** Continue until all students have participated.

EL VERBO "HABER" PARA EXPRESAR EXISTENCIA

Spanish conveys the idea of **there is/there are** by using **hay**:

_____

---

[12] The parenthesis means that you do not need to use the pronoun. In Spanish the verb carries the subject. Sometimes we use personal pronouns to make an emphasis.

[13] In some places like Argentina, Uruguay, and most Central American countries speakers use **vos** instead of **tú**. Sometimes the use of **vos** requires a different type of conjugation that we will not cover here. Like: Vos **sos** estudiante.

Hay un profesor en la clase.	There is a professor in class.
Hay muchos alumnos en la clase.	There are many students in class.
Hay doce chicos y trece chicas en la clase de español.	There are twelve boys and thirteen girls in the Spanish class.

Note that this kind of expressions are related with visual experiences, you can express the existence because you can see what is there.

Note that regardless of the number of people, animals or things, the form of **hay** doesn't change.

Note also that Spanish only uses **indefinite articles** (un/una/unos/unas) with hay:

Hay **unas** papas en la canasta.	There are some apples in the basket.
Hay **un** perro en la clase.	There is a dog in the class.

Note also that the expression "**Hay que**" is used also to express obligation or duty ("must"). You will study this in chapter 2 under the form "tener que": Hay que levantarse temprano   One must get up early to go to school.
para ir a la escuela.

Expresiones útiles:

¡Hola!	Hello/hi!
¡Buenos días!	Good day!
¡Buenas tardes!	Good afternoon!
¡Buenas noches!	Good evening/good night!
¡Escuche!	Listen!
¡Repita, por favor	Repeat, please!
¡Levántese! (formal)	Get up!
¡Siéntese!	Sit down!
¡Siga derecho!	Walk straight ahead!
¡Avance!	Forward!
¡Doble a la derecha!	Turn to the right!
¡Doble a la izquierda!	Turn to the left!
¡Deténgase!	Stop!
¡Abra la puerta!	Open the door!
¡Cierre la puerta!	Close the door!

¡Abra la ventana!	Open the window!
¡Cierre la puerta!	Close the door!
¡Abra el libro!	Open the book!
¡Cierre el libro!	Close the book!
¡Hable más fuerte, por favor!	Speak louder, please!
¡Hable más despacio!	Speak slowly!
¡Despiértese!	Wake up!
¡Contésteme!/	
¡Respóndame!	Answer me!
Gracias.	Thank you.
Muchas gracias.	Thank you very much.
De nada.	You're welcome.
Por nada	You're welcome.
Con permiso	Excuse me!
Perdón!	Pardon me!
Lo siento.	I am sorry.
Adiós.	Good-bye.
Chao.	Bye.
Hasta luego.	See you later.
Hasta pronto/Hasta la vista.	See you soon.
Hasta mañana.	See you tomorrow.
¡Qué tenga un buen fin de semana!	Have a good weekend!
¡Qué pase buenas noches!	Have a good night!

Más vocabulario: En el salón de clase

Repeat each sentence after your instructor

Aquí está el profesor.	The teacher is here.
Hay un profesor.	There is a teacher.
Aquí están los estudiantes.	The students are here.
Hay unos estudiantes.	There are some students.
Aquí está el salón de clase.	The classroom is here.
Hay un salón de clase.	There is a classroom.

El profesor está hablando.	The teacher is speaking.
Los estudiantes están escribiendo.	The students are writing.
Aquí está el libro.	Here is the book.
Hay un libro.	There is a book.
Hay unos libros.	There are some books.
Aquí está la bandera.	The flag is here.
Hay una bandera.	There is a flag.
¿Qué es esto?	What is this?
Es un estudiante.	It is a student. (male)
Es una estudiante.	It is a student. (female)
Es una silla.	It is a chair.
Es un escritorio.	It is a desk.
Es un pupitre.	It is a desk.
Es una pizarra.	It is a blackboard.
Es un borrador.	It is an eraser.
Es una pluma/ un bolígrafo.	It is a pen.
Es un cuaderno.	It is a notebook.
Es un libro.	It is a book.
Es un lápiz.	It is a pencil.
Son unos lápices.	These are pencils.
Es un marcador.	It is a marker.
Es una computadora.	It is a computer.
Es un diccionario.	It is a dictionary.
Es un proyector.	It is a projector.
Son unos estudiantes.	Those are students.

EJERCICIOS PRÁCTICOS

☺ ☺

A. Now quiz a class partner about the items in the classroom.
   Modelo: ¿Qué es esto?
                 Es un libro.

CAPITULO 1: LA SALIDA

En este capítulo...

You will learn how to say your name and ask other people's names. You will practice some Spanish expressions used to greet people, name eating utensils, and describe family relationships. You will also discover how to express how you feel and where you are going.

To help you do these things, you will learn about the verbs **ser/estar** (to be), the progressive tense, the verbo **ir** (to go), you will get familiar with the numbers 1 to 15, and you will learn how to ask questions using information words like ¿**cómo**?, ¿**dónde**?, etc. and you will get familiar with the numbers 1 to 15.

Contexto

Cuatro estudiantes estadounidenses van a México. Ellos son parte de un grupo más grande de estudiantes que pasarán un semestre estudiando español en la ciudad de Puebla. Los estudiantes se llaman Thomas, John, Anna y Lisa. Ellos son buenos amigos y están viajando juntos. Ellos están en un avión, con el resto del grupo. El avión va a México. Ellos tratan de hablar español durante esta "experiencia mexicana". La azafata les trae la comida.

Azafata:	Hola, buenas tardes. ¿Cómo están? ¿Van a comer?
Thomas:	Yo sí, muchas gracias, pero mi amigo va mal no va a comer, creo.
Azafata:	¿Está cansado o se siente mal, señor?
John:	Estoy cansado señorita. Estoy muy cansado.
Azafata:	¿Quieren descansar o prefieren ver la película?
Thomas:	Yo también estoy cansado, pero deseo ver la película.
John:	Yo prefiero dormir. No me despierte (*él busca las palabras*) no me despierte hasta llegar a la ciudad de México.
Azafata:	(*ella se ríe*) De acuerdo. Buen provecho. Le traeré los audífonos e en un momento, joven.
Thomas:	Gracias, señorita.
John:	Hasta luego, señorita.

VOCABULARIO: LA CHAROLA (BANDEJA)

Thomas y John están contentos. Ellos van a México. La azafata (aeromoza) les trae la comida. Sobre la bandeja hay un tenedor, una cuchara, un cuchillo, una servilleta, un vaso, una taza y un plato, además de la comida.

Dichos

Ser el abogado del diablo.	To play the devil's advocate.
Tomársela con calma.	Take it easy.
Hay más tiempo que vida.	There's more time than life.

Más vocabulario: El árbol genealógico de Martín.

1. José Zurita y Yolanda González de Zurita son los padres de Martín.
2. José es el padre.
3. Yolanda es la madre.

4. Pedro Zurita es el tío de Martín.
5. Ana González es la tía.
6. Las hijas de José y Yolanda se llaman Yolanda y Cecilia.
7. El único hijo se llama Martín.
8. Yolanda, Cecilia y Martín son los hijos de José y Yolanda.
9. Yolanda y Cecilia son las hermanas de Martín.
10. Yolanda es la hija mayor.
11. Martín es el segundo hijo.
12. La Srta.[14] Cecilia es la hija menor
13. Hay cinco personas en la familia Zurita González.
14. Los abuelos paternos de Martín son el Sr. Mario Zurita y su esposa la Sra. Guadalupe Marín de Zurita.
15. Los abuelos maternos de Martín son Don Carlos González y su esposa Cecilia Orozco de González
16. Los abuelos de Martín están muertos
17. Las abuelas de Martín están vivas.

Preguntas

1. ¿Quiénes son los señores Zurita?
2. ¿Cómo se llama el papá de Martín?
3. ¿Cómo se llama la mamá de Martín?
4. ¿Cómo se llaman las hermanas de Martín?
5. ¿Cómo se llama el tío de Martín?
6. ¿Cómo se llama la tía de Martín?
7. ¿Cómo se llama la hermana menor de Martín?
8. ¿Cómo se llama la hermana mayor de Martín?
9. ¿Cómo se llaman los abuelos de Martín?
10. ¿Cómo se llaman las abuelas de Martín?

Más vocabulario:

los hijos (m. pl.) the children   la familia (f.) the family

---

[14] Srta. is the abbreviation of Señorita (Miss)
Sr. is the abbreviation of Señor (Mr.)
Sra. is the abbreviation of Señora (Mrs.)

los padres (m. pl.) the parents
el padre (m.) the father
la madre (f.) the mother
el tío (m.) the uncle
la tía (f.) the aunt
las hijas (f. pl.) the daughters

el hermano (m.) the brother
las hermanas (f. pl.) the sisters
el chico/el muchacho (m.) the boy
los abuelos (m. pl.) the grandparents
el hijo (m.)   the son
las abuelas (f. pl.) the grandmothers

Más vocabulario: Los saludos

Here are some other expressions that you may use to vary your responses.
You meet a friend and he/she greets you with a hearty: **¡Hola!**
You may answer: **¡Hola! ¿Cómo está? ¿Cómo le va? ¿qué tal?**
He/she answers: **Bien**[15].
Estoy muy bien ¿y usted? (formal) ¿y tú? (informal)
Me va bien/ estoy bien/ me siento bien/ bien.
Regular.
Más o menos. Las cosas no están muy bien.[16]

EJERCICIOS PRÁCTICOS

☺ ☺

A. Now practice greeting your classmates using as many different expressions as possible.

---

[15] In Spanish, as in formal English, you have to use an adverb rather than an adjective to answer the question: how are you?

[16] In Spanish when you're not feeling well you blame the situation rather than yourself.

NOTA CULTURAL[17]: MÉXICO

1. When you are in Mexico, you will discover many similarities and many differences from your own world. These cultural phenomena define people, Americans and Mexicans alike.
2. Mexico is the country with the largest Spanish speaking population, with about 127 (ciento veintisiete) million people; the United States is the second largest Spanish speaking country with about 52 million people.
3. About 500 million people speak Spanish in 22 countries (including Puerto Rico). This book will prepare you to enter this vast territory as a knowledgeable person who appreciates the similarities and respects the differences that will be encountered.

APUNTES GRAMATICALES
1. LOS VERBOS "SER" Y "ESTAR"

1. Verbs are parts of speech that indicate some kind of action. Verbs may also convey the idea of motion, condition, existence, or relations.

[17] Each **Nota cultural** will provide you with information to help you communicate sensitively with the inhabitants of the Spanish-speaking community.

2. Some sets of verbs, known as regular, share a common conjugation pattern. Other verbs, known as irregular, exhibit exceptional behavior that is unique to them or to a very small set of verbs.

3. In declarative usage (in a sentence that is neither a question nor a (command) the subject (when expressed) usually precedes the verb. Remember that when the subject is one of the pronouns it is often not expressed.

4. The verb **Ser** (to be) is an irregular verb. In a very general sense, "ser" used to express the meaning "to be" when talking about where you are from ("Soy de Estados Unidos." / "Soy mexicano").

SUBJECT NOUN	SUBJECT PRONOUN	VERB	COMPLEMENT
yo	soy	estudiante.	
tú	eres	estudiante.	
vos[18]	sos	estudiante.	
usted	es	estudiante.	
(Thomas)			
(El estudiante) }	él	es	estudiante.
(La azafata)	ella	es	estudiante.
nosotros	somos	estudiantes.	
Vosotros	sois	estudiantes.	
(Thomas y John)			
(Thomas, John, y			
Lisa) }	ellos	son	estudiantes.
(Anna y Lisa)	ellas	son	estudiantes.

5. **Estar** (to be) is also an irregular verb. In a very general sense, "estar" is used to express the meaning of "to be" when you wish to talk about how you are doing (¿Cómo estás?) or to express location (¿dónde estás?). It also used as "to stay" like in the phrase "stay there" (Estate/estese ahí).

---

[18] If the plural informal in Spain is **vosotros** it is easy to make the singular informal form **vos**.

SUBJECT NOUN	SUBJECT PRONOUN	VERB	COMPLEMENT
yo	estoy	en el avión.	
tú	estás	en el avión.	
vos	estás	en el avión.	
usted	está	en el avión.	
(Thomas)			
(El estudiante) }	él	está	en el avión.
(La azafata)	ella	está	en el avión.
nosotros	estamos	en el avión.	
vosotros	estáis	en el avión.	
(Thomas y John)			
(Thomas, John y Lisa) }	ellos	están	en el avión.
Anna y Lisa	ellas	están	en el avión.

Note If you want to practice your verb conjugations, there are several websites that you can use. Here is one of those http://www.spaleon.com/

6. El verbo "ser" contrastado con "estar"

A. **El verbo ser is used in following situations:**

a. With an adjective that expresses basic characteristics that are unlikely to change soon:

Él **es** guapo.	He **is** handsome.

b. With a profession, religion, or nationality.

Él **es** doctor.	He **is** a doctor.
Ellos **son** católicos.	They **are** Catholic.
Ellas **son** canadienses.	They **are** Canadians.

Note that these situations express an unmodified condition therefore the definite article is not used. But if you express a modified profession, religion or nationality then you have to use the indefinite article:

Él **es un** buen estudiante.	**He's** a good student.

c. With a proper name or to introduce someone including yourself:

Él **es** Thomas.	He **is** Thomas.

Yo **soy** Pedro.	I **am** Pedro.

d. To translate the expression "It is X who…" or "X is the one who…":

Es ella quien hizo el trabajo.	**It is she who** did the job.
Ella **es** quien hizo el trabajo.	**She is the one who** did the job.

e. To express destination or recipient:

Los libros **son** para Thomas.	The books **are** for Thomas.
El regalo **es** para la cumpleañera.	The present **is** for the birthday girl.

Note that the preposition **para** is required in this situation because she is receiving something. You will study **por** and **para** in Chapter 7.

f. When the subject of the sentence is a phrase following an infinitive:

Esquiar en invierno **es** fantástico.	Skiing in winter **is** fantastic.
Hablar español no **es** difícil.	Speaking Spanish **is** not difficult.
Dormir **es** muy importante.	To sleep (sleeping) **is** very important.

g. In impersonal phrases:

Es importante…	It **is** important…
Es mejor…	It **is** better…

h. To refer to a place of origin. Note the need for the preposition de:

Thomas **es de** los Estados Unidos.	Thomas **is** from the U.S.

i. To express possession or relationship:

El coche **es** mío.	The car **is** mine.
Ella **es** su hermana.	She **is** his/her sister.

j. To describe what material an object is made of:

Mi chamarra **es** de cuero.	My jacket **is** made of leather.

k. To express time, dates, days, months or seasons:

Es tarde.	**It's** late.
Hoy **es** lunes.	Today **is** Monday.
Agosto **es** todavía verano.	August **is** still summer.

l. To express where an event is taking place:

La fiesta **es** en la casa de la familia Bernal.	The party **is** at the Bernals' house.

m. To express purpose, similar to the verb servir:
Los coches **son** para viajar.   Cars **are** for travel.

n. In passive voice sentences:
El estadio va a **ser** construido por los ingenieros.
   The stadium will **be** constructed by the engineers.

ñ. To express math results:
Cuatro más cuatro son ocho.   Four plus four equals eight.

    Note that with marital status you can use either **ser** or **estar**:
    Yo **soy** casado.   I **am** married.
    Ella **está** divorciada.   She **is** divorced.

B. **The verb** estar **is used in the following situations:**

a. To express a current situation or condition that is temporary (Note that current condition can be mental, emotional or physical):
Thomas **está** cansado.   Thomas **is** tired.
John **está** enfermo.   John **is** sick.

b. With adjectives that express emotion:
Los Zurita **están** contentos con Thomas. The Zuritas **are** happy with Thomas.
La chica **está** triste.   The girl **is** sad.

c. To express the result of an action:
La ventana **está** rota.   The window **is** broken.

d. To express location:
Mi madre **está** en Madrid.   My mom **is** in Madrid.
La oficina **está** cerca.   The office **is** close.

e. When one makes an observation based on the senses:
El agua del mar **está** tibia.   The ocean water **is** warm.
El café **está** caliente.   The coffee **is** hot.
La comida **está** deliciosa.   The food **is** delicious.

f. To form the progressive tense, as was seen in the Capítulo Preliminar:

Estoy leyendo.   I **am** reading.

g. The expression "estar a punto de..." is used in Spanish to express near future (*to be about to*):
   Ella **está a punto de** comer.   She **is about to** eat.
   Nosotros **estamos a punto de** llegar.   We **are about to** arrive.

h. With the preposition **con** to express some feelings or needs[19]:
   Estoy con hambre.   I **am** hungry.
   Estamos con sueño.   We **are** sleepy.
   Ella **está con** prisa.   She **is** in a hurry.
   Él **está con** mucho coraje.   He **is** very angry.

i. With other prepositions to express a temporary situation:
   Estoy de novio/de novia   I **am** dating[20].
   Están de manteles largos.   They**'re** celebrating a special occasion.
   Él **está de** balde.   He **is** unoccupied.
   Estoy de luto.   I **am** in grief/I am mourning the loss of...
   Estamos **de** pie.   We **are** standing.
   Estamos para servirle.   We **are** here to serve you.
   Usted **está por** empezar a comer   You **are about** to eat.

   Note that because of the differences between **ser** and **estar** expressed here, some adjectives have a different translation in English whether they are used with **ser** or **estar**. Por ejemplo:

   Ella **es** lista. ->   She **is** clever.
   Tú **eres** bonita ->   You **are** beautiful.
   Ella **está** lista. ->   She **is** ready.
   Tú **estás** bonita (hoy). ->   You **look** beautiful (today).
   Nosotros **somos** felices ->
        We are happy (as an emotion/feeling happy)
   Nosotros **estamos** felices. ->   We **are** happy (as temperament)

   _____

[19] The meaning here is very similar to that of some idiomatic expressions using the verb **tener** that you will learn in Chapter 2.

[20] Note that the choice of gender here depends on the subject of the sentence and *not* on the gender of the person he/she is dating.

La manzana **es** verde ->   The apple **is** green.

La manzana **está** verde. ->   The apple **is** unripe.

EJERCICIOS PRÁCTICOS

☺ ☺

A. Complete these sentences using **ser** or **estar**.

Modelo: Thomas _____ su amigo. (relationship)

Thomas **es** su amigo.

1. Ella _____ en la escuela.
2. Nosotros _____ estudiantes.
3. Yo no _____ guapo.
4. La fiesta _____ en mi casa.
5. La computadora _____ encendida.
6. Sus padres _____ divorciados.
7. Ellas _____ de Argentina.
8. Él _____ irlandés.
9. El café _____ caliente.
10. Ellas _____ amigas.

B. Complete the sentences using the verb **ser** or **estar**.

Modelo: Thomas _____ con su amigo. (location)

Él **está** con su amigo.

1. Los estudiantes y la azafata _____ en el avión.
2. La charola _____ de plástico.
3. Thomas, John, Anna y Lisa _____ amigos.
4. Thomas y John _____ altos.
5. El libro _____ de Anna.
6. La azafata _____ de Perú.
7. Mi papá _____ mecánico.
8. La azafata _____ trabajando.
9. John _____ estadounidense.
10. Thomas _____ soltero.

C. Complete the paragraph using **ser** or **estar**.

Yo _____ en el avión y tú también _____ en el avión. Ellas _____ en el avión. Las azafatas y los estudiantes _____ en el avión que va a México. Thomas _____ estudiante y John _____ estudiante también. John _____ mal. Thomas _____ viendo la película. Anna y Lisa _____ sentadas juntas. Nosotros _____ cansados.

D. Complete the paragraph using **ser** or **estar**.

Ahora nosotros _____ frente al Palacio Nacional. A la izquierda _____ la catedral. Esa _____ la bandera de México, _____ muy grande y _____ en el centro de lo que los mexicanos llaman el zócalo. Toda esa gente que ven allí _____ haciendo fila para entrar al Palacio Nacional; y esta gente que ven aquí _____ saliendo del metro que _____ debajo de la plaza. Como se puede ver por el decorado de los edificios, los mexicanos _____ muy festivos y les gusta celebrar en grande. Bueno, eso _____ todo por hoy ya _____ hora de irnos.

E. Insert the appropriate form of **ser** o **estar.**

Anna y su mamá _____ a punto de salir a hacer las compras. Anna _____ muy contenta de poder acompañarla. Al llegar al supermercado se queda sorprendida, "___ un mercado muy grande" le dice a su mamá. La señora Bernal _____ con hambre y le pregunta a Anna si quiere comer. Las dos _____ ya buenas amigas y les gusta _____ juntas. La mamá de Anna _____ casada, _____ mexicana y _____ dentista. Anna, por su parte quiere _____ enfermera. Anna _____ alta y la señora Bernal _____ gordita. Y aunque no se parecen en nada, ellas _____ como madre e hija.

2: PRESENTE PROGRESIVO[21]

1. In Spanish the progressive tense is formed in a similar way to English using the verb **estar** (to be) and the **gerundio** (gerund) of another verb (the -ing form in English). Spanish has two ways to form a **gerundio** depending on the ending of the verb in the infinitive: **—ando** (for verbs ending in **—ar**, like hablar), and **—iendo** (for verbs ending in **—er** or **—ir**, like comer or vivir).

2. There are some irregular **gerundios** that you will learn later in Chapter 12. These include those formed from the verbs **poder, dormir, reír, pedir,** etc.

3. The verb **ir** has an irregular **gerundio** **—yendo** although it is used less frequently than "going" is used in English. **"—yendo"** is also the ending for a small group of verbs with consecutive vowels such as **caer, leer, oír, poseer, creer,** and **traer**[22], but NOT with the verb **reír**.

4. The present progressive is used for an action that is happening at the moment that the speaker lives it; in other words, the speaker is speaking about it as an action that is in progress[23].

EJERCICIOS PRÁCTICOS

A. Use **ir a** to change these sentences.
   Modelo: Yo estoy _____ (**escribir**).
   Yo estoy **escribiendo**.

   1. Ella está _____ (**trabajar**).
   2. El profesor está _____ (**enseñar**).
   3. Thomas y John están _____ (**viajar**) a México.
   4. Las chicas están _____ (**jugar**) **fútbol**.
   5. Mi mamá está _____ (hablar) por teléfono.

   _____

[21] You will have the opportunity to study other forms of the progressive in Capítulo 15.

[22] Note that the verb **reír** (to laugh) does not follow this pattern.

[23] Whereas English refers to current positions of the body using the present progressive (e.g., "I'm standing," "They're sitting," "She's lying on the bed"). Spanish expresses the same thoughts using the past participle (e.g., "Estoy parado," "Están sentados," "Está recostada") as a temporal adjective or a current condition.

6. El perro está _____ (comer) pizza.
7. Mis hermanas están _____ (oír) música.
8. Tú estás _____ (leer) un libro.
9. Nosotros estamos _____ (correr) en el parque.
10. Ellos están _____ (lavar) ropa.

3.   EL VERBO "IR"

1. Like the verbs **ser** and **estar**, the verb **ir** is also irregular. Its conjugation is:

yo	voy	nosotros	vamos
tú	vas	*vosotros*	*vais*
vos	vas	*vosotros*	*vais*
usted	va	ustedes	van
él	va	ellos	van
ella	va	ellas	van

2. The verb **Ir** means "to go".
   Ellos **van** a[24] México.   They are **going** to Mexico.

3. The present tense of **ir** has the following English equivalents:
   { They are **going** to Mexico.
   Ellos **van** a México.   { They do **go** to Mexico.
   { They **go** to Mexico.

4. In the **Contexto** you saw **ir** used in the following forms:
   El avión **va a** México.   The airplane **goes** to Mexico.

5. Sometimes, **Ir** is used, instead of the verb **estar**, with the adverbs **bien** and **mal** to describe one's state of health or well-being:
   (Yo) **estoy** bien, pero mi amigo **va** mal. I **am** doing well but my friend is not.
   ¡Me **va** muy mal!   I **am** having a very hard time.

6. **Ir** + a verb in infinitive form the near (informal) future[25]:

_____

[24] Ellos van **a** México. In expressing direction you can also use the preposition **para** that you will learn in **Chapter 7**.

[25] You will learn the use of regular future in **Chapter** 12.

| (Yo) **voy a traer** los auriculares inmediatamente. | **I am going to bring** the headsets immediately. |
| Mañana ella **va a** hablar con él. | Tomorrow she **is going** to speak with him. |

7. The negative is formed by placing the adjective **no** before the conjugated verb:

Él **no** va a hablar con el profesor.

He is **not** going to speak to the professor.

8. The verb ir can be use with the preposition **de** to express purpose or to describe an action like:

| Ellas van de compras. | They are going shopping. |
| Los estudiantes van de paseo. | The students go for a walk. |

9. The verb ir can be use with the preposition **con** to express company, like in the following sentences:

| Voy con mi madre al mercado. | I go with my mother to the market. |
| Usted va con su amiga al cine. | You go with your friend to the movies. |

10. The verb ir can be use with the preposition **en** or **por to express means of transportation.**

EJERCICIOS PRÁCTICOS

A. Use **ir a** to change these sentences.

Modelo: Él mira el reloj.

Él **va a** mirar el reloj.

1. Tú entras en la sala de espera.
2. Nosotros documentamos el equipaje.
3. El empleado compra un bocadillo.
4. El señor acomoda el equipaje de los pasajeros.
5. Ella consulta el horario.
6. Vosotros verificáis la hora de partida.
7. Los estudiantes suben al autobús.
8. El conductor revisa los boletos.
9. En el autobús pasan una película.
10. Los pasajeros llegan a Puebla.

☺ ☺

B. With a friend create sentences using the verb ir with the countries and languages that they speak in those places.

Modelo: El avión va a **México** donde se habla **español**[26]

Francia	francés
Brasil	portugués
Italia	italiano
Inglaterra	inglés
Alemania	alemán
Arabia Saudita	árabe

☺ ☺

C. Work with a partner and use all the names of countries in the map above and all the forms of **ir** to ask and answer questions.

Pointing to Mexico on the map, you say: **¿A dónde vas (tú)?** Your partner answers: **(Yo) voy a México.** You point to another country, for example Paraguay, and ask: **¿A dónde vamos nosotros?** Your partner answers **Nosotros vamos a Paraguay.** Continue until you have covered most of the countries with your partner. Make sure that you use a different subject pronoun or noun for each one.

You can repeat this type of exercise using all the forms of the verb **estar** to ask and answer questions: Pointing to Mexico on the map, you say: **¿Dónde estás (tú)?** Your partner answers: **(Yo) estoy en México...**

The same can be done with the verb **ser.** Pointing to Mexico on the map, you say: **¿De dónde eres (tú)?** Your partner answers: **(Yo) soy de México...**

Note how the prepositions in the questions change according to the verb used in each exercise.

---

[26] Note that the names of languages are not capitalized in Spanish.

México

Cuba

República Dominicana

Puerto Rico

Guatemala Honduras

El Salvador Nicaragua

Costa Rica

Panamá Venezuela

Colombia

Ecuador

Perú Brasil

Bolivia

América Latina

Paraguay

Chile

Uruguay

Argentina

4. LOS NÚMEROS DEL UNO AL QUINCE

1. As you will learn, the counting system in Spanish is quite easy, and very logical. Nevertheless, you still have to learn these numbers by heart.

1 Uno
2 Dos
3 Tres
4 Cuatro
5 Cinco
6 Seis
7 Siete
8 Ocho
9 Nueve
10 Diez
11 Once
12 Doce
13 Trece
14 Catorce
15 Quince

2. The number **uno** agrees with gender so it can be **una** in front of a feminine object:

Tengo **una** fruta.　　I have **a** fruit.

3. The number **uno** also drops the —o in front of a masculine noun always:

Tengo **un** coche.　　I have **a** car.

EJERCICIOS PRÁCTICOS

☺ ☺

A. Repeat the numbers after the instructor so you can be familiar with them.

5. ¿CÓMO HACER PREGUNTAS?

Questions may be asked in several ways.

1. By inverting (reversing) the order of the subject, the pronoun or noun and the verb:

    Tú estás cansado   ¿Estás tú cansado?

2. By adding ¿verdad?, ¿cierto? or ¿no? to the end of the sentence:

    John va mal, ¿verdad?
    La azafata va a traer la comida, ¿no?
    Jesús es el copiloto, ¿cierto?

3. In spoken Spanish, you can change your intonation so that your voice rises at the end of the sentence[27]:

    (Tú) estás enojado. ↗ (Tú), ¿estás enojado?

4. By using interrogative words[28]:

a. **¿Cómo?** (how) asks for a description or condition: ¿Cómo es ella? (What is she like?) ¿Cómo está usted? (How are you?)

b. **¿Dónde?** (where) asks for places: ¿Dónde están los estudiantes? (Where are the students?)

c. **¿Cuándo?** (when) asks about placement in time: ¿Cuándo vas a México? (When are you going to Mexico?)

d. **¿Quién/quiénes?** (who) asks about people: ¿Quién les trae la comida? (Who is bringing them food?) ¿Quiénes son ellos? (Who are they?)

e. **¿Por qué?** (why) asks about the reason for doing something: ¿Por qué estudias español? (Why are you studying Spanish?)

f. **¿Cuánto/a/?** (How much) asks about cost, the duration of an action or qualitative nouns: ¿Cuánto cuesta el pasaje a México? (How much does the trip to

---

[27] In all those kind of questions (numeral 1 to 4) the speaker is expecting a yes/no answer.

[28] Questions using an interrogative words cannot be answered with a simple yes/no answer.

Mexico cost?) ¿Cuánto tiempo van a estar en México los estudiantes? (How long will the students be in Mexico?) ¿Cuánta arena hay en el mar? (How much sand is there in the ocean?)

g. **¿Cuántos/as?** (How many) asks about quantitative nouns, number of people or things: ¿Cuántos años tienes? (How old are you?) ¿Cuántas azafatas hay en el avión? (How many flight attendants are there on the airplane?)

h. **¿Qué?** (What) asks for **a definition** if followed by the verb **ser,** or **an explanation** if followed by other verbs: **¿Qué es** la libertad? (What is freedom?) ¿Qué está haciendo Thomas? (What is Thomas doing?). ¿Qué? is also used as **identification** followed by a noun to ask specific information or identify something, but quite often in conversational Spanish people use ¿cuál? because there is a choice implied: ¿En **qué** piso vives? (identification) ¿En **cuál** piso vives? (choice).

i. **¿Cuál/cuáles?** (Which) asks for **a choice among of a set of options.** ¿Cuál es tu número de vuelo? (What/which is your flight number?) ¿Cuáles botas quieres? (Which boots do you want?)

5. In many cases you can modify the type of question if you include a preposition before the interrogative word as in the following examples:

¿**A** dónde van los estudiantes?	(**To**) Where are the students going?
¿**A** qué hora llega el vuelo?	**At** what time will the flight arrive?
¿**De** dónde llega el avión?	**From** where is the plane coming from?

EJERCICIOS PRÁCTICOS

A. Make your own questions using 'question words'.

Modelo: ¿Quién?
        ¿Quién es él?

1. ¿Cómo?	6. ¿Dónde?	11. ¿Cuántos?
2. ¿Cuál?	7. ¿Por qué?	12. ¿A dónde?
3. ¿Qué?	8. ¿De dónde?	13. ¿Quiénes?
4. ¿Cuánto?	9. ¿Para qué?	14. ¿Desde cuándo?
5. ¿Cuándo?	10. ¿Dónde?	15. ¿De quién?

B. Answer these questions freely.

Modelo: ¿Dónde están los estudiantes?
Los estudiantes están en el avión.

1. ¿Dónde está la servilleta?
2. ¿Dónde hay un menú?
3. ¿Dónde está la profesora de español?
4. ¿Cuándo es la clase de español?
5. ¿Cuándo es tu cumpleaños?
6. ¿Cuándo es el partido de fútbol?
7. ¿Dónde es la fiesta?
8. ¿Quién es el profesor de español?
9. ¿Quién va a mirar la película?
10. ¿Cuánto dura el vuelo a México?

VOCABULARIO

Words listed here should become part of your active vocabulary. Memorize them. Nouns are grouped logically whenever possible.

VERBOS

ser	estar	ir

NOMBRES

la familia	el aeropuerto	el amigo/la amiga
los países y los idiomas	el avión	el/la camarada
la bandeja	el copiloto	el/la colega
el desayuno	la salida	los compañeros
el almuerzo	los audífonos	los auriculares
la comida	la experiencia	la mujer
la cena	la película	los/las jóvenes
el postre	la azafata	la señora (Sra.)
el menú	el itinerario	el señor (Sr.)
el helado	el pasaporte	la señorita (Srta.)
el agua	el pasajero	la profesora

la soda
el jugo
el número
el árbol
la fiesta
el grupo
Martín

el piloto
el policía
la nota
los padres
la clase
los/las estudiantes
José

el profesor
los alumnos
el apunte
los abuelos
el aire
la servilleta
Yolanda

ADJETIVOS

alerta
malo/a
bueno/a
inteligente
capaz
genealógico/a
libre

contento/a
alegre
feliz
triste
cansado/a
vivos/as

mexicano/a
estadounidense
argentino/a
brasileño/a
peruano/a
muertos/as

ADVERBIOS

también
bien
mal
sí
no

inmediatamente
en general
juntos
si

luego
muy
¿cómo?
¿dónde?

EXPRESIONES UTILES

¡hola!
delante,
buen provecho
buenas tardes
muchas gracias
hasta mañana

de acuerdo
al lado
de nada
buenas noches
adiós
¿cómo está?

detrás
entre
buenos días
hasta luego
hasta pronto
las cosas no están muy bien.

CAPÍTULO 2: LA LLEGADA

En este capítulo...

You will learn how to describe the airport, and ways of transport in the city. At the end you will learn about the extended family. To help you learn this, you will continue learning the numbers beyond 15 as well as learning how to ask and tell time, then you will study the verb **tener** (to have), and you will learn to conjugate regular verbs from the three verb families: —**ar**, —**er**, —**ir** verbs. These verbs include **hablar** (to talk), **comer** (to eat), and **vivir** (to live). You will also learn to use negative expressions.

Contexto

El avión llega al Aeropuerto Internacional Benito Juárez, de la Ciudad de México, a las tres de la tarde. El vuelo llega a la terminal dos, a la puerta 59. Después de desembarcar, Thomas y John buscan a Anna y Lisa, que son

también parte del grupo. Todos van a recoger sus maletas en la banda número cinco. Los trámites de migración y la recogida del equipaje están en la planta baja de la terminal.

Inspector de migración: Hola joven, buenas tardes.

Thomas: Buenas tardes, señor.

Inspector: ¿Cuánto tiempo se va a quedar en nuestro país?

Thomas: Todo un semestre señor.

Inspector: Muy bien. Bienvenido a nuestro país.

Thomas: Muchas gracias. Hasta luego.

Un poco después, mientras esperan el equipaje:

Anna: (Yo) no tengo mi raqueta de tenis.

John: ¡Ahí está!

Anna: ¿Tienen ustedes todas sus cosas... quiero decir todo su equipaje?

Thomas: Yo tengo todas mis maletas, pero no tengo mi saco de dormir. (Él lo busca)

Lisa: ¡Aquí lo tienes! (Lo toma de la banda y se lo pone en el carrito con las otras maletas)

Los cuatro amigos le preguntan a un policía ¿dónde hay una casa de cambio? Antes de ir a la estación de autobuses, necesitan cambiar dinero.

Thomas (al cajero): ¡Hola! ¡Buenas tardes! Necesitamos cambiar dólares por pesos.

El cajero: ¡Muy buenas tardes, joven! ¿Cuánto es lo que usted desea cambiar?

Thomas (se voltea a ver a sus amigos): Cien dólares cada uno, pienso que es suficiente ¿no?

El cajero: Muy bien, caballero, cómo usted ordene. Necesito sus pasaportes por favor, es un requisito para cambiar dinero en nuestro país.

Thomas (cuenta veinte billetes de 20 dólares y se los da al cajero junto con los cuatro pasaportes): Aquí tiene 400 dólares y los cuatro pasaportes.

El cajero: ¡Muchas gracias! En un momento le regreso los pasaportes y su cambio en pesos.

Thomas: Muy bien.

Vocabulario

¿A qué hora llega el vuelo?	At what time does the flight arrive?
El avión llega **a tiempo.**	The flight is on time.
El avión viene **retrasado.**	The flight is delayed.
El vuelo está **demorado**.	The flight is delayed.
El vuelo está **cancelado.**	The flight has been cancelled.
¿Qué busca él? ¿Qué está buscando él?}	What is he looking for?
¿Qué van a hacer antes de tomar el autobús?	What are they going to do before taking the bus?
¿Quién busca su saco de dormir? ¿Quién está buscando su saco de dormir?	Who is looking for his sleeping bag?
¿Cuánto dinero necesitan cambiar los estudiantes?	How much money do the students need to change?

Preguntas

1. ¿A qué horas llega el avión al aeropuerto de México?
2. ¿A quién buscan los dos estudiantes?
3. ¿Qué busca Thomas?
4. ¿Dónde está la sala para recoger el equipaje?
5. ¿En qué número de banda llega su equipaje?

NOTA CULTURAL: INFORMACIÓN PRÁCTICA

1. La **planta baja** is the ground floor.

2. Once you get to Mexico you may need to exchange money at the airport. It is customary to present your passport in order to complete this business transaction. If you prefer, you can use an ATM (un cajero automático), especially if you are planning to use your debit card. Many places now accept credit cards, so you do not need to carry a lot of cash (efectivo).
   Do not forget to inform your bank here in the US that you are planning to use your card in Mexico.

3. If you are staying in Mexico City it is better to use a certified taxi (**taxi de sitio**) to take you to your destination; Uber also operates in Mexico. You can also use **el metro** (**subway**), which is the least expensive and often the quickest means of transportation.

4. Once arriving at Mexico City's airport, you can take a bus to many cities that are relatively close by, such as **Puebla, Toluca, Cuernavaca,** and **Pachuca**.

5. You can buy your tickets at the bus station using Mexican currency or credit cards. All seats on these buses are preassigned.

6. **Un autobús**, is a bus that travels between cities that are far apart.

7. **Camión** used to be the name for the public buses in Mexico City, but now there is a new bus system called **Metrobús**.

8. In a very few places in the city you still can use a **trolebús** (tram).

Dichos

A Dios rogando y al mazo dando.	God helps those who help themselves.
Al que madruga, Dios lo ayuda.	The early bird catches the worm.
Poner las cartas sobre la mesa.	To lay your cards on the table.

VOCABULARIO: TRANSPORTES Y COMERCIOS

En la ciudad de México hay muchos medios (*means*) de transporte. Hay por ejemplo bicicletas (bicis) motocicletas (motos) coches, taxis, peseros, metrobuses, trolebuses, metro y el tren ligero.

En una ciudad típica **uno** (*a person*) encuentra diversas tiendas y negocios (*shops*). Hay **entre otros** (*among others*), restaurantes y cafeterías donde uno puede comer un **bocadillo** (*sandwich*), cines para ver **películas** (*films*), tiendas donde se puede comprar **ropa** (*clothing*), librerías (*bookstores*) para comprar libros, bibliotecas públicas (*public libraries*), cyber cafés, oficinas de correos para enviar **cartas** (*letters*), oficinas de telégrafos para enviar telegramas y dinero, kioscos donde se pueden comprar periódicos y revistas, tarjetas postales, chicles y **dulces** (*candies*) y **tarjetas telefónicas** (*phone cards*).

Preguntas

1. ¿Hay metro en su ciudad (*your city*)?
2. Si no hay (*if not*) ¿Cuáles son los medios de transporte?
3. ¿Tiene usted coche? ¿De qué marca es (*make*)?
4. ¿Cómo llega usted a la escuela (*school*)? ¿En bicicleta, en coche, a pie (*on foot*), o en autobús?
5. En su escuela los estudiantes tienen ¿bicicletas, coches, patinetas (skateboard)?

Más vocabulario: El aeropuerto

la forma migratoria	tourist immigration form
verificar los pasaportes	to check passports
el agente de migración	the immigration officer
nada que declarar	nothing to declare
el agente de aduanas	the customs agent
los/las turistas	tourists
extrañar su país	to be homesick
la declaración de aduanas	the customs declaration form
enseñar	to show / to teach
abrir	to open

bromear	to joke
llegar a tiempo	to arrive on time
el botón del semáforo[29]	the "red light/green light" custom button.

EJERCICIOS PRÁCTICOS

✎

A. Complete the paragraph with the appropriate words from **Más vocabulario**
El avión de los jóvenes va a _____ a tiempo. En el avión, las azafatas les dan a los pasajeros _____ y la declaración de _____. Los agentes de migración van a revisar la forma _____ junto con los _____. Después se pasa con el agente de aduana y se le entrega _____ de aduanas. Thomas y John le dicen (*tell*) al agente de aduana que ellos no tienen _____ y dicen bromeando (*joking*) : "Nosotros no vamos a _____ como todos (*like all*) los turistas". A Anna le toca el **semáforo en rojo** (*red light*) y tiene que _____ su maleta donde sólo hay cosas de uso personal.

☺☺
B. Now ask your partner questions about the paragraph in item A.
1. ¿A qué hora va a llegar el avión?
2. ¿Quién da las formas migratorias en el avión?
3. ¿Quién verifica los pasaportes de los pasajeros?
4. ¿Qué es lo que Anna tiene que abrir?
5. ¿A quiénes les enseñan sus bolsas y maletas?
6. ¿Qué le dicen los jóvenes al agente de aduana?

---

[29] This was an old practice in México City, where every person or the head of a family coming from another country has to press a button to clear customs. If you get a green light you are clear to go, but if you get a red light, your luggage has to be searched.

APUNTES GRAMATICALES

6. LOS NÚMEROS CARDINALES A PARTIR DEL 16

As you will see the counting system in Spanish is quite easy. There are a few basic and logical rules to learn. Note the combination of the tens and units:

16	diez **y** seis or dieci**s**éis
17	diez **y** siete or diec**i**siete
18	diez **y** ocho or diec**i**ocho
19	diez **y** nueve or diec**i**nueve
20	veinte
21	veinte **y** uno/**a** or veintiuno[30]/**a** **o** **veintiún (if is in front of a masculine noun)**
22	veinte **y** dos or veint**i**dós
23	veinte **y** tres or veint**i**trés
30	treinta
31	treinta **y** uno/**a**
40	cuarenta
41	cuarenta **y** uno/**a**
50	cincuenta
60	sesenta
70	setenta
80	ochenta

Note the sound of the "i" when you link two numbers.
That happens always between 16 and 99.

---

[30] Remember that **uno** always drops the "o" in front of a masculine noun. Example: **Yo tengo veintiún años**; remember also that **uno** can be transformed into feminine **una; in fact all the numbers that end in "o" can be transformed into a feminine by changing the "o" for an "a"**. In all the other numbers the gender depend on the person or object they refer to.

90	noventa	
100	cien	
101	ciento uno/**a**	**Note** the change from **cien** to **ciento** in all forms other than "100" and so on.
102	ciento dos,	
200	doscientos/**as**[31]	**Note** that since **dos** is plural, **ciento** becomes plural as well.
300	trescientos/**as**	
400	cuatrocientos/**as**	
500	quinientos/**as**	
600	seiscientos/**as**	
700	setecientos/**as**	
800	ochocientos/**as**	
900	novecientos/**as**	**Note** the changes in **500, 700** and **900**
1,000	mil	
1,001	mil uno/**a**	
2,000	dos mil	**Mil** is invariable
1,000,000	un millón	**Millón** is treated as a noun and requires **de** when followed by a noun: **un millón de dólares**.
2,000,000	dos millones	**Note** the plural of millón is millon**es**.

---

[31] From **doscientos** to **novecientos** all the hundreds also can be feminine.

EJERCICIOS PRÁCTICOS

Do the following math equations.

A. Suma (*Addition*)
   modelo: 1 + 1 = 2:   uno más uno es igual a dos
   1. (18 + 75 =   )   4. (45+ 88901 =   )
   2. (29 + 701 =   )   5. (521 + 7 =   )
   3. (300 +12 =   )   6. (62 + 909 =   )

B. Resta (Subtraction)
   modelo: 3 - 1 = 2   Tres menos uno es igual a dos
   1. (91 - 6 =   )   4. (100 - 50 =   )
   2. (150- 131 =   )   5. (13 - 13 =   )
   3. (127- 101 =   )   6. (710 - 30 =   )

C. Multiplicación (*Multiplication*)
   modelo:2 X 6 = 12   dos por seis es igual a doce
   1. (21 X 7 =   )   4.   (3 1X 5 =   )
   2. (60 X 2 =   )   5.   (10 X 10 =   )
   3. (30 X 30 =   )   6.   (45X 3 =   )

D. Read the numbers aloud.
   1. 21, 31, 41   6. 6, 67, 78
   2. 51, 61, 71   7. 8, 80, 88
   3. 81, 91,101   8. 1,000, 2,002, 3,003
   4. 201, 301, 401   9. 1,978, 2,005, 2,011
   5. 500, 700, 900   10. 1,000,000

   ☺☺

E. A little bit of Mexican History:

Llegada de los Aztecas a México-Tenochtitlán	1325
La conquista española	1519 - 1521
Caída del Imperio Azteca	1521
Inicio de la Independencia de México	1810
Separación de Texas	1836
Guerra México - Estados Unidos	1846 - 1848
Firma del Tratado de Guadalupe	1848
Batalla de Puebla (5 de mayo)	1862
Maximiliano, Emperador de México	1864 - 1867

El Porfiriato[32]	1887 -1910
Inicio de la Revolución Mexicana[33]	1910
La Guerra Cristera	1926 - 1929
PRI (único partido en el poder)	1929 - 2000
TLC (NAFTA)	1994
Movimiento Zapatista	1994
PAN (inicio de la alternancia política)	2000
Celebración del Bicentenario	2010
Regreso del PRI a la presidencia	2012
Inicio del neo-populismo político	2018

7. LA HORA

1. In Spanish, the verb **ser** is used to ask and give the time. In Spanish the use of the feminine article is mandatory:

¿Qué hora es?	Son las dos.
¿Qué horas son?	Es la una[34].
¿Qué hora tiene?[35]	Son las tres en punto[36].

2. Minutes after the hour is indicated by using **y** (and):

¿Qué horas son?	Son las tres y quince.
	Son las tres y cuarto. (*Quarter after three*)
¿Qué horas tiene?	Son las seis y media.

3. Minutes before the hour are stated as follows:

¿Qué hora tiene?	Son las seis menos quince.
	Son las seis menos cuarto. (*Quarter to six*)

4. This is another way of expressing the time:

---

[32] The era of Porfirio Díaz's government from 1876-1911 is known as the **Porfiriato** and its motto was "Order and Progress". During his 33 year rule, Mexico entered into the industrial age.

[33] The Mexican Revolution was brought on by, among other factors, tremendous disagreement among the Mexican people over the dictatorship of Porfirio Díaz.

[34] **La una** is the only singular time.

[35] The above forms are normal ways to ask time in some Latin American countries.

[36] Sharp.

| ¿Qué hora es? | Faltan quince minutos para las seis. |
| | Falta un cuarto para las seis. (*Quarter to six*) |

5. Midnight is **medianoche** noon is **mediodía**:
   | ¿Qué horas son? | Es medianoche. |
   | ¿Qué horas tiene? | Es mediodía. |

   Note the following expressions:
Son las ocho **de la mañana.**	It's 8 o'clock **in the morning** (8:00 a.m.).
Son las cuatro **de la tarde.**	It's 4 o'clock **in the afternoon** (4:00 p.m.).
Son las nueve **de la noche**[37]	It's 9 o'clock **in the evening** (9:00 p.m.).

EJERCICIOS PRÁCTICOS

A. Tell us the time answering this question: ¿Qué hora es?
   Modelo: Son las 7:10 (siete y diez)

   1:25
   5:15
   9:30
   11:42
   2:45
   12:00

☺ ☺

B. Read Monica's schedule on typical school day,
7:00 de la mañana:	Mónica desayuna (has breakfast)
7:45 de la mañana:	Mónica llega a la escuela.
8:00 de la mañana:	Mónica tiene su primera clase.
Mediodía:	Mónica tiene su clase de inglés.
2:00 de la tarde:	Las clases terminan.
2:45 de la tarde:	Mónica llega a casa.
3:00 de la tarde:	Mónica ayuda con la comida.
5:00 de la tarde:	Mónica estudia sus lecciones.
8:30 de la noche:	Mónica cena.
9:00 de la noche:	Mónica ve la televisión.

---

[37] This form is rarely used in situations other than on the radio or television.

10:00 de la noche: Mónica se va a dormir.

☺ ☺

C. Now answer these questions.
   1. ¿A qué horas desayuna Mónica?
   2. ¿A qué horas llega a la escuela?
   3. ¿A qué horas tiene su primera clase?
   4. ¿A qué horas tiene su clase de inglés?
   5. ¿A qué horas se terminan las clases?
   6. ¿A qué horas mira la televisión?
   7. ¿A qué horas se va a la cama?

☺ ☺

D. Complete using the appropriate times.
   Un día en mi vida. (A day in my life.)
   (Yo)me levanto a las _____, después me baño y luego desayuno a las
   _____. (Yo) me voy a trabajar a las _____ y salgo a comer a
   las _____. Por la tarde regreso a casa a las _____ después
   preparo la cena y a las _____ veo las noticias en la televisión. Por lo
   general me acuesto a las _____.

☺ ☺

E. Now ask a classmate about a typical day. Include the following questions:
   1. ¿A qué horas desayunas?
   2. ¿A qué horas revisas el Internet?
   3. ¿A qué horas dejas la residencia universitaria?
   4. ¿A qué horas tienes tu clase de español?
   5. ¿A qué horas termina la clase de español?
   6. ¿A qué horas entra a trabajar tu papá/mamá?
   7. ¿A qué horas van al cine?
   8. ¿A qué hora te vas a la cama?

8.   EL VERBO TENER (TO HAVE)

1. **Tener** (to have) is an irregular verb. Its conjugation **en el presente indicativo** (in the present indicative) is:

yo tengo   nosotros tenemos

tú tienes	*vosotros tenéis*
vos tenés	*vosotros tenéis*
usted tiene	ustedes tienen
él tiene	ellos tienen
ella tiene	ellas tienen

(Yo) tengo una maleta.	Nosotros tenemos un carrito.
¿Tú tienes todas tus cosas?	*Vosotros tenéis* el dinero.
Thomas no tiene su saco de dormir.	Ellos tienen los pasaportes.

2. The interrogative with **tener** is formed as follows:
    ¿Es que tienes (tú)...?   ¿Tiene ella...?
    ↗¿Usted tiene...?

    or one may use question words:
    ¿Qué tienen ellos?[38]   ¿Cuál tiene él?
    ¿Dónde lo/la/los/las tienen ustedes?   ¿Quién tiene el pasaporte?
    ¿Cómo es que nosotros tenemos esta maleta?

3. It is very common in Spanish to use the verb **tener** plus the word "que" to express obligation or duty[39]. Here are some examples using the form **tener que**:
    (Yo) tengo que trabajar.   I have to work.
    (Nosotros) tenemos que hacer la tarea. We have to do our homework.

4. The verb **tener** is also used in several idiomatic expressions[40] whose English equivalents use the verb "to be":

tener sueño	to be sleepy	tener hambre	to be hungry
tener calor	to be hot	tener sed	to be thirsty
tener frío	to be cold	tener miedo	to be afraid
tener cuidado	to be careful	tener razón	to be right

---

[38] This expression is also used idiomatically to mean "What is happening with them?" or "what's wrong with them?"

[39] Many Spanish speakers prefer to use **deber de, hay que, es necesario que** to express the same idea of obligation or duty because **tener que** is a direct translation of the English **to have to**.

[40] In chapter 4 you will learn that **estar con** can also be used to express some of these feelings or needs.

| tener prisa | to be in a hurry | tener ... años | to be ... years old |
| tener suerte | to be lucky | tener mala suerte | to have bad luck |

5. The expression **tener ganas de** is used to indicate a desire or a mood:

¿*Tenéis* ganas de nadar?　　　　　　Do you feel like swimming?

Sí tenemos ganas de nadar.　　　　　Yes, we are in the mood to swim.

EJERCICIOS PRÁCTICOS

A. Conjugate the verb according to the subject in the parentheses.
   Modelo:　　Ella tiene un baúl. (nosotros)
   　　　　　　Nosotros tenemos un baúl.
   1. Ella tiene un baúl. (Thomas)
   2. Nosotros tenemos una bicicleta. (ellos)
   1. Anna tiene que abrir la maleta. (yo)
   4. Lisa tiene ganas de dormir. (tú y yo)
   5. El profesor tiene ganas de salir a pasear (tú)

9.　LOS VERBOS REGULARES TERMINADOS EN —AR[41], —ER, —IR

1. There are three groups of regular verbs in Spanish. These verbs are considered regular because they follow common patterns of conjugation. A verb is classified into one of the three groups according to the ending of its infinitive. In English an infinitive is preceded by the preposition "to" (to walk, to talk).

2. Regular verbs in the first group end in **—ar**, like the verb **hablar** (to speak). The present indicative stem of these verbs is formed by dropping the **—ar** ending of the infinitive. For example, the stem of **hablar** is **habl—**. In order to conjugate the verb, the following endings are added to the stem: **—o, —as, —a, —amos, —áis, —an.**

3. The present indicative conjugation of **hablar** is as follows:
   SUBJECT PRONOUN　　　　　　STEM　　　　ENDING

---

[41] In Spanish, this is the most common category of verbs and it includes almost all verbs imported from other languages like **esquiar** (from English to ski).

(yo)	habl	+	o[42]
(vos)	habl	+	ás
(tú)	habl	+	as
usted[43], él, ella	habl	+	a
(nosotros)	habl	+	amos
(*vosotros*)	habl	+	áis
ustedes, ellos, ellas,	habl	+	an

4. **Note** that the present tense in Spanish has at least two meanings in English:

(Yo) hablo español	I **speak** Spanish. I **am speaking** Spanish.

5. In general, questions are formed by switching the order of the verb in the sentence with the subject pronoun for a yes/no answer:

¿Habla usted español?	Sí (yo) hablo español. No[44], (yo) no hablo español.

Remember that you can also ask questions using question words, as you learned in chapter 1.

6. The following verbs are common regular —**ar** verbs:

abrazar	to embrace/to hug	desayunar[45]	to have breakfast
adorar	to adore	donar	to give/to donate
amar	to love	escuchar	to listen/to heed advise
aportar	to bring/to contribute	estudiar	to study

---

[42] **Notice** that all present tense verbs regardless of the family end in —**o** in the yo form, except the verb **dar, estar, ir, ser** which end in —**oy**, the verb **saber**, whose conjugation for **yo** is **sé**, and the verb **haber** whose conjugation for **yo** is **he**.

[43] In some countries like Guatemala the formal form **usted** is used to refer to family members instead of **vos** as a form of respect.

[44] The first **no** is answering the question. The second **no** is reinforcing the negative character of the answer.

[45] Be aware that it is quite common in Spanish that a conjugation can also turn into a noun as in the case of the verb desayunar. "Yo desayuno" (means I eat breakfast) but "desayuno" in a different context just means breakfast: "El desayuno se sirve temprano siempre".

atrapar	to catch	llegar	to arrive
bailar	to dance	llevar	to carry
besar	to kiss	parar	to stop
borrar	to erase	pasar	to show (a film)/to pass
brincar	to jump	quitar	to take away/to remove
buscar	to look for	regresar	to return/to come back
cantar	to sing	repasar	to review
cenar	to have dinner	sacar	to put out/to take away
dejar	to leave	saltar	to jump/to leap
demandar	to ask for	trabajar	to work
desear	to wish/to want	viajar	to travel

B. Los verbos regulares —er/—ir

1. The verb **comer** (*to eat*) is typical of the second group of regular verbs in Spanish ending in —**er**. For the —**ir** group, a typical verb is **vivir** (*to live*).

2. To form the present tense of these verbs, drop the —**er** or —**ir** from the infinitive and add the appropriate ending:
   —**er: —o, —es, —e, —emos, —éis, —en**
   —**ir: —o, —es, —e, —imos, —ís, —en**

   Note that the two groups of verbs have the same endings in their conjugations, except for **nosotros** and *vosotros* forms:

SUBJECT/PRONOUN	STEM	ENDING
Yo	com/viv	o
tú	com/viv	es
vos	**comés**	**vivís**[46]
usted	com/viv	e
él	com/viv	e
ella	com/viv	e
nosotros	**com**	**emos**

---

[46] Remember that the form **vos** is used instead of **tú** in several countries in Latin America specially in South and Central America.

	viv	imos
vosotros	*com*	*éis*
	viv	*ís*
ustedes	com/viv	en
ellos	com/viv	en
ellas	com/viv	en

3. The following verbs are conjugated like **comer**:

beber	to drink	correr	to run
aprender	to learn	comprender	to understand
leer	to read	deber	must, to be supposed to
prender	to turn on	romper	to break
toser	to cough	vender	to sell
creer	to believe	meter	to place/to insert

4. The following verbs are conjugated like **vivir**:

escribir	to write	añadir	to add
abrir	to open	describir	to describe
recibir	to receive	asistir	to attend/to assist
decidir	to decide	discutir	to discuss
subir	to go up/ raise	interrumpir	to interrupt
sufrir	to suffer	ocurrir[47]	to occur/to happen

Here is another web site that you can use to practice your verbs conjugations and more: http://www.spanishdict.com/

EJERCICIOS PRÁCTICOS

☺ ☺

A. Choose five verbs from the list, and create a simple scenario using the verbs you have chosen.
Modelo: Todos los estudiantes **llevan** sus libros a clase. La profesora siempre **llega** temprano. Mis amigas **escuchan** música antes de clase. Yo **busco** mi lápiz. Anna **repasa** los verbos todos los días.

---

[47] This verb is impersonal, therefore it's only used with third person singular and plural.

B. Rewrite the sentences using the subjects in the parentheses to conjugate the verbs.
   Modelo: Los estudiantes suben al autobús. (yo)

   Yo subo al autobús.

   1. Los estudiantes suben al autobús. (tú)
   2. Thomas decide hablar español. (Anna y John)
   3. Anna y John discuten sobre los boletos. (el chofer)
   4. El chofer abre la ventana. (las mamás)
   5. El piloto canta una canción. (las azafatas/aeromozas)

C. Rewrite the sentences using the subjects in the parentheses to conjugate the verbs.
   Modelo: Yo aprendo del profesor. (Nosotros)

   Nosotros aprendemos del profesor.

   1. Nosotros subimos los pupitres. (ellas)
   2. Un alumno enfermo tose. (los chicos)
   3. Nosotros rompemos las ventanas. (yo)
   4. El profesor interrumpe la clase. (las mamás)
   5. El piloto come mucho. (tú)

D. Rewrite the sentences using the verbs in the parentheses.
   Modelo: Tú corres mucho. (comer)

   Tú comes mucho.

   1. Tú corres mucho. (leer)
   2. La azafata sufre demasiado. (discutir)
   3. El hombre come poco. (beber)
   4. El profesor abre el libro. (vender)
   5. Los policías escriben mucho. (interrumpir)

E. Create full sentences using these clues.

1. Yo/beber/leche.
2. La mujer/meter/la/comida.
3. *Vosotros*/vender/apartamentos.

4. Los estudiantes/discutir/mucho.
5. Ella/abrir/la ventana.
6. El niño/escribir/una/carta.

10. EXPRESIONES NEGATIVAS:

1. The negative form in Spanish is created by adding **no** before the verb, which translates to English "not" or "don't":

   No bailo salsa.   I **don't** dance salsa.

2. In a question that has **no** as an answer, it is customary to add the information coming from the same question in a negative form:

   ¿No bailas salsa?   Don't you dance salsa?
   No, no bailo salsa.   No, I do not dance salsa.
   Yo **tampoco**.   Me neither.

3. There are many negative expressions that you can use in Spanish:

   Nunca tengo dinero. }   I **never** have money.
   Jamás tengo dinero.

4. Other negative expressions that you should learn are:

nada	nothing
nadie	nobody, no one
ninguno/a }	none, not any
ningún[48]	
nunca	never
jamás	never
nunca jamás[49]	never ever
tampoco	neither
ni ... ni	neither ... nor

---

[48] **Ninguno** drops the **-o** before a masculine singular noun. In this case, it requires the addition of a written accent mark.

[49] **Nunca jamás** is used to emphasize negativity on the answer. These two words also work as adverbs of frequency.

Note that when the negative precedes the verb, as in "Aquí nadie baila salsa.", or "Nunca comemos fuera.", there is no "double" negative.

5. When these negative expressions appear in a position in the sentence after the verb, as they usually do, you must place a "no" before the verb:
    No tengo dinero **nunca**.   I never have money.
    No tengo **nada**.   I have nothing./I don't have anything.
    No mira **ningún** programa.   She isn't watching any program.

    Note that in Spanish it is quite common to use double negative in a sentence; be aware that in English some of those negative expression like **nada** can be translated as "nothing" or "anything", and **nadie** can be translated as "no one" or "anyone"

6. Be aware that in Spanish you may use the adverb **poco** (*very little*) or the preposition **sin** (*without*) to give a negative meaning of an adjective:
    Es una cosa **poco interesante**.   It is an **uninteresting** thing.
    Es una teoría **sin** probar.   It is an **untried** theory.

EJERCICIOS PRÁCTICOS

Fill in the blank using negative expressions
  1. Yo _____ (never) voy al cine.
  2. Aquí no hay _____ (nobody).
  3. No tengo dinero, _____ (neither) chequera, _____ (nor) tarjeta de crédito.
  4. Ellas no tienen _____ (nothing) en su garage.
  5. No tenemos _____ (none) coche caro.
  6. Ella no tiene _____ (none) hermana.
  7. Tú no tienes coche, yo_____. (neither)
  8. Yo no tengo _____ (none) hermano.
  9. El profesor _____ _____ (never ever) ha matado a una persona.
  10. Ellas _____ (never) han ido a la luna.

B. Answering in a negative form.
  Modelo: ¿Es que el profesor va a México?
                 No, el profesor no va México.
  1.   ¿Es que ellos tienen los pasaportes?
  2.   ¿Es que los estudiantes tienen las formas migratorias?

3. ¿Es que tú tienes una hermana?
4. ¿Es que el piloto tiene dolor de cabeza?
5. ¿Es que la azafata cambia dinero?
6. ¿Es que el policía viaja en el avión?
7. ¿Es que están enfermos los turistas?
8. ¿Es que el copiloto usa un cajero automático?
9. ¿Hay alguna mujer casada en (la) clase?
10. ¿Hay algún lugar frío en México?

ARBOL GENEALOGICO DE MARTIN (CONTINUACIÓN)

1. José es **el marido** de Yolanda y el mayor de la familia.
2. Yolanda es **la esposa** de José.
3. Ignacio es **el menor** de la familia. Él tiene un mes.
4. Yolanda y Cecilia son **las sobrinas** de Pedro Zurita.
5. Martín es **el sobrino** de Pedro Zurita.
6. Don[50] Mario Zurita es **el abuelo** de Martín.
7. Doña[51] Guadalupe Marín de Zurita es **la abuela** de Martín.
8. Daniela Pérez es **la prima** de Martín.
9. Ignacio Pérez es **el sobrino** de Martín.
10. ¿Cuántos años tiene Daniela? Daniela tiene siete años.
11. ¿Quién es Ana González de Pérez? Es **la tía** de Martín.
12. Martín es **el nieto** de don Mario y doña Guadalupe.
13. Ana es **la hermana** de Yolanda.
14. Ana es **la cuñada** de José.
15. José es **el cuñado** de Ana.

VOCABULARIO

el mayor	the oldest
un mes	one month
la menor	the youngest
el primo/la prima	the cousin
la esposa	the wife

---

[50] **Don** is a form of respect used in Spanish for a man.

[51] **Doña** is a form of respect for a woman.

el marido (el esposo)	the husband
el sobrino/la sobrina	the nephew/the niece
el abuelo/la abuela	the grandfather/the grandmother
el nieto/la nieta	the grandson/the granddaughter
el cuñado/la cuñada	the brother-in-law/the sister-in-law
el tío/la tía	the uncle/the aunt
los abuelos	the grandparents

EJERCICIOS PRÁCTICOS

A. Answer the following questions related to the Árbol genealógico de Martin.
 1. Yolanda Zurita es la esposa de José. ¿Quién es la esposa de Mauricio?
 2. José es el marido de Yolanda. ¿Quién es el marido de Ana?
 3. Yolanda Zurita es la hermana de Ana. ¿Quién es la hermana de
 4. Ignacio?
 5. Yolanda es la hermana de Martín. ¿Quién es la otra hermana de Martín?
 6. Martín es el primo de Ignacio. ¿Quién es la prima de Martín?
 7. Cecilia es la prima de Daniela. ¿Quién es la otra prima de Daniela?
 8. Yolanda es la hija de José y Yolanda. ¿Quién es la otra hija de José y Yolanda?
 9. Ignacio es el hijo de Mauricio y Ana. ¿Quién es el hijo de José y Yolanda?
 10. Yolanda es la tía de Ignacio. ¿Quién es el tío de Martín?
 11. Ana es la tía de Yolanda y Cecilia ¿Quién es la tía de Daniela?

B. Answer the following questions.
 1. ¿Cuántos años tiene Daniela?
 2. ¿Cuántos años tiene Ignacio?
 3. ¿ Cuántos años tiene usted?
 4. ¿Quién es el mayor en su casa?
 5. ¿Quién es el menor de sus hermanos?
 6. ¿Es usted hijo/a único/a?
 7. ¿Tiene usted abuelos?
 8. ¿Tiene usted tíos y tías?
 9. ¿Tiene usted primos y primas?
 10. ¿Tiene usted sobrinos y sobrinas?
 11. ¿Es usted el/la menor de la familia?

☺☺

C. Ahora es su turno. Pregúntele a su compañero/a...

1. ¿Cuántos años tiene él/ella?
2. ¿A qué horas desayuna?
3. ¿A qué horas entras a la escuela?
4. ¿A qué horas termina la clase?
5. ¿Quién busca su raqueta de tenis en el aeropuerto?
6. ¿Quiénes cambian dinero en la casa de cambio?
7. ¿Cómo se llama el estudiante delante de él/ella?

MINIRELATO: LOS AEROPUERTOS DE NUEVA YORK Y LA CIUDAD DE MÉXICO

A. Sólo hay un aeropuerto en la ciudad de México y se llama Aeropuerto Internacional Benito Juárez, pero en el 2020 va a ser inaugurado el Nuevo Aeropuerto (the new airport) en el área de Texcoco. Hoy por hoy, el Aeropuerto Internacional Benito Juárez, es **el más grande y más importante del país** (the most important, and the biggest). Se llama así en honor al presidente Benito Juárez. El aeropuerto está ubicado en el **oriente** (East)de la ciudad, en la **colonia** (neighborhood) El Peñón de los Baños. **Es el aeropuerto más transitado** (this is the busiest airport) de América Latina y cada año pasan por sus puertas unos 40 millones de pasajeros (about 40 million passengers each **year**). El aeropuerto tiene dos terminales internacionales que están conectadas por un **tren aéreo** (air train). La línea cinco del metro conecta al aeropuerto con otras líneas del sistema de transporte colectivo.

Preguntas

1. ¿Cuántos aeropuertos hay en la ciudad de México?
2. ¿Cómo se llama el aeropuerto?
3. ¿Dónde está ubicado?
4. ¿Qué línea de metro conecta al aeropuerto con la ciudad?
5. ¿Cómo se puede ir de una terminal a otra?
6. ¿Cuántas terminales internacionales tiene el aeropuerto?

B. **Now let's compare airports in New York with airports in Mexico City.**
En Nueva York hay dos aeropuertos. Ellos se llaman John F. Kennedy y La Guardia. Los aeropuertos son nombrados en honor a un presidente de los Estados Unidos y a un **alcalde** (mayor) de la ciudad de Nueva York. Estos aeropuertos están ubicados en el barrio de Queens. El trayecto entre Nueva

York y La Guardia es corto y **no pasa** (does not exceed) de 30 minutos; el trayecto entre Nueva York y John F. Kennedy no pasa de 45 minutos en taxi, claro está que **todo depende del tráfico** (everything depends on the traffic conditions). Además está el Newark Liberty International Airport que está ubicado en los suburbios (the suburbs) en la ciudad de Newark, en el estado de Nueva Jersey.

Preguntas

1. ¿Cuántos aeropuertos hay en el área de Nueva York?
2. ¿Cómo se llaman?
3. ¿En honor a quiénes han sido nombrados estos dos aeropuertos?
4. ¿En qué barrio están situados estos aeropuertos?
5. ¿Cuánto tiempo (how long) dura (lasts) el trayecto desde la ciudad al aeropuerto JFK en taxi?
6. ¿Cómo es el trayecto de la ciudad al aeropuerto de La Guardia?
7. ¿Qué aeropuerto está ubicado en la ciudad de Newark?

EJERCICIOS PRÁCTICOS

☺☺

A. Ask your partner the following questions:
1. ¿Hay un aeropuerto en su ciudad? Si no, ¿dónde está el aeropuerto más cercano?
2. ¿Cómo se llama ese aeropuerto?
3. ¿Cuánto dura el trayecto entre su ciudad y el aeropuerto?
4. ¿Hay transporte público? para llegar al aeropuerto?
5. ¿Es un aeropuerto grande e importante?

VOCABULARIO

VERBOS

hablar	abrazar	desayunar	adorar
donar	conectar	bailar	cantar
amar	escuchar	aportar	estudiar
atrapar	llegar	borrar	llevar
besar	parar	pasar	buscar
brincar	quitar	regresar	repasar
preguntar	ser	tener	estar

NOMBRES

la familia	el marido/el esposo	la esposa	el abuelo
la abuela	el menor	la menor	el sobrino
la sobrina	el primo/a	el tío	el nieto
la nieta	el mes.	la tía	la maleta
la hora	el dinero	las revistas	el policía
el aeropuerto	el metro	el autobús	
el cajero automático	los medios de transporte		
las formas migratorias	el dólar	las monedas	el metrobús
la casa de cambio	la suma	el agente de migración	
el agente de aduanas	la resta	la estación de autobuses	
la multiplicación	la división	la maleta	el peso
el cochecito	el árbol	el aeropuerto	el trolebús

ADJETIVOS
interés   grande

ADVERBIOS
poco   más

PREPOSICIONES
sin en entre de a con

EXPRESIONES UTILES

El avión llega **a tiempo.**	¿Qué hora es?
El avión llega **retrasado.**	¿A qué horas llega el vuelo?
El vuelo está **cancelado.**	¿Cuántos años tiene usted?
Tengo que trabajar	¿De qué tiene ganas?

CAPÍTULO 3: EN LA ESTACION DE AUTOBUSES

En este capítulo...

You will ask for information, check schedules, reserve and buy bus tickets, and have a snack while waiting for the bus. To help you do these things, you will study how to form contractions with the prepositions **a** and **de** and the masculine singular article **el**. You will also learn about the uses of the prepositions **a, de, en** and **con;** some vocabulary related to days, months, and seasons of the year, and you will be introduced to the possessive adjectives and possessive pronouns as well as the use of the demonstratives adjectives. Finally, you will discover how to use the **mini relato** as a model for conveying information about yourself, your city, and other objects of interest.

Contexto

Después de salir de la casa de cambio, los cuatro amigos cargan sus cosas y juntos buscan la taquilla de los autobuses. Ellos están muy emocionados de que van a conocer a sus familias en Puebla.

Lisa: ¡Qué amable el señor de la casa de cambio! ¿verdad?

John: La gente de México tiene fama de ser amable.

Anna: Eso lo vamos a ver durante el semestre que estemos en Puebla.

Thomas: ¡De prisa chicos, que se nos hace tarde para tomar el autobús de las cinco de la tarde!

Anna: ¿Cómo vamos a estar tarde? ¿Qué hora es?

John: Son las cinco menos cuarto.

Lisa: ¡Dios mío, sí que ya es tarde!

Mientras hace cola en la ventanilla...

Thomas: Cuatro boletos a la ciudad de Puebla, por favor.

Empleado: Hay dos terminales, ¿a cuál quiere ir usted?

Thomas: Yo no sé.

Empleado (*incrédulo*): Hay una terminal que está a las orillas de la ciudad, cerca de la autopista a Orizaba. Y la otra está en el centro.

Thomas: A la que está en el centro, pienso. (*desconcertado*)

Empleado: A la que está en el centro entonces, ¿verdad?

Thomas (*dudoso*): Sí...sí, a la del centro.

Empleado: Muy bien señor. Sus boletos, ¿los quiere de ida y vuelta?

Thomas: No, sólo de ida, por favor.

Empleado: Está bien. La siguiente corrida es a las cinco y media. ¿Está bien?

Thomas: ¿Ya no tiene para el de las cinco?

Empleado: No joven, se nos agotaron los boletos.

Thomas: (*buscando ayuda de sus amigos*): Sí, está bien.

Empleado: Muy bien. Entonces aquí tiene cuatro boletos a la Terminal de la Cuatro Poniente. En total son 776 pesos.

Thomas: ¿Cuánto cuesta cada pasaje?

Empleado: 194 pesos por cada boleto, joven.

Thomas: Aquí tiene ochocientos pesos (*le entrega seis billetes de cien y cuatro de cincuenta*).

Empleado: Muy bien, veinticuatro pesos de cambio.

John: ¿Dónde tomamos el autobús?

Empleado: Esperen en la sala. Los van a llamar por el altavoz. ¡Buen viaje y gracias por preferirnos!

Anna y Lisa (*en coro*): ¡Muchas gracias, señor!

Preguntas

1. ¿Es que los cuatro amigos están emocionados por encontrarse con sus familias?
2. ¿Es que ellos tienen una buena impresión del cajero en la casa de cambio?
3. ¿Quién dice "de prisa que ya estamos tarde"?
4. ¿Qué hora es?
5. ¿Qué hacen en la ventanilla?
6. ¿A qué hora encontraron boletos?
7. ¿Cuánto cuesta el pasaje a Puebla?
8. ¿Cuánto dinero le da Thomas al empleado?
9. ¿Cuánto le da de cambio el empleado a Thomas?

NOTA CULTURAL: LA RED DE AUTOBUSES DE MÉXICO

1. Thomas chose well. It is much better to travel to Puebla directly from the airport; it saves you time and money, because there is no need to take a taxi to one of the other three bus stations in Mexico City.

2. Taking an express bus from the airport to Puebla is very convenient. From Benito Juárez International Airport you can also take buses to closer cities like Cuernavaca, Toluca, Pachuca, Tlaxcala, and Puebla.

3. There are reduced fares for children under 12, for senior citizens 65 and up, and for students with a valid ID during the school year.

Dichos

¡Más vale tarde que nunca!	Better late than never!
¡Hay que ver para creer!	Seeing is believing!
¡A lo hecho pecho!	it's no use crying over spilt milk!

VOCABULARIO: Las emociones[52]

Uno expresa (express) frecuentemente sus emociones por los gestos y muecas. Uno describe (describes) estas reacciones con adjetivos. Trate (*try*) de visualizar y de sentir (*to feel*) los sentimientos de las expresiones de cada una de las imágenes.

A. Draw the right face according to the emotion in writing.

Él/ella está alegre.   Él/ella está desorientado/a.

Él/ella está intimidado/a.   Él/ella está enojado/a.

Él/ella está irritado/a.   Él/ella está impaciente.

Él/ella está emocionado/a.   Él/ella está exasperado/a.

EJERCICIOS PRÁCTICOS

☺ ☺

A. Acting out your emotions.
1. ¿Qué gestos o muecas hace usted cuando está exasperado/a, intimidado/a, impaciente, enojado/a, desorientado/a, alegre, emocionado/a, ilusionado/a?

2. Now say, act out, and feel each emotion listed in item 1.
    Modelo: Cuando estoy irritado, yo... (*make appropriate face*)

    Más vocabulario: La terminal de autobuses
    la sala de espera   waiting room
    el kiosco de información   information desk
    la cafetería   the cafeteria

---

[52] The Spanish language uses **estar** to express feeling and emotions because it is seen as a temporary situation/ current condition that may change if the circumstances change.

reservar un asiento	to reserve a place (a seat)
la paquetería	to check the baggage/parcel service
la consignación	locker
el reloj	clock/watch
el horario	schedule
el andén	platform
la parada	stop
la correspondencia	change, connection (transportation)
esperar	to wait for
subir	to get on board/ to get on/to climb
salir/partir	to leave
abordar	to board
saber	to know (a fact)

EJERCICIOS PRÁCTICOS

✎

A. Complete using Más vocabulario.

Thomas, John, Anna y Lisa esperan el autobús de las cinco y media en _____. Para estar puntuales a la hora de la salida, ellos documentan su equipaje en _____. Después ellos van a comprar un bocadillo en _____. Ellos miran el _____ para saber la hora. Ellos consultan el _____ para verificar la hora de salida del autobús y estar a tiempo. Después, ellos caminan hacia el _____ donde está el autobús que les toca. Ellos le muestran sus boletos al chofer y _____ al autobús.

☺ ☺

B. Now ask your partner questions about the paragraph in item A.
   1. ¿Dónde es que los jóvenes van a tomar el autobús?
   2. ¿Dónde se hace la documentación del equipaje?
   3. ¿Dónde se puede comprar un bocadillo?
   4. ¿Dónde verifican la hora de la salida?
   5. ¿Por qué miran el reloj?

APUNTES GRAMATICALES

11. LAS PREPOSICIONES "A" Y "DE" + EL ARTÍCULO DEFINIDO "EL"

1. The preposition **a** usually means 'to', 'for', or 'at'. When **a** is followed by the masculine singular article **el** (**a + el**), together they form the contraction **al**:
   Voy **al** baño.   I am going to the restroom.
   Ellos van **al** cine.   They are going to the cinema.

2. The preposition **de** usually means 'of', 'from' or 'about'. When **de** is followed by the masculine singular article **el** (**de + el**), together they form the contraction **del**:
   (Yo) vengo **del** baño.   I am returning from the restroom.
   Ellos vienen **del** cine.   They are returning from the cinema.

3. When followed by the definite article **la**, **a** and **de** never form a contraction:

Ellas van a la biblioteca.　　　　They are going to the library.
Ellas no vienen de la cafetería.　They are not coming from the cafeteria.

4. When followed by a plural definite article, **a** and **de** never form a contraction:
Nosotros vamos **a** los partidos de fútbol.
We go **to** the football games.

EJERCICIOS PRÁCTICOS

A. Change the contraction to change the meaning.
Modelo:　　Ella va al parque. (venir de)
　　　　　　Ella viene del parque.
1. Tú vas al cine. (venir de)
2. Ellos van al comedor. (venir de)
3. Nosotros vamos al partido de fútbol. (venir de)
4. Él va al gimnasio. (venir de)
5. Usted va al aeropuerto. (venir de)

12. LAS PREPOSICIONES: A, DE, EN, CON

1. Prepositions are words that generally precede nouns or pronouns and indicate their relationship to other elements in a sentence.[53]

2. Spanish uses the preposition "**a**" to express 'to', 'at', or 'in', in the following situations:
 a. To express direction (motion toward a place):
Thomas va **a** México.　　　　　Thomas goes **to** Mexico.
Bienvenidos **a** Puebla.　　　　　Welcome **to** Puebla.

 b. To refer to a person acting as a direct object ("a" personal). You will learn more about this in **Chapter 6**:
Thomas busca **a** John.　　　　　Thomas looks **for** John.

---

[53] El escritor argentino Jorge Luis Borges, afirma que las preposiciones son: "obligatorios y modestos sonidos que el uso añade a ciertas palabras y sobre los que no se puede ejercer originalidad", Obras Completas, Tomo I, Emecé Editores, 1996, España, p. 240.

c. To indicate the time (hour) of an action or event:
   El examen de español es **a** las de la mañana.
      The Spanish test is **at** eight o'clock in ocho the morning.
   Llegamos **a** las cuatro de la tarde.
      We will arrive **at** four o'clock in the afternoon.

d. To make explicit the indirect object in a sentence accompanied by the indirect object pronoun:
   A Lisa no le gusta andar en moto.
   Lisa does not like **to** drive a motorcycle.

e. To connect verbs of motion (**salir, venir**) with the infinitive that follows them:
   Los estudiantes salen **a** comer.   The students go out **to** eat.
   El profesor cree que ellos vienen a   The teacher thinks that they come
   aprender.   **to** learn.

f. It is also used after certain verbs, such as **enseñar, aprender, comenzar** and **empezar**, when they are followed by an infinitive:
   El profesor les **enseña a** hablar   The professor teaches them **to**
   español.   speak Spanish.
   Los estudiantes **empiezan a**   The students start **to** practice
   practicar español en sus casas.   Spanish at home.

g. To identify the frequency of an action when is more that one time:
   Thomas debe tomar la medicina   Thomas has to take the medicine
   cuatro veces **al**[54] día.   four times **per** day.

h. To level the distance, equivalent to the preposición **hasta**:
   De aquí **a** tu casa hay dos kilómetros.   From here **to** your home there
                                                 are two kilometers.

i. Some common idiomatic expressions with **a**:
   a menudo   often   a bordo   on board
   a veces   sometimes   a tiempo   on time
   a mano   by hand   a doble espacio double space

_____

[54] Remember that a + el = **al**

a caballo	by horse	a sus anchas	to be comfortable
uno a uno	one by/on one	a regañadientes	reluctantly
a gatas	crawling	paso a paso	step by step
a nado	swimming	a pie	by foot

3. The preposition **de** is used in Spanish to express of, from, about in the following situations:

a. To indicate a specific time of day:
   Son las siete **de** la mañana.   It is seven in the morning.

b. To indicate motion from another place:
   Los estudiantes llegan **de** Nueva York.   The students arrive from NY.

c. To express place of origin:
   Thomas es **de** Colorado.   Thomas is from Colorado.

d. To indicate possession or relationship. **Note** that here there are sometimes two possible English translations, but in Spanish there is only one possible structure:
   La bicicleta es **de** José.   The bicycle is José**'s**.
   Yolanda es la esposa **de** José.   Yolanda is the wife **of** José./
                                                        Yolanda is José**'s** wife.

e. To indicate the material that something is made of:
   El teléfono es **de** plástico.   The telephone is **made of** plastic.

f. To introduce a topic of conversation (equivalent to English "about"):
   Los chicos iban a hablar **del**[55] viaje a Oaxaca.
   The kids were going to talk **about** the trip to Oaxaca.

g. To indicate a personality trait or other characteristic:
   El profesor es un hombre **de** carácter fuerte.
   The teacher is a man **of/with a** strong character.

---

[55] Remember this is the second type of contraction in Spanish: de + el = **del**

h. To express **just finished** (acabar de + a verb in infinitive) that you will study in
   Chapter 5:
   Acabo de llegar.   I just arrived.

i. The preposition **de**, is used in several idiomatic expressions like:
   de veras/de verdad   truly/really
   de nada   you're welcome
   de ida   one way
   de vuelta   returning
   de ida y vuelta   round trip
   de mala gana   unwillingly
   de mala manera   with an attitude/bad intentions
   ir de compras   to go shopping
   estar de luto   to be in mourning
   de vez en cuando   sometimes
   saltar de alegría   to jump for joy
   loco de remate   to be extremely crazy
   gritar de dolor   to scream in pain
   morir de hambre   to starve to death

4. The preposition **en** is used in Spanish to express "at", "in", "on", "inside", and
   "over" in the following situations:
a. To indicate location in a fixed place:
   Los estudiantes están **en** Puebla.   The students are **in** Puebla.
   Estamos **en** casa.   We are **at** home.

b. To indicate a period of time:
   Voy a estar de vuelta **en** quince minutos   I'll be back **in** fifteen minutes.

c. To indicate a means of transportation:
   Los estudiantes llegan **en** avión[56].   The students are arriving **by** plane.

d. As a synonym of the preposition **sobre** (on):
   Los libros están **en** el escritorio/   The books are **on** the desk.
   (Los libros están **sobre** el escritorio)

_____

[56] **Note**: the exceptions **a pie** 'by foot' or **a caballo** "by horse", as was established in page 7.

e. To identify a price (in exchange):
Venden el coche **en** quince mil pesos.   They are selling the car for 15,000 pesos.

f. **En** is used in some idiomatic expressions like:

en serio	seriously
en broma	as a joke
estar en contra	to be against
lo reconocí en la voz	I recognized him by his voice
ni en sus peores tiempos	Not even on his/her worst days
en paz	In peace
en calma	calmly

5. **Con**[57] is used in Spanish to express "with" if "by", "of" in the following situations:

a. To indicate accompaniment:
Vamos al cine con nuestros amigos.
We are going to the movies with our friends.

b. To identify the means of completing an action:
(Ella) cierra la casa **con** llave.   She locks the house **with** a key.
Como la sopa **con** una cuchara.   I eat the soup **with** a spoon.

c. To identify the manner in which something is done:
Nos mira **con** desconfianza.   He is looking at us **with** distrust.

d. To identify the content of a container (although some speakers will use **de** instead in this context):
Tengo una bolsa **con** comida.   I'm carrying a bag **of/with** food.
Tengo una bolsa **de** comida.   I'm carrying a bag **of** food.

e. **Con** is used in few idiomatic expressions like:

con todo	with everything
con valor	with courage

---

[57] **Sin** is the preposition that expresses without. Example: Estoy sin dinero.

con determinación   with determination

f.   The opposite of **con** is **sin** ("without"):
    Bebo el café **sin** azúcar.   I drink coffee **without** sugar.

EJERCICIOS PRÁCTICOS

A. Complete these sentences using prepositions:
    La casa está _____ la playa.
    La botella es _____ plástico.
    Ella viene _____ Cancún.
    Voy al cine _____ mis amigos.
    Vamos a hablar _____ deportes.
    Ellos son _____ Nueva York.
    No sé quién está _____ la casa.
    No me gusta el café _____ leche.
    La computadora es _____ Aarón.
    Ella llega siempre _____ carro.
    Ellos son los hijos _____ la directora.
    Yo vengo a la clase _____ pie.

B. Complete the paragraph using the correct prepositions.
    Los estudiantes estadounidenses van _____ Puebla _____ estudiar por un se-
    mestre; ellos van _____ vivir _____ una familia en la ciudad y van _____ poder
    practicar español todos los días. Los estudiantes vienen _____ distintas ciuda-
    des _____ los Estados Unidos, pero este semestre van _____ vivir todos _____
    la ciudad _____ Puebla. Todos los estudiantes están muy contentos _____ te-
    ner la oportunidad de estudiar _____ el extranjero por un semestre y saben
    que van _____ aprender mucho ____ la lengua y la cultura ____ México.

C. Complete the paragraph using the correct prepositions.
    Roberto va ____ ir ____ su novia ____ Nueva York. Ellos van ____ tomar el tren
    _____ media noche y van _____ ir _____ museo de Arte Moderno. Después
    piensan ir _____ ver la Estatua de la Libertad y van _____ comer en un restau-
    rante cubano que está en el Soho. Antes de regresar _____ Boston van ____
    comprar boletos para ver una obra de teatro _____ Broadway. Después van a
    regresar _____ tren.

13. LOS DÍAS, LOS MESES, LAS ESTACIONES DEL AÑO

1. In Spanish all the days of the week are masculine. Los días de la semana son: **lunes, martes, miércoles, jueves, viernes, sábado, y domingo**[58]. In most Spanish-speaking countries, the week starts on Monday (**lunes**).

   To indicate that something is occurring **on** a certain day of the week, use the singular definite article **el**:
   Ella va a la iglesia **el** domingo.   She is going to church **on** Sunday.

   To indicate that something occurs regularly on a certain day of the week, use the plural definite article **los**:
   Ella va a la iglesia **los** domingos.   She goes to church on Sundays.

2. All months are masculine. Los meses del año son: enero, febrero, **marzo, abril, mayo, junio, julio, agosto, septiembre, octubre, noviembre, y diciembre.**

3. Las cuatro estaciones son: la **primavera,** (*spring*), el **verano** (*summer*), el **otoño** (*fall/autumn*) y el **invierno** (*winter*).
   Note that all seasons are masculine, except for **primavera**.

   The definite article is used with the seasons:
   Mi estación favorita es **el** verano.   Summer is my favorite season.

   To say that something happens in a particular season, use the preposition **en** with the definite article:
   En la primavera hace buen tiempo.   In the spring the weather is fine.
   En el verano hace calor.   In the summer it's hot.
   En el otoño llueve.   In the fall it rains.
   En el invierno hace frío.   In the winter it is cold.

4. Dates are expressed as follows:

---

[58] In Spanish, the days of the week, months, and seasons are not capitalized.

¿Qué fecha es hoy?
¿En qué fecha estamos? }   What's today's date?

Hoy es el 4 de julio.
Estamos a 4 de julio.   }   It's the fourth of July.
The ordinal number is used only for the first day of the month:
Es **el primero** de enero.   It's **the first** of January.

5. There is only one way of saying the year in Spanish, which equates to "two
    thousand eleven" (and never "twenty eleven"):
    2011: Dos mil once

    ¿En qué año nació usted?   In what year were you born?
    (Yo) nací en mil novecientos cincuenta y siete. I was born in 1957.

6. In Spanish, the day always comes first, then the month, then the year:
    10 de octubre de 1957.   October 10th, 1957.

7. When a date is written in figures, the day comes first. Note that this differs
    from the American practice of putting the month first:
    7/11/1960 = July 11, 1960 (United States)
    11/7/1960 = 11 de julio de 1960 (Spanish)

EJERCICIOS PRÁCTICOS

A. Escriba la fecha en palabras.
    modelos: 1/1/2013
                 Primero de enero del[59] dos mil trece.

1. 7/11/1960	5. 20/4/1987	9. 23/12/1990
2. 10/10/1957	6. 20/11/1910	10. 22/1/2009
3. 5/5/1862	7. 12/12/1900	11. 4/7/1776
4. 16/9/1810	8. 11/11/1935	12. 1/1/2000

☺ ☺

---

[59] Starting with the year 2000 in Spanish you have to use the contraction **del**.

B. Ahora es su turno. Quiz a partner on the following material. Then have your partner take you through the same exercise.
1. ¿Cuáles son los días de la semana?
2. ¿Cuáles son los meses del año?
3. ¿Cuántos días tienen los meses de enero, marzo, mayo, julio, agosto, octubre y diciembre?
4. ¿Cuántas semanas tiene el año?
5. ¿Cuántos días hay en un año?
6. ¿Cuáles son las cuatro estaciones?
7. ¿Cuándo comienza (*starts*) cada estación?
8. ¿Qué estación prefiere usted?
9. ¿En qué día estamos hoy?
10. ¿Cuáles son los meses que tienen 30 días?

☺ ☺

C. Match the date with the event.

24/12	Día del trabajo
1/5	Día de la Independencia
12/12	Nacimiento de Benito Juárez
16/9	Noche Buena[60]
21/3	Día de la Virgen de Guadalupe

☺ ☺

D. Match the year with the event.

1.	1910	Caída del Imperio Azteca
2.	1325	Inicio de la Revolución Mexicana
3.	2000	Llegada de los Aztecas a México
4.	1810	Independencia de México
5.	1521	Inicio de la Alternancia Política.

FIESTAS MEXICANAS

Estudie el calendario de las fiestas mexicanas.

---

[60] Mexico and all other Latin America countries celebrate Christmas on the night of December 24.

In Mexico, a different saint is honored on each day of the year. Many Mexicans still celebrate the saint's day after whom they are named. But in Mexico, people tend to have a bigger celebration for their birthdays.

Many holidays are celebrated throughout the year. Some of these holidays are national, some historical, some religious, and some local. Workers are entitled to paid time off on all legal holidays.

Banks, schools, and public offices are closed on legal holidays.

NATIONAL HOLIDAYS

Primero de enero (New Year's Day) **Año Nuevo.** People visit friends to wish them a Happy New Year on January 1st.

Primer lunes de febrero (Constitution's Day) **Día de la Constitución.** It used to be celebrated in Mexico on February 5th., but now it is celebrated on the first Monday.

Tercer lunes de marzo (President's Day) The birthday of President **Benito Juárez** used to be celebrated on March 21st. in Mexico, but now it is celebrated on the third Monday in March.

Primero de mayo (Labor Day) **Día del Trabajo.** It is celebrated with parades of laborers, and political protests.

16 de septiembre (Independence Day) **Día de la Independencia**. The celebration starts the evening before with a massive gathering at the Zócalo (in downtown Mexico City) where the president addresses the people with the same words pronounced by Miguel Hidalgo y Costilla: ¡**Viva México**! The next day (September 16th.), the celebration continues with a military parade.

Tercer lunes de noviembre (Revolution Day) **Aniversario de la Revolución**. This holiday is celebrated with an athlete's parade. It used to be celebrated on November 20th., but now it is celebrated on the third Monday in November.

Navidad (Christmas) Traditional Christmas in Mexico is celebrated on the evening of December 24th. It is a tradition to have **la Cena de Navidad** (Christmas dinner) with the whole family. Christmas is observed as a national holiday throughout Mexico.

Año nuevo (New Year's Eve) celebrated on the night of December 31th. This day, Mexicans celebrate with a **cena** similar to the one on Christmas.

RELIGIOUS HOLIDAYS

Los Santos Reyes (Epiphany) January 6th. The night before this holiday, the Three Wise Men arrive. Children set their shoes under the Christmas tree in hopes that **Los Reyes Magos** (The Three Wise Men) will bring them gifts.

Pascua (Easter) y la **Semana Santa** (Holy Week). Some people participate in religious celebrations, but many use this week to vacation at the beach.

El Día de Todos los Santos (All Saints' Day) Is observed on November 1st., and **el Día de los Muertos** (All Souls' Day) on November 2nd. Families and friends visit the cemeteries to clean, paint and place flowers on the graves of the deceased. Some people will eat at the cemetery and bring musicians to play their loved ones' favorites songs.

El Día de la Virgen de Guadalupe (Celebration of the Virgin of Guadalupe) **Diciembre 12**. This is the major religious celebration of Mexico. The night before (December 11th.) people go to the Basilica of the Virgin of Guadalupe to sing her **las mañanitas** (The happy birthday song to her) with a mariachi[61] band. Famous musicians show respect to the Virgin by singing for her.

14. LOS ADJETIVOS Y PRONOMBRES POSESIVOS

1. The possessive adjectives expresses ownership. In Spanish only the plural form of the possessive adjective **nuestro/a**, and **vuestro/a** agrees in gender. But remember, all the forms agree in number with the noun they modify.

---

[61] A traditional group of musicians.

2. The forms of the possessive adjectives are as follows:

	SINGULAR MASCULINO	SINGULAR FEMENINO	PLURAL MASCULINO Y FEMENINO
my	mi hermano	mi hermana	mis hermanos/ hermanas
your	tu hermano	tu hermana	tus hermanos/ hermanas
his, her, its, one's	su hermano	su hermana	sus hermanos/ hermanas
our	**nuestro** hermano	**nuestra** hermana	**nuestros** hermanos **nuestras** hermanas
your	*vuestro* hermano	*vuestra* hermana	*vuestros* hermanos *vuestras* hermanas
their	su hermano	su hermana	sus hermanos/ hermanas

Aquí viene **mi tren**.	Here's **my train**.
Tu casa está cerca de la tienda.	**Your house** is near the store.
Thomas trae **sus cosas**.	Thomas bring **his things**.
Nuestro coche está en la calle.	**Our car** is on the street.
No están **vuestras maletas**.	**Your bags** are not here.
Los García reconocen a **sus** estudiantes.	The Garcias recognize **their** Students.

3. The possessive pronouns also express ownership. All the Possessive pronouns have to agree with gender and number. The forms of Possessive pronouns are as follows:

Mine	mío/mía	ours	nuestro/nuestra
yours	tuyo/tuya	yours (informal)	vuestro/vuestra
his/hers	suyo/suya	theirs	suyo/suya
Ese coche es mío.		That car is mine	
Esta corbata es suya.		This tie is his.	

4. Remember, agreement in gender and number is determined by the noun in possession, not by the possessor:
Su casa es amarilla.   His/her house is yellow.
Mi coche es azul y el suyo es negro.   My car is blue and his is black.

EJERCICIOS PRÁCTICOS

A. Rewrite the sentences using the pronouns in the parentheses.
    Modelo: Yo miro mis tarjetas postales. (él)
                   Él mira sus tarjetas postales.
    1. Él compra sus timbres postales. (nosotros)
    2. Yo verifico mi dirección. (ustedes)
    3. Nosotros mandamos nuestras cartas. (ellas)
    4. Ellas reciben su correspondencia. (yo)
    5. Vosotros cuidáis a vuestro hijo (él)

    ☺ ☺
B. Answer each question, using the appropriate possessive adjective.
    Modelo: ¿Quién es el hermano de mi padre?
                   El hermano de mi padre es **mi** tío.
    1. ¿Quién es el marido de mi madre?
    2. ¿Quién es la hermana de mi madre?
    3. ¿Quién es la madre de mi madre?
    4. ¿Quién es el marido de mi hermana?
    5. ¿Quién es la mujer de mi hermano?
    6. ¿Quién es el hijo de mi hermana?
    7. ¿Quiénes son los hijos de mi tío y tía?

C. Fill in the blank using the correct possessive adjective.
    Modelo: _____ hermano tiene un coche.
                  Mi hermano tiene un coche.
    1. _____ padres trabajan en una fábrica. (his)
    2. _____ perro es grande. (my)
    3. _____ casa es blanca. (their)
    4. _____ clases son fáciles. (our)
    5. _____ computadora está encendida. (your)

D. Fill in the blank using appropriate possessive pronoun.
    Modelo: La computadora es _____.

La computadora es **mía**.
1. La manzana es _____. (mine)
2. Mi casa es grande y ¿la _____? (yours)
3. Nuestra casa es pequeña y ¿la _____? (his)
4. El teléfono es _____. (our)
5. Los libros son _____. (hers)

15. LOS ADJETIVOS DEMOSTRATIVOS

1. The demonstrative adjective is used to make reference to a specific noun. In English, *this* and *that* are demonstrative adjectives:
   Ese señor es amable.   That man is nice.

2. The demonstrative adjectives agrees in gender (masculine or feminine) and in number (singular or plural) with the noun it modifies:

	SINGULAR	PLURAL
MASCULINE:	**Este** señor	**Estos** señores
	Ese señor	**Esos** señores
	Aquel señor	**Aquellos** señores
FEMININE:	**Esta** señora	**Estas** señoras
	Esa señora	**Esas** señoras
	Aquella señora	**Aquellas** señoras

3. As you can see, Spanish has three types of demonstrative adjectives. They are related with the distance in space or in time between the speaker and the person(s) or object(s):

   a. Use **Este/Esta/Estos/Estas** for people or things close to you (close enough that you can touch them). These forms are most often the equivalent of "this" in English.

   b. Use **Ese/Esa/Esos/Esas** for people or things that are still relatively close, but which are too far for you to touch them. These forms generally correspond to "that" in English.

   c. Use **Aquel/Aquella/Aquellos/Aquellas** for people or objects that are far from the speaker.

EJERCICIOS PRÁCTICOS

A. Practice using all of the demonstratives you have learned for each of the sentences below.

    Modelo: El muchacho está enfadado. (este)
                    Este muchacho está enfadado.

1. El estudiante está intimidado.
2. El piloto está asustado.
3. El policía está enojado.
4. El empleado está sorprendido.
5. El chofer está alegre.

B. **Modelo:**   La muchacha está enfadada. (esa)
                    Esa muchacha está enfadada.

1. La estudiante está triste.
2. La azafata está ocupada.
3. La mujer está asustada.
4. La chica está enojada.
5. La empleada está aburrida.

C. **Modelo:**   Las muchachas están ocupadas. (aquellas)
                    Aquellas muchachas están ocupadas.

1. Las chicas están enfadadas.
2. Las enfermeras están desesperadas.
3. Las mujeres están incómodas.
4. Las empleadas están ocupadas.
5. Las azafatas están tristes.

D. Point out the places one finds in a city. Use the appropriate demonstrative adjective.

    Modelo: La tienda está lejos de aquí.
                    Aquella tienda está lejos de aquí.

1. La oficina de correos está detrás del hotel.
2. La estación de autobuses está delante de la escuela.
3. El banco está cerrado.
4. La iglesia está abierta.
5. El museo es famoso.

MINIRELATO: Las ciudades

La ciudad de México es una de las ciudades más grandes (*biggest cities*) del mundo. La ciudad está situada en el centro de México. La ciudad está a 2,400 metros de altura (*7,200 feet above sea level*). Los veranos **no son tan calientes** (*aren't that hot*) por la altura a la que está y por el viento que viene de las montañas (*mountains*) que la rodean. En invierno **hace frío, pero no nieva** (*it is cold but doesn't snow*). La ciudad fue fundada (*founded*) por los Aztecas en 1325, y actualmente viven en la ciudad más de doce millones (*twelve million*) de personas. La ciudad es el centro político, cultural y financiero del país.

Preguntas

1. ¿Cuál es la altura a la que está la ciudad?
2. ¿Por qué no hace tanto calor en verano?
3. ¿Cuándo fue fundada la ciudad?
4. ¿Quiénes fundaron la ciudad?
5. ¿Cuántas personas viven en la ciudad?

La ciudad de Nueva York es la más grande del estado de Nueva York. Ella está situada al sur del estado, entre el río Hudson y el río East. En verano hace calor y en invierno hace frío. La ciudad tiene más de trescientos años de fundada. Nueva York es l**a capital artística del mundo entero** (*the artistic capital of the entire world*). En Nueva York, hay **un montón de teatros, cines, museos y salas de conciertos** (*a lot of theaters, cinemas, museums and concert halls*). Y hay muchísimos taxis y restaurantes para todos los gustos y bolsillos. En la ciudad de Nueva York viven más de dos millones de hispanohablantes. En la región metropolitana, hay casi tantas personas que hablen español como en Panamá o en Uruguay.

Preguntas

1. ¿Es Nueva York una ciudad grande?
2. ¿Está situada al sur del estado?
3. ¿Cómo se llaman los ríos entre los que está ubicada la ciudad?
4. ¿Hace frío en invierno?
5. ¿Hace calor en verano?
6. ¿Tiene la ciudad más de doscientos años?
7. Hay muchos taxis ¿no?

8. Nueva York tiene casi tantas personas que hablan español como ¿cuáles países latinoamericanos?

VOCABULARIO

VERBOS

ir	sumar	restar	dividir	llamar(se)
llegar	escribir	comer	hacer	vivir

NOMBRES

los días	el empleado	la maleta/el equipaje
los meses	el cliente	la sala de espera
las estaciones	los jóvenes	las vacaciones
el boleto/los boletos	la ventanilla	los días de trabajo
la tarjeta de crédito	el andén	los días de descanso
la cafetería	un bocadillo	las personas
el dinero	las monedas	el cambio
el teléfono	una llamada	un museo
el teatro	el tren	el país
el nombre	la hora	la ciudad
la región	el estado	los taxis
el frío	el río	el/la capital

ADJETIVOS

triste	emocionado/a	desorientado/a
alegre	enojado/a	exasperado/a
disgustado/a	descorazonado/a	molesto/a
intimidado/a	impaciente	irritado/a
frustrado/a	enfadado/a	trastornado/a
cubano/a	hispano/a	metropolitana
financiero/a	grande	efectivo/a

PREPOSICIONES

a   de   en   con   sin   conmigo   contigo   consigo

ADVERBIOS

hoy   a menudo   rápidamente   alrededor

CAPÍTULO 4: EN EL AUTOBUS

En este capítulo...

You will learn about the train system in Mexico, and something about kilometers, temperatures, and weight conversions. You will learn more about buses, and discover how to point things out, and describe the weather.

To help you do these things, you will study how to use **muy** and **mucho**. Then you will become familiarized with the positioning of descriptive adjectives, and the concordance between nouns and adjectives. You will also learn when to use the verb **hacer** (to do/to make) as well as how to talk about the weather; and the use of **la hora oficial**, that is normal in some countries like Argentina, and is used in all official business in all Latin American countries.

Contexto

(Por los altavoces se oye que llaman para subir al autobús 214 con salida hacia la ciudad de Puebla a las diecisiete horas y treinta minutos.)
John y Anna discuten sobre el empleado de la taquilla de autobuses y su actitud. Thomas va sentado en el asiento de al lado y Lisa va tres asientos más atrás. En este autobús van todos los estudiantes que van a pasar un semestre en México. El autobús comienza a avanzar; atrás queda la ciudad. Ellos ven el paisaje por la ventana, algunos ven cosas interesantes.

John: ¿Qué piensas del empleado que nos vendió los boletos?
Anna: Fue muy pedante y agresivo.
John: ¿Y hablando de boletos, ¿qué vamos a hacer con estos boletos?
Anna: Los vamos a guardar, por si el revisor los quiere ver.
John: ¿Tú crees que hay un revisor? Este es un autobús de lujo, no puede haber un revisor.
Anna: Si no los revisan, nos van a servir de recuerdo, los podemos poner en nuestros diarios.

Junto a Thomas va sentada una señora. Después de un rato de viaje, la señora le pregunta con cierta emoción:
Señora: Perdone la indiscreción joven, pero ¿a qué va a Puebla?
Thomas: Vamos a estudiar español por un semestre.
Señora: ¡Qué bien! De verdad los felicito.
Thomas: Muchas gracias. Y usted, ¿vive en Puebla?
Señora: Sí soy poblana y vivo en la ciudad.
Thomas: ¿Cuánto tiempo se hace hasta Puebla?
Señora: No está muy lejos, sólo hay 129 kilómetros, pero en autobús se hace entre hora y media y dos horas, dependiendo del tráfico.
Thomas: Y, ¿cómo es el clima en Puebla?
Señora: Hace buen tiempo. En esta época llueve menos que en el Distrito Federal. No se preocupe, Puebla es una ciudad muy bonita. Les va a encantar; tiene muchos lugares para divertirse, y además es de las ciudades más seguras que hay.
Thomas: ¡Me alegro mucho!

Preguntas

1. ¿De qué discuten los amigos?
2. ¿Qué ven por la ventana los jóvenes estadounidenses?
3. ¿Por qué guardan los boletos?
4. ¿De dónde es la señora que platica con Thomas?
5. ¿Es ella joven o mayor[62]?
6. ¿Es que Puebla está lejos de la Ciudad de México?
7. ¿A cuántos kilómetros está Puebla?
8. ¿Cómo se llama la capital de México?
9. ¿Los amigos van a hacer sus estudios en Puebla?
10. ¿Cuánto tiempo van a pasar en Puebla los jóvenes?

NOTA CULTURAL: LA DESAPARICIÓN DEL FERROCARRIL EN MÉXICO (FNM)

1. Trains used to be an important part of Mexican history. The Mexican Revolution could not have been successful without the uses of trains, especially in the northern part of Mexico.

2. Ferrocarriles Nacionales de México (FNM) suspended passenger rail service in 1997. Currently there is only one route in service in the northern state of Chihuahua —the Copper Canyon route.

3. The first train route started in 1903 from Mexico City to the northern city of Nuevo Laredo, which is across the border from Laredo, Texas.

4. As you probably already know, distances in Mexico are measured in kilometers. A kilometer is five-eighths of a mile. A quick estimate of miles can be made by dividing kilometers by 10 and then multiplying by 6. Puebla is 125 kilometers (125/10*6= 75 miles) from Mexico City. (See conversion chart on the following page)

---

[62] Note that in Mexico the adjective **viejo/a** may be offensive so they use **mayor** to suggest that a person is a senior citizen. Note that **mayor** also means the oldest one.

Conversions

Peso (*weight*)

1 oz. = 28.36 grams

1 lb. = 454 grams

1 gram = 0.035 oz.

1 kg. = 1,000 grams or 2.2 lbs.

Longitud (*Length*)

1 inch = 0.0254 m

1 foot = 0.3048 m

1 yard = 0.9144 m

1 mile = 1.6 km

1 cm = 0.393 inches

1 meter = 1.0938 yards

1 km. = 1,093 yards

Temperatura (*temperature*)

0° centigrade = 32° Fahrenheit

5° C = 41° F

10° C = 50° F

15° C = 59° F

20° C = 68° F

25° C = 77° F

30° C = 86° F

35° C = 95° F

100° C = 212° F

Dichos

Después de la tempestad viene la calma.

It's always darkest before the dawn.

El sol brilla para todos.

The sun shines for everyone.

VOCABULARIO: POR LA VENTANA SE OBSERVA

el paisaje	**una casa**
la montaña	**una escuela**
las vacas	**una iglesia**
el caballo	**un castillo**
el perro	**un puente**
el gato	**un anuncio**
las nubes	**unos niños**

EJERCICIOS PRÁCTICOS

☺ ☺

A. Answer these questions.

Modelo: ¿Cómo se llama su gato?
              Mi gato se llama Manolo.

1. ¿Qué animales producen leche?
2. ¿Quién monta el caballo?
3. ¿Quién cuida la casa?
4. ¿Quién caza los ratones?

5. ¿Le gusta la leche?
6. ¿Monta usted un caballo?
7. ¿Tiene usted un perro?
8. ¿Tiene usted un gato?

Más vocabulario: En el autobús.

el chofer/el conductor	the bus driver
los pasajeros	the passengers
la canastilla (para el equipaje)	the net that holds baggage
el pasillo	the aisle
los asientos	the seats
entregar los boletos al chofer	to give the tickets to the driver
un asiento disponible	an open seat
número de asiento	seat number
el paisaje	the view
un refrigerio	a snack
el chofer pone una película	the driver plays a movie
la mochila	the backpack
las maletas	the luggage
una película	a movie/film

EJERCICIOS PRÁCTICOS

🖎

A. Complete the paragraph with the appropriate words from **Demos un paso adelante**.

Antes de subir al autobús, los estudiantes _____ al chofer. Al subir, caminan por _____ y buscan un _____ disponible. Después, ponen sus _____ en _____. Puebla no está lejos del Distrito federal, pero van a ver _____ que va a poner el chofer. Por la ventana si quieren pueden ver

_____.

☺ ☺

B. Ahora su turno. Now ask your partner questions based on the paragraph in item A.

1. ¿A quién le entregan los boletos los pasajeros?
2. ¿Qué buscan los pasajeros al subir al autobús?
3. ¿Dónde ponen sus mochilas?
4. ¿Es que Puebla está lejos de la Ciudad de México?
5. ¿Por dónde caminan los pasajeros?
6. ¿Qué pueden ver por la ventana?
7. ¿Es que el chofer va a poner una película?

APUNTES GRAMATICALES
16. POSICIÓN DE LOS ADJETIVOS

1. Most adjectives in Spanish follow the noun. Adjectives that follow the noun or the verb **ser** often:
a. Describe colors:

La manzana es **roja.**	The apple is **red**/It's a **red** apple.
El portero lleva un suéter **amarillo.**	The goalkeeper is wearing a **yellow** jersey.

b. Describe nationality:

El volkswagen es un coche **alemán.**	The volkswagen is a **German** car.
Thomas es un joven **estadounidense.**	Thomas is a young person from the US.

c. Describe religion:

México es un país cada vez menos **católico.**	México is a country that is becoming less and less **Catholic.**

d. Describe physical qualities such as shape, size, states, age:

El rey Arturo fue el líder de los caballeros de la mesa **redonda.**	King Arthur was the leader of the Knights of the **Round** Table.
Cuando hace frío, uno toma café **caliente.**	When it's cold, one drinks **hot** coffee.
Ella tiene el pelo **corto.**	She has **short** hair.
Martín es **joven;** José es **viejo.**	Martin is **young;** Jose is **old.**

e. Are derived from past participles of verbs (similar to **–ed** forms in English):

El presidente es una persona **distinguida**.	The president is a **distinguished** person.
La puerta está **cerrada**.	The door is **closed**.

f. Some of these adjectives are irregular:

romper	roto	La ventana está rota. (*broken*)
abrir	abierto	El libro está abierto. (*open*)
escribir	escrito	Todo está por escrito. (*in writing*)
hacer	hecho	La tarea está hecha. (done)
morir	muerto	John Lennon está muerto. (*dead*)

2. The colors in Spanish are as follows:

rojo	red	blanco	white
verde	green	anaranjado	orange
negro	black	café/marrón[63]	brown
plateado	silver	rosa/rosado	pink
amarillo	yellow	azul	blue
violeta	violet	gris	gray
dorado	golden	celeste	light blue
morado	purple	azul marino	navy blue

Hair colors include:

rubio/güero[64]	blonde
castaño claro	light brown
castaño oscuro	dark brown
negro	black
pelirrojo	red
canoso	gray

Skin colors include:

blanco	white, caucasian

---

[63] **Marrón** is used more in Spain rather than in Latin American countries.

[64] **Rubio, and** güero can be used as descriptive adjective for a person, as can **pelirrojo** and **canoso**. In those cases the adjective has to agree with the gender of the person.

moreno	dark-skinned
negro	black
mulato	bi-racial

Note that in Spanish-speaking countries people often make reference to skin color, whereas in the United States such comments would not necessarily be considered polite.

3. Do not forget that adjectives agree in gender and number with the nouns they modify:

La casa es **pequeña**.	The house is **small**.
Los estudiantes son **altos**.	The students are **tall**.
Esos coches son **grandes**.	Those cars are **big**.
Esa chica es **rubia**.	That girl is **blonde**.

4. Only the adjectives ending in **–o** agree with gender and can change into **–a** for the feminine forms:

El chico es alto alto.	The boy is **tall**.
Las chicas son altas.	The girls are **tall**.

If an adjective ends in **–r** it will add an **–a** to become feminine:

Ellos son unos hombres **trabajadores**.	They are **hard-working** men.
Ellas son unas mujeres **trabajadoras**.	They are **hard-working** women.

If the adjective ends in **–ón, it** will change into **–ona**:

(Tú) eres un **preguntón**.	You are a **questioning** boy.
Ellas son unas **preguntonas**.	They are **curious** girls.

If the adjective ends in **–án, it** will change into **–ana**:

El es un **haragán**.	He is **lazy**.
Nosotras somos unas **haraganas**.	We are **lazy**.

5. If a masculine adjective ends in **–e**, the same form is used for the feminine adjective:

MASCULINE SINGULAR:	Él es inteligente/fuerte/interesante.
	(*He is smart/strong/interesting*).
FEMININE SINGULAR:	Ella es inteligente/fuerte/interesante.
	(*She is smart/strong/interesting*).

6. In almost all other cases in which a masculine adjective ends in a consonant, the same form is used for the feminine adjective:
   MASCULINE SINGULAR: Él es ágil/joven/veloz.
                              (*He is agile/young/fast*)
   FEMININE SINGULAR: Ella es ágil/joven/veloz.
                              (*She is agile/young/fast*)

7. Spanish do not add an **–s** to last names. The use of the plural definite article indicates that it is plural:
   Los **Zamora** viven cerca del río.   The **Zamoras** live near the river.

EJERCICIOS PRÁCTICOS

✎

A. Read the paragraph, translate each adjective to complete the paragraph properly.
   Hace _____ tiempo, (long ago) bajo un cielo muy _____ (clear) una joven leía un libro _____ (small) para niños. En el libro se hablaba de un príncipe _____ (blue) que tenía un caballo _____ (white) muy hermoso. El príncipe era muy _____ (handsome) pero estaba muy _____ (sad) porque no había encontrado a la mujer de sus sueños. La chica se empezó a aburrir con la lectura y, poco a poco, se fue quedando _____ (asleep). Horas más tarde, cuando despertó, cabalgaba en un caballo blanco acompañada de un hombre muy _____ (young) como el príncipe del libro. Al llegar al palacio del príncipe, se casaron y desde entonces viven muy _____ (happy).

☺ ☺

B. Complete these sentences by choosing one of the following words: gris, verde, café, anaranjado, colores.
   1. El arco iris (*rainbow*) contiene todos los _____.
   2. Con el blanco y el negro usted puede obtener el color _____.
   3. Con el verde y el rojo usted puede sacar el color_____.
   4. Si se mezcla el amarillo y el azul se obtiene el color _____.
   5. Si usted mezcla rojo y amarillo se obtiene el color_____.

C. Pluralize the noun and its corresponding parts.
   Modelo: El animal es grande.
                 Los animales son grandes.

111

1. El perro es grande.
2. El pájaro es pequeño.
3. El león es rápido.
4. La zebra es rayada.
5. El tiburón es largo.

17. MUY VS MUCHO

1. Learning how and when to use **muy** or **mucho** in Spanish can be a little bit confusing.

2. **Muy** is an adverb and can be translated into English as *very*.

   Tú eres **muy** inteligente.   You are **very** intelligent.
   Ellas son **muy** altas.   They are **very** tall.

   Note that since **muy** is an adverb, it does not agree with gender or number. So it will always be **muy**.

3. The adverb **muy** can be use with an adjective or another adverb.
   a. Normally **muy** is used before an **adjective** to increase the intensity of it.
   Mi hermana está **muy** triste.   My sister is (currently) **very** sad.

   b. In certain occasions we use **muy** with an adverb to intensify that adverb.
   Mi abuela oye **muy** bien.   My grandma hears **very** well.

   Note that you cannot use the word **muy** by itself. It always needs to be in company of an adjective or an adverb.
   ¿Estás cansado?   Are you tired?
   Sí, estoy **muy** cansado.   Yes, I am **very** tired.

4. **Mucho** means in English a **lot** - **a lot of** - **much** - **many**.
   a. **Mucho** also can be used as an adjective or as an adverb.
   When **Mucho** is used as an adjective, it must agree with gender (masculino/femenino) and number (singular/plural)
   Hay **mucha** comida.   There is **a lot of** food.
   Hay **muchos** chicos en clase.   There are **many** boys in class.

   b. In certain occasions **mucho** can be used as an **adverb** after a verb. In those occasions, **mucho** does not agree with gender or number:
   El perro ladra **mucho**.   The dog barks **a lot**.

Ellas trabajan **mucho**.	They work **a lot**.

c. The most common use of **mucho** is as an adjective:

El presidente tiene **mucho** dinero.	The president has **a lot of** money.
Hoy hace **mucho** calor	Today is **really** hot.
Mi madre tiene **mucha** paciencia	My mom has **a lot of** patience.

Note that the opposite of **mucho** is **poco (little)**, and it's used in the same way as **mucho**:

Tengo **poco** dinero.	I have **little** money.
Trabajo **poco.**	I work **very little**.

Note also that mucho, mucha, muchos, muchas, or poco, poca, pocos, pocas is placed alway in front of a noun.

d. In Spanish in a short yes/no answer you have to say: Sí, **mucho**/ No **mucho**.

¿Estás cansado?	Are you tired?
Sí, **mucho**.	Yes, a **lot**.
No **mucho**.	Not **much**.

EJERCICIOS PRÁCTICOS

A. Fill in the blanks using **muy** or **mucho, mucha, muchos or muchas**

    Modelo: Ella tiene _____ ropa. (a lot)

                 Ella tiene **mucha** ropa.

1. El está _____ cansado.
2. Nosotros vamos a la playa _____.
3. El perro duerme _____.
4. Hace _____ calor.
5. En Centro América llueve _____.
6. Ellos tienen _____ hijos.
7. Ustedes tienen _____ trabajo.
8. Las mamás trabajan _____.
9. Los profesores dejan _____ tarea.
10. Pedro es _____ guapo.

B. Fill in the blanks using muy, mucho, mucha, muchos, muchas, poco, poca, po-cos, pocas

Modelo: Nosotros tenemos _____ paciencia. (little)
Nosotros tenemos **poca** paciencia.

1. Ella tiene _____ dinero. (little)
2. Ustedes tienen _____ tarea. (a lot)
3. Tú trabajas _____. (a lot/too much)
4. Ellas duermen _____ _____. (very little)
5. (Yo) tengo _____ hermanos. (many)
6. Ustedes compran _____ _____ libros. (very few)
7. José baila _____ bien. (very)
8. Yolanda gasta _____ en perfumes. (a lot)
9. Los estudiantes estudian _____. (a lot)
10. Ellos hablan español _____ bien. (very)

18. EL VERBO HACER

1. **Hacer** is an irregular verb in the **yo** form, as you will study in **Chapter 5**. The verb hacer has many meanings. When used alone, it usually means 'to do' or 'to make'. It is commonly used to ask questions, but it is also used in many idiomatic expressions, including weather expressions:

¿Qué estás **haciendo?**	What are you doing?
¿Qué **haces**?	What are you doing?
¡**Hace** buen tiempo!	It's a nice day!
Él no **hace** ejercicio.	He does not do any exercise.

2. **Hacer** has the following conjugation in the present tense:

yo **hago**	nosotros **hacemos**
tú **haces**	*vosotros **hacéis***
vos **hacés**	*vosotros **hacéis***
usted **hace**	ustedes **hacen**
él **hace**	ellos **hacen**
ella **hace**	ellas **hacen**

3. Although a question and its answer often contain the same verb, a question containing **hacer** may require a different verb in its answer:

¿Qué **haces?**	What are you doing?/ What do you do?
¿Qué **hace** usted?	What are you doing?/ What do you do?
Yo **trabajo**.	I work, I am working.
Yo **estoy trabajando**.	I am working.

4. Hace is used in Spanish to express the length of time. You will study this in detail in **Chapter 7**:
    Hace dos años que **estudio** español.
    I have been studying Spanish for two years.

5. Hace is also used to express the adverb "ago". You will study this in more detail in **Chapter 9**:
    Hace dos años que **estudié** español.
    It's been two years since I **studied** Spanish.

6. Here are some expressions con **hacer**:

hacer preguntas	to ask questions
hacer deportes	to play sports
hacer ejercicio	to exercise
hacer la tarea	to do homework
rehacer la tarea	to redo the homework.
hacer un viaje	to take a trip
hacer las maletas	to pack one's bags
deshacer la maleta	to unpack one's bag
hacer el mandado/las compras	to go shopping
hacer la comida	to cook
hacer la cama	to make the bed
hacer el aseo/la limpieza	to clean the house
hacer la cola/fila	to stand in line
hacer un papel	to play a role
hacer una casa	to build a house
hacer las paces	to make peace
hacer caso	heed/to take notice/to pay attention

    Note, as you can see many physical activities are expressed with the verb **hacer**.

EJERCICIOS PRÁCTICOS

☺ ☺
A. Complete the following statements.
    Modelo: Antes de hacer un viaje, una persona ....

Antes de hacer un viaje una persona **hace** un presupuesto (*budget*)

1. Para hacer la comida, una persona...
2. Para estar en forma, un atleta...
3. Antes de cocinar, las mamás...
4. Todas las tardes, los estudiantes...
5. En las universidades, los cocineros...

19. EL TIEMPO/EL CLIMA

El tiempo/el clima
Cielo despejado durante la mañana, con posibilidad de lluvia durante la tarde. Viento leve del noreste durante la noche. La temperatura mínima será de diez grados centígrados (10° C) con una de máxima de veinte grados centígrados (20° C).

The weather
Clear skies during the morning, with a chance of rain late afternoon. Light wind from the northeast during the evening. Lows, 50° highs 68°.

Vocabulario

Hace buen tiempo.	It's nice out.
Hace (poco) calor.	It's (not that) hot.
Hace (mucho) frío.	It's (very) cold.
Hace sol.	It's sunny.
Hace viento.	It's windy.
Hace un tiempo espantoso.	It's a nasty day.
Hace fresco.	It's brisk/cool.
Llueve[65]/Está lloviendo.	It's raining.
Está cayendo un aguacero.	It's raining cats and dogs.
Nieva/Está nevando.	It's snowing.
Está nublado.	It's cloudy.
Está soleado.	It's sunny.

---

[65] The infinitive of the verbs **llover** and *nevar* are commonly used to express weather conditions. They are impersonal verbs that are only conjugated in third person singular: **llueve/nieva**.

Está húmedo.	It's muggy.
Está lluvioso.	It's rainy.
Está fresco.	It's brisk/cool.
Está caliente.	It's hot.
Está muy frío.	It's very cold.
Hay viento.	It's windy.
Hay sol.	It's sunny.
Hay nubes.	It's cloudy.
Hay lluvia.	It's raining.
Va a llover	It's going to rain.
Va a nevar	It's going to snow.
Tengo frío[66]	I'm cold.
Tiene frío	He/she is cold.
Siento calor	I feel hot.
Tengo calor	I'm hot.

EJERCICIOS PRÁCTICOS

☺ ☺ ✎

A. Ask these questions to your partner. Have your partner answer orally and draw the weather conditions on the board. Take turns asking and answering questions.

1. ¿Qué tiempo hace en invierno? ¿en otoño? ¿en primavera? ¿en verano?
2. ¿Hace frío seco en Londres?
3. ¿Hace calor seco en Phoenix?
4. ¿Hay humedad en el desierto?
5. ¿Qué tiempo hace hoy?
6. ¿Cuándo es tiempo para esquiar?
7. ¿Cuándo es buen tiempo para nadar?
8. ¿Generalmente, qué tiempo hace en Puebla?
9. ¿Está húmedo hoy?
10. ¿Qué tiempo prefiere usted?

---

[66] When you are talking about how you feel use either **tener** or **sentir**.

20. LA HORA OFICIAL

1. Official time/military time (the time listed on flight schedules, for instance) is based on a 24-hour clock. Note the differences between official time and standard time:

STANDARD		OFFICIAL
La una	de la mañana	1 h[67]
Las dos		2 h
Las tres y cuarto		3 h 15 minutos 12 s
Las cuatro		4 h
Las cinco y media		5 h 30 minutos
Las seis		6 h
Las ocho menos cuarto		7 h 45 minutos
Faltan diez para las nueve		8 h 50 minutos
Las nueve y veinte		9 h 20 minutos
Las diez		10 h
Las once y cinco		11 h 5 minutos
Las doce/mediodía		12 h
La una	de la tarde	13 h
Las dos		14 h
Las tres		15 h
Las cuatro		16 h
Las cinco		17 h
Las seis		18 h
Las siete	de la noche	19 h
Las ocho		20 h
Las nueve		21 h
Las diez		22 h
Las once		23 h
Las doce/ medianoche		24 h
Las doce y veinte		0 h 20 minutos

2. For official times, hours are indicated by numbers from 0 to 24:

---

[67] In Spanish, "**h**" is the abbreviation for either **hora** or **horas**. The official time is always expressed in numbers, and will also be displayed with seconds. You will only hear the official time on public radio stations, but you may see it on transportation schedules at the airport or bus stations.

Official: **Son las cero horas y/con veinte minutos.**
Standard: **Son las doce y veinte de la noche.**

3. For official times from 1:00 p.m. to midnight, hours are indicated by numbers from 13 to 24:
   Official: Son las trece horas con treinta minutos.
   Standard: Es la una y media de la tarde.

4. In official time minutes are displayed from 1 to 59:
   Official: Son las tres horas con trece minutos.
   Standard: Son las tres y trece de la mañana.

5. Official time expresses exact or precise time using **cero** minutes, Standard time will use **en punto**:
   Official: Son las diez horas y cero minutos.
   Standard: Son las diez en punto.

EJERCICIOS PRÁCTICOS

☺ ☺ ✎

A. Give the time using the oficial time.
   Modelo: 4:45 Son las dieciséis con cuarenta y cinco minutos.
   1. 8:30
   2. 15:22
   3. 19:58
   4. 22:30
   5. 13:40
   6. 20:25
   7. 11:15
   8. 1:28
   9. 14:24
   10. 21:00

MINIRELATO: EL METRO DE LA CIUDAD DE MÉXICO

En la ciudad de México el metro es un medio de transporte **muy fácil de usar** (*very easy to use*). Es rápido, práctico y eficaz; además es **limpio** (*clean*). El metro atraviesa la ciudad en todos los **sentidos** (*directions*). Las líneas del metro tienen **colores diferentes** (*different colors*) y esto facilita el moverse de una línea a otra sin correr el riesgo **de perderse** (*get lost*). **El precio del boleto** (*the ticket price*) del metro es sumamente barato, veinticinco **centavos** (*cents*) de dólar por viaje. Con un sólo boleto es posible recorrer todas las líneas siempre y cuando no se salga del metro.

Preguntas

1. ¿Cómo es el metro de la ciudad de México?
2. ¿Es que es un medio práctico de transporte?
3. ¿Cómo atraviesa la ciudad?
4. ¿Es que es posible perderse?
5. ¿Cómo se pueden identificar las líneas en el plano?
6. El precio del boleto es barato, ¿verdad?
7. ¿Hay metro en su ciudad?
8. ¿Cuál es el medio de transporte más común en su ciudad?

Vocabulario

VERBOS

hacer	comer	vivir	tener
haber	estar	sentir	viajar
ver	revisar	ser	comer

NOMBRES

el conductor	el asiento	la ventana	el chofer
la canastilla	el paisaje	la montaña	el/la capital la
ciudad	la película	el tráfico	el pasillo
el autobús	la lluvia	las cosas	el sol
el viento	el tiempo	las nubes	el calor
el tiempo	el metro	el mapa	el frío
líneas	estaciones	el chico	la nieve
un aguacero	el precio	la voz	el boleto

ADJETIVOS

amable	gentil	brusco/a	caliente
interesante	joven	mayor (viejo/a)	frío/a
paciente	amigable	sabio	húmedo/a

bueno/a	malo/a	fresco/a	poco/a
mucho/a	espantoso/a	listo/a	rojo/a
guapo/a	contento/a	inteligente	pasivo
bonito/a	listo/a	pelirrojo/a	verde
blanco/a	amarillo/a	azul	gris

ADVERBIOS

mucho	normalmente	sumamente	bien
fácilmente	hoy	poco	mal

EXPRESIONES UTILES

no se preocupe

le va a gustar

perdonar la indiscreción

les va a encantar

siempre y cuando

CAPÍTULO 5: EL ENCUENTRO CON LA FAMILIA MEXICANA

En este capítulo...

You'll learn how to describe a person's physical characteristics, and how to ask for and give directions to key locations in a city. You'll also discover how Mexico City is divided into districts (delegaciones), and read a poem by Octavio Paz, Nobel Prize laureate in literature in 1990.

To help you accomplish these goals you'll learn about irregular verbs in general, as well as those that are irregular in the "yo" form. You will learn the ordinal numbers, the use of **todo** to express quantity, and the three families of stem-changing verbs like the verb **pensar** (*to think*), volver (to return), and pedir (to ask for something concrete). You will also practice the form **acabar de** to express the immediate past.

Contexto

El autobús llega a la terminal 4 Poniente en Puebla de los Ángeles. Hay mucha gente en la sala esperando a que lleguen sus familiares y amigos. Son las 7 y veinte de la noche cuando el autobús 214 arriba a la terminal. Las familias que van a hospedar a los chicos están inquietas porque no saben si podrán identificar a los estudiantes que van a hospedar. Los estudiantes, a la vez, están ansiosos por saber cómo los van a recibir las familias y cuál va a ser la primera impresión que ellos van a darles.

Yolanda Zurita: ¡Por fin, ya está aquí el autobús!

El señor García: ¡Vaya ya era hora! Yo creo reconocer al que me toca allá en la ventanilla. Lo ven, el que está saludando.

Maribel Bernal: ¡Cómo va a ser eso, Jesús, si están bien lejos!

Yolanda Zurita: Es verdad, y además ni se parecen a los de las fotos, dice bromeando.

Maribel Bernal: ¡Dios del cielo! Allí viene bajando la primera chica. Y la muchachita que voy a hospedar ¿será alta? ¿será rubia? y los demás estudiantes ¿cómo serán? ¿serán estudiosos o flojos, ordenados o desordenados?

Yolanda Zurita: Me basta con que sean buenas gentes, además de guapos, ¡claro!, continúa bromeando.

El señor García: Yo espero que este sea conversador, alegre, locuaz, como Justin, el que nos tocó el año pasado.

Maribel Bernal: Yo sólo espero que mi niña no sea mala para comer.

Jesús: Es que a algunas chicas les cuesta adaptarse a la comida mexicana, yo por eso prefiero hospedar solo muchachos", con ellos es más fácil.

Yolanda Zurita: No te preocupes Maribel, vas a ver que te la vas a pasar muy bien con tu nueva hija.

El profesor: Espero que vengan todos los chicos en este autobús, si no habrá que esperar al siguiente (*se prepara para revisar la lista y después empieza a contar: doce, trece y catorce*.) ¡Gracias a Dios ya están todos!

Dirigiéndose a los estudiantes: ¿ya tienen todas sus cosas?

Maribel Bernal: ¿Ya me puedo llevar a mi niña, Profesor?

El profesor: ¡Atención a las familias que han venido a recoger a sus chicos, ya se los pueden llevar! *Y (dirigiéndose a los estudiantes)*: chicos nos vemos el lunes a primera hora. Espero que vengan con muchas ganas de aprender y qué pasen un muy buen tiempo con sus familias.

Preguntas

1. ¿En qué autobús los cuatro amigos arribaron?
2. ¿Quiénes estaban en la terminal esperándolos?
3. ¿A qué hora llega el autobús?
4. ¿Por qué las familias están inquietas?
5. ¿Qué se pregunta la señora Bernal de los americanos?
6. ¿Qué dice Yolanda Zurita bromeando?
7. ¿Cómo espera el señor García que sea su hijo?
8. ¿Cuántos estudiantes son en total?
9. ¿Qué espera el profesor?
10. ¿Qué les pregunta el profesor a los estudiantes?

NOTA CULTURAL: LA FAMILIA

In today's society, we frequently speak of blended families, as well as extended or nontraditional families. If your parents are divorced, you would say: Mis padres están divorciados (or: Mis padres son divorciados).
You can use either **ser** or **estar** in this case.

You may also have a half-brother or a half-sister. You would refer to these as **medio hermano**, **media hermana.**

If you are adopted, you may refer to your mother as **mi madre adoptiva** and your father as **mi padre adoptivo.**

A widow is **una viuda**, and a widower is **un viudo.**

Your stepfather is **mi padrastro**, while your stepmother is **mi madrastra.**

Your brother-in-law is **mi cuñado**, and your sister-in-law is **mi cuñada.**

When you study abroad, you might wish to talk about your host family, in which case you would say: Mi familia mexicana. Mi mamá mexicana, etc…

Dichos

A caballo regalado no se le mira   Don't look a gift horse in the mouth.

el diente (no se le busca colmillo)
En boca cerrada no entra mosca.　　　　A closed mouth gathers no flies.

VOCABULARIO: Las formas físicas

Ellos son altos

atléticos	esqueléticos
gordos	flacos
guapos	feos
débiles	fuertes
jóvenes	viejos
morenos	bajos
rubios	musculosos

La cara

el cabello/ el pelo	la cabeza,	los ojos	la boca
la mejilla/el cachete	la frente	la nariz	el mentón
el cuello	las cejas	los dientes	la lengua

EJERCICIOS PRÁCTICOS

☺☺

Two students go to the board and stand so they cannot see each other. The remaining students take turns calling out vocabulary related to the face and adjectives to describe them. As each body part or characteristic is named, the students at the board must draw it and label it in order (1, 2, 3, etc.) When the drawings are complete, the class should describe and compare them.

VOCABULARIO: El plano de la ciudad

En esta página electrónica encontrará el plano de la ciudad de Puebla
http://hotelpueblaplaza.com.mx/mapa53527.html

Más vocabulario: direcciones

Los cuatro puntos cardinales: **norte** (*north*), **sur** (*south*), **este/oriente** (*east*), **oeste/poniente** (*west*).

¡Atraviese el puente!	Cross the bridge!
¡Váyase todo derecho!	Go straight ahead!
El Palacio Municipal está en la calle Juárez.	City Hall is on Juárez Street.
La zona industrial está en la zona **sur.**	The Industrial park is in the south end.
La catedral está en el centro.	The cathedral is in the center.
(Yo) estoy perdido.	I am lost.
(Yo) busco el museo universi-tario.	I am looking for the university museum
Tome la primera calle a la dere-cha.	Take the first street on your right.
Se va hasta la tercera calle y allí doble a la izquierda.	Go to the third street and turn to the left.

¿Dónde se toma el autobús?	Where is the bus stop?
¿Dónde se toma el metro?	Where is the subway?
Visitar un monument	To visit a monument
Visitar un museo	To visit a museum
Preguntar por el camino	To ask for directions
Policía	Police Officer

EJERCICIOS PRÁCTICOS

A. Using the city map, give your partner directions to a requested location.
   Modelo: Usted está de frente al palacio de gobierno

   (alguien le pregunta) ¿Cómo se llega a la biblioteca Palafoxiana?

   (Usted le responde) pase frente a catedral hasta la calle 3era Oriente, allí doble a la izquierda, la biblioteca está a su derecha.

   1. De la biblioteca, ¿cómo se llega a la rectoría de la Universidad?
   2. De la rectoría, ¿cómo se va al mercado El Parián?
   3. Del mercado El Parián, ¿cómo se va a la iglesia de San Francisco?
   4. De la iglesia de San Francisco, ¿cómo se va al Centro de Convenciones?
   5. Del Centro de Convenciones, ¿cómo se llega al mercado de los Sapos?

   ☺ ☺
B. You are at the Catedral. Using the map of Puebla, ask your partner to answer these questions:
   1. ¿Dónde queda la estación de autobuses (la CAPU)?
   2. ¿Dónde queda el estadio de fútbol?
   3. ¿Cómo se llega a la iglesia de la Compañía?
   4. ¿Cómo se llega al mercado Parián?
   5. ¿Dónde está el mercado de los Sapos?

C. Complete this paragraph using the correct vocabulary.

Los cuatro amigos visitan el centro histórico de Puebla. Ellos quieren visitar el _____Universitario. Ellos se sienten _____ y deciden preguntarle a un _____. Thomas le dice: "Perdón oficial, ¿dónde _____ el Museo Universitario?" El agente responde: "Para llegar al Museo Universitario, se va todo derecho hasta la Segunda Norte, allí se _____ a la izquierda. El museo _____ a la izquierda, a un costado del Palacio Municipal y es conocido como la Casa de los Muñecos.

APUNTES GRAMATICALES

21. VERBOS IRREGULARES[68]

1. En español algunos verbos son irregulares como los verbos ser, estar, ir, dar, ver, oír, caber, saber:

Dar (to give):

yo	doy	nosotros	damos
tú	das	vosotros	dais
vos	dás	vosotros	dais
él	da	ellos	dan
ella	da	ellas	dan
usted	da	ustedes	dan

Nosotros les **damos** comida a los animales.   We **give** food to the animals.

Ver (to see):

yo	veo	nosotros	vemos
tú	ves	vosotros	veis
vos	ves	vosotros	veis
él	v e	ellos	ven
ella	ve	ellas	ven
usted	ve	ustedes	ven

---

[68] You already know some irregular verbs in present tense like ser, estar, ir, you can add the verbs dar, ver, and oír to that list.

(Yo) **veo** un pájaro en la rama.　　　**I see** a bird on the branch.

oír (to hear):

yo	oigo	nosotros	oímos
tú	oyes	vosotros	oís
vos	oís	vosotros	oís
él	oye	ellos	oyen
ella	oye	ellas	oyen
usted	oye	ustedes	oyen

La mujer **oye** a su hijo cantar.　　　The woman **hears** her son sing.

2. There are also a couple verbs that are irregular only in the "yo" form without forming a group:

Saber: **to know** (information, facts, know how to do something, and to taste)

yo **sé**	nosotros sabemos
tú sabes	vosotros sabéis
vos sabés	vosotros sabéis
él sabe	ellos saben
ella sabe	ellas saben
usted sabe	ustedes saben

Yo no **sé** nadar.　I do not **know how** to swim.

Caber	**To fit in**
yo **quepo**	nosotros cabemos
tú cabes	vosotros cabéis
vos cabés	vosotros cabéis
él cabe	ellos caben
ella cabe	ellas caben
usted cabe	ustedes caben

¿**Quepo** en tu coche?　Can I fit in your car?

3. There are 4 type of ending changes for the **yo** form:

a. The first group form ends in **—go**:

poner	to put	(Yo) **pongo** el libro en la mesa.
salir	to leave	(Yo) **salgo** para México.
valer	to be worth/to have value	(Yo) **valgo** mucho.

componer	to fix, to make up	(Yo) **compongo** la televisión.
caer[69]	to fall	(Yo) **caigo** en el hoyo.
traer	to bring	(Yo) **traigo** mi camisa azul.

Note that there are other verbs like **tener** (*to have*), **venir** (*to come*), **seguir** (*to follow*), **decir** (*to tell*) that are also irregular in the **yo** form; but since they are also stem-changing verbs, you will learn about them later on.

b. Verbs that ends in **−zco** in the **yo** form:

conocer	to know (be familiar with)	(Yo) **conozco** al profesor.
agradecer	to be thankful for	(Yo) **agradezco** sus atenciones.
conducir	to drive	(Yo) **conduzco** un taxi.
parecer	to look like	(Yo) me **parezco** a mi padre.
aparecer	to appear	(Yo) **aparezco** en la película.
obedecer	to obey	(Yo) **obedezco** a mi madre.
producir	to produce	(Yo) **produzco** buenos frutos.
pertenecer	to pertain, to belong	(Yo) **pertenezco** a la sociedad protectora de animales.

c. Verbs that end in **−jo** in the **yo** form:

dirigir	to direct	Yo **dirijo** el tráfico.
escoger	to choose	Yo **escojo** la ropa.
exigir	to demand	Yo **exijo** libertad.
proteger	to protect	Yo **protejo** a mi mamá.
corregir	to correct	Yo **corrijo** a mi hermanito.

The verb **elegir** (*to elect*) is also irregular in the **yo** form. Since it is also a stem-changing verb, you will learn more about it later on.

d. Verbs that ends in **−zo** in the **yo** form:

| vencer | to defeat/ to conquest | Yo **venzo** a mi oponente. |
| convencer | to convince | Yo **convenzo** a mi madre de ir a México. |

_____

[69] Note that the verbs **caer** and **traer** have a unique conjugation in the **yo** form besides ending in **−igo: Traigo un libro. (I bring a book)** Ca**igo en un hoyo. (I fall in a hole)**

The verbs **torcer** (*to twist*) and **retorcer** (*to twine/to wring out*), and **destorcer** (to unwind) are also irregular in the **yo** form, but they are also stem-changing verbs that you will learn more about later:

Yo me **tue**rzo el tobillo.	I strain my ankle.
Yo re**tue**rzo la toalla.	I twist the towel.
Yo des**tue**rzo la soga.	I unwind the rope.

EJERCICIOS PRÁCTICOS

☺ ☺

A. Using these irregular verbs, ask and answer the following questions
   Modelo: ¿Tienes hambre?
                Sí, tengo hambre.
   1.   ¿Pones la mesa?
   2.   ¿Sales de la casa?
   3.   ¿Cabes en ese coche tan pequeño?
   4.   ¿Oyes música en español?
   5.   ¿Das dinero a los pobres?
   6.   ¿Le dices la verdad a tu madre?
   7.   ¿Conoces México?
   8.   ¿Obedeces a tus padres?
   9.   ¿Conduces un Ferrari?
   10.   ¿Diriges el tráfico?

☺ ☺

B. Change into the negative.
   Modelo: Yo conozco Madrid.
                Yo no conozco Madrid.
   1.   Yo salgo de vacaciones.
   2.   Yo tengo dos hermanos.
   3.   Yo obedezco al profesor.
   4.   Yo exijo la verdad.
   5.   Yo digo mentiras.
   6.   Yo oigo la radio.
   7.   Yo vengo del baño.
   8.   Yo dirijo la orquesta.
   9.   Yo conduzco una moto.
   10.   Yo escojo el libro.

☺ ☺

C. Fill in the blanks with the correct verb conjugation
1. Yo _____ (conocer) Perú.
2. Yo no _____ (saber) cocinar.
3. Yo le _____ (dar) dinero a la Universidad.
4. Ellos _____ (oír) el canto del pájaro.
5. Ella _____ (ver) el paisaje por la ventana.
6. Yo _____ (dirigir) el concierto.
7. Yo me _____ (torcer) el tobillo.
8. Yo _____ (poner) la mesa.
9. Yo no _____ (tener) dinero.
10. Yo _____ (obedecer) a mi madre.

22. LOS NÚMEROS ORDINALES

1. Ordinal numbers define the order of items in a series: first, second, third, etc.

primero/a	first	**sexto/a**	sixth
segundo/a	second	**séptimo/a**	seventh
tercero/a	third	**octavo/a**	eighth
cuarto/a	fourth	**noveno/a**	ninth
quinto/a	fifth	**décimo/a**	tenth

2. Ordinal numbers agree in gender and number with the nouns they modify:

Yo soy el **segundo** hijo.   I am the second son.
Mi esposa es la **quinta** hija.   My wife is the fifth daughter.

3. In general, when cardinal and ordinal numbers occur together, the cardinal number precedes the ordinal one:

Los **tres** primeros de la fila.   The first **three** in the line.

4. The ordinal numbers **primero** and **tercero** drop the -o in front of a masculine noun:

Es mi **primer** coche.   It's my **first** car.
Este es mi **tercer** trabajo.   This is my **third** job.

5. In Spanish, ordinal numbers are seldom used after "tenth", instead, Spanish speakers use cardinal numbers:

John vive en el piso **once**.   John lives on the **eleventh** floor.

Vivimos en el siglo **veintiuno**.   We live in the **twenty first** century.

6. Ordinal numbers are used in Spanish to refer to the first day of the month only. After that, cardinal numbers are used:

Hoy es **primero** de enero.   Today is January **first**.

Hoy es cinco de mayo.   Today is May fifth**.**

7. Ordinal numbers may also be abbreviated as follows:

1ero/1era/1er (if a masculine noun follows the number), **2do/2da**, **3ero/3era/3er** (if a masculine noun follows the number), **4to/4ta, 5to/5ta**, etc.:

John vive en la **5ta.** calle Oriente.   John lives on **5th** Street East.

EJERCICIOS PRÁCTICOS

A. Transform the sentences using ordinal numbers, days of the week, and months of the year.

Modelo: El primer día de la semana es lunes (el segundo día)

            El segundo día de la semana es martes.

  1. El primer día de la semana es lunes. (el segundo, el tercero, el cuarto, el quinto, el sexto, el séptimo)

  2. El primer mes del año es enero. (el segundo, el tercero, el cuarto, el quinto, el sexto, etc…)

☺ ☺

B. Working with a partner, practice using ordinal numbers in a variety of contexts. Take turns asking and answering questions such as the following:

    1.   ¿Cuáles son los dos días del fin de semana?

    2.   ¿Cuál es el primer día de la semana?

    3.   ¿Cuál es el primer mes de la primavera?

    4.   ¿Cuál es el primer día del año?

    5.   ¿Cómo se llama el Primer Ministro de España?

    6.   ¿Cuál es su segundo nombre?

    7.   ¿Cuál es su primer apellido?

    8.   ¿Quiénes viven en el tercer piso?

    9.   ¿Quién es el primero de la lista?

    10.   ¿Quién está en primer lugar?

23. TODO Y OTRAS EXPRESIONES DE CANTIDAD

1. When used as an adjective, **todo** agrees in gender and number with the noun it modifies. It can be followed by a definite article, a possessive adjective, or a demonstrative adjective:
    El profesor lee **todo** el periódico.   The teacher reads the **entire** newspaper.

2. As a pronoun, **todo** means everything or all:
    Todas las personas somos mortales.   We **all** are mortal.

3. Here are some other expressions with **todo**:
Todo el mundo llega temprano.	**Everybody** arrives early.
Todo el tiempo habla el profesor.	**The whole** time the professor speaks.
Todos juntos cantan el himno nacional.	They sing the National Anthem **in unison.**
Todo pasa y **todo** queda.	Everything passes and everything stays.

4. Varios, pocos, algo, alguno, bastante, and cualquier are some other indefinite expressions of quantity:
Varios países forman la coalición militar.	**Several** countries form the military coalition.
Muy **pocos** exámenes son fáciles.	**Very few** tests are easy.
¿Está buscando **algo** bonito?	Are you looking for **something** beautiful?

    Ella llama a **algunos** de sus amigos.
    Los niños suelen querer que se les compre **cualquier** cosa.

5. Otras formas de cantidades indefinidas son:
 a. Spanish adds **—ena** to the end of certain numbers to indicate an indefinite or approximate number that forms a group or a number of days. This is possible with the following numbers:

10	una decena
11	una oncena
12	una docena
15	una quincena
20	una veintena
30	una treintena
40	una cuarentena
100	una centena

Note that the construction number + **—ena** is always feminine. Because it is an expression of quantity, it may be followed or preceded by **de**:

Una treintena de estudiantes.

Es el salario de **una quincena**[70].

b. Another way to express a group of numbers is with the following expressions:

2 dúo
3 trío
4 cuarteto
5 quinteto
6 sexteto
1000 millar

c. Fractional numbers other than **un medio** (1/2) and **un tercio** (1/3) have the same form as the ordinal number:

un cuarto (1/4) **un quinto** (1/5) **un décimo** (1/10)

EJERCICIOS PRÁCTICOS

A. Complete the following sentences using these expressions of quantity: trío, novena, oncena, todo, dúo, docena, quincena, decena.

Los ricos lo tienen _____.

Me gusta como tocan los _____.

En México pagan cada _____.

Diez es igual a una _____.

El esposo compra una _____ de rosas para su esposa.

Esta semana es la _____ a San Antonio.

En un equipo de fútbol hay una _____ de jugadores.

Batman y Robin son el _____ dinámico.

El doctor puso al enfermo en _____.

La música de cámara la toca un _____.

☺ ☺

_____

[70] In Spanish, when determining dates, you include the day from which you are counting. You say **ocho días** to indicate one week and **quince días** to express two weeks. Two weeks makes **una quincena**.

B. Working with a partner, answer these questions using expressions of quantity. Take turns asking and answering questions such as the following:
1. ¿Cuántos jugadores hay en un equipo de béisbol?
2. ¿Cuántos jugadores hay en un equipo de fútbol?
3. ¿Cuántos jugadores hay en un equipo de rugby?
4. ¿Cuántos jugadores hay en un equipo de baloncesto?
5. ¿Cuántos jugadores hay en un equipo de hockey sobre hielo?
6. ¿Cuántos integrantes hay en un dúo?
7. ¿Cuántos integrantes hay en un sexteto?
8. ¿Cuántas integrantes hay en un quinteto?

24. LOS VERBOS QUE CAMBIAN SU RAÍZ

There are three groups of verbs that are stem-changing.

A. The first group is formed by verbs like **pensar** (*to think*), **querer** (*to want/to desire*) or **sentir** (*to feel*), and are known as stem-changing verbs, since in most forms of the present tense, the —**e**— of the stem changes to —**ie**—Their conjugations are as follows:

Pensar (to think/to believe):

(yo) **pienso**	nosotros pensamos[71]
tú **piensas**	*vosotros pensáis*
vos **pensás**	*vosotros pensáis*
usted **piensa**	ustedes **piensan**
él **piensa**	ellos **piensan**
ella **piensa**	ellas **piensan**

Los estudiantes piensan comer pizza.   The students think of eating pizza.

Querer (to want):

(yo) **quiero**	nosotros queremos
tú **quieres**	*vosotros queréis*
vos **querés**	*vosotros queréis*
usted **quiere**	ustedes **quieren**
él **quiere**	ellos **quieren**

---

[71] Note that **pensar**, like all stem-changing verbs, has a regular conjugation in the **nosotros** and **vosotros** forms of the present tense.

ella **quiere**   ellas **quieren**

Ellas **quieren** ir a la playa.   They want to go to the beach.

Sentir (to feel):
(yo) **siento**   nosotros sentimos
tú **sientes**   *vosotros sentís*
vos **sentís**   *vosotros sentís*
usted **siente**   ustedes **sienten**
él **siente**   ellos **sienten**
ella **siente**   ellas **sienten**

Él **siente** dolor en su brazo. He **feels** pain in his arm.

A.1 Forms of stem-changing verbs that are modified by a prefix are conjugated in the same way:
repensar (*to rethink*)   dispensar (*to excuse/to waive*)

A.2 The following verbs are conjugated like **pensar, querer** and **sentir**:

comenzar	to begin
confesar(se)	to confess
negar	to refuse/ to deny
renegar	to deny vigorously/ to complain
mentir	to lie
perder	to lose
sentar(se)	to sit
sugerir	to suggest
tropezar	to trip
preferir	to prefer
empezar	to start
entender	to understand
referir(se)	to refer
cerrar	to close
tener	to have
venir	to come
requerir	to require
presentir	to have a feeling

Él **comienza** la tarea.   He **starts** to do his homework.

Ellas **tropiezan** con la piedra.	They **trip** on the rock.
El hombre **pierde** su cartera.	The man **loses** his wallet.
Nosotros **negamos** la verdad.	We **deny/denied** the truth.
Ellos **prefieren** la carne.	They **prefer** red meat.
El juez **requiere** pruebas.	The judge **requires** proofs.

Note that the stem-change occurs on the second to last syllable.

EJERCICIOS PRÁCTICOS

A. Answer these questions
   1. ¿Qué tienes que hacer hoy?
   2. ¿Piensas que va a hacer buen tiempo hoy?
   3. ¿Qué prefieres hacer hoy con este clima tan bonito?
   4. ¿Qué quiere hacer hoy el profesor?
   5. ¿Qué sugieren los estudiantes hacer en México?

☺ ☺

B. Pick a verb from the list for your partner to put in a sentence.
   comenzar, tener, confesar(se), querer, negar, perder, sentar(se), sugerir, tropezar, preferir, empezar, sentir(se), entender, referir(se), mantener, mentir,
   venir, (re)pensar.

B. The second group of verbs are known as stem-changing verbs, because in
   most forms of the present tense, the —**o**— of the stem changes to —**ue**— like
   the verb **almorzar** (*to have lunch*):

yo **almuerzo**	nosotros almorzamos
tú **almuerzas**	*vosotros almorzáis*
vos **almorzás**	*vosotros almorzáis*
usted **almuerza**	ustedes **almuerzan**
él **almuerza**	ellos **almuerzan**
ella **almuerza**	ellas **almuerzan**

El profesor **almuerza** solo.	The professor **has lunch** alone.

The conjugations of the verb **poder** (*to manage to/ to be able to*) is:

yo **puedo**	nosotros podemos
tú **puedes**	*vosotros podéis*
vos **podés**	*vosotros podéis*

usted **puede**	ustedes **pueden**
él **puede**	ellos **pueden**
ella **puede**	ellas **pueden**

¿**Puede** mostrarme mi cuarto, por favor?
Can you show me my room please?

The conjugation of the verb **dormir** (to sleep) is:

yo **duermo**	nosotros dormimos
tú **duermes**	*vosotros dormís*
vos **dormís**	*vosotros dormís*
usted **duerme**	ustedes **duermen**
él **duerme**	ellos **duermen**
ella **duerme**	ellas **duermen**

B.1 Other verbs with a similar change in the stem as **poder** and **almorzar**:

colgar	to hang up the phone or the clothes
contar	to count/to tell a story
costar	to cost
morir	to die
mostrar	to show
mover	to move
probar	to try/to taste
soler	to be accustomed/to be used to
soñar	to dream
sonar	to ring the bell/to hit somebody/to blow your nose
torcer	to twist
volar	to fly
volver	to return/to come back

EJERCICIOS PRÁCTICOS

A. Make sentences using the given words. Remember to conjugate the stem-changing verbs.

¿poder/usted/español?/hablar
Ellas/volver/de/la/fiesta/tarde.
La policía/resolver/el/rápidamente/crimen.
Un niño/soñar/ser/piloto/con.

Martín/mover/el/coche/mamá/de/su.

☺☺

B. You and your classmates divide into groups of five, and each individual choo-ses a verb. The first person acts out the selected verb and the rest of the classmates identify it. The second student repeats the verb of the first student and adds his or her own and so on, until it is the last student's turn. He/she must repeat and act out all five verbs. Use verbs like **poder**, and **almorzar,** so you can improve your control of stem-changing verbs.
After the class has identified the verbs, you and your group of five make up a story using the verbs in logical order.
Modelo: Después de practicar muchas horas, por fin yo **puedo** tocar el violín. Se lo **cuento** a mi mamá y le **pruebo** que no **miento**. ¡Qué, por fin, **recuerdo** como hacerlo sin tener al profesor a mi lado!

Repeat the same process with verbs like **almorzar, colgar, sonar,** etc.

C. The third group of verbs is formed by verbs that in most forms of the present tense, the —**e**— of the stem changes to —**i**—. Like the verb **pedir** (*to ask for something material or concrete*).
Its conjugation is as follows:

yo **pido**	nosotros pedimos
tú **pides**	*vosotros pedís*
vos **pedís**	*vosotros pedís*
usted **pide**	ustedes **piden**
él **pide**	ellos **piden**
ella **pide**	ellas **piden**

El piloto **pide** una ensalada.   The pilot **asks** for a salad.

C.1 Other verbs with a similar change in the stem as **pedir**:

decir	to tell
despedir	to fire
despedir(se)	to say goodbye to somebody else
elegir	to elect
impedir	to impede
medir	to measure
reír	to laugh
reelegir	to reelect

repetir	to repeat
servir	to serve
seguir	to follow
sonreír	to smile
vestir(se)	to dress
desvertir(se)	to undress

Note that this type of change (e: i) only can occur with verbs ending in –ir.

Note that all the stem-changing verbs in the present tense have a regular stem in the **nosotros** and *vosotros* forms.

Note also that in all the stem-changing verbs, the stem-change occurs in the second to last syllable.

EJERCICIOS PRÁCTICOS

✎

A. Construct sentences using the given words. Remember to conjugate the stem-changing verbs!
Usted/servir/la/comida/en/el/comedor.
Ellas/pedir/permiso/para/ir a/la/fiesta.
La policía/impedir/el/crimen.
La/mamá/vestir/a/su/hija/pequeña.
Martín/medir/la/sala/de/su/casa.

☺ ☺

B. You and your classmates divide into groups of five, and each individual chooses a verb. The first person acts out the selected verb and the rest of the classmates identify it. The second student repeats the verb of the first student and adds his or her own and so on until it is the last student's turn. He/she must repeat and act out all five verbs. Use verbs like **pedir** so you can improve your control of stem-changing verbs.

After the class has identified the verbs, you and your group of five make up a story using the verbs in logical order.

Modelo: La policía **impide** el asalto al banco. Yo **sigo** la noticia en la televisión y **repito** la historia a todos mis amigos. Después de un rato mi mamá me

llama para comer. Ella **sirve** la mesa con amor. Después de comer yo **digo** que su comida es la mejor del mundo y mi mamá **sonríe**.
Repeat the same process with verbs like **pedir, reír, despedir, vestir,** etc.

25. ACABAR DE + INFINITIVO

1. The verb **acabar de** + an infinitive can be translated as "to have just" done something (in the very recent past)[72].
    Acaba de terminar la clase.   The class **has just** finished.

2. The verb **acabar** is a regular verb, and it conjugation is as follows:
    yo acabo   nosotros acabamos
    tú acabas   *vosotros acabáis*
    vos acabás   *vosotros acabáis*
    usted acaba   ustedes acaban
    él acaba   ellos acaban
    ella acaba   ellas acaban
    Acabo de llegar de la escuela.   I **just** arrived from the school.

3. The expression **acabar de** is always formed by the conjugated form of the verb **acabar** and the preposition "de". It is always followed by a verb in the infinitive:
    Ellas **acaban de** comprar una casa.   They **have just** bought a house.
    Acabamos de comer.   We **have just** finished our meal.

EJERCICIOS PRÁCTICOS

A. Complete the following sentences using the immediate past. (**acabar de**)
    Modelo: El agente de migración... (acabar de llegar de trabajar)
                   El agente de migración acaba de llegar de trabajar.
    1. El presidente y su gabinete...   4. Yo...
    2. Las aeromozas y la tripulación...   5. Tú...
    3. Ellos...   6. Él...

---

[72] In some Latin American countries like Uruguay, they prefer to use the form **recién** or **recientemente** (recently) instead of **acabar de** to express "to have just done something".

B. Change from present tense to immediate past using **acabar de**.
   Modelo: Él compra una casa (acabar de)
               Él **acaba de** comprar una casa.
   1. Él viaja a México.   4. Nosotros pintamos la casa.
   2. Ellos regresan de la escuela.   5. Usted limpia el coche.
   3. Tú vendes tu computadora.   6. Yo hago la tarea.

☺ ☺

C. Working with a partner, take turns asking and answering questions.
   Modelo: (*Ask him/her*) ¿Acabas (tú) de terminar de trabajar?
               Sí, acabo de terminar de trabajar./ No, yo no acabo de terminar de
               trabajar.
   1. ¿Acabas de llegar a México?
   2. ¿Acaba de venir de la escuela?
   3. ¿Acaba de ver llegar al Capitán América?
   4. ¿Acabas de venir del cine?
   5. ¿Acabas de conocer a Lady Gaga?

MINIRELATO: LAS ZONAS Y ALCALDIAS (ANTES LLAMADAS DELEGACIONES) DE LA CIUDAD DE MÉXICO

Si se observa el plano de la ciudad de México se verá que hay dieciséis **alcaldías** (*boroughs*). **Cada una** (*each one*) de esas delegaciones tiene su propio carácter distintivo. Por ejemplo, en la zona centro está la parte histórica, lo que queda de las ruinas prehispánicas, los edificios coloniales, la **catedral** (*cathedral*), todo lo que le dio a la Ciudad de México el **título** (*title*) de *la Ciudad de los Palacios*. En la parte norte **se asienta** (*sits*) la zona industrial, en la zona **sur** (*South*) está la Universidad Nacional; muchas de las librerías, **galerías** (*galleries*) y teatros están en esta zona. Al poniente se encuentra **el corazón financiero** (*financial district*) y la zona residencial donde está la mayoría de las **embajadas** (*embassies*). Si se pasea por el paseo de la Reforma verá que allí están los mejores hoteles, además **a un costado** (*on one side*) del Paseo de la Reforma, está la zona Rosa, un lugar muy frecuentado por turistas, donde hay muchos bares y discotecas. El **aeropuerto** (*airport*) Internacional Benito Juárez está al **oriente** (*East*) de la ciudad en la delegación Venustiano Carranza.

Preguntas

1. ¿Qué se descubre al ver el plano de la Ciudad de México?
2. ¿En qué zona de la ciudad están las embajadas?
3. ¿En qué parte de la ciudad está la Universidad Nacional Autónoma de México?
4. ¿En qué parte están los edificios coloniales?
5. ¿En qué alcaldía se asienta el distrito financiero?
6. ¿En qué parte de la ciudad se asienta la zona industrial?
7. ¿En qué alcaldía está ubicado el aeropuerto?
8. ¿En qué zona están los bares y discotecas?
9. ¿Conoce usted la Ciudad de México?

LECTURA: PRIMAVERA A LA VISTA

Pulida claridad de piedra diáfana,
lisa frente de estatua sin memoria:
cielo de invierno, espacio reflejado
en otro más profundo y más vacío.

El mar respira apenas, brilla apenas.
Se ha parado la luz entre los árboles,
ejército dormido. Los despierta
el viento con banderas de follajes.

Nace del mar, asalta la colina,
oleaje sin cuerpo que revienta
contra los eucaliptos amarillos
y se derrama en ecos por el llano.

El día abre los ojos y penetra
en una primavera anticipada.
Todo lo que mis manos tocan, vuela.
Está lleno de pájaros el mundo.

Octavio Paz

Preguntas

1. ¿Qué palabras reconoce(s) en el poema?
2. ¿Quién escribe el poema?
3. ¿De dónde es este escritor?
4. ¿Cuál es el premio más importante que él recibió?
5. ¿De qué está lleno el mundo?
6. ¿Cuál es el título del poema?
7. ¿Recuerda qué es la primavera?
8. ¿Qué pasa con todo lo que tocan las manos del poeta?
9. ¿De qué nace el viento?

VOCABULARIO

VERBOS

pensar	creer	venir	acabar (de)	conocer	dirigir
hacer	incluir	querer	renegar	caber	oír
dar	ver	tener	negar	saber	llamar
obedecer	sentir	requerir	poner	agradecer	

NOMBRES

el carro	el plano	la primavera	el restaurante
la ciudad	el museo	la torre	el país
la orquesta	los hijos	la estatua del caballito	
el puente	el instituto	la zona industrial	
el viento	el/la poeta	el centro financiero	
las manos	el poema	el Museo de Antropología e Historia	
la vista	la biblioteca	el mercado	la alcaldía

ADJETIVOS

precoz	distintivo	prehispánicas	mejores
hermoso/a	negro/a	rojo/a	azul
verde	violeta	morado/a	gris
dorado/a	plateado/a	rosa	amarillo/a
anaranjado/a	celeste	azul marino/a	blanco/a
café	canoso/a	pelirrojo/a	rubio/a
castaño	primero/a	segundo/a	tercero/a
cuarto/a	quinto/a	sexto/a	séptimo/a
octavo/a	noveno/a	décimo/a	violeta

ADVERBIOS
así   siempre   muy

CONJUNCIONES
porque   y/e

PREPOSICIONES

delante (de)	atrás (de)	debajo (de)	abajo (de)
sobre	encima (de)	por	para
hasta	hacia	entre	sin
de	con	en	a

146

CAPÍTULO 6: EN CASA DE LOS ZURITA

En este capítulo...

You'll learn how to describe furnishings and rooms in a house. We will also discuss how to cope with common Mexican expectations of American visitors. To help you accomplish these goals, you'll learn about the adjectives that precede nouns in Spanish. You'll also learn about the direct object pronouns and the uses of the personal "a", and about the differences between the verbs **saber** and **conocer**. Finally, you'll also learn about other verbs like **jugar, oler, inquirir, guiar,** and **continuar** that have special conjugations and behave as if they were stem-changing verbs.

Contexto

Después de despedirse de sus amigos, Thomas sale de la estación de autobuses y se va con Yolanda Zurita. Pone sus maletas en la cajuela del coche y se sube al lado de Yolanda. Ella se pone al volante para ir a casa. En ese instante empieza a llover.

Yolanda Zurita: ¡Qué lástima, se nos vino la lluvia encima!

Thomas: (*Está un poco mojado*) Perdone pero se me mojó un poco mi camisa.

Yolanda: Está bien. Verás que mañana va a hacer buen tiempo.

Después de un rato, Yolanda y Thomas llegan a casa.

Yolanda (*al ser recibidos por su marido*): José, este es el estudiante que vamos a hospedar.

José Zurita: Ya lo sé. Lo he reconocido por la foto. ¡Bienvenido a casa, joven! (*dice esto mientras le extiende la mano para saludarlo*)

Thomas: Muchas gracias señor (*extendiendo la mano tímidamente*). Es un honor y un gusto conocerlo.

José: El gusto es todo nuestro.

Yolanda: Y este es nuestro hijo Martín.

Thomas: ¡Hola Martín!

Martín: ¡Hola! (*mientras le extiende la mano*) ¿y el viaje?

Thomas: Bien; un poco largo, pero todo bien.

Yolanda (*interrumpiendo*): Ven Thomas, te voy a mostrar tu cuarto.

Thomas: Voy en seguida señora. Primero necesito tomar agua. Tengo mucha sed.

Yolanda: ¡Está muy bien!

Todos ellos suben al segundo piso.

Yolanda: Aquí está tu cuarto, es un cuarto sencillo, pero verás que vas a estar muy cómodo y nadie te va a molestar.

Thomas: Muchas gracias, de nuevo. Y, ¿dónde está el ...?

Yolanda (*adivinando la frase*): El baño está aquí mismo, pero hay otro al fondo y uno más en el primer piso, bajando las escaleras. Puedes usar el que quieras.

Thomas: Un cuarto con baño propio. ¡Qué maravilla! Muchas gracias.

Yolanda: De nada. Hay un jabón sobre el lavabo y las toallas están limpias; si necesitas algo más, me avisas. Estás en tu casa.

Thomas: Muchas gracias de nuevo. Ya sé que voy a estar muy bien con ustedes.

José: Mañana vamos a salir para que conozcas un poco la ciudad.

Thomas: ¿Vamos a ir en su nuevo coche?

José: Vamos a ir en mi único coche.

Preguntas

1. ¿Cuánto tiempo llevan las familias esperando en la terminal?
2. ¿Quién conduce el coche en que se sube Thomas?
3. ¿Cómo está el clima hoy?
4. ¿Qué tiempo va a hacer mañana, según Yolanda?
5. ¿A quién más conoce Thomas esa noche?
6. ¿Dónde está el cuarto de Thomas?
7. ¿Cómo es su cuarto?
8. ¿Tiene baño su cuarto?
9. ¿Dónde están los otros baños?
10. ¿Qué hay en el baño del cuarto de Thomas?

NOTA CULTURAL: LA PLANTA AUTOMOTRIZ EN PUEBLA

La ciudad de Puebla es famosa por muchas cosas, entre otras porque aquí está la planta de autos Volkswagen. En esta ciudad se producen todos los autos "Jettas" que hay en el mundo. Aquí también se producía el viejo volkswagen Beetle, conocido en México como "vochito" que dejó de hacerse hace algunos años y que le dio fama a esta planta automotriz.

Dichos

El fin justifica los medios.	The end justifies the means.
Querer es poder.	Where there's a will, there's a way.
En el país de los ciegos, el tuerto es rey.	In the kingdom of the blind, the one-eyed man is king.

VOCABULARIO: La casa

La planta baja: La cocina: la estufa, el refrigerador, el microondas
el comedor: la mesa, las sillas, el mantel, las cortinas, una vitrina (chinero).
La sala: Tres sofás, una televisión, un estéreo, un cuadro, unas lámparas.

Segundo piso:
Las recamaras: una cama, un tocador, un clóset/armario, un baño.
El cuarto: una cama, un respaldo, un buró, una lámpara, un reloj despertador, una cómoda.
La cama: una sábana, dos almohadas, un cobertor, un muñeco de peluche.

El baño: La taza, el rollo de papel higiénico, el bote de basura, el lavabo, la tina de baño, la regadera, la toalla, el jabón, el champú.

El estudio u oficina: un escritorio, una silla, una lámpara, un librero, los libros, un teléfono, una computadora[73], un cesto para basura, un ventilador.

Más vocabulario: La casa de los Zurita

la casa	the house
la colonia/ el barrio	the neighborhood
el garaje	the garage
una recámara	a bedroom
un cuarto	a room
al fondo	at the end
el aire acondicionado	the air conditioning
la planta baja	the ground floor
la planta alta	the upper floor

---

[73] In Spain they use **el ordenador** instead.

el primer piso	the first floor
el ático	the attic
la despensa	the pantry
el sótano	the basement
la escalera	the stairs
está muy claro	it's very clear
el vino	the wine
descender/bajar	to go downstairs
ascender/subir	to go upstairs

EJERCICIOS PRÁCTICOS

✎

A. Complete these sentences with the correct vocabulary.

La _____ de los Zurita es grande. Es una casa de dos pisos. En la planta _____ está la cocina con una _____ grande, la sala y el comedor, además del _____ para dos carros. En la planta _____ están las _____. La casa no tiene _____, la verdad es que casi ninguna casa en México tiene, ni tampoco suelen tener _____. En el primer piso también hay un baño que está _____, aunque el cuarto de Thomas tiene _____ propio. Para subir o bajar los Zurita usan las _____. La casa está en la _____ San Manuel, una de las más antiguas de Puebla.

☺ ☺

B. Now ask the following questions to a partner.
  1. ¿Cuántos pisos tiene la casa de los Zurita?
  2. ¿Cuántos pisos tiene su casa?
  3. ¿Tiene ático para guardar las maletas la casa de los Zurita?
  4. Y su casa, ¿tiene ático?
  5. ¿En qué piso están las recámaras?
  6. Y en su casa ¿en qué piso están las recámaras?
  7. ¿En qué planta está la sala en la casa de los Zurita?
  8. ¿Dónde guardan sus coches los Zurita?
  9. ¿Hay otros baños en la casa?
  10. ¿Tiene sótano la casa de los Zurita?

☺ ☺

C. Here you have the answers. Make the proper questions.
  Modelo: La casa es de dos plantas.

¿Cuántas plantas tiene la casa?
1. La sala es grande.
2. Hay tres recámaras en la casa de los Zurita.
3. Sí, el cuarto de Thomas tiene baño propio.
4. Yolanda conduce su coche.
5. El hijo se llama Martín.
6. Hay un baño al fondo.
7. No, no tiene ni sótano ni ático.

APUNTES GRAMATICALES

26. ADJETIVOS QUE PRECEDEN A LOS NOMBRES.

1. As you may remember, adjectives describe qualities of nouns and pronouns:

   Este es un **buen** libro.   This is a **good** book.

   Thomas es **alto.**   Thomas is **tall.**

2. You may also remember that adjectives agree with the nouns and pronouns they modify in gender and number:

   Yo tengo una recámara **pequeña.** I have a **small** bedroom.

   Las chicas son **bonitas.**   The girls are **pretty.**

3. Most adjectives follow the noun they modify. However, certain adjectives usually precede the noun they modify. These include descriptive adjectives that express inherent characteristics of the noun, numerical adjectives, possessive adjectives, demonstrative adjectives, adjectives that express a subjective judgment, and adjectives following the expression ¡**Qué**!:

   La **blanca** nieve.   **White** snow (since snow is inherently white).

   Los Zurita tienen **dos** coches.   The Zuritas have **two** cars.

   Su casa es grande.   **His/her/their** house is big.

   Este chico es guapo.   **This** boy is handsome.

   Sergio es el **peor** profesor de todos.   Sergio is the **worst** professor of all.

   ¡Qué **mala** suerte!   What **bad** luck!

4. Some masculine adjectives drop the **-o** in front of a masculine singular noun: **bueno, malo, primero, tercero, uno, alguno, ninguno**:

   Yo soy el **tercer** hijo.   I am the **third** son.

   Thomas es un **buen** estudiante.   Thomas is a **good** student.

Note that a**lguno** and **ninguno** add a written accent mark when they drop the —**o**:

¿Hay **algún** doctor aquí?   Is there **any** doctor here?

No, no hay **ningún** doctor.   No, there is **no doctor**.

5. The adjective **grande** and **cualquiera** (any) shorten to **gran** and **cualquier** when they precede a singular noun:

Cualquier día de estos me voy para México.   Any one of these days I will go to Mexico.

La madre Teresa fue una **gran** mujer.   Mother Teresa was a **great** woman.

6. Some adjectives change meaning depending on whether they are placed before or after the noun they modify: **alto, antiguo, cierto, cualquiera, diferente, grande, justo, mismo, nuevo, puro, solo, simple, única, viejo**:

Él está en un **alto** puesto.   He is in a **higher** position.

Él es un hombre **alto**.   He is a **tall** man.

Mi mujer es la **única** hija.   My wife is the **only** child.

Mi mujer es **única.**   My wife is **unique.**

Tenemos el **mismo** profesor.   We have the **same** professor.

El profesor **mismo** arregló el problema.   The professor **himself** solved the problem.

Note that if the adjectives are placed before the noun they modify, they express a subjective or personal judgment. When they are placed after the noun they modify, they qualify or describe the noun or person.

7. The adjective **Santo** ('holy' or 'saint') is abbreviated before all masculine saints' names except **Santo Domingo, Santo Tomás,** and the expressions **¡Santo Cristo! ¡Santo Cielo! ¡Santo Padre!**, and this popular prayer **¡Santo Dios, Santo Fuerte, Santo Inmortal!**:

San Francisco

San Diego

San Antonio

8. All the female saints keep the adjective Santa:

Santa Bárbara

Santa Clara

Santa Mónica

EJERCICIOS PRÁCTICOS

A. Fill in the blank using the right adjective.
1. Tengo un coche _____. (new)
2. Tengo un _____ (new to me) coche.
3. Mi esposa es una mujer _____. (unique)
4. Ella es mi _____(only) esposa.
5. Los atletas beben agua _____. (pure)
6. Este café es _____(nothing but water) agua.
7. FDR fue un hombre _____. (big)
8. FDR fue un _____ (great) hombre.
9. El tiene un _____ (high) puesto.
10. El es un hombre _____. (tall)

B. Use the adjectives provided to create new sentences.
Modelo: Los niños están en el comedor. (pocos)
          Los **pocos** niños están en el comedor.
1. Mis alumnos no vienen a clase. (peores)
2. Nuestras nietas estudian español. (primeras)
3. Los invitados toman vino en la sala. (algunos)
4. Mis amigos llegan a tiempo. (muchos)
5. Vuestra hermana canta muy bien. (única)
6. Él es profesor de química. (el mejor)

C. Describe a family photo using the adjectives provided.
Modelo: Este es el patriarca. (primero)
          Este es el **primer** patriarca.
1. Este es el nieto. (segundo)
2. Ellas son las sobrinas. (mejores)
3. Este es el hijo. (peor)
4. Este es el retrato de la hija. (tercera)
5. Este es Francisco de Asís. (Santo)

27. LOS PRONOMBRES DE OBJETO DIRECTO

1. Sometimes in Spanish, a verb may require one or more objects. The role of those objects is either to receive the action of the verb ("direct object") or to receive the indirect action ("indirect object").

2. A direct object pronoun replaces an object of the verb which is a noun and which follows the verb directly (that is, an object that is not preceded by a preposition). A direct object pronoun thus shares the gender and number of the noun it replaces:

Tú ves **la cama**.	You see **the bed**.
Tú **la** ves.	You see **it**.

3. These are the direct object pronouns:
FOR PERSONS[74] OR THINGS

me	me	**nos**	us
te	you (singular)	**os**	you (plural)
lo	him, it	**los**	them (masculine)
la	her, it	**las**	them (feminine)

4. In Spanish, a direct object pronoun is placed before the conjugated verb:

Él mira **la televisión**.	He watches **television**.
Él **la** mira.	He watches **it**.
Ellas no prefieren **las cosas simples**.	They do not prefer **simple things**.
Ellas no **las** prefieren.	They do not prefer **them**.
Thomas saluda **a Martín**.	Thomas greets **Martin**.
Thomas **lo** saluda.	Thomas greets **him**.

5. ¡Attention! Certain Spanish verbs have a direct object where their English counterparts would take indirect objects:

Ella escucha **al profesor.**	She listens **to the professor**.
Ella **lo** escucha.	She listens **to him**.
Él mira **a los niños.**	He looks **at the children**.
Él **los** mira.	He looks **at them**.
Ellos buscan el hotel.	They are looking **for the hotel**.
Ellos **lo** buscan.	They are looking **for it**.
Nosotros pedimos **la foto**.	We are asking **for the photo**.
Nosotros **la** pedimos.	We are asking for **it**.

---

[74] In some regions of Spain, if the direct object is a male person, speakers will replace the form **lo** with **le**, and if the direct object is a mixed group of persons (male and female), the forms **los** and **las** with **les**. This usage is not considered incorrect, but it is virtually absent from speech in Latin America.

6. In constructions where two verbs are used together, there is a choice as to the position of the object pronoun. It may precede the verb that is conjugated, or may be attached to the verb that is in the infinitive or gerund form:

Voy a traer **los audífonos.**	I will bring **the earphones.**
Los voy a traer/ Yo voy a traer**los.**	I will bring **them.**
Él está mirando **el partido.**	He is watching **the game.**
Él **lo** está mirando/ Él está mirándo**lo.**	He is watching **it.**

EJERCICIOS PRÁCTICOS

A. Replace the object nouns with direct object pronouns.
   Modelo:　Ella lleva al chico a casa.
   　　　　　　Ella lo lleva a casa.
   1. José reconoce al estudiante.
   2. El saluda a Thomas.
   3. Thomas saluda a Martín.
   4. Thomas ve la recámara.
   5. El busca el baño.

B. Convert the sentence from an affirmative one to a negative one and replace the direct object with a direct object pronouns.
   Modelo:　El taxista conduce a los estudiantes a la estación.
   　　　　　　El taxista **no los** conduce a la estación.
   1. Ellos encuentran a Anna debajo del reloj.
   2. Ellos pierden sus maletas.
   3. Ellos traen sus mapas.
   4. Ellos ponen todas sus cosas en el carrito.
   5. Ellos compran los boletos.
   6. Ellos ven el paisaje por la ventana.
   7. Lisa mira la película.

C. Replace the object with a direct object pronouns.
   Modelo:　¿Completan ellos la carta de desembarque?
   　　　　　　¿**La** completan ellos?
   1. ¿Hacen ellos la cola?
   2. ¿Muestran ellos sus pasaportes?
   3. ¿Abre Thomas su maleta?
   4. ¿El agente de aduana inspecciona el equipaje?
   5. ¿Cambian dinero los turistas?

D. Place the direct object pronoun in one of the two possible locations.
    Modelo: Nosotros vamos a estudiar a Octavio Paz.
                Nosotros **lo** vamos a estudiar.
                Nosotros vamos a estudiar**lo**.
    1. Octavio Paz va a escribir sus libros.
    2. Él piensa describir la democracia mexicana.
    3. Nosotros tenemos que estudiar su poesía.
    4. John no cree comprender su filosofía.
    5. ¿Van a leer los estudiantes *El laberinto de la soledad*?

28. EL USO DE LA "A" PERSONAL

1. When a direct object noun is a person (or sometimes an animal, such as
    a pet), it is preceded by the preposition a. The personal "a" has no English
    equivalent:
    Los estudiantes ven **al** profesor.   The students see the teacher.
    José besa **a** su novia.   José kisses his girlfriend.

2. The Personal "a" is used before the indefinite pronouns **alguien,**
    (*someone*), **nadie** (*nobody*), **alguno** (*somebody*), **ninguno** (*none*),
    cualquiera (*anybody*), and any other pronoun or number that refers to people:
    No puedo llamar **a nadie**.   I can't call anyone.
    Invito **a** dos amigas.   I invite two (girl) friends.

3. The Personal "a" is not generally used after the verb **tener**:
    Martín **tiene** una novia.   Martin has a girlfriend.
    Yolanda **tiene** un hijo.   Yolanda has a son.

4. The personal "a" is not used before nouns that do not refer to a specific
    person:
    Este restaurante busca varios   This restaurant is looking for
    meseros.   some waiters.

    Note that personal a is optional when referring to animals, and is not used
    with inanimate objects:
    Los Bernal llaman **a** su perro.   The Bernals are calling their dog.
    Ellos compran cuatro boletos de autobús.
    They buy four bus tickets.

EJERCICIOS PRÁCTICOS

A. You have to decide if you use the personal "a" or not.
   Modelo: ¿Qué miran las muchachas? (las bolsas)
                Las chicas miran las bolsas.
                ¿**A** quién miran las chicas? (Cristiano Ronaldo)
                Miran **a** Cristiano Ronaldo.
   1. ¿Qué compra la esposa del presidente? (la ropa)
   2. ¿A quién busca el profesor? (los alumnos)
   3. ¿Qué compran las mamás? (la comida)
   4. ¿A quién llama el profesor? (los bomberos)
   5. ¿Qué estudian los alumnos? (español)
   6. ¿Quién está hablando? (el profesor)

B. Write the personal "a" when needed to complete the sentences.
   1. El profesor busca _____ la lista de asistencia.
   2. Los alumnos llaman _____ sus papás por teléfono.
   3. La mujer abraza _____ su esposo.
   4. José tiene _____ las facturas.
   5. Thomas busca _____ John.
   6. Anna ayuda a cruzar la calle _____ un anciano.
   7. Anna tiene _____ un hijo.
   8. Yo busco _____ el profesor.
   9. Nadie puede encontrar _____ la dirección.
   10. No veo _____ ningún estudiante.

29. "SABER" CONTRASTADO CON "CONOCER"

1. **Saber** and **conocer** both translate to the verb "to know" in English, but they are not interchangeable.

2. **Saber** means to know something by heart, to know a fact. As you may remember, **saber, in the present tense,** has an irregular conjugation in the **yo** form:
   Sé hablar español.   I **know how** to speak Spanish.
   Los estudiantes **saben** que van a Puebla.
   The students **know** they are going to Puebla.
   Ella **sabe** como te llamas.   She **knows** your name.

¿Sabes la respuesta? Do you **know** the answer?
Nosotros sabemos la verdad. We **know** the truth.

3. **Saber** + infinitive is the equivalent of "to know how to do something":
   Los estudiantes **saben** hablar español.
   The students **know how** to speak Spanish.
   Note that **conocer** cannot be used in this way. Note also that the word "how"
   (*como*) is not needed in Spanish.

4. **Saber** also means to have a flavor:
   Esta comida sabe mal. This food tastes bad.
   Los panes saben a queso. These breads taste like cheese.

5. **Conocer** is also translated as "to know" but it means to be acquainted or
   familiar with a person, a place, an object or a situation:
   Conocer, as you may remember, is also irregular in the **yo form** in the present tense:
   Conozco a tu padre. I **know** your father.
   Ellos **conocen** México. They **know** Mexico.
   ¿**Conoce** usted las novelas de Carlos Fuentes?
   Do you **know** Carlos Fuentes' novels?
   Conozco la obra de Picasso. I am familiar with Picasso's paintings.

6. Verbs that are conjugated like **conocer** are: **reconocer** (to recognize),
   parecer (to look like) **aparecer** (to appear), **obedecer** (to obey), **conducir** (to
   drive), **producir** (to produce) **reproducir** (to reproduce):
   Yo **reconozco** que ella tiene razón. I **admit** that she is right.

EJERCICIOS PRÁCTICOS

☺ ☺ ✎

A. With a classmate construct both affirmative and negative sentences using the
   words provided.
   1. Los estudiantes/saber/español/mucho.
   2. Los Zurita/saber/cocinar/muy bien.
   3. Martín/saberse/los poemas de Octavio Paz/de memoria.
   4. Los chicos estadounidenses/muy bien/saber/bailar.
   5. ¿Saber/los estudiantes estadounidenses/cantar/en español?

B. Fill in the blank using 'saber' or 'conocer'.

1. Nosotros no (conocer) _____ Puebla muy bien, pero (saber) _____ que hay lugares buenos donde comer.

2. La familia Zurita (saber) _____ tratar muy bien a sus invitados y (saber) _____ hacerlos sentir como en su propia casa.

3. Mi madre (conocer) _____ Madrid y ella (saber) _____ bailar flamenco muy bien.

4. El profesor (conocer) _____ la mayoría de poemas de Octavio Paz y (saberse)_____ muchos de memoria.

5. El piloto no (saber) _____ hablar español, pero las azafatas sí (saber) _____ hacerlo muy bien.

30. LOS VERBOS JUGAR, OLER, INQUIRIR, GUIAR, CONTINUAR Y LOS VERBOS TERMINADOS EN —UIR

1. The verb **jugar** (to play a sport or a game) has a unique conjugation; where – **u**— turns into —**ue**— except with the subjects **vos, nosotros** and **vosotros**:

yo **juego**	nosotros jugamos
tú **juegas**	vosotros jugáis
vos **jugás**	vosotros jugáis
usted **juega**	ustedes **juegan**
él **juega**	ellos **juegan**
ella **juega**	ellas **juegan**
Él **juega** futbol.	He **plays** futbol.
Nosotros **jugamos** ajedrez.	We **play** chess.

2. The verb **oler** (to smell) also has a conjugation that differs from other verbs because includes an h in the conjugation **o**— to **hue**—, other than that behaves like the verb **poder**:

yo **huelo**	nosotros olemos
tú **hueles**	vosotros oléis
vos **olés**	vosotros oléis
usted **huele**	ustedes **huelen**
él **huele**	ellos **huelen**
ella **huele**	ellas **huelen**
¡Ella **huele** muy bien!	She **smells** so good!

Vosotros **oléis** muy bien.   You **smell** very good.

3. The verb **inquirir** (to inquire) has also a unique conjugation **–i** to **– ie** except in **vos**, **nosotros** and **vosotros**:

yo **inquiero**   nosotros inquirimos
tú **inquieres**   *vosotros inquirís*
vos **inquirís**   *vosotros inquirís*
usted **inquiere**   ustedes **inquieren**
él **inquiere**   ellos **inquieren**
ella **inquiere**   ellas **inquieren**

El policía **inquiere** información sobre el accidente.
The police officer **inquires** about information concerning the accident.

4. The verb **guiar** (*to guide*) is irregular because you must add an accent mark to the **–í** in most forms of the conjugation:

yo **guío**   nosotros guiamos
tú **guías**   *vosotros guiáis*
vos **guiás**   *vosotros guiáis*
usted **guía**   ustedes **guían**
él **guía**   ellos **guían**
ella **guía**   ellas **guían**

Jorge **guía** a los estudiantes hacia la catedral.
Jorge **guides** the students to the Cathedral.

Note that several other verbs follow the same pattern as **guiar**: **confiar** (*to trust*), **enviar** (*to send*), **espiar** (*to spy*), **fiar** (*to sell merchandise on credit*), **enfriar** (*to cool/to chill*), **variar** (*to vary*).

Note also that the verb guiar will be accompanied by the "a" personal when is related to people: Ella guía **a** los padres de familia.

5. The verb **continuar** (to continue) like **guiar**, is special because the **-u** of the stem has an accent mark in most of the forms:

yo **continúo**   nosotros continuamos
tú **continúas**   *vosotros **continuáis***
vos **continuás**   *vosotros **continuáis***
usted **continúa**   ustedes **continúan**

él **continúa**	ellos **continúan**
ella **continúa**	ellas **continúan**

El profesor **continúa** dando clases.	The professor continues teaching.

Other verbs like **continuar** are: **actuar** (*to act*), **rehusar** (*to refuse*).

Note that the verb continuar when followed by a verb will require the use of the gerund form, because it is one of the verbs that express progression in the action. You will study some of these verbs later on in the **Chapter 12**.

6. Verbs ending in **–uir**, like **incluir** (*to include*) changes the "i" to "**y**" except in **vos**, **nosotros** and **vosotros**:

yo **incluyo**	nosotros incluimos
tú **incluyes**	*vosotros incluís*
vos **incluís**	*vosotros incluís*
usted **incluye**	ustedes **incluyen**
él **incluye**	ellos **incluyen**
ella **incluye**	ellas **incluyen**

El juez **incluye** todas las pruebas en el expediente.
The judge includes all the evidence in the file.

Other verbs like **incluir** are: **atribuir** (*to attribute*), **concluir** (*to conclude*), **construir** (*to build*), **contribuir** (*to contribute*), **destruir** (*to destroy*), **influir** (*to influence*), **sustituir** (*to substitute*), **huir** (*to run away/to escape*).

7. The verb **erguir** (*to raise, to* erect; *to lift up*) admits to different types of conjugations; in the first one, its stem changes from —**er**— to —**yer**—, the second one (less common) its stem changes from —**e**— to **i**—:

yo **yergo**	nosotros erguimos	yo **irgo**	nosotros erguimos
tú **yergues**	*vosotros erguís*	tú **irgues**	*vosotros erguís*
vos **erguís**	*vosotros erguís*	vos **erguís**	*vosotros erguís*
usted **yergue**	ustedes **yerguen**	usted **irgue**	ustedes **irguen**
él **yergue**	ellos **yerguen**	él **irgue**	ellos **irguen**
ella **yergue**	ellas **yerguen**	ella **irguen**	ellas **irguen**

EJERCICIOS PRÁCTICOS

☺ ☺

A. Ask your partner the following questions. Then switch roles.
1. ¿A qué huele tu casa?
2. ¿Qué/cuál deporte juegas?
3. ¿Quién guía a los turistas?
4. ¿Quién huye de la policía?
5. ¿Sobre qué asunto inquieren los policías?
6. ¿A quién más incluyes en la lista?
7. ¿Qué/cuál flor huele más, la rosa o el clavel?
8. ¿Quién construye la casa?
9. ¿Qué envía Thomas en este sobre?
10.　¿En quién confías tú?

B. Change these sentences from the near future to the simple present tense of the verb in parentheses.
Modelo:　El ladrón va a oír los cargos. (rehusar)
　　　　　El ladrón rehúsa los cargos.
1. Ella va a construir su casa. (destruir)
2. Tú vas a salir con dinero. (contribuir)
3. El entrenador va a ver al jugador. (sustituir)
4. Anna y Armando van a salir juntos. (huir)
5. Ellos van a ver un partido de fútbol en su viaje. (incluir)

C. Change these sentences from the near future to the simple present tense of the verb in parentheses.
Modelo:　El guía va a estar hablando. (continuar)
　　　　　El guía continúa hablando.
1. Yolanda va a llevar a Thomas hacia la Central de Abastos. (guiar)
2. El profesor va a confiar en los alumnos. (desconfiar de)
3. Los artistas van a estar esta noche en el teatro. (actuar)
4. David va a mandar la carta por correo. (enviar)
5. Thomas va a oír sobre la carta robada. (inquirir)

MINIRELATO: OCTAVIO PAZ

Octavio Paz representa el **espíritu ilustrado** (*the spirit of Enlightenment*) de México. Él nace en la ciudad de México el 31 de marzo de 1914.

Comienza a escribir **a temprana edad** (*at an early age*) En 1937 él participa del Segundo Congreso de Escritores Antifascistas celebrado en Valencia, España. En 1939 Paz **se considera a sí mismo** (*he considers himself*) como un poeta. En 1943 viaja con fondos de la **beca** (*fellowship*) Guggenheim a los Estados Unidos donde participa activamente de la Poesía Modernista estadounidense. En 1945 comienza a trabajar en el **servicio diplomático mexicano** (*foreign service*) como tercer secretario de la embajada de México en París; allí conoce a numerosos escritores que **influyen** (*influence*) en su vida como Benjamín Peret y André Breton.

En 1968 **renuncia** (*resigns*) a su cargo de Embajador de México en la India en **protesta** (*as a protest*) por la **masacre estudiantil** (*student massacre*) del 2 de octubre de 1968[75].

En 1990 Octavio Paz **recibe el Premio Nobel de Literatura (***Nobel Prize of Literature***)** y **muere** (*he dies*) en la ciudad de México el 19 de abril de 1998.

Preguntas

1. ¿Qué representa Octavio Paz?
2. ¿Cuándo nace?
3. ¿Dónde nace?
4. ¿Cuándo comienza a escribir?
5. ¿A dónde viaja en 1937?
6. ¿En qué año viene a los Estados Unidos?
7. ¿A quiénes conoce en París?
8. ¿Por qué renuncia a su cargo de embajador de México en la India?
9. ¿Cuándo recibe el Premio Nobel de Literatura?
10. ¿Qué otros escritores mexicanos conoce usted?

CONVERSACIÓN: La primera reunión del grupo

El profesor estadounidense les habla a los estudiantes que se encuentran en el salón de clase en Puebla.

---

[75] This student **massacre** (also known as the Tlatelolco massacre), was a government killing of student and civilian protesters and bystanders that took place during the afternoon and night of October 2, 1968, in the Plaza de las Tres Culturas in Mexico City. This massacre occurred days before the 1968 Summer Olympic Games celebrated in Mexico City.

El profesor: Hola chicos, hoy vamos a comenzar hablando sobre lo que las familias mexicanas **esperan de ustedes** (*expect from you*). ¿Quién tiene alguna idea que quiera compartir?

Thomas: Como usted ha dicho **siempre** (*always*), **las familias esperan de nosotros** (*the families expect from us*): ¡la cortesía, el tacto, la comprensión, la paciencia, la discreción, la disponibilidad, el buen humor y la capacidad de adaptación!

El profesor: **En efecto** (*indeed*), ese es el **secreto** (*the secret*) de toda la experiencia. Si ustedes hacen, todos los días, el mayor esfuerzo posible por comprender y respetar los hábitos de la vida cotidiana mexicana **estarán** (*you will be*) al final de su estancia muy satisfechos **con ustedes mismos** (*with yourselves*).

John: Usted ha hablado del "choque cultural" ¿Podría **añadir algo más** (*add something*) sobre este tema?

El profesor: El "choque cultural" es simplemente **la actitud mental** (*the mental state*) de **alguien** (*someone*) que no ha alcanzado aún un estado de **comodidad** (*comfort*) en una cultura diferente. Hay **por supuesto** (*of course*) diferencias en el estilo de vida y en la mentalidad entre los distintos países y cuando no se respetan esas diferencias **uno sufre** (*one suffers*) y además **se deja una mala impresión** (*one makes a bad impression*).

Jane: **Eso es lo que me ha pasado a mí** (*That's what has happened to me*).

El profesor: ¿Si? Cuando eso pasa, **uno se siente** (*one feels*) detestado, humillado, aplastado y **uno reacciona mal** (*one reacts poorly*).

Anna: Es verdad, al llegar a México, e ir a la **ventanilla donde se venden los boletos** (*ticket counter*) para el autobús yo me sentí **intimidada** (*intimidated*) por la actitud del empleado. No sé qué habría hecho si Thomas no hubiera estado allí.

El profesor: ¡No se trata de ponerse paranoicos, ni agresivos! Ese señor, es un mexicano **que no los conoce** (*who doesn't know you*); él reaccionó **como lo haría con cualquiera** (*as he would with anyone else*) en las mismas circunstancias.

Preguntas

Working with a partner, take turns asking and answering the following questions.

1. ¿Quiénes escuchan al profesor?
2. ¿Dónde se encuentran los estudiantes?
3. ¿Qué es lo que los mexicanos esperan de los estadounidenses?
4. ¿Cuál es el secreto de la experiencia de vivir en el extranjero?
5. ¿Por qué es importante que todos hagan el mayor esfuerzo posible por respetar los hábitos de la vida cotidiana mexicana?
6. ¿Qué es "el choque cultural"?
7. ¿Hay diferencias en la forma de vida y mentalidad de los países?
8. ¿Dónde se sintió intimidada Anna?
9. ¿Por qué ella se sintió protegida por Thomas?
10. ¿Qué afirma el profesor?

VOCABULARIO

VERBOS

poder	pedir	soñar	comprar
saber	conocer	contar	escribir
reír	dormir	medir	decir
probar	sonar	volver	volar
almorzar	despedir	mentir	esperar
seguir	elegir	reelegir	preferir
venir	conocer	afirmar	ser

NOMBRES

el interior de la casa
la planta alta
la taza del baño
la tina del baño
el garaje
el ventilador
el cesto/la cesta para la basura
el papel higiénico/papel de baño
la ventanilla
el premio
la cama

las toallas
el lavabo
la cocina
las escaleras
el escritorio
la computadora

los hábitos
la literatura
el buró

la planta baja
el primer piso
la sala
la regadera
la recámara
los meseros
la despensa
el poema
el zócalo
el servicio

el jabón
el baño
la oficina
la puerta
la estufa
el comedor
los boletos
la capital
la ciudad
la avenida

ADJETIVOS

estadounidense
varios/as
diplomático/a
mexicano/a

ADVERBIOS

rápidamente
allí

simplemente
tímidamente

activamente
siempre

mal

EXPRESIONES UTILES

por supuesto
en efecto
esa es la clave
el choque cultural
¡no puede ser!

aprender de memoria
una mala impresión
espíritu ilustrado
la capacidad de adaptación

temprana edad
una beca
¡qué caray!
claro que sí

CAPÍTULO 7: THOMAS SE INSTALA

En este capítulo...

You'll learn more about Thomas and how he settled in to the Zurita's home. You will start learning about the uses of the pronominal verbs, and learn how to convey the meaning of "to become" in Spanish. You will learn about the uses of the prepositions "por" and "para", and how "yo" and "tú" change after a preposition. You'll be introduced to the uses of the indirect object pronoun, and you will also learn the differences between the verbs **pedir** and **preguntar**.

Contexto

Thomas está en su cuarto. Yolanda lo está ayudando a instalarse y le muestra cómo y dónde acomodar la ropa que ha traído.

Yolanda: Te voy a poner tus cosas en este armario. ¿Cuántas maletas tienes? ¿Es todo lo que tienes para todo el semestre?

Thomas: Sí. Traje solo esta maleta gris que es bastante grande e incómoda para viajar; esta pequeña maleta café y mi saco de dormir que había perdido en el aeropuerto y que recuperé finalmente.

Yolanda: ¿Y este suéter es tuyo?

Thomas: Sí, me lo puse en el aeropuerto, pues sentí frío.

Yolanda: Te voy a poner estas tres playeras, los calzoncillos, los pañuelos y los calcetines en este cajón. Las camisas te las colgué en un gancho al igual que los pantalones para que no se te arruguen. La chaqueta, que no vas a necesitar para nada, la puedes dejar en la maleta.

Thomas: Usted cree que no voy a necesitar ponerme la chamarra, ¡mire que soy bien friolento!

Yolanda: No hombre, si nunca hace frío en Puebla, es siempre primavera. ¡Ay que pesadas son tus maletas, muchacho! Las tendrás que subir tú mismo.

Thomas: No se preocupe, yo lo hago.

Yolanda: Si dices que eres friolento, aquí te dejo otra frazada para que te cubras si tienes frío por la noche.

Thomas: Muchas gracias.

Yolanda: Por cierto, en el baño te puse la pasta dental, el cepillo, el peine, tu champú, tu enjuague bucal y demás cosas del aseo personal. Ahora ven para darte las toallas.

Después, Yolanda y Thomas bajan a la sala.

José: Thomas, por cierto, si quieres puedes usar una de las bicicletas mientras estés con nosotros. Martín te puede mostrar cómo usarla, sobre todo porque el freno tiene su maña. Ahora yo me tengo que ir a trabajar a la florería.

Thomas: Gracias don José, es usted muy amable. Se lo agradezco muchísimo.

Martín: Sólo si quiere usarla, ¡eh! No se sienta obligado.

Thomas: Me vendría bien, así no tengo que caminar todos los días a clase.

Los jóvenes salen a dar una vuelta en las bicis.

Yolanda: Martín de paso vayan a la panadería y compren unos bolillos que
estén bien dorados porque voy a hacer unos molletes para la cena.
Martín: ¿Y el dinero?
Thomas: Yo los compro.
Yolanda: ¡Cómo crees!
José: ¿Cuánto necesitas?
Martín: Unos cien pesos, yo creo.
Thomas: Yo le doy el dinero.

Preguntas

1. ¿En qué tono ocurre la conversación?
2. ¿Cuántas maletas tiene Thomas y de qué color son?
3. ¿Dónde pone Yolanda las cosas de Thomas?
4. ¿Qué puso Yolanda en el cajón del armario?
5. ¿Qué pone Thomas en el baño?
6. ¿Cómo son las maletas de Thomas?
7. ¿Qué le ofrece José a Thomas?
8. ¿Cuál es el problema con la bicicleta?
9. ¿A dónde tiene que ir José?
10. ¿Qué le pide que traiga Yolanda a Martín?

NOTA CULTURAL: LAS TALLAS Y MEDIDAS EN MÉXICO

Vestidos

México[76]	28	30	32	34	36	38	40	42
USA	6	7/8	10	12	14	16	18	20

[76] As a general rule the sizes used in Mexico for clothing and shoes are valid in Latin America as well as Spain.

Zapatos para dama

Mé-xico	21	22	23	24	25	26	27	29	30	31	32
USA	51/2	6	61/2	7	71/2	8	81/2	9	91/2	10	101/2

Trajes para hombre

México	38	40	42	44	46
USA	S	M	L	XL	XXL

Camisas

México	151/2	16	161/2	17	171/2
USA	28/29	30/31	32/33	34/35	36/37

Zapatos para hombre

México	28	29	30	31	32	33	34
USA	81/2	9	91/2	10	101/2	11	11/12

Dichos

El hábito no hace al monje.	The suit does not make the man/ The cowl does not make the monk.
Aunque la mona se vista de seda se queda.	You can't make a silk purse out of a sow's ear.
Es el último grito de la moda.	Up-to-the-minute trend/The newest cool teen craze.

VOCABULARIO: Prendas para mujer

los lentes de sol[77]	sunglasses	las joyas	jewels
la bufanda	scarf	las botas	boots
la blusa	blouse	el abrigo	coat

---

[77] In Spain they use **gafas** instead of **lentes**, and you may also hear **anteojos** in places like Central America.

los guantes	gloves	la bolsa	purse
las pulseras	bracelets	el traje	a suit
el reloj	a watch	el saco	blazer
la falda	skirt	las playeras	t-shirts
el vestido de algodón	cotton dress	la ropa interior	underwear
la blusa de seda	silk blouse	las medias	pantyhose
chamarra de nylon	nylon jacket	las calcetas	socks
los guantes de piel	leather gloves	el pantalón	pants
los guantes de lana	wool gloves	tacón alto	high heels
el suéter	sweater	las chancletas	sandals
el pantalón de mezclilla/los vaqueros			jeans
los pantalones cortos			shorts

VOCABULARIO: Prendas para hombre

una corbata	a tie	un abrigo	a coat
un sombrero	a hat	los zapatos	shoes
una camisa	a shirt	un traje	a suit
un saco	a jacket	un pantalón	pants
un reloj	a watch	los calcetines	socks
un saco	blazer	los tirantes	suspenders
la chamarra de cuero	leather jacket	el chaleco	vest
las sandalias	sandals	la/el pijama	pajamas
el cinturón	belt	la cartera	wallet
el traje de baño	swimsuit		

Más vocabulario: La bolsa de viaje de Anna

los tenis	sneakers	broncearse	to tan
el bikini	bikini	un libro	a book
las gafas de sol	sunglasses	la bolsa	bag
el bloqueador solar	sunblock	la playera[78]	t-shirts
el barniz para las uñas	nail polish	las licras/mallas	leggings/lycra

---

[78] In some countries like Chile you may hear **polera**, or in Central America, **camiseta.**

EJERCICIOS PRÁCTICOS

Estudie y comprenda.

Anna espera poder hacer distintos tipos de deportes mientras viva en México. En su maleta ha traído dos pares de tenis, dos trajes de baño para ir a nadar, un par de licras para hacer ejercicio y yoga. También ha traído playeras y varios pantalones cortos de varios colores y estilos, así como muchos calcetines, también de distintos colores. Sus padres incluso le han ofrecido una nueva raqueta, que si necesita van a comprarle en una tienda de deportes. Además, Anna no podía olvidar su Ipod para escuchar su música favorita ni su bronceador solar, sus lentes de sol y una crema para broncearse. Y como buena chica ha traído todos los productos de belleza que necesita: máscara, perfumes, cremas, delineadores, sombras y pintalabios.

☺ ☺

Ahora haga las preguntas siguientes a otro estudiante.

1. ¿Qué espera hacer Anna mientras esté en México?
2. ¿Qué trae para ir a nadar?
3. ¿Qué le ofrecen sus padres?
4. ¿Cómo son sus pantalones cortos?
5. ¿Qué productos de belleza ha traído?
6. Para protegerse del sol, ¿qué productos trae?
7. ¿Trae Anna su Ipod?
8. ¿Cuántos pares de tenis ha traído?
9. ¿Trae Anna sus gafas (lentes) de sol?
10. ¿Qué trae para hacer yoga?

APUNTES GRAMATICALES
31. LOS VERBOS PRONOMINALES

1. As we have already seen, a verb in Spanish may be preceded by an object pronoun:

   (Yo) Veo a la chica.   I see the girl.

   (Yo) **La** veo.   I see **her.**

2. In some cases, both the subject of a verb and its object refer to the same person or thing. Verbs of this kind are called "pronominal", and they may demonstrate either a reflexive or a reflexive or a reciprocal:

REFLEXIVE:	Yo **me** lavo.	I wash **myself.**
	Ella **se** baña	She bathes **herself.**
RECIPROCAL:	Nosotros **nos** miramos.	We look at **each other.**
	Ellas **se** saludan	They greet each other.

3. A pronominal construction consists of a subject or pronoun, a reflexive pronoun, and the appropriate verb form. The reflexive pronoun is placed just before the conjugated form of the verb (except in the infinitive or the gerund, as in "estoy bañándome" and, as you will learn in **Chapter 8**, in the imperative affirmative form).

Let's take for example the verb **lavarse**:
yo **me** lavo (*I wash myself*)   nosotros **nos** lavamos (*We wash ourselves/*
We wash each other)

tú **te** lavas	vosotros **os** laváis
vos **te** lavás	vosotros **os** laváis
usted **se** lava	ustedes **se** lavan
él **se** lava	ellos **se** lavan
ella **se** lava	ellas **se** lavan

4. All pronominal infinitives are indicated by the pronoun **se** attached to the end. There are two types of pronominal verbs:

a. Those that are always pronominal:

arrepentirse	to repent	**Me** arrepiento de mis malas acciones.
atreverse	to dare	Ella **se** atreve a hablar en español.
ausentarse	to take leave/ to be absent	**Nos** ausentamos todos.
casarse	to get married	Nosotros **nos** casamos apenas.
comportarse	to behave	Tú **te** comportas muy bien.
graduarse	to graduate	Los estudiantes **se** gradúan en mayo.
quejarse	to complain/ groan	Él **se** queja de dolor.
suicidarse	to kill oneself/ To commit suicide	El hombre **se** 174uicide.

Other verbs may be turned into pronominal verbs by adding a reflexive pronoun, but they also exist as transitive verbs:

lavar	to wash	Yo lavo el coche.

lavarse[79]	to wash oneself	Yo **me** lavo las manos.
levantar	to lift, to raise	Yo levanto la mesa.
levantarse	to stand up/to get up	Nosotros **nos** levantamos tarde.
aburrir	To bore, to tire	(Yo) aburro a mis alumnos.
aburrirse	to get bored	Ella **se aburre** en la clase.
confundir	to confuse/ to mix up/ to mislead	
confundirse	to get confused	
confesar	to confess/ to admit/	
confesarse	to confess oneself/to own up	

Note the differences in translation for each pair of sentences:

(Yo) **llamo a** Thomas.	I **call** Thomas.
(Yo) **me llamo** Thomas.	I **call myself** Thomas.

Él **para** el coche.	He **stops** the car.
Él **se para** frente al coche.	He **stands** in front of the car.

(Nosotros) **encontramos** el coche.	We **find** the car.
(Nosotros) **nos encontramos** en el coche.	We **meet** in the car.

5. Here are some commonly used pronominal verbs:

despertarse	to wake up
levantarse	to get up/to stand up
bañarse/ducharse[80]	to take a bath/shower
rasurarse/afeitarse[81]	to shave
depilarse	to remove hair
maquillarse	to put on make up
peinarse	to comb one's hair
vestirse	to dress
desvestirse	to undress
acostarse	to go to bed
dormirse	to fall asleep
recostarse	to rest

---

[79] All reflexive verbs are indicated by the pronoun **-se** attached to the infinitive.
[80] There is a preference in countries like Mexico for the verb **bañarse**, meanwhile in places like Spain **ducharse is** the preferred verb used.
[81] In Mexico, there is a preference for **afeitarse**, but in other countries like in Central America you may hear **rasurarse**.

apurarse	to hurry
enojarse	to become irritated/to get angry

Note that many of these pronominal verbs refer to daily routines.

6. In a negation, **no** precedes the reflexive pronoun:

AFFIRMATIVE: El niño **se** acuesta.
NEGATIVE: El niño **no se** duerme todavía.

7. The reflexive pronoun may serve as the direct object, as we have seen in most of the examples above, or as an indirect object. Verbs like **ponerse** + article of clothing (to put on), have a direct object (the article of clothing) in addition to the reflexive pronoun:

El piloto **se pone el uniforme.**	The pilot **puts on** his uniform.
Ella **se** lava las manos.	She washes **her** hands.
Ellas **se** preparan una ensalada.	They prepare **themselves** a salad.

8. In the case of a sentence with two verbs (conjugated verb + infinitive or gerund), the reflexive pronoun may be placed in front of the conjugated verb (general rule) or attached to the end of the infinitive or the gerund:

Me estoy cambiando.	Estoy cambiándo**me**[82].
Él **se** va a lavar las manos.	Él va a lavar**se** las manos.

9. The Spanish verb **ponerse** is equivalent to the verb "to become" when followed by an adjective that expresses emotion:
Thomas **se pone contento** con   Thomas **is happy** with the Zuritas.
la familia Zurita.

10. When the verb "to become" implies a change in status, the verb **volverse** is commonly used in Spanish:
El profesor **se vuelve** famoso.   The professor **becomes** famous.

---

[82] Note that this verb needs a written accent mark because the position of the stressed syllable has changed.

Note that you may also use the verb **hacerse** in this very same situation:

El profesor **se hace** famoso.   The professor **becomes** famous.

11. The following verbs change their meaning if they are used as transitive or reflexive.

abonar	to pay on monthly basics/to fertilize a plant	**abonarse**	to subscribe
acordar	to agree/to decide	**acordarse**	to remember
acusar	to accuse	**acusarse**	to incriminate oneself
aparecer	to show/to appear	**aparecerse**	to appear (often as a supernatural event)
cambiar	to change	**cambiarse**	to change clothing to move (house)
despedir	to say goodbye to/ to fire	**despedirse**	to say goodbye.
dormir	to sleep	**dormirse**	to fall asleep
estar	to be	**estarse**	to stay
hacer	to do	**hacerse**	to become
ir	to go	**irse**	to go away
llevar	to carry	**llevarse**	to take
parecer	to seem like	**parecerse**	to look like/to be alike
poner	to put	**ponerse**	to put on (clothing) to become (emotions)
quedar	to remain/plan to meet/agree to meet.	**quedarse**	to stay
recordar	to remember	**recordarse**	to remind
salir	to leave	**salirse**	to get away with/ to leave by your own will
saltar	to jump	**saltarse**	to jump over/to skip
volver	to return	**volverse**	to become/to turn around.

EJERCICIOS PRÁCTICOS

Fill in the blanks using the reflexive pronouns.

Modelo: Tú _____ cambias para ir a la escuela.

          Tú **te** cambias para ir a la escuela.

1.   Ella _____ cepilla el cabello para ir a la fiesta.

2. Los jóvenes _____ rasuran antes de salir.
3. Yolanda _____ baña siempre.
4. Yo _____ cambio de ropa los domingos.
5. Superman y yo _____ ponemos nuestros trajes de combate.
6. Tú _____ acuestas temprano siempre.
7. Ellas _____ sienten mal porque tomaron tequila.
8. Lisa _____ despierta tarde los sábados.
9. El policía _____ pone su uniforme.
10. Tú y yo _____ ponemos de acuerdo para hacer el proyecto.

Change these sentences from positive to negative.
Modelo: Tú te cambias para ir a la escuela.
              Tú **no** te cambias para ir a la escuela.
1.   Ella se cepilla el pelo para ir a la fiesta.
2.   Los estudiantes estadounidenses se rasuran antes de salir.
3.   Los Zurita se preparan para ir a Oaxaca.
4.   Thomas se desviste al llegar de la fiesta.
5.   Anna se acuesta temprano.
6.   John se siente mal.
7.   Lisa se decide a ir a la fiesta.
8.   El policía se pasea enfrente del lugar de la fiesta.

C. Describe your morning routine, using the pictures in your textbook and the following pronominal verbs: levantarse, lavarse, bañarse, cepillarse, vestirse,
   ponerse la ropa, cepillarse el cabello, rasurarse, maquillarse.
   Modelo: Yo me despierto y me levanto a las siete de la mañana. Después
   me lavo las manos con jabón, me cepillo los dientes, después me baño y
   me...

   ☺ ☺
D. Complete each sentence using an appropriate pronominal verb.
   Modelo: Cuando uno está tarde para una cita...
                 Cuando uno está tarde para una cita, uno se apura.
   1. Cuando uno no pone atención al manejo del cuchillo...
   2. Cuando uno tiene una pesadilla...
   3. Uno busca su ropa para...
   4. Para quitarse la barba uno...
   5. Antes de salir una dama...
   6. Delante de un semáforo en rojo uno...

7. Ante una injusticia usted...
8. Cuando dos amigos se ven en México, ellos...
9. Si hace frío uno...
10. Si se le olvida el nombre de un amigo, usted trata de...

32. LAS PREPOSICIONES POR Y PARA

1. The preposition **por** is used to express:
a. **Motion** (by, along, through), even referring to an unspecified location. For example:

Ellos caminan **por** el parque.
Pasan **por** la panadería.
Thomas y Martín salen **por** el zaguán. (garage)
Él anda **por** allí.

b. On behalf of, per, authorship, means of transportation, unit of measure, for the sake of (by, for, per). For example:

Thomas habla **por** todos sus compañeros.
Solo el uno **por** ciento de la población es extremadamente rica.
El libro está escrito **por** Sergio Pitol.
La carta llega **po**r correo.
El autobús viene a 95 kilómetros **por** hora.
Por el amor de Dios, deja de fumar.
Ellos ganan doce dólares por hora.

c. Some sort of exchange. For example:

Los estudiantes pagan 194 pesos **por** cada boleto de autobús.

d. Period of time during which an action takes place (during, in, for). For example:

Los estudiantes van a estar en México **por** un semestre[83].
Los chicos van a ir a la fiesta el sábado **por** la noche.

e. Cause, motive or reason for an action (because of, on account of, on behalf of). For example:

John estudia español **por** necesidad.
Thomas está en México **por** el profesor.
Lisa estudia español **por** su novio colombiano.

f. To refer to the agent of passive constructions. For example:
Los edificios están siendo construidos **por** los albañiles.

g. An action that favors another. For example:
Paso **por** ustedes a las siete y media de la noche.

h. When expressing something in favor or support of. For example:
En el 2008, la mayoría de los jóvenes votaron **por** Obama.

i. Labeling the number of times or occasions something occurs. For example:
Van a ir a México **por** cuarta vez.

j. To represent the number of times something is multiplied by. For example:
Tres **por** nueve son veintisiete.

k. In common expressions that use it. They are:

por cierto	by the way	por ahora	for now
por casualidad	by any chance	por añadidura	in addition
por completo	completely	por consiguiente	consequently
por culpa de	the fault of	por lo demás	furthermore
por desgracia	unfortunately	por ejemplo	for example
por escrito	in writing	por eso	therefore
por favor	please	por fin	finally
por lo general	generally	por lo menos	at least

---

[83] Note that some people prefer not to use the preposition **por** in sentences with a period of time because these sentences already express their meaning without the use of the preposition. For example: **Los estudiantes van a estar en México un semestre.**

2. The preposition **para** is used to express the following concepts:
a. To name a final destination, toward, in the direction of. For example:
Vamos **para** México.
Ella va **para** el baño.

b. Reference to employment (to work for). For example:
Trabaja **para** la Universidad Nacional de Chile.

c. To express for whom, or what something is for (recipients), in benefit of or directed towards. For example:
La ensalada es **para** Thomas.

d. To announce a deadline (due date) in the future (by, for). For example:
La entrega de los documentos es **para** el lunes.

e. To express a "purpose", "goal"; or "in order to" or "so that". For example:
Estudio español **para** conseguir un trabajo.

f. To express someone's opinion. For example:
Para Thomas los Zurita son la mejor familia del mundo.

g. To represent comparisons that are only used when people talk about a person or thing. It can mean "considering that", for example:
Para ser profesor se tiene que tener poca paciencia.

h. To be used for. As an example:
La pizarra se usa **para** escribir.

I. With common expressions that use **it**. They are:

para entonces	by that time	para otra vez	for a later occasion
para siempre	forever	para variar	just for a change
¿para qué?	what for?	ser tal para cual	to be two of a kind
para nada	not at all	para que	so that/in order to

EJERCICIOS PRÁCTICOS

A. Una película fascinante! Answer the questions using **por**.
   Modelo: ¿Por qué te gustó tanto la película?

Fue por el trabajo de dirección.
1. ¿Por qué te atrae tanto la película?
2. ¿Por qué te impresiona tanto?
3. ¿Por qué estás tan entusiasmado por volverla a ver?
4. ¿Por qué la consideras tan buena?
5. ¿Cuánto vas a pagar por verla de nuevo?

B. Make your own call! Complete with **por** or **para**.
   Modelo: Ella paga 50 dólares _____ el libro. (por or para)
   Ella paga 50 dólares **por** el libro.
   1. Voy _____ Honduras.
   2. _____ ellos el mejor actor es Robert de Niro.
   3. Siempre paso _____ tu casa.
   4. No tengo dinero _____ pagar el taxi. (In order to)
   5. Thomas habla _____ los estudiantes estadounidenses (on behalf).
   6. John maneja su moto a cien kilómetros _____ hora.
   7. El regalo es _____ Lisa.
   8. Yolanda no trabaja _____ el gobierno. (employment)
   9. Jim está sin trabajo _____ la crisis. (cause)
   10. _____ ser doctor uno tiene que estudiar muchos años.
   11. El regalo tiene un 15 _____ ciento de descuento.
   12. La entrevista va a ser escrita _____ el mejor periodista. (authorship)
   13. Los edificios van a ser construidos _____ los albañiles.
   14. El libro me va a llegar _____ correo.
   15. Dos _____ seis son doce.
   16. El proyecto es _____ mañana.
   17. La pizarra es _____ escribir.
   18. El taxi pasa _____ ustedes a las ocho de la noche.
   19. Ellas van al gimnasio _____ estar en forma. (goal)
   20. Voy a Costa Rica _____ tercera vez.
   21. Ella gana quince dólares _____ hora.
   22. Yo estudio solo _____ pasar el examen.

C. Complete the paragraph using **por** or **para**.
   Los estudiantes estadounidenses van _____ México. Después de pasar
   _____ la aduana van a ir a cambiar dólares _____ pesos. Después deberán
   ir a la taquilla de los autobuses _____ comprar los boletos _____ Puebla.
   Subirán al autobús _____ la puerta. Algunos de ellos verán el paisaje _____

la ventana, otros dormirán _____ olvidarse de los nervios que tienen. Al llegar a Puebla verán a sus familias _____ primera vez; después cada uno se
va a ir _____ su lado con sus familias.

33. PRONOMBRES COMO OBJETOS DE UNA PREPOSICIÓN

1. Let's remember the Spanish pronouns:

yo	nosotros/as
tú	vosotros/as
vos	vosotros
usted	ustedes
él	ellos
ella	ellas

2. Out of all of these pronouns, only the first person singular **yo** and second person singular **tú** have special forms after a preposition. The rest of the pronouns remain the same. Let's look at the list again as they are transformed into prepositional pronouns:

mí	nosotros/as
ti	vosotros/as
vos	
usted	ustedes
él /sí	ellos /sí
ella /sí	ellas /sí

3. When used with the preposition **con** (with), the first person singular (**yo**) and the second person singular (**tú**) become: **conmigo**, and **contigo.**
¡Venga **conmigo**!
¿Puedo ir **contigo**?

4. There is another form of the third person pronouns (él, ella, uno, ellos, ellas, unos) that have a form called "reflexivo tónico": the pronoun **sí**. This form remains unchanged in gender or number. When **con** is the preposition that precede "sí" then we should use "consigo":

El hombre habla **consigo** mismo.	The man is talking to himself.
Ella lleva el pasaporte **consigo**.	She carries her passport with her.

183

EJERCICIOS PRÁCTICOS

A. Complete this exercise using the correct prepositional pronoun.
    Modelo: Yo voy al cine con _____ (ustedes)
                    Yo voy al cine con ustedes.

   1.   Ella compra unos zapatos para _____. (tú)
   2.   El profesor corrige el examen de _____. (ellos)
   3.   José arregla la bicicleta para _____. (yo)
   4.   Yolanda prepara la comida para _____. (nosotros)
   5.   El policía le da una infracción a _____. (John)
   6.   ¿Ellos viajan con _____ (tú) o con_____ (yo)?
   7.   Pienso que mis amigos siempre hablan de _____. (yo)
   8.   Qué va, ellos nunca hablan de _____. (tú)
   9.   La motocicleta es para _____. (ella)
   10.   Alfredo habla _____. (con él mismo)

   ☺☺

B. Interview a classmate using the following questions. Use the correct prepositional pronouns.
    Modelo: ¿Hablas con tu mamá a menudo?
                    Sí, hablo con **ella** a menudo.

   1.   ¿Quieres ir a dar un paseo conmigo?
   2.   ¿Quieres ir al cine con nosotros?
   3.   No trabajas para ellas, ¿verdad?
   4.   ¿Todavía vives con tus padres?
   5.   ¿Vas a la playa con tu novia/o?
   6.   ¿Le vas a comprar un helado a tu amiga?
   7.   ¿Para quién es el regalo?

34. LOS PRONOMBRES DE OBJETO INDIRECTO.

1. An indirect object pronoun replaces an indirect object noun. The action of the
   verb is transmitted indirectly to the object noun via the preposition "a" with
   third person (le/les), and "a or para" with other indirect object pronouns:

   INDIRECT OBJECT NOUN: Yo le hablo **al hombre.**   I speak **to the man.**
   INDIRECT OBJECT PRONOUN: Yo **le** hablo.   I speak **to him.**

INDIRECT OBJECT NOUN:	Ella nos habla (**a nosotros**).	She speaks **to us.**
INDIRECT OBJECT PRONOUN:	Ella **nos** habla.	She speaks **to us.**

2. The indirect object pronouns are:

me	to me	**nos**	to us
te	to you	**os**	to you
le	to him, to her	**les**	to them

3. Like the direct object pronoun, the indirect object pronoun is placed before the verb even in negative sentences:

Le doy un dulce **al niño**.	I give a candy to the child.
No le hablo **al chico**.	I do not speak to the boy.

Note that in Spanish when the indirect object is in the third person, singular or plural, it is normal to keep the indirect object in the sentence even when the indirect object has been replaced by an indirect object pronoun. These pronouns are generally used to replace **a + people** or other **living things**. The main reason for that is to keep the meaning of the sentence clear. For example: La azafata **les** trae los audífonos a los estudiantes.

4. When a conjugated verb and an infinitive or a gerund are used together, the speaker can choose whether to place the indirect object pronoun before the verb (general rule) or to attach it to the infinitive or gerund (optional):

La azafata **les** va a traer la comida.
La azafata va a traer**les** la comida.

La azafata **les** está trayendo los audífonos.
La azafata está trayéndo**les** los audífonos.

5. The forms of the indirect object do not change according to the gender of their referent:

¿Siempre **le** dice Ana la verdad a su madre?
Sí, siempre **le** dice la verdad.
¿Siempre **le** dice Juan la verdad a su madre?
No, casi nunca **le** dice la verdad.

6. As a general rule, we can say that all verbs can work with indirect objects; but certain verbs like pedir, decir, preguntar, doler, gustar, hacer falta, dar, utilize it with more frequency:

Thomas **le** pide vino tinto al mesero.
José **le** pregunta la hora a Thomas.

EJERCICIOS PRÁCTICOS

A. Make up your own wish list. Answer the questions using indirect object pronouns.
Modelo: ¿Qué **les** vas a dar a tus amigos?
                Les voy a dar una sorpresa.
1.   ¿Qué le vas a ayudar a hacer a Yolanda?
2.   ¿A quiénes les vas a presentar a tu novia?
3.   ¿Qué les vas a dar de regalo?
4.   ¿Qué le vas a mostrar a Martín?
5.   ¿Qué les vas a comprar a tus padres?
6.   ¿Qué le vas a decir a tu profesor?
7.   ¿Qué les va a comprar Thomas a sus padres?
8.   ¿Qué le dice José a Thomas?
9.   ¿Qué les responde Thomas en el brindis?

35. "PEDIR" CONTRASTADO CON "PREGUNTAR"

1. The verb **pedir** means to ask for, to request something, or to ask somebody to do something:
Thomas **pide** unas palomitas grandes y seis sodas con poco hielo.
Thomas asks for some big popcorn and six sodas with little ice.

2. The verb **preguntar** means to ask a question or sometimes to request information:
Anna y Lisa **preguntan** a qué horas es la función en español.
Anna and Lisa ask what time the movie is in Spanish.

3. The expressions **preguntar por** means to ask about someone or to inquire about something:
José le **preguntó** a Thomas **por** la profesión de sus padres.
Joseph asked Thomas about his parents' profession.

EJERCICIOS PRÁCTICOS

A. Fill in the blank using **pedir** or **preguntar**.
1. ¿Qué le va a _____ a Santa Claus?
2. ¿Cuánto dinero le _____ a tu mamá para este viaje?
3. ¿Por quién le _____ José a Thomas?
4. Cuando tienes un problema, ¿a quién le _____ consejo?
5. Cuando necesitas saber una dirección tú ¿a quién le_____?
6. Anna no tiene reloj y necesita saber la hora, ¿qué le _____ Anna a su amiga Lisa?

B. Choosing between one verb or another can make a difference. Help Thomas make the right call by circling the correct verb.
1. Thomas necesita saber la hora.   (pedir o preguntar)
2. Thomas quiere saber el precio de este CD   (pedir o preguntar)
3. Thomas necesita dinero.   (pedir o preguntar)
4. Thomas quiere saber dónde nació Yolanda   (pedir o preguntar)
5. Thomas necesita usar la bicicleta   (pedir o preguntar)
6. La mamá de Thomas quiere fotos de los Zurita   (pedir o preguntar)
7. Thomas quiere que Santa le traiga un regalo   (pedir o preguntar)
8. ¿Qué va a _____ Thomas en el cine?   (pedir o preguntar)
9. Thomas necesita saber más sobre la tarea   (pedir o preguntar)
10. Thomas necesita saber la dirección de Allan   (pedir o preguntar)

MINIRELATO: LA MODA

La moda refleja, en parte, acontecimientos de cada periodo. Por ejemplo, en México, a finales del **siglo** (*century*) XIX y principios del XX, durante el tiempo conocido como "el Porfiriato", los hombres de la ciudad solían usar sombrero negro de ala pequeña, **a la usanza francesa** (*French style*), mientras que las mujeres acostumbraban llevar **sombrillas** (*parasols*) para protegerse del sol. No olvidemos que en aquella época Francia tenía una gran influencia sobre la cultura mexicana en todos sus aspectos y no sólo en cuanto a la moda.

Después de la **Revolución Mexicana** (*Mexican Revolution*) el uso del sombrero por parte de los hombres acomodados de la ciudad **decayó** (*decreased*) y sólo se conservó su uso en el campo, aunque se trataba de un tipo de sombrero muy diferente al usado por **los catrines** (*dandies*) como los apodaba la población. El sombrero del campesino era de palma, de falda ancha para defenderse del sol; las películas sobre la revolución permiten apreciar este tipo de sombrero, pues todos los revolucionarios llevaban sombreros; **ellos eran los sombrerudos** (*guys that wear big hats*) como los llamaban despectivamente los citadinos (*people from the city*) conservadores.

Preguntas

1. ¿Qué país influyó en la cultura mexicana a finales del siglo XIX y principios del XX?
2. ¿Cómo se llama el período histórico a finales del siglo XIX y principios del siglo XX en México?
3. ¿Qué suelen usar los hombres acomodados de la ciudad?
4. ¿Qué suelen usar las mujeres de la ciudad?
5. ¿Cómo llama la gente del pueblo a los hombres acomodados?
6. ¿Cómo es el sombrero que usan los campesinos?
7. ¿Por qué el ala del sombrero campesino es tan ancha?
8. ¿Cómo llama la gente conservadora de la ciudad a los campesinos?

CONVERSACIÓN: La familia (continuación)

Peter: Tengo la impresión de que mi familia no me quiere, ni siquiera me hablan. Nos la pasamos viendo la televisión todo el día, **incluso** (*even*) a la hora de comer.

El profesor: De todas formas, tú puedes **aprender mucho** (*you can learn a lot*) de esa familia. Puedes aprender a conocer **los hábitos** (*the habits*) de esa familia, así como sus **manías** (*idiosyncrasies*). Ver la **tele** (*tv*) es una manía como cualquier otra. **Adáptate** (*adapt yourself*) completamente a la vida de esa familia y **todo será para mejor** (*all will be for the best*) **incluso si** (*even if*) al principio te parece difícil o incluso **absurdo** (*absurd*). Empieza por organizar tu vida en torno al **horario** (*schedule*) de la familia. Toma el desayuno y las demás comidas con ellos, **en la medida de lo posible** (whenever *possible*).

Eleanor: ¿Podría usted hacer el perfil del mexicano promedio (*average*)?

El profesor: Lo puedo intentar. **Por una parte** (*on one hand*), el mexicano ama la espontaneidad, lo casual, **el azar** (*chance*). **Por ello mismo** (*therefore*), al mexicano le gustan las reuniones familiares y de amigos y **disfrutar** (*enjoy*) de la buena cocina y de un buen ambiente, con música, con muchas bebidas y con mucha **algarabía** (*uproar*). En fin, que al mexicano le gustan las fiestas o como las llaman ellos, "**las pachangas**" (*parties*).

Lisa: ¿Y la política?

El profesor: Yo diría que no. No es que el mexicano no se interese en la política, pues se discute mucho de política y por lo general, los mexicanos votan en las elecciones, al menos en las que se elige presidente, pero la política no es su motivación principal. Los mexicanos **respetan** (*respect*) sus instituciones, pero **desprecian** (*despise*) a los políticos, pues los **consideran** (*they are considered*) **corruptos, inmorales y mezquinos** (*corrupt, immoral, mean*).

PREGUNTAS

1. ¿Qué es lo que uno aprende viviendo con una familia?
2. ¿Cómo debe un estudiante organizar su vida en México?
3. ¿Qué ama un mexicano promedio?
4. ¿Aman los mexicanos las fiestas?
5. ¿Aman la buena comida?
6. ¿Les gusta la política?
7. ¿Qué respetan los mexicanos?
8. ¿Qué piensan de los políticos?
9. ¿Usted cómo valora el azar?
10. En su familia, ¿cómo se valora a los políticos?

VOCABULARIO

VERBOS

hacer(se)	gustar	guiar
encantar	fascinar	enloquecer
doler	conocer	jugar
oler	inquirir	rehusar

continuar
rasurarse
vestirse
arrepentirse
mirar(se)
confundir(se)
estar(se)
votar

erguir
acostar(se)
desvestirse
ir(se)
saludar(se)
apurar(se)
dormir(se)

volver(se)
levantar(se)
acordarse
olvidarse
llamar(se)
abonar(se)
salir(se)

NOMBRES

el vino tinto
el cepillo de pelo
la comida
las bebidas
el desayuno
el cepillo de dientes
las guayabas
la Revolución Mexicana
el balde
los rostros
los sombreros
la política

el vino blanco
la rasuradora
los postres
las comidas
el almuerzo
la merienda
la moda

la familia
la vestimenta
la cocina

la pasta dental
la crema de afeitar
las instituciones
los políticos
la cena
los postres
los acontecimientos
los campesinos
los hábitos
el ala
las elecciones

ADJETIVOS

católicos
corruptos
mucho/a
mexicanos/as

mezquinos
sombrerudos
citadinos
presidenciales

inmorales
catrines
conservadores

ADVERBIOS

inmediatamente

completamente

típicamente

EXPRESIONES UTILES

¡a tu salud!
las manias
por cierto

hacer un brindis
los hábitos
beber de un solo trago

¿te gusta?
estar sediento

CAPÍTULO 8: ¡A DESAYUNAR!

En este capítulo...

You will discuss Mexican food and eating habits. You'll find out what a typical Mexican family eats during their midday meal and what types of foods are available at Mexican shops and supermarkets.

In this chapter, you will learn how to use the indirect object pronoun using a variety of verbs. You will also learn how to do double substitutions and how to use the verb gustar and similar verbs with indirect object pronouns. You will also learn how to express length of time. Finally, you will learn about the formation of the imperative through the creation of formal and negative commands. Towards the end of the chapter, you will read an excerpt of the poem "Oda a la papa" by Pablo Neruda, Nobel Prize laureate in literature in 1971.

Contexto

José Zurita entra al comedor, se le ha hecho un poco tarde. Él tiene hambre y tiene que regresar a trabajar a la florería en menos de una hora. En la mesa, Yolanda sirve la ensalada de lechuga, tomates, zanahorias y pepinos. ¡Se ve deliciosa!

José: ¿Cuántos años tienes Thomas?

Yolanda: José tú ya lo sabes; Thomas tiene veinte años. ¿Por qué le preguntas eso?

José: Es para hacerlo hablar.

Yolanda: Entiendo, pero no lo incomodes.

Yolanda sirve la ensalada.

Yolanda: Te gustan las ensaladas, ¿verdad?

Thomas: Me encantan.

Yolanda: ¡Qué bueno! Ahora, ¡pásenme el pan, por favor!

José: Un momento, Martín ¿dónde está la botella de vino? Antes de empezar a comer, tenemos que brindar por Thomas, por el gusto de que esté en casa.

Yolanda: A mí no me sirvas mucho.

Todos (menos Thomas): ¡A su salud!

Thomas no dice nada.

Yolanda: Thomas, tú debes decirle "¡A la suya señor!"

Thomas: ¡A la de todos nosotros!

Martín: A ti, ¿te gusta el vino tinto?

Thomas: Oh, sí (se toma el vino de un solo trago)

Martín: Te lo bebes como si fuera agua.

José: Déjalo, a lo mejor está sediento.

Yolanda entra al comedor trayendo el resto de la comida, después de que todos han terminado la ensalada.

Thomas: Y ahora, ¿qué sigue?

Yolanda: Pásenme sus platos para servirles, ¿Te sirvo pierna de puerco?

Thomas: Sí, por favor.

Yolanda: Ahora si quieren sírvanse, arroz, zanahorias, espárragos y todavía queda ensalada por si alguien quiere más.

Martín: Y de postre ¿qué tenemos?

Yolanda: Arroz con leche y café.

José: Después de esta primera comida formal en familia, Thomas ya nos puedes tutear[84].

Thomas: ¿Qué quiere decir eso?

José: Que nos podemos llamar por nuestros nombres sin necesidad de decir señor.

Yolanda: Significa que podemos ser más informales en el trato.

Thomas: ¡Ah!

Preguntas

1. ¿En dónde están los Zurita y Thomas?
2. ¿En cuánto tiempo tiene que regresar a trabajar José?
3. ¿Cuántos años tiene Thomas?
4. ¿Por qué José le pregunta la edad a Thomas?
5. ¿Le encantan las ensaladas a Thomas?
6. ¿Por quién es el brindis?
7. Cuando se hace un brindis en su honor, ¿qué debe responder usted?
8. ¿Cómo se bebe el vino Thomas?
9. ¿Qué van a comer?
10. ¿Por qué José le dice a Thomas "ya nos puedes tutear"?

NOTA CULTURAL: LAS COMIDAS

1. During the week, the Mexicans take a shorter or longer lunch break depending on whether they are active or sedentary, male or female, alone or with their families. They eat at home less and less, due to the increased popularity of the continuous workday, which often prevents workers from returning home at lunch time. Also, a larger proportion of women work and don't have time to return home to prepare meals.

2. Everyday meals are less formal and more health-conscious than traditional "Mexican cooking". Lunch is being eaten faster and faster. People are satisfied with a soup, a main course, followed by a dessert and a coffee.

---

[84] "Tutear" means that you address someone by using the Spanish pronoun, "tú" instead of "usted". In the Spanish spoken in Spain and some other Latin American countries "tú" is used when you have a close relationship with the person you address.

3. Sunday and holiday meals are completely different experiences. Mexicans take advantage of every opportunity to spend some time with their family and friends and to enjoy the atmosphere created by a good meal.
Traditionally, before the meal, **un aperitivo** is served, to "increase one's appetite". It is usually a drink, could be a shot of tequila, a "cuba libre", or a beer. At the table, the meal begins with a **sopa**, salad, or a first course, followed by the main course, consisting of meat, chicken, pork or fish and vegetables. After that, fruit may be served or any other type of dessert. Some people may prefer a **digestivo** drink "to digest the food", other may prefer **un postre**, or just coffee afterwards. And for the kids any kind of soda is customary, but in some homes they will prefer to serve fresh fruit water (a fresh fruit juice drink).

4. Many Mexicans are trying to maintain a more balanced diet in an attempt to stay thin and healthy; But at the same time, many families are increasingly relying on frozen food (**comida congelada**) consumption. This trend was accelerated by the arrival of the microwave oven as a complement to the freezer.

5. Mexicans still drinks a great amount of **cerveza, tequila, ron** and sodas. However, consumption of wine is increasing during meals, especially in middle class families. Many are also choosing to ditch the drinks and opt for water as a healthier alternative.

Dichos

Lo agarraron con las manos en la masa.   To get caught red-handed.
Es más bueno/a que el pan.   He/she is good as gold.
Se vende como pan caliente.   It's selling as a hot cakes.

VOCABULARIO: UNA VARIEDAD DE ALIMENTOS

El cuerno de la abundancia: las legumbres.
Los espárragos, la col, los pepinos, las calabacitas, las espinacas, la lechuga, las zanahorias, los champiñones, los chícharos, los ajos, las cebollas, el chile morrón, las papas, los tomates, los elotes, la coliflor, los aguacates, los nopales, el cilantro, el perejil.

LAS CARNES ROJAS: el puerco, el cordero, la carne de res, la ternera, el jamón, las salchichas.

LAS CARNES BLANCAS: el pollo, el pavo, el pescado.

LAS BEBIDAS: la cerveza, el té, la leche, el agua, las aguas frescas, los refrescos, el vino, el tequila, el ron, los licores de sabores.

LAS FRUTAS:
la piña, la sandía, los limones, las cerezas, el durazno, los plátanos, las peras, el melón, las manzanas, las fresas, las uvas, las ciruelas, los mangos, las naranjas, las mandarinas, las limas, las toronjas.

Más vocabulario:

Páseme **la sal**, por favor.	Pass me **the salt**, please.
Páseme **la pimienta.**	Pass me **the pepper.**
Quiero más **azúcar** en mi café.	I want more **sugar** in my coffee.
Me gustaría **mostaza** para la carne.	I would like my steak with **mustard.**
Generalmente se pueden comprar **legumbres** en latas o bolsas.	Generally one can buy **vegetables** in cans or bags.
Se puede hacer **paté** de puerco.	You can use pork to make **pâté.**
En México se suele comer **sopa** como primer platillo.	**Soup** is normally the first course in Mexico.
Una baguette es un pan largo y delgado.	**A baguette** is a long, thin loaf of bread.
Los chilaquiles son típicos en el desayuno o almuerzo en México.	**Chilaquiles** is a typical breakfast or lunch dish in Mexico.
Las tortas son típicas y muy populares en México.	**Tortas** are typical and very popular in Mexico.
El panadero hace el **pan** y los **pasteles.**	The baker bakes **bread** and **cakes.**
De la leche se hace el **queso**, **la mantequilla** y **la crema.**	**Cheese, butter**, and **cream** are made from milk.
¿Cuál es su **helado** favorito?	Which is your favorite **ice-cream?**
Vainilla, fresa y chocolate son **mis favoritos.**	Vanilla, strawberry and chocolate are my favorites.

Más vocabulario: De compras en el mercado

Estudie el vocabulario.

la carnicería	the butcher shop	el aceite	oil
el carnicero	the butcher	los frijoles	the beans
el arroz	rice		
departamento de salchichonería		the butcher shop for pork and sausage/deli	
la panadería	the bakery	el vinagre	vinegar
el panadero	the baker	las pastas	pasta
la pollería	the butcher shop for poultry	un kilo	a kilogram
		la caja	the cashier/the box
la pescadería	seafood shop	la cremería	the dairy store
la verdulería	vegetable shop		
la tienda de abarrotes		the grocery store	
los camarones	the shrimp	las ostras	oysters
la langosta	the lobster	los dulces	sweets
pagar	to pay (for)	comprar	to buy
cocinar	to cook	hervir	to boil
freír	to fry	servir	to serve

EJERCICIOS PRÁCTICOS

El supermercado.

México ha cambiado mucho. Por ejemplo, hoy en día ya no se trata de ir al supermercado sino que ya hay lo que se conoce como hipermercados. Son como los viejos mercados de los pueblos, pero con el lujo y la comodidad de los tiempos modernos. En ellos se encuentra de todo. Si no le gusta comprar carne empacada, se va a la sección de las carnes y el carnicero le puede preparar los cortes a su gusto: chuletas, carne para asar, carne molida, lomo, bistec. En el departamento de salchichonería, se encuentra el jamón, las salchichas, el salami y el paté. En la pescadería usted puede encontrar además de pescado, una variedad de productos del mar como calamares, camarones, ostras, langosta y pulpo. En la panadería usted puede escoger el pan dulce, los bolillos, la baguette y los pasteles para festejar un cumpleaños.

En la cremería usted puede comprar todo tipo de productos lácteos: cremas, quesos, mantequilla, margarina y requesón. En la sección de verduras usted puede encontrar una variedad de legumbres y frutas de la estación. En la amplia sección de abarrotes se pueden conseguir la sal, los frijoles, el arroz, el café, el chocolate, las latas de chile, el vinagre, el aceite, la mostaza y demás aderezos, las cervezas, el vino, el tequila y, por supuesto, los refrescos.

Después de hacer todas sus compras en un solo lugar, usted pasa a la caja para hacer su pago. Puede hacerlo en efectivo, con cheque o con su tarjeta de débito o crédito. En los supermercados hay personas que empacan sus productos, pero en México se acostumbra darles propina. Y no olvide llevar sus propias bolsas para empaquetar sus productos.

☺ ☺

B. Ahora hágale estas preguntas a su compañero/a:
1. ¿En qué lugar se puede comprar carne?
2. ¿Qué se puede encontrar en el departamento de salchichonería?
3. ¿Qué se puede encontrar en la pescadería?
4. ¿Qué se puede pedir en la panadería?
5. ¿Qué tipo de productos se encuentran en la cremería?
6. ¿Dónde se compran las legumbres?
7. ¿Qué se puede comprar en la sección de abarrotes?
8. ¿Por qué se acostumbra darle propina a quienes empaquetan los productos?

C. You are going to prepare a first-rate meal. The following stores contain some of the items you'll need. Fill in the blank to complete the story.

Como primer platillo voy a servir sopa seca, consistente en arroz con un huevo frito encima; tanto el arroz como los huevos los voy a comprar en la sección de _____. Como plato principal voy a preparar pescado al mojo de ajo acompañado con verduras salteadas. El pescado lo compro en la _____ y las verduras las consigo en la _____. De postre voy a servir unas mantecadas muy sabrosas que voy a comprar en la _____. El café lo voy a encontrar en la sección de _____; y si alguien quiere crema para el café tengo que llevarla de la sección de _____. Por cierto, llevaré mis propias bolsas para no _____ pagarlas y también para ayudar al medio ambiente.

APUNTES GRAMATICALES
36: VERBOS USADOS CON PRONOMBRES DE OBJETO INDIRECTO

1. Almost any verb can be used with an indirect object pronoun, as long as the sentence implies that someone is receiving a direct object. **Dar, pedir, guardar, decir, comprar, preguntar, mentir, vender, tirar**, are common verbs used with indirect object pronouns:

Sus amigos **le** dicen la verdad a Thomas.   His friends tell Thomas the truth.
Le doy dinero a los pobres.   I give money to the poor.
Le compro una casa a mi hijo.   I buy a house for my son.
Nos venden las frutas.   They sell us the fruit.
Le tiro la pelota al receptor.   I throw the ball to the catcher.

2. The indirect object in Spanish is often the equivalent to the English possessive with regard to articles of clothing, and body parts:

Le pongo los zapatos a mi hijo.   I put my son's shoes on.
Al bebé su mamá **le** lava la cara.   The mom washes **her** baby's face.
Ese suéter **le** queda muy bien.   This sweater fits **him/her** very well.

3. Remember that the indirect object tells us for whose benefit or for whose disadvantage something is done:
La mamá **les** prepara la comida.
The mom prepares the food for **them.**

4. The indirect object pronoun can be added to a **se** construction with verbs that suggest unplanned situations. These constructions focus on the object affected rather than the person that is involved:

El vaso se **le** rompió.	The glass was broken.
Las llaves se **les** perdieron.	They lost their keys.
Se **me** olvida la tarea.	I'm forgetting my homework.

5. The Indirect object pronouns can be added to certain impersonal expressions like:

| A los ancianos, **les** es difícil cuidarse solos. | Elderly people have a hard time taking care of themselves. |

EJERCICIOS PRÁCTICOS

A. Change the indirect object pronoun according to the indirect object in parentheses.

Modelo: ¿A ti, qué te dice el profesor? (a los estudiantes)
          ¿Qué **les** dice el profesor?
1.   (A los padres de familia)
2.   (A los Zurita)
3.   (A los niños y sus papás)
4.   (A las azafatas)
5.   (A mí)
6.   (A la mamá)
7.   (A ti)
8.   (A *vosotros*)
9.   (A nosotros)
10. (A los padres del niño)

✎

B. Fill in the blank using the correct indirect object pronoun.
1.   José _____ da las llaves a Thomas.
2.   Yolanda _____ dice "hola" a sus hijas.
3.   Mi esposa _____ pone las gotas en los ojos (a mí).
4.   Los estudiantes _____ entregan la tarea al profesor.
5.   Yo _____ compro un perro a mis hijos.
6.   La abuela _____ da los dulces a nosotros.
7.   Ellas _____ piden dinero para una buena causa (A nosotros).

37. ORACIONES CON DOBLE SUSTITUCIÓN (OBJETO DIRECTO E INDIRECTO)

1. In Spanish a direct object pronoun and an indirect object pronoun can occur in the same sentence:

   Le compro **una casa a mi madre**.   I buy a house for my mom.
   A mi madre is the receiver (the indirect object)
   Le is the indirect object pronoun
   Una casa is the direct object

2. If a sentence has a direct object and an indirect object, the indirect object pronoun comes first followed by the direct object pronoun:

   Yo **me** compro **una casa** para mí.   ⇒ Yo **me la** compro.

3. Sentences with a third person singular or plural indirect object pronoun (**le** or **les)** and a third person direct object pronoun (**lo, la, los, las**), the indirect object pronoun always changes to **se**:

   Yo **le** compré una casa a mi madre.   ⇒ Yo **se** la compré.

4. Double object pronouns cannot be separated from each other:

   Le voy a prestar la bicicleta.   ⇒ **Se la** voy a prestar.

5. Double object pronouns follow the same rules of position as single object pronouns. They are placed before the conjugated verbs, except for positive commands when they are attached to the command or following and attached to infinitive, or gerund:

   Dime la verdad.   ⇒ Dí**mela**[85]

   Voy a comprarle una casa a mi madre.   ⇒ Voy a comprársela.

   Estoy comprándole una casa a mi madre.   ⇒ Estoy comprándosela.

6. In order to clarify the meaning in sentences with **se** out of context

---

[85] Note that when the objects are attached to positive commands the verb has a written accent mark.

Spanish uses **a** + a prepositional pronoun even though it may sound redundant:

A ella se le cayó el café.

A ellos se les perdió la llave del coche.

7. In negative sentences the adverb **no** precedes the pronouns:
Ella **no** se lo vendió.

EJERCICIOS PRÁCTICOS

A. Rewrite the sentences using double object pronouns.

Modelo: Me explican las razones.

Me las explican.

1. Me cuentan la historia completa.
2. Le dicen una mentira grande al juez.
3. No les cuentan la verdad a las familias.
4. Les dan una carta con detalles falsos a los padres.
5. Nos inventan una excusa tonta.
6. Les cuento un chiste a los estudiantes.
7. Me ven la cara de tonto.
8. Les explican mal el problema a los alumnos.
9. Me dan gato por liebre.
10. Te mandan la información incompleta.

B. Transform these sentences by attaching the pronouns to the infinitive or the gerund.

Modelo: Se lo voy a dar.

Voy a dárselo.

Modelo: Le estoy mandando la carta. (A usted)

Estoy mandándosela.

1. Se las voy a mandar.
2. Me la voy a comprar.
3. Se la estoy enviando ahora.
4. Le estoy apagando la televisión.
5. Le voy a comprar una bici.
6. Le acabo de arreglar la silla.
7. Quiero que me muestre las fotos.
8. Le voy a vender la casa a mi hermano.

38. EL VERBO GUSTAR Y OTROS VERBOS USADOS CON PRONOMBRES DE OBJETOS INDIRECTOS.

1. The verb **gustar** is translated as "to like" in English, but its literal meaning is "to please":

   A Thomas **le gusta** Puebla.   Puebla **pleases** Thomas.
   A los estudiantes **les gusta** el español.   Spanish **pleases** them.

2. Usually **gustar** is used with an indirect object pronoun indicating the person who is pleased[86]:

   A ellas les gustan las frutas. They like fruits. (They are pleased
                                    by fruits)

3. The verb **gustar** agrees with the subject of the sentence that is always expressed after the verb:

   Al profesor le gusta **la leche.**   The professor likes **milk**.
   A Yolanda le gustan **las ensaladas.**   Yolanda likes **salads**.
   Me gustas **tú.**   I like **you**.

4. When the verb **gustar** is followed by another verb in the infinitive, the singular form of **gustar** is used:

   A mi esposa **le gusta** ver películas   My wife likes to watch horror mo- te-
   rror.   vies.

5. The preposition **a** is always used to emphasize or clarify who is pleased:

   A los Zurita **les gusta** recibir   The Zurita family **likes** to receive
   estudiantes internacionales.   international students.

6. Other verbs like gustar are: encantar, fascinar, enloquecer, doler, importar, hacer falta, interesar, entusiasmar, incomodar, molestar, quedar bien/mal, sobrar, convenir, caer bien, caer mal, sentar bien:

   Me encanta bailar.   I love to dance.
   A los chicos **les fascina** mucho   The boys love American Football.
   el fútbol americano.

_____

[86] In Mexico, it is common to hear expressions like "Como usted guste" (as you wish/as you prefer) or "¿Gusta tomar asiento?" (Would you like to take a seat?) which are using "gustar" as in English "to like".

A Martín **le duele** la cabeza.	Martin has a headache.
A mí **me** interesa la política.	I am interested in politics.
Al niño **le** hace falta dormir.	The child needs to sleep.

7. You can intensify a sentence by placing the adverbs **mucho, poco, menos** and **más** after the verb:

A Yolanda **le enloquecen** más las joyas.	Yolanda is more crazy about the jewelry.

EJERCICIOS PRÁCTICOS

A. Complete the following sentences using indirect object pronouns.
   1. A ella, _____ gusta nadar en el mar.
   2. A nosotros, _____ duelen los pies.
   3. A los estudiantes estadounidenses, _____ gusta estudiar español.
   4. A Adán y a Eva, _____ gustan las manzanas.
   5. Al presidente de Estados Unidos, _____ encanta hablar.
   6. A Thomas, _____ hace falta su mamá.
   7. A Yolanda Zurita, _____ encanta bailar.
   8. A las mujeres de hoy, _____ molestan los piropos.
   9. A los hombres de hoy, _____ interesan los deportes.
   10. A la señora Marín, _____ fascinan los zapatos.

☺ ☺

B. Ahora es su turno de hacerle preguntas sobre lo que le gusta y no le gusta a su compañero/a de clases.
   1. A ti, ¿qué te gusta hacer en tu tiempo libre?
   2. En tu casa, ¿qué te disgusta hacer?
   3. En la clase de español, ¿qué ejercicio te fascina más?
   4. De la gramática, ¿qué parte te cuesta más?
   5. ¿Qué comida te gusta más?
   6. ¿Qué bebida no te gusta para nada?
   7. ¿Qué tipo de postre te enloquece más?
   8. ¿Cuál es la película que más les gusta a tus papás?
   9. ¿Qué deporte le gusta más a tu papá?
   10. ¿Qué te hace falta para ser feliz?

C. Complete the paragraph using the correct form of the verbs in parentheses.
A la hora de comer lo que más me (gustar) _____ es la sopa, pero no me (gustar) _____ los postres; de hecho me (molestar) _____ comer postre. Para acompañar la comida me (encantar) _____ los jugos de frutas. Debo confesarles que no me (entusiasmar) _____ tener que pagar la cuenta; eso se lo dejo a mi papá, aunque a él tampoco le _____ (gustar) hacerlo.

✎

D. Now complete the paragraph using the correct form of the indirect object pronoun.
A la señora Zurita _____ gusta ir de compras al mercado. A ella _____ encanta ir con su marido; de hecho a ambos _____ gusta comprar juntos. Y a usted, ¿_____ gusta ir de compras con su mamá? En nuestra casa, a mi mujer y a mí _____ enloquece ir al mercado juntos para comprar frutas de la estación; pero lo que no _____ gusta es tener que manejar tan lejos.

39. "HACE" PARA EXPRESAR LA DURACIÓN DE TIEMPO (*LENGTH OF TIME*) QUE SE HA ESTADO HACIENDO ALGO.

1. The formula used to express the length of time that something has been occurring for, or that someone has been in at a place is: **hace** + period of time + **que** + a verb in present tense:

Hace dos días que no duermo.	I haven't slept for (in) two days.
Hace cinco años que el profesor conoce a los Zurita.	The professor has known the Zuritas for five years.

2. It is also very common in Spanish to use **desde** (*since*) in combination with **hacer** to express a duration of time:

Vivo en Miami **desde hace** siete años.	I have been living in Miami since seven years ago.

Note that when you choose to use **desde + hace** the relative pronoun **que** is not used.

Note also that sometimes, as in English, you can use **desde** with a verb in the present tense without having to use **hace.** For example, in the following sentence:

Vivo en Miami **desde** el 2005.   I live in Miami **since** 2005.

3. If you want to pose a question asking the period of time that something
   has been going on:
   ¿**Hace cuánto tiempo** que .....? or ¿**Cuánto tiempo hace** que...?
   (*How long have you been...?*)

   Note that the equivalent sentences in English often use a form of "to have" +
   the past participle, but in Spanish the present tense is used to express this
   meaning.

4. You can also pose the question using **desde:**
   "¿**Desde hace** cuánto vives en los Estados Unidos?"
   How long have you been living in the U.S.?

   Note that when using **desde** without **hace** makes the question word change
   from **cuánto** ("how much (time)/how long") to **cuándo** ("when"):
   ¿**Desde cuándo** vives en los Estados   **Since** when have you been
   Unidos?   living in the US?

EJERCICIOS PRÁCTICOS

☺ ☺
A. Ask the following questions to your classmates.
   Modelo: Estamos en noviembre/ Thomas se fue a México en agosto.
   Hace tres meses que Thomas vive en México.
   1.   Son las cinco de la tarde/el paciente espera desde las tres y media.
   2.   Estamos en el año 2011/El presidente vive en la Casa Blanca desde el
         2009.
   3.   Es el año 2025/mi familia y yo llegamos a Estados Unidos en el 2000.
   4.   Es mitad de enero/El señor García está en el hospital desde navidad.
   5.   Son las ocho y media/el profesor está enseñando desde las ocho.

☺ ☺
B. Ask the following questions to your classmates.
   Modelo: Estamos en noviembre/ Thomas se fue a México en agosto.
   Thomas vive en México **desde hace** tres meses.
   1.   Son las cinco de la tarde/el paciente espera desde las tres y media.
   2.   Estamos en el año 2017/El presidente vive en la Casa Blanca desde el

1. 2009.
2. Es el año 2025/mi familia y yo llegamos a Estados Unidos en el 2000.
3. Es mitad de enero/El señor García está en el hospital desde navidad.
4. Son las ocho y media/el profesor está enseñando desde las ocho.

☺ ☺

C. Below are some questions your classmate can ask you.
   1. ¿Hace cuánto que estudias español?
   2. ¿Hace cuánto que juegas en el equipo de fútbol?
   3. ¿Hace cuánto que tu familia vive en los Estados Unidos?
   4. ¿Hace cuántos años que tus padres están casados?
   5. ¿Hace cuánto que no vas a México?
   6. ¿Hace cuánto que somos compañeros?

☺ ☺

D. Ask the following questions to your classmates.
   1. ¿Desde cuándo estás en los Estados Unidos?
   2. ¿Desde cuándo estás casado?
   3. ¿Desde cuándo tomas clases de español?
   4. ¿Desde cuándo trabajas en esa compañía?
   5. ¿Desde cuándo haces ejercicio?
   6. ¿Desde cuándo conoces al profesor de español?

40. EL USO DEL MODO IMPERATIVO

1. The imperative is used to give commands. The imperative in Spanish has two forms: the formal, which you will study here, and the informal, which you will study in **Chapter 11**.

2. Commands are typically softened by adding **por favor**:
   ¡Siéntese, por favor! (formal)

3. Formal commands are for the second person singular (**usted**)[87], the second person plural (**ustedes**), and for **nosotros**:

---

[87] Formally speaking, **usted** and ustedes are **second person** pronouns, but practically, the verbs are conjugated in the **third person**.

¡**Abra** el libro!	Open the book! (you formal)
¡**Abran** el libro!	Open the book! (you all)
¡**Abramos** el libro!	Let's open the book! (we)

4. Commands may be affirmative:

¡**Cierre** la puerta, por favor!	Close the door, please!
Por favor, ¡**escriban** la tarea!	Please write down the homework!
¡**Abramos** las ventanas, por favor!	Let's open the windows, please!

Note that when the command is affirmative, pronouns are always attached at the end of the command:

¡Venda el coche! ⇒ ¡vénda**lo**!   ¡Deme el libro! ⇒   ¡Dé**melo**!

¡Cómprame un dulce! ¡Cómpra**melo**!
Buy me a candy!   Buy it to me!

5. Commands can be negative:

¡**No cierre** la puerta!	Do not close the door!
¡**No la cierre**![88]	Do not close it!
¡**No cierres**[89] **la puerta!**	**Do not close the door!**

6. Some verbs have irregular formal imperatives:
Ser:

¡**Sea** bueno!	**Be** good!
¡**Seamos** prudentes!	**Let's be** careful!
¡**Sean** amables!	**Be** nice!

Estar:

¡**Esté** tranquilo!	**Be** calm!
¡**Estemos** pendientes!	**Be** aware!
¡**Estén** a tiempo!	**Be** on time!

Dar:

¡**Dé** dinero a los pobres!	**Give money** to the poor!
¡**Démosle** una sorpresa!	**Let's give him/her** a surprise!

---

[88] Note that in negative commands, the pronouns are before the command.
[89] This is an informal command. You will study those in Chapter 11, but notice that all the negative commands follow the formal structure.

¡**Denle** una mano!	**Give him/her** a hand!

Ir:

¡**Vaya** pronto!	**Go** immediately!
¡**Vayamos** con cuidado!	**Let's** go carefully!
¡**Vayan** confiados!	**Go** with confidence!

Saber:

¡**Sepa** hablar con propiedad!	**Know** who to speak correctly.
¡**Sepamos** más sobre México!	Let's find out more about Mexico!
¡**Sepan** la lección de memoria!	Learn the lesson by heart!

7. All the verbs ending in **—car, —gar, —zar** change for phonetic reasons:

Llegar:	¡**Lleguemos** temprano!	**Let's get** there early!
Cargar:	¡**Cargue** la maleta!	**Carry** the luggage!
Almorzar:	¡**Almuercen** bien!	**Eat** well! (Lit: Have a good lunch!)

8. An easy and practical way to form these commands is to write a sentence in present tense **yo** form, (with the only exception of **irregular verbs, and verbs ending in –car, -gar, and –zar**). **Then, drop the "o", and add the "opposite" ending, that is, "a" for "—er" and "—ir" verbs, and "e" for "—ar" verbs**:

Yo abro la puerta.	→ **Abra** la puerta.	(-er/ir verbs change to a)
Yo como menos.	→ **Coma** menos.	(-ar verbs change to e)

EJERCICIOS PRÁCTICOS

A. Tell your classmates to perform the following activities at an imaginary bus station, converting the infinitive to the proper form of the imperative.
Modelo: Ir a la ventanilla.
            ¡Vayan a la ventanilla, por favor!
    1.   Verificar la hora.
    2.   Consultar el horario.
    3.   Comprar un bocadillo.
    4.   Mostrar los boletos.
    5.   Subir al autobús.

B. Tell someone what to do during a ride in an imaginary taxi. Use the imperative.

Modelo: Parar un taxi.

¡Pare un taxi, por favor!

1. Hablar con el taxista.
2. Subir las maletas a la cajuela.
3. Ver por la ventana.
4. Pagar el servicio.
5. Dar la propina al taxista.

C. Tell your classmates to join you in performing these actions. Use the imperative form.

Modelo: Proponer a la clase hablar sólo en español.

¡Propongamos a la clase hablar sólo en español!

1. Estudiar los verbos.
2. Hablar solamente español.
3. Ver películas en español.
4. Escuchar al profesor.
5. Poner mucha atención.

D. Change the verbs to the imperative.

Modelo: Usted no está a tiempo.

¡Esté a tiempo!

1. No está atento.
2. No está concentrada.
3. No es amable.
4. No ve a todos lados antes de cruzar.
5. No va despacio en la carretera.
6. No abraza a su mamá.
7. No paga la cuenta.
8. No busca estacionamiento.
9. No da propina al mesero.
10. No es cuidadoso.

☺ ☺

E. Using the verbs **buscar, traer y poner**, tell one or more classmates to look for specified objects, find them, and put them in various places.

Modelo: ¡Busque el libro!

¡Traiga el libro!

¡Ponga el libro sobre la mesa!

☺ ☺

F. Use direct object pronouns in the following commands. Express the commands in a negative way.

Modelo: Compre el libro.
No **lo** compre.

1. ¡Abra el armario!
2. ¡Escoja las toallas!
3. ¡Tome las sábanas!
4. ¡Cierre el armario!
5. ¡Haga la cama!
6. ¡Ponga las toallas en el baño!

LECTURA: FRAGMENTO DEL POEMA "ODA A LA PAPA"

PAPA,
te llamas
papa
y no patata,
no naciste castellana:
eres oscura
nuestra piel,
somos americanos,
papa,
somos indios.
Profunda
y suave eres,
pulpa pura, purísima
rosa blanca
enterrada,
floreces
allá adentro
en la tierra,
en tu lluviosa
tierra
originaria,
en las islas mojadas
de Chile tempestuoso,
en Chiloé marino,
en medio de la esmeralda que abre
su luz verde
sobre el austral océano.

Pablo Neruda

Preguntas

1. ¿Por qué dice el poeta que "no naciste castellana"?
2. ¿Cómo es la piel de la papa?
3. ¿Cómo se llamaría la papa si fuera castellana?
4. ¿Qué significa que el poeta diga somos americanos?
5. ¿Qué significa que diga somos indios?
6. ¿De dónde es originaria la papa según el poema?
7. ¿Le gustan a usted las papas?
8. ¿Sabe usted cuál es el origen de la papa?
9. ¿De dónde era Pablo Neruda?
10. ¿En qué año recibió el premio Nobel de Literatura Pablo Neruda?

MINIRELATO: UN DESAYUNO MUY MEXICANO

Una vez que los niños se han ido a la escuela, la señora Bernal se pone a cocinar unos chilaquiles verdes que va a acompañar con unos **huevos** (eggs) fritos. En casa está Berta, su hija mayor, que está de **vacaciones** (on vacation) y Yolanda que ha sido invitada a desayunar con ellas. Berta **pone la mesa** (sets the table) mientras la señora Bernal rebana la cebolla para adornar los chilaquiles. Yolanda les ha traído una bolsa de **pan dulce** (pastries) para acompañar el café después del almuerzo. Pero la señora Bernal la sorprende con un **chocolate caliente** (hot chocolate) que de todas formas viene bien con el pan.

Preguntas

1. ¿Cuándo empieza la señora Bernal a preparar el almuerzo?
2. ¿Qué platillo típico está preparando?
3. ¿Quién está poniendo la mesa?
4. ¿Por qué está Berta en casa?
5. ¿Con qué van a acompañar los chilaquiles?
6. ¿Quién es la invitada de la señora Bernal?
7. ¿Qué está rebanando la señora Bernal?
8. ¿Qué lleva Yolanda para el almuerzo?
9. ¿Con qué bebida la sorprende la señora Bernal?

CONVERSACIÓN: La familia (continuación)

David: Mi madre mexicana me dice que cuide el agua y no la desperdicie, pues el agua es un recurso no renovable y en México el agua es muy escasa y **no se puede dejar correr de forma innecesaria** (*don't let the water run*) antes de meterse a bañar. También me dijo que al salir del baño es importante **apagar la luz** (*turn off the light*) para no gastar dinero inútilmente.

El profesor: Yo espero que esas indicaciones no te molesten. Estoy seguro que tu mamá te diría **lo mismo** (*the same*) en los Estados Unidos. Escúchenme bien todos, yo espero que la imagen **que estamos pintando** (*are describing*) en clase **concuerde** (*concurs*) con la visión general... y que a través de los casos concretos aprendamos de la cultura del ahorro de los recursos. Y ahora, ¿de qué quieren hablar?

Andrew: ¡Háblenos de la comida!, profesor.

El profesor: Bien. En cada comida observe los buenos modales, **las reglas** (*the rules*) de urbanidad, ¿qué detalles son diferentes de los que tenemos en casa? Haga las preguntas sobre lo que no entienda.

Jesse: Yo he observado que los mexicanos mientras comen tienen siempre las dos manos sobre la mesa y no como hacemos nosotros.

Andrew: Y también usan el tenedor con la mano izquierda y el cuchillo con la derecha, lo cual es, **después de todo** (*after all*), más práctico.

El profesor: De acuerdo. Hoy en la comida que les hemos preparado se les servirán cosas que les parecerán **extrañas** (*unknown*) aunque todos los platos son deliciosos. Por ejemplo: tacos de **ojos** (eyes), de **sesos** (*brains*), de **criadillas** (*testicles*), **hígado** (*liver*) encebollado, una **riñonada** (kidneys), tacos de **gusano** (*worm*) de maguey, **chapulines** (*grasshoppers*). ¡Cómanselo todo! Tomen un poco para comenzar y si quieren más ¡pidan más! pero, ¡No **desperdicien** (*waste*) nada! ¡No se queden sentados! ¡Cómanselo todo! Las tortillas de maíz azul es una tradición entre los mexicanos. El uso del maíz, como saben **se remonta** (*goes back*) a los tiempos prehispánicos, mucho antes de que se usara para hacer etanol. Díganle **de vez en cuando** (*from time to time*) a la señora que cocina, que les gusta su comida ¡**Esa será su mayor recompensa**! (*That will please her most!*).

Preguntas

1. ¿Por qué la mamá de David recomienda no desperdiciar el agua?

2.	¿Qué se debe hacer al terminar de usar el baño?
3.	¿Qué espera el profesor respecto a estas prácticas?
4.	¿De qué quieren hablar los estudiantes hoy?
5.	¿Qué recomienda el profesor observar en la mesa?
6.	¿Qué deben hacer los estudiantes sino entienden algo?
7.	¿Qué piensa de las comidas que van a probar los estudiantes hoy?
8.	¿Cuál platillo le parece más extraño?

VOCABULARIO

VERBOS

hacer	saber	conocer	aparecer
tener	poder	querer	parecer
caer	decir	dar	gustar
estar	sacar	almorzar	encantar
enloquecer	fascinar	doler	comprar
ser	ir	prestar	correr
dejar	poder	apagar	florecer

NOMBRES

la bicicleta	la ropa	el vestido	los sesos
los chapulines	los tacos	los gusanos	el libro
la sombrilla	los guantes	la corbata	la leche
las películas	el maíz	los platillos	el océano
los modales	la familia	la comida	el agua
la luz	las mujeres	los hombres	los piropos
la papa	una oda	las islas	la piel
la rosa	la tierra	la pulpa	la patata/la papa

ADJETIVOS

catrines	típicos	pobre	buenos/as
sentado/a	mojados/as	mejor	marino/a
austral	blanco/a	oscuro/a	

ADVERBIOS

evidentemente	ayer	esta mañana
finalmente	inútilmente	despectivamente
solo	no	

EXPRESIONES UTILES
le dieron gato por liebre buenos modales
las reglas de urbanidad su mayor recompensa
les vieron la cara de tonto

CAPÍTULO 9: LA MOTOCICLETA

En este capítulo...

You'll learn a bit about the Mexican rules of the road and how to discuss health and parts of the body. You will also learn about the preterite to express actions which occurred in the past, and how to use it to express the adverb "ago". You will also learn about the uses of the imperfect tense to make descriptions, express ongoing actions, age, and time setting in the past. You'll learn about contrasting the preterit and the imperfect, and you will study four verbs that slightly change their meaning if they are used in the preterit or in the imperfect.

Contexto

Es Domingo por la mañana, y John está ansioso por contarles a sus amigos sobre su viaje en moto al African Safari, pero solo pudo hablar con Anna.

Anna: Mira nomás, ¡qué guapo te ves en esa moto! Pero, ¿te sirve la licencia de los Estados Unidos en México?

John: ¡Claro que sí! ¿Quieres venir a dar una vuelta?

Anna: ¿Me llevarías?

John: Por supuesto. ¡Vamos! ¡Súbete!

Anna: ¿Desde cuándo manejas moto?

John: Desde que tenía diecisiete años, solía tomar clases ya en mi segundo año de preparatoria.

Anna: ¿Tú crees que yo podría aprender a andar en moto?

John: ¿Por qué no? Es lo mismo que en los Estados Unidos.

Anna: Pero hay que tener más cuidado aquí en México que en Estados Unidos, ¿no crees?

John: Sí, pero una vez que te familiarizas con las reglas de tránsito y la forma de manejar de los mexicanos, no debes tener ningún problema. Es tan seguro aquí como allá.

Los dos jóvenes se detienen a tomar un café.

Anna: Bueno, y, ¿qué es lo que querías contarme?

John (dudando): Bueno es que ayer Manuel, mi hermano mexicano, y yo fuimos al African Safari.

Anna: ¡Qué bien! y ¿qué pasó?

John: Pues que él manejó la moto de ida y yo me la traje de regreso. Estuvo como dicen los mexicanos: "de pelos".

Anna: ¡Qué suerte la tuya! Me da gusto por ti. ¿Y te gustó?

John: Mucho, es muy bonito. Deberías decirle a tu familia que te lleven. Anna: Les voy a decir.

John: Bueno. Ya vámonos ya.

Anna: Deja voy a pagar la cuenta.

John: Ya la pagué.

Anna: Muchas gracias, eres todo un caballero.

John: Soy el caballero de la moto.

Preguntas

11. ¿Desde qué edad maneja moto John?
12. ¿Le sirve la licencia de los Estados Unidos en México?
13. ¿No es arriesgado manejar moto en un lugar como México?
14. ¿A dónde fueron los jóvenes?
15. ¿A dónde fue John el sábado?
16. ¿Con quién fue?
17. ¿Quién manejó la moto de regreso?
18. ¿Quién pagó el café?
19. ¿Qué le dice Anna a John?
20. ¿Sabe usted andar en moto?

NOTA CULTURAL: EL LENGUAJE DE LOS ANIMALES

Animals, too, speak a different language from country to country. Here are the sounds that some common animals make in Mexico:

el asno/burro (a donkey)	¡íja! ¡íja!
el gallo	(rooster)	¡Kikirikí!
el gato	(cat)	¡Miau! ¡Miau!
el perro	(dog)	¡Guau! ¡Guau!
la vaca	(cow)	¡Muuuuu!
la oveja	(sheep)	¡Beeee!
el león	(lion)	¡grgrgrgr!
el pollo	(chicken)	¡pío! ¡pío!
la rana	(frog)	¡croc! ¡croc!

You can check out the following website to learn more sounds:
http://www.slideshare.net/lisibo/los-sonidos-de-los-animales

Dichos

¡Ojo por ojo y diente por diente!   An eye for an eye, a tooth for tooth!
Quien ríe al último ríe mejor. He who laughs last laughs best.

VOCABULARIO: Señales de tránsito

Con cuidado al doblar a la izquierda
Paso de peatones
Vías del tren
Calle resbaladiza
Curvas peligrosas
Hombres trabajando
Alto

Calle angosta
No rebasar
No dar vuelta en U
No hay paso
No hay vuelta a la derecha
No se permite el paso a los
Ciclistas

Aquí tiene una página de internet con las señales de tránsito:
http://www.portalplanetasedna.com.ar/transito.htm

EJERCICIOS PRÁCTICOS

☺ ☺

Working with a partner, take turns asking and answering the following questions:
1. ¿Qué hace usted cuando ve una señal que indica "Prohibido doblar a la derecha"?
2. ¿Qué hace usted cuando ve una señal que indica "No hay entrada"?
3. ¿Qué hace usted cuando ve una señal que indica "Vías del tren"?
4. ¿Qué hace usted cuando ve una señal que indica "Alto"?
5. ¿Qué hace usted cuando ve una señal que indica "Paso de peatones"?

VOCABULARIO: EL CUERPO HUMANO

la cabeza
el cuello
la espalda
el pecho
el vientre
las caderas
los brazos
los codos
las uñas
el estómago/la panza

el muslo
la rodilla
la pantorrilla
los tobillos
los pies
las piernas
las manos
los dedos
los glúteos/las nalgas

Partes de la cara

los cabellos   las orejas
la frente   la nariz
los ojos   la boca
las pestañas   los labios
los dientes   el mentón
la lengua   las mejillas/los cachetes

Preguntas

1. ¿Con qué toca usted las cosas?
2. ¿Con qué saborea usted?
3. ¿Con qué mira usted?
4. ¿Con que olfatea usted?
5. ¿Con qué corre usted?
6. ¿Con qué piensa usted?
7. ¿Qué le gusta mirar?
8. ¿En dónde le gusta caminar?
9. ¿Le gusta su cabello?

Más vocabulario: Thomas se siente mal.

Estudie el vocabulario

sentirse	to feel oneself	estornudar	to sneeze
ojos llorosos	watery eyes	tener fiebre	to have fever
toser	to cough	un resfriado	a cold
escurrimiento nasal	runny nose	dolor de cuerpo	body aches
la tos	a cough	la prescripción	prescription
4 veces al día	4 times a day	un comprimido	tablet
los pulmones	lungs	el corazón	heart
el té	tea	atrapar	to catch
descansar	to rest	tomar líquidos	drink enough liquids
hidratarse	to hydrate oneself		
un antigripal	cold medicine	la miel de abeja	honey
agarrar un resfriado	catch a cold	dolor de cabeza	headache

EJERCICIOS PRÁCTICOS

☺ ☺

A. Escuche y comprenda.

Thomas no se siente bien hoy. Él está fatigado. Él estornuda constantemente, tiene congestión nasal, fiebre y le duele la cabeza. Yolanda le da un té de manzanilla y un antigripal que lo hace dormir; pero le telefonea al doctor para ver si puede pasar a la casa y ver al paciente. Al llegar el doctor González tiene el siguiente diálogo con Thomas:

Dr. González: ¿Le duele el cuerpo?
Thomas: Sí doctor.
Dr. González: ¡Abra la boca, por favor y diga aaa!
Thomas: Sí doctor.
Dr. González: ¡Déjeme escuchar sus pulmones y su corazón! (El doctor saca su estetoscopio y lo pone en el pecho de Thomas) ¡Tosa fuerte!

Thomas está resfriado. El doctor le recetó unos comprimidos antigripales cuatro veces al día para bajar la fiebre y tomar jugo de limón con miel de abeja, al menos tres veces al día, para limpiar la garganta y aliviar la tos; además le recomendó tomar muchos líquidos, especialmente jugos de frutas y, por supuesto, descansar.
A Yolanda le pidió que le tomara la temperatura cada ocho horas y si hay un aumento brusco que lo llame.

☺ ☺

B. Ahora su turno. Haga las siguientes preguntas a su compañero/a.
1. ¿Cómo se siente Thomas?
2. ¿Qué hace Yolanda?
3. ¿Qué le pregunta el doctor a Thomas?
4. ¿Qué es lo que Thomas tiene?
5. ¿Qué le recetó el doctor?
6. ¿Qué tiene que hacer Thomas?
7. ¿Qué debe hacer Yolanda?
8. ¿Qué hace usted cuando tiene resfriado?

☺ ☺

C. You and four classmates describe a visit to the doctor, putting the following vocabulary to work: **el estetoscopio, abrir la boca, decir aaa, toser, respirar hondo, tomar los comprimidos, beber el jugo de fruta, descansar**.

APUNTES GRAMATICALES
41. EL USO DEL PRETÉRITO PARA REFERIRSE A ACCIONES TERMINADAS EN EL PASADO.

1. The preterite tense is used to express:
   a. actions or events that were completed in the past,
   b. actions that were performed only once,
   c. when you need to narrate a series of events in the past,
   d. when an ongoing action in the past is interrupted,
   e. when the beginning or the endpoint of an action is indicated regardless the duration of that action.
   f. to express "ago". (You will learn that next in **Apunte Gramatical 42**)

2. For regular verbs preterite tense endings are added to the stem. Let's consider the verb **hablar**:

yo **hablé**	nosotros **hablamos**
tú **hablaste**	*vosotros* **hablasteis**
vos **hablaste**	*vosotros* **hablasteis**
usted **habló**	ustedes **hablaron**
él **habló**	ellos **hablaron**
ella **habló**	ellas **hablaron**

3. —**er** and —**ir** verbs have the same ending in the preterite, such as the verbs **comer:**

yo **comí**	nosotros **comimos**
tú **comiste**	*vosotros* **comisteis**
vos **comiste**	*vosotros* **comisteis**
usted **comió**	ustedes **comieron**
él **comió**	ellos **comieron**
ella **comió**	ellas **comieron**

   vivir:

yo **viví**	nosotros **vivimos**
tú **viviste**	*vosotros* **vivisteis**
vos **viviste**	*vosotros* **vivisteis**
usted **vivió**	ustedes **vivieron**
él **vivió**	ellos **vivieron**
ella **vivió**	ellas **vivieron**

Note that the first and the third person singular always have a written accent mark. This is the case with all verbs except those that are absolutely irregular.

4. The **nosotros** form for —**ar** and —**ir** verbs is the same as the present tense conjugation, the meaning is clarified by the context:
conjugation. The meaning is clarified by the context:

PRESENT TENSE:	Nosotros **hablamos** español siempre.
PAST TENSE:	Nosotros **hablamos** español ayer.
PRESENT TENSE:	Nosotros **vivimos** en México.
PAST TENSE:	Nosotros **vivimos** en México hace muchos años.

5. Verbs that ends in —**car**, —**gar**, —**zar** change only in the **yo** form for phonetic reasons. Some of those verbs are:

Ex: **sacar**

yo **saqué**	nosotros sacamos
tú sacaste	*vosotros sacasteis*
vos sacaste	*vosotros sacasteis*
usted sacó	ustedes sacaron
él sacó	ellos sacaron
ella sacó	ellas sacaron

Yo **saqué** la basura ayer.

Other verbs like **sacar** are: **atacar, buscar, acercar(se), explicar, pescar, publicar, tocar, colocar, fabricar, marcar, mascar, masticar, indicar, dislocar.**

Ex: **llegar**

yo **llegué**	nosotros llegamos
tú llegaste	*vosotros llegasteis*
vos llegaste	*vosotros llegasteis*
usted llegó	ustedes llegaron

él llegó   ellos llegaron
ella llegó   ellas llegaron

Yo **llegué** en tren a la universidad.

Other verbs like **llegar** are: **agregar, ahogar, apagar, cargar, castigar(se), colgar, descolgar, negar, renegar, pagar, pegar, rogar, tragar, jugar, encargar, madrugar.**

Ex: **almorzar**

yo **almorcé**	nosotros almorzamos
tú almorzaste	*vosotros almorzasteis*
vos almorzaste	*vosotros almorzasteis*
usted almorzó	ustedes almorzaron
él almorzó	ellos almorzaron
ella almorzó	ellas almorzaron

Yo **almorcé** con mis padres el fin de semana pasado.

Other verbs like **almorzar** are: **abrazar, comenzar, alcanzar, amenazar, cruzar(se), empezar, gozar, rezar, lanzar(se), tranquilizar(se), tropezar(se).**

6. **—ir** verbs that change in the stem in the present tense also have a stem-change in the preterit, but that change only occurs in the third person (singular and plural). There are two types of changes:

a. Verbs like the verb **pedir** that change from **—e** to **—i**:

yo pedí	nosotros pedimos
tú pediste	*vosotros pedisteis*
vos pediste	*vosotros pedisteis*
usted **pidió**	ustedes **pidieron**
él **pidió**	ellos **pidieron**
ella **pidió**	ellas **pidieron**

Ellas **pidieron** arroz con pollo ayer en el restaurante.

Some verbs like **pedir** are: **servir(se), divertir(se), repetir(se), advertir, con-sentir(se), medir(se), convertir(se), hervir, (son)reír, seguir**[90]**, sentir(se), vestir(se), desvestir(se), mentir, preferir.**

b. The verbs **dormir** and **morir** change their stem from **—o** to **—u**:

yo dormí	nosotros dormimos
tú dormiste	*vosotros dormisteis*
vos dormiste	*vosotros dormisteis*
usted **durmió**	ustedes **durmieron**
él **durmió**	ellos **durmieron**
ella **durmió**	ellas **durmieron**

7. Verbs **—er** and **—ir** with a double vowel also change in the third person singular and plural. Every subject except for the third person plural has a written accent mark:

Ex: **Leer**

yo leí	nosotros leímos
tú leíste	*vosotros leísteis*
vos leíste	*vosotros leísteis*
usted **leyó**	ustedes **leyeron**
él **leyó**	ellos **leyeron**
ella **leyó**	ellas **leyeron**

Tú **leíste** un libro entero anoche.

Verbs like **leer: caer(se), creer, oír, poseer.**

8. Verbs ending in **—uir** also change, like the double vowel verbs; however, they follow the normal pattern of accentuation for verbs in the preterit:

Ex: **Construir**

yo construí	nosotros construimos
tú construiste	*vosotros construisteis*
vos construiste	*vosotros construisteis*
usted **construyó**	ustedes **construyeron**
él **construyó**	ellos **construyeron**

---

[90] The verbs **reír, sonreír** and **seguir** are double vowel verbs but they follow the stem-changing pattern.

ella **construyó**   ellas **construyeron**

El sábado él **construyó** un castillo de arena en la playa.

Verbs like **construir: destruir, concluir, huir, distribuir, contribuir, intuir, incluir.**

9. The verbs **ser** and **ir** have one and the same conjugation; only the context can clarify the meaning:

    yo **fui**   nosotros **fuimos**
    tú **fuiste**   *vosotros* **fuisteis**
    vos **fuiste**   *vosotros* **fuisteis**
    usted **fue**   ustedes **fueron**
    él **fue**   ellos **fueron**
    ella **fue**   ellas **fueron**

    Vos **fuiste** a Buenos Aires el verano pasado.

Nosotros **fuimos** a México.	We **went** to Mexico.
Nosotros **fuimos** estudiantes hace tiempo.	We **were** students long ago.

10. The verbs **dar** and **ver** are also irregular and since they are monosyllables they do not carry "acentos":
    dar: **di, diste, dio, dimos, disteis, dieron**
    ver: **vi, viste, vio, vimos, visteis, vieron.**

    Ayer le **di** dinero a mi hermano menor.
    Ayer **vi** una película en la televisión.

11. There are three small groups of verbs that are irregular[91] in the preterite:
  a. In the first group the verbs are: **andar, estar** and **tener; all three** have the same declination:
    andar: and**uve**, and**uviste**, and**uvo**, and**uvimos**, and**uvisteis**, and**uvieron**
    estar: **estuve, estuviste, estuvo, estuvimos, estuvisteis, estuvieron**
    tener: **tuve, tuviste, tuvo, tuvimos, tuvisteis, tuvieron**

    _____

[91] There is no written accent mark for any irregular verb.

¡Los estudiantes **tuvieron** suerte!   The students **were** lucky!
Ella **estuvo** en el partido ayer.
Mis padres **anduvieron** por el parque esta tarde.

b. In the second group this verbs have the same conjugation, with a change in the third person singular of the verb **hacer**:
caber: **cupe cupiste, cupo, cupimos, cupisteis, cupieron**
poder: **pude, pudiste, pudo, pudimos, pudisteis, pudieron**
poner: **puse, pusiste, puso, pusimos, pusisteis, pusieron**
saber: **supe, supiste, supo, supimos, supisteis, supieron**
hacer: **hice, hiciste, <u>hizo</u>, hicimos, hicisteis, hicieron**
querer: **quise, quisiste, quiso, quisimos, quisisteis, quisieron**
venir: **vine, viniste, vino, vinimos, vinisteis, vinieron**

Él **hizo** los goles.   He **scored** the goals.
Ellos **pusieron** las mesas.   They **set** the tables.

c. The third group are verbs ending in -cir, and verbo traer; this verbs have the same conjugation as in the group b, with a change in the third person plural (ellos, ellas, ustedes) that drop the —**i**—. For example:
– **conducir**: conduj**e**, conduj**iste**, conduj**o**, conduj**imos**, conduj**isteis**, **condujeron**
traer: traj**e**, traj**iste**, traj**o**, traj**imos**, traj**isteis**, traj**eron**

Ellos **trajeron** a sus perros a mi casa.
Ellas **condujeron** su coche anoche.

Verbs similar to conducir are: **deducir, reducir, inducir, traducir, producir, decir.**

Note that the verb **decir** is also a stem-changing verb and its conjugation goes as: **dije, dijiste, dijo, dijimos, dijisteis, dijeron**:
(Yo) les **dije** la verdad.   I **told** them the truth.

EJERCICIOS PRÁCTICOS

A. Tell us about a trip to Argentina that took place in the past. Change the verbs from the present tense to the preterite tense.

Modelo: Yo voy a Buenos Aires.
　　　　　　 Yo fui a Buenos Aires.

1.   Nosotros estamos en Argentina.
2.   Los choferes de autobuses van a trabajar.
3.   Tú estás en el café.
4.   Thomas compra muchos regalos para sus amigos.
5.   El profesor se siente fatigado después del viaje.

B. Change the verbs from the present tense to the preterite tense.
Modelo: Tú estás de vacaciones.
　　　　　　 Tú estuviste de vacaciones.

1.   Tú gastas todo tu dinero.
2.   Él va al banco.
3.   Nosotros tomamos un taxi.
4.   Ellas compran regalos.
5.   (Yo) llego tarde al aeropuerto.

C. Change the verbs form the present to the preterite to celebrate your   mother's birthday.
Modelo: Yo encuentro un buen restaurante para celebrar.
　　　　　　 Yo encontré un buen restaurante para celebrar.

1.   Mi padre escoge la mesa.
2.   El capitán nos trae el menú.
3.   Mi esposa pide una copa de vino.
4.   Nosotros ordenamos la comida.
5.   Mi hermano propone un brindis.
6.   El mesero nos sirve la comida.
7.   Yo saco la cartera.
8.   Yo pago la cuenta.
9.   Yo abrazo a mi madre.
10. Ella está muy feliz.

☺ ☺

D. It's gratifying to be successful! Working with a partner, take turns asking the following questions and answering them in the affirmative.
Modelo: Ayer hablamos español todo el día, ¿verdad?

Sí, ayer hablamos español todo el día.

1. ¿Ustedes conversaron en español mientras estuvieron en México?
2. ¿Ya terminaste de leer el capítulo siete?
3. ¿Ya vieron la película en español?
4. Ya tomó el examen, ¿verdad?
5. Salisteis bien en el examen ¿cierto?

☺ ☺

E. Answer these questions using double negative.
   .**Modelo**: ¿Cumplió siete años el niño?
   No, el niño **no** cumplió siete años.

1. ¿Sacaste buena nota en el examen de ayer?
2. ¿Ya leyó tu hermana todo el libro?
3. ¿Creíste que tu hermana lo lograría?
4. ¿Tradujiste el poema?
5. ¿Estuviste cansado después de la práctica?
6. ¿Fueron tus papás a verte jugar?
7. ¿Le diste las gracias a la profesora?

F. Complete the paragraph using the preterite of the verb in parentheses.
   Ayer, yo _____ (ir) al mercado a comprar comida para la semana. Al salir de
   la casa me _____ (encontrar) con mi primo Juan. Él quería saber a
   dónde iba y yo le _____ (contestar) que a la tienda y lo _____ (invitar) a venir conmigo. Por el camino, él me _____ (decir) que se iba a casar
   y yo le _____(dar) el pésame. Al llegar a la tienda nosotros _____
   (comprar) el mandado y _____ (regresar) en taxi. Mi primo ____
   _____ (quedarse) a comer y nosotros la _____ (pasar) muy bien.

42. EL VERBO "HACER" PARA EXPRESAR "AGO"

1. Spanish uses the formula "**hace** + period of time + relative pronoun **que** + a
   verb in preterite = the adverb 'ago'", that is to express the moment when an
   action took place or started:

   Hace cinco años que lo conocí   I **met** him, for the first time, **five**
   por primera vez.   **years ago.**

2. You can change the order of the elements of the sentence without altering the meaning:

Lo conocí por primera vez **hace cinco años.**

I **met** him for the first time **five years ago.**

EJERCICIOS PRÁCTICOS

A. Pose questions about the following statements using the verb "hacer".
Modelo: Ir a la playa.
¿**Hace** cuánto que fuiste a la playa?

1. Trabajar en una tienda.
2. Irse de vacaciones.
3. Aprender español.
4. Visitar a tus abuelos.
5. Aprender a nadar.
6. Ir con los amigos al cine.

B. Talk about the last time you did the following things using "hacer".
Modelo: La última vez que fui al cine.
La última vez que fui al cine fue hace dos años.
1. La última vez que comiste helados.
2. La última vez que viste a tu novio/a.
3. La última vez que hiciste yoga.
4. La última vez que hablaste con tu mamá.
5. La última vez que compraste una corbata.
6. La última vez que hablaste español.

☺ ☺

C. Ask the following questions to a partner. When you have finished, switch roles.

1. ¿Hace cuánto que empezaste a estudiar español?
2. ¿Hace cuánto que conociste a tu novio/a?
3. ¿Cuánto tiempo hace que llegaste a esta ciudad?
4. ¿Cuánto tiempo hace que fuiste a Santiago de Chile?
5. ¿Hace cuánto tiempo que trabajaste en la librería?

6. ¿Hace cuánto tiempo que te graduaste de la preparatoria?

7. ¿Hace cuánto tiempo que aprendiste a hablar español?

43. EL IMPERFECTO

1. All **—ar** verbs are regular in the imperfect. All the conjugations are formed by adding **—aba, —abas, —aba, —ábamos, —abais, —aban** to the stem:
hablar:

yo **hablaba**	nosotros **hablábamos**
tú **hablabas**	*vosotros* **hablabais**
vos **hablabas**	*vosotros* **hablabais**
usted **hablaba**	ustedes **hablaban**
él **hablaba**	ellos **hablaban**
ella **hablaba**	ellas **hablaban**

2. All **—er, —ir** verbs are regular except these three: **ser**, **ir**, and **ver**. All the conjugations are formed by adding **—ía, —ías, —ía, —íamos, —íais, —ían** to the stem.
comer:

yo **comía**	nosotros **comíamos**
tú **comías**	*vosotros* **comíais**
vos **comías**	*vosotros* **comíais**
usted **comía**	ustedes **comían**
él **comía**	ellos **comían**
ella **comía**	ellas **comían**

vivir:

yo **vivía**	nosotros **vivíamos**
tú **vivías**	*vosotros* **vivíais**
vos **vivías**	*vosotros* **vivíais**
usted **vivía**	ustedes **vivían**
él **vivía**	ellos **vivían**
ella **vivía**	ellas **vivían**

Note that the first person singular and the third person singular have the same conjugation. This is valid also for irregular verbs.

3. As noted above, there are only three irregular verbs in imperfect: **ser, ir** and **ver**.
   Ir: iba, ibas, iba, íbamos, ibais, iban
   Ser: era, eras, era, éramos, erais, eran
   Ver: veía, veías, veía, veíamos, veíais, veían

4. The imperfect tense is used to describe the past. It conveys a number of meanings and is used in a number of ways.

   a. The imperfect is used to express a customary or habitual action in the past:
   Ellas **iban** al cine **todos los días.**   They **used** to go to the movies **every day.**

   b. The imperfect also describes two actions that occurred simultaneously and continued indefinitely:
   Ellas **hablaban** mientras que yo **trabajaba.**
   They **were speaking** while I **was working.**

   Note that **"mientras que"** is the most common way of connecting two actions happening at the same time.

   c. The imperfect is used to describe conditions in the past:
   Todas las tiendas **estaban** cerradas.   All the stores **were** closed.

   d. The imperfect is used to describe a past state of mind or health:
   Yo no **sabía** que ella me **tenía** miedo.   I **didn't know** that she was afraid of me.

   Él **estaba** enfermo.   He **was** sick.

   e. The imperfect is used to set a scene:
   Estaba lloviendo y todos **los animales tenían** miedo. De pronto Noé les dijo: "Cálmense pequeños".
   It was pouring and all **the animals were** frightened. Suddenly, Noah told them: "Be calm, little ones".

   f. To refer to ongoing actions in the past without any reference to their beginning or end:
   Ella **estaba** preparando el café.   She **was preparing** coffee.

   g. The imperfect is used to express age in the past:

Cuando **tenía** quince años Anna fue a Cancún.

h. The imperfect is used to express time in the past:
Eran las cuatro de la tarde.

5. The imperfect is used to express an ongoing action or an action in progress in the past:
Estaba lloviendo…   It **was** raining.
Note that when there is an ongoing action, and something interrupts that action, that interruption is expressed using the preterite:
Todos **estábamos** bailando cuando se **fue** la luz.

EJERCICIOS PRÁCTICOS

A. Use the preterite tense in order to complete the following sentences.
   Modelo: Estaba viendo el partido cuando... (llegar mi papá)
                 Estaba viendo el partido cuando llegó mi papá.

   1.   Ellas estaban durmiendo cuando...
   2.   Él estaba corriendo cuando...
   3.   Nosotros íbamos al cine cuando...
   4.   Yo estaba conduciendo cuando...
   5.   Los policías estaban comiendo cuando…

B. Change the verbs from the preterite to the imperfect and add the information in parentheses.
   Modelo: Usted nadó en la alberca/piscina ayer. (todos los días)
                 Usted nadaba en la alberca/piscina todos los días.

   1.   Tú caminaste dos kilómetros ayer. (todas las tardes)
   2.   Él practicó con el balón ayer. (generalmente)
   3.   Ellas danzaron toda la noche. (cada vez que podían)
   4.   Él fue al gimnasio ayer. (todas las mañanas)
   5.   Thomas anduvo en bicicleta ayer. (mientras vivía en México)

44. VERBOS QUE CAMBIAN SU SENTIDO SI SE USAN EN PRETÉRITO O IMPERFECTO

1. A very few verbs like **saber, conocer, poder, querer**, slightly change meaning depending on whether they are used in preterite or imperfect.

2. The verb **querer**, when used in the preterite expresses "to try" (intentar), "have been trying to", "to attempt":
Muchas veces ella **quiso** ir a España. She has been **trying** to go to Spain.

When **querer** is used in the negative form in the preterite it means "to refuse":
Yo **no quise** ir al partido.   I **refused** to go to the game.

In the imperfect **querer** expresses the infinitive meaning "**to want**":
Yo **quería** ir al viaje y fui.   I **wanted to** go to the trip, and I went.
Yo **quería** ir al baile, pero no   I **wanted to** go to the gala, but in fact, I
pude ir.   wasn't able to go.

When used in the negative, the imperfect of **poder** means "to express the lack of desire":
El profesor **no quería** ir al viaje,   The teacher **didn't want** to go on the
pero el director lo obligó a ir.   trip, but the director forced him to go.

3. The verb **poder**, in the preterite, expresses the idea of "managed to" or "to succeed in doing something":
Él **pudo** ir a la fiesta.   He **managed to** go to the party.
                                     He **succeed in going** to the party

The negative in the preterite **no poder** expresses "to fail to do something":
Yo **no pude** ir a la fiesta.   I **could not** (I failed to) to go to the party.

When used in the imperfect **poder** is translated as the infinitive "to be able to" or "have the ability to":
Cuando era joven, él **podía** correr muy rápido.
When he was young he **could** run fast.

El **podía** haberlo hecho, pero no lo hizo.
He **had the ability to** do it, but he did

not do it.

When used in the negative the imperfect **no poder** means "not to be able":
Cuando era niño **no podía** correr. When I was a child I **wasn't able** to run.

4. The verb **saber** in preterite suggests "found out" something at a specific moment in the past:
   Supe la verdad hoy.   I **found out** the truth today.

   The verb **saber** in imperfect suggests that somebody had had that knowledge
   for quite some time:
   Todos **sabíamos** la verdad.   We **knew** the truth.

5. The verb **conocer**, in the preterite means **met** or **got to know** for the first
   time:
   Ella **conoció** al profesor hoy.   She **met** the professor today.

   The verb **conocer** in imperfect suggests the idea of that two people **had already been acquainted** for some time or somebody had been familiar with a
   place or thing:
   Ellos ya **conocían** al profesor.   They already **knew** the teacher.
   Yo ya **conocía** San Francisco.   I already **have been** in San Francisco.

EJERCICIOS PRÁCTICOS

☺ ☺
A. Ask the following questions to your partner. He/she has to decide whether to
   use the preterite or imperfect.
   1.   ¿Cuándo conociste a tu nuevo primo?
   2.   ¿Ya sabías qué clases ibas a tomar este semestre?
   3.   ¿Tuviste una fiesta de cumpleaños el año pasado?
   4.   ¿Querías tomar una clase de español este semestre?
   5.   ¿Ya conocías al profesor de inglés?
   6.   ¿Siempre quisiste estudiar en esta universidad?
   7.   ¿Podías correr cuando eras niño?
   8.   ¿Tenías un perro cuando vivías con tus padres?

✎

B. Change the sentence from the imperfect to the preterite.

Modelo:　Yo no sabía que el profesor era viudo.
　　　　　Lo **supe** hoy.

1.　Thomas no conocía a Yolanda.
2.　John no sabía de la fiesta sorpresa.
3.　José no conocía a Thomas.
4.　Los estudiantes no conocían a las familias.
5.　Los estudiantes no conocían Puebla.

C.　Complete the exercise with the correct verb form, do not forget what these questions imply and answer accordingly.

1.¿Ya _____ (conocer/knew) **usted** a la profesora de español?
　No, la _____ (conocer/met) esta mañana.

2.¿_____ (Saber/knew) **ustedes** que Felipe Calderón fue presidente de México?
　No, lo _____ (saber/found out) hoy en la clase.

3.¿_____ (querer/wanted to) **tú** ir al viaje organizado por la escuela?
　No _____, (querer/wanted to) pero tuve que ir.

4.¿_____ (poder/manage to) **el profesor** ir al partido anoche?
　No, no _____ (poder/manage to) ir, pues se enfermó del estómago.

5.¿_____ (querer/wanted to) usted vender su coche a mejor precio?
　Sí _____. (querer/wanted to) ¿Lo vendió?
　No, no _____ (poder/managed to) porque se arruinó.

6.¿ _____ (saber/knew) tú nadar antes de entrar a la escuela?
　Sí, ya _____ (saber/knew) nadar.

7.¿_____ (querer/wanted to) los estudiantes hacer la tarea de español?
　No, no _____ (querer/wanted to), pero la tuvieron que hacer.

8.¿ _____ (saber/knew) Cristóbal Colón que iba a América?
　No lo _____ (saber/knew), lo _____ (saber) después.

9.¿Ya _____ (conocer/knew) tus papás a tus compañeras de cuarto?
　Sí, las _____ (conocer/met) en el verano.

10.¿_____ (saber/knew) los estudiantes que la comida en la universidad era tan mala?
　Sí, ya lo _____ (saber/knew)

45. REPASO: EL PRETÉRITO CONTRASTADO CON EL IMPERFECTO

1.　Remember that preterite and imperfect tenses reflect different forms of actions or events expressed in the past.

2. Spanish uses preterite in various situations:
 a. When an ongoing action is interrupted in the past you have to use the preterite to express that interruption:
   Cuando **estábamos** celebrando **llegó** la policía.

 b. Spanish uses the preterite to narrate in the past:
   Ayer yo **fui** al cine con mis hermanos y nos **divertimos** mucho.

 c. Spanish uses the preterite to report actions that have been completed in the past:
   Él **compró** un boleto de autobús.

 d. Spanish also uses the preterite for singular actions which occurred in the past:
   La policía **llegó** a las ocho.

3. Spanish uses the imperfect in various situations:
 a. To describe a situation that occurred in the past:
   Anna **tenía** puesto su vestido azul.

 b. To indicate a continuous action without any reference to the beginning or the end:
   Ella **estaba** estudiando para el examen.

 c. To express a habitual action in the past:
   Cuando Thomas **vivía** en casa de los Zurita **comía** muchas ensaladas.

 d. To express time in the past:
   Eran las cinco de la mañana cuando se despertó Martín.

 e. To express age in the past:
   John **tenía** veinte años cuando fue a México.

 f. To make a setting or to elaborate a framework:
   El día en que se **iba** a casar Santiago...

 g. To describe mental, physical or emotional states in the past:
   Los estudiantes **estaban** cansados de tantos exámenes.

h. To express simultaneous actions in the past:
El detective fumaba mientras esperaba la llamada telefónica

EJERCICIOS PRÁCTICOS

A. ¿Pretérito o imperfecto? Decide whether to use the preterite or the imperfect based on the context clues.
   Modelo: Ella va a la escuela. (todos los días)
   Ella iba a la escuela todos los días.

   1.   Ella compra el mandado. (ayer)
   2.   Ellos se sientan a desayunar. (todas las mañanas)
   3.   Tú te pones tus botas de cuero. (siempre)
   4.   El piloto vive en México. (cuando niño)
   5.   Anna va al cine. (ayer)
   6.   John no pasa el examen. (la semana pasada)
   7.   El profesor compra unos libros. (esta mañana)
   8.   Lisa quiere ver a su novio. (todos estos días)
   9.   John maneja la moto. (siempre)
   10. Martín estudia poco. (cuando estaba en la preparatoria)

   ☺ ☺
B. Change the sentence in the preterite and put it in imperfect. Do not forget to change the adverb of time when the action occurred as suggested.
   Modelo: Yo fui al cine **ayer por la tarde**.
   Yo **iba** al cine **cuando era niño**.

   1.   Él cantó muy mal **ayer**.
   2.   Ella fue a la clase de baile **anoche**.
   3.   El hombre leyó un libro **ayer por la tarde**.
   4.   Los niños jugaron fútbol **el domingo en la tarde**.
   5.   El profesor enseñó la lección **esta mañana**.

   ✎
C. Complete the paragraph using the preterite or the imperfect.
   _____ (ser) las nueve de la mañana cuando Carlos _____ (llegar) a mi casa. Él _____(sentarse) a esperarme en el comedor, nosotros

dos _____ (desayunar) juntos y después nos _____(ir) a esperar el autobús. Carlos _____ (vestir) una camisa verde y un pantalón de mezclilla. Al llegar el autobús nos _____ (subir). Yo _____ (pagar) el pasaje de ambos y nos _____ (sentar) en el asiento de atrás. Yo me _____ (poner) a cantar pero, según Carlos lo _____ (hacer) muy mal, así que me _____ (pedir) que me callara. Después de ese día no _____ (volver) a cantar. Ese día _____ (ser) mi debut y despedida.

✎

D. Complete the paragraph using the preterite or the imperfect.
En tres ocasiones, el año pasado, mi hermana _____ (querer) visitar el Museo de Arte Contemporáneo de Nueva York. Ayer mi madre le _____ (preguntar) si _____ (querer) acompañarla a Nueva York. Mi hermana le _____ (decir) que sí. Las dos _____ (salir) hoy a las 5 de la mañana. Cuando yo ____ _____ (despertarse) ellas ya se habían ido. Antes de salir de casa, mi mamá me _____(dejar) el desayuno listo. Yo ___ _____ (levantarse), ___ _____ (bañarse) y _____ (desayunar) solo y después ___ _____(irse) a la escuela. Hoy _____ (ser) un día muy largo y aburrido.

✎

E. Complete the paragraph using the preterite or the imperfect.
Cuando yo era pequeño _____ (ir) de vacaciones a México todos los años. En cada uno de los viajes yo _____ (conocer) distintos lugares; a menudo _____ (ir) a los centros comerciales, a las plazas, a los restaurantes y a bailar a las discotecas y también _____ (soler) comprar muchas cosas para mis amigos. En uno de esos muchos viajes, yo _____ (entrar) a una librería y le _____ (comprar) un libro a mi hermana menor. Recuerdo que la última noche _____ (ir) a la Plaza Garibaldi y cuando _____ (estar) oyendo a los mariachis, _____ (sacar) a bailar a una chica mexicana. La verdad es que yo no _____ (saber) que México _____ (ser) tan divertido.

✎

F. Preterite vs. Imperfect! Underline the correct conjugation.
Cuando era pequeño no sabía/supe nada sobre México, pero el semestre pasado viajaba/viajé a México para aprender/aprendí sobre nuestro vecino del sur. Durante mi visita, conocía/conocí a varios estudiantes y fui/iba a muchos centros comerciales, discotecas, restaurantes, librerías y lugares turísticos

como el zócalo y recorrí/recorría el Centro Histórico. Durante este viaje, también podía/pude visitar muchas iglesias y museos interesantes. La última noche fui/iba a la Plaza Garibaldi para escuchar/escuché a los mariachis; allí siempre había/hubo mucha gente y algunas personas querían/quisieron bailar con los turistas, pero éstos no siempre querían/quisieron, pues creo que les dio/daba pena y un poco de miedo. Gracias a este viaje sabía/supe que México es un país muy moderno y a la vez, con mucha historia.

MINIRELATO: LOS BARRIOS INDÍGENAS

Del otro lado del Río San Francisco estaban los barrios indígenas: San Francisco, El Alto, Analco, San Baltazar, San Pablo, San Sebastián y el Barrio de Santa Ana, entre otros.

Al empezar la construcción de la Ciudad de Puebla en 1531, los indígenas se establecieron **en barrios propios** (their own neighborhoods) alrededor de la ciudad española. Entre los barrios que aún conservan un ambiente laborioso y popular, San Francisco El Alto es el barrio **más antiguo** (the oldest) en Puebla.

En estos barrios fueron típicas, y **todavía lo son** (they still are) las **actividades artesanales** (hand made crafts) como la construcción de **loza roja** (red pottery) y la elaboración de **las famosas semitas** (a typical type of bread) de Puebla.

Algunos de estos barrios todavía conservan sus calles **angostas** (narrow streets) y **empedradas** (cobblestone pavements). En estos barrios los primeros **Frailes Franciscanos** (Franciscan Friars) construyeron muchas iglesias, **pero sin duda** (without a doubt) **la más famosa** (the most famous one) es la iglesia de San Francisco, terminada en 1585.

Preguntas

1. ¿Puede mencionar los nombres de tres barrios indígenas?
2. ¿Dónde se ubicaban estos barrios?
3. ¿Por qué se llaman barrios indígenas?
4. ¿Cuál es el barrio más antiguo?
5. ¿Cómo son las calles en estos barrios?
6. ¿Qué tipo de actividades son típicas de estos barrios?
7. ¿Cómo se llama el pan típico de Puebla?
8. ¿En qué año fue fundada la ciudad de Puebla?
9. ¿Cuál es la iglesia más famosa construida por los franciscanos?

10. ¿En qué año fue terminada esta iglesia?

CONVERSACIÓN: La familia (continuación)

Peter: ¿Podemos pedir que no nos sirvan tanta comida?

El profesor: ¡**Por supuesto**! (*of course*) pero tienen que ser **muy cuidadosos** (very careful) para **no lastimar la sensibilidad** (*not hurt the feelings*) de sus madres. Ellas, **estoy seguro,** (*I am sure*) lo hacen para agradarlos; ofrecerles más comida es una forma **de mostrarles que aprecian** (*to show that they are glad*) su estancia en casa.

Andrew: Y con respecto a las bebidas, ¿qué nos recomienda?

El profesor: Bueno, recuerden que en México es, en algunas familias, normal tomar una cerveza con la comida; pero **nadie los puede obligar** (*no one can force you*) a tomar alcohol, ni la familia **se va a sentir ofendida** (*they won't feel offended*) si dicen que no. Siempre pueden cortésmente **declinar** (to decline) una cerveza y pedir un vaso con agua. Si usted es **sensible** (*sensitive*) a los efectos del alcohol simplemente pida o sírvase agua. **Además** (*besides*) no todas las familias mexicanas ofrecen alcohol con las comidas, otras ponen sodas o agua de frutas o simplemente sirven agua.

Lisa: Pero algunas veces no es fácil decir no.

El profesor: ¡Es verdad! Pero mi recomendación sería, **usen el sentido común** (*use your common sense*), la oportunidad de compartir y socializar con la familia y no olviden que su **comportamiento** (*behavior*) habla de su educación, de su cultura y que **en resumidas cuentas** (*at the end of the day*) ustedes son **embajadores** (*ambassadors*) de su país en México. **Eviten la vulgaridad** (*avoid bad manners*) no sean **ruidosos** (*noisy*) o **descorteses** (*impolite*)

Kevin: ¿Nos puede dar ejemplos?

El profesor: Si algo **molesta** (*bother*) a las familias mexicanas es que la gente ponga los pies sobre un mueble, como la mesa de la sala. No sean desconsiderados con los bienes ajenos, sean más bien comprensivos, **pacientes** (*patient*) y **conserven el buen humor** (*maintain a good attitude*).

Andrew: Y con respecto a la ropa, ¿qué nos puede decir?

El profesor: **Su ropa debe ser apropiada** (*your clothes should be appropriate*) y debe estar limpia, **evite andar sin camisa** (*don't go around the house with your shirt off*) y **sin zapatos** (*barefoot*).

Preguntas

1. Si le sirven mucha comida, ¿qué pueden hacer los estudiantes?
2. ¿De qué forma se puede evitar comer demasiado?
3. Si no se hace correctamente, ¿qué pasaría?
4. ¿Es obligatorio tomar alcohol con la comida en México?
5. Si usted no toma alcohol, ¿qué puede hacer?
6. ¿Es que todas las familias toman alcohol con las comidas?
7. ¿Qué recomienda el profesor usar para acertar con la familia?
8. ¿Es que para el profesor los estudiantes son embajadores de su país?
9. ¿Qué les pide el profesor que eviten ser?
10. ¿Qué molesta sobremanera a las familias mexicanas?

VOCABULARIO

VERBOS

levantar(se)	bañar(se)	vestir(se)
cepillar(se)	acordar(se)	acostar(se)
desvestir(se)	sacar	apagar
dormir	pedir	andar
pegar	negar	traer
conocer	saber	poder
querer	evitar	fumar
esperar		

NOMBRES

la licencia de conducir	la multa	el peatón
las partes de cuerpo	el policía	la moto
el motor	la gasolina	el aceite
las llantas/ruedas	el acelerador	el freno
las señales de tránsito	el pueblo	la arena
las artes	el país	la loza
la semita	el barrio	las danzas
el quetzal	el rector	el palacio

la ciudad
el humor
los embajadores
la ropa
las mesas
las bebidas
la llamada
una silla

las calles
una vulgaridad
el penacho
la gente
la sala
la casa
la comida
un antigripal

la iglesia
el sentido
los zapatos
los muebles
las familias
la educación
los zapatos
los frailes

ADJETIVOS
blanco/a
rojo/a
propio/a
ruidoso/a
apropiado/a

moderno/a
indígenas
antiguo/a
paciente
urduo/a

bellos/as
famosos/as
último/a
fácil
delicado/a

ADVERBIOS
cortésmente
alrededor
buen

simplemente
especialmente

todavía
constantemente

EXPRESIONES UTILES
evitar la vulgaridad
¡por supuesto!
tu día de suerte
tiempo libre
debut y despedida

usar el sentido común
¡no te tardes!
calles angostas y empedradas
con el alma en un hilo
de pelos

CAPÍTULO 10: EN FRENTE DE CATEDRAL

En este capítulo...

You'll visit the cathedral with the tallest towers in Puebla, Mexico. You will learn how to express two kinds of actions in the past: those that began in the past and continue into the present, and those that took place in the past before another past action. You'll also learn how to talk about cities, countries, and other geographical locations.

To help you do these things, you'll study the past participle, the present perfect and the past perfect tenses.You will also learn more simple and compound prepositions, and the use of the infinite after a preposition.

Contexto

Los estudiantes hacen una visita guiada al centro histórico de la ciudad. El profesor ha contratado a su amigo Jorge Fernández, quien es reconocido en la ciudad como el mejor guía de todos.

Thomas: Señor, ¿Qué son aquellas torres tan altas?

Jorge: ¡Pongan atención! Aquellas torres que se ven a la distancia, son las torres de la catedral.

Thomas: Deben de ser las torres más altas que he visto.

Jorge: Puede ser. En México la catedral de Puebla tiene las torres más altas de todas las iglesias del país. Ambas torres miden 70 metros de altura.

Jesse: ¿Puede hablar un poco más despacio, por favor señor?

Jorge: ¡Claro que sí!

Todos siguen a Jorge que los guía a través del zócalo hacia el atrio de catedral.

Jorge: Antes de continuar tengo una pregunta para ustedes, ¿alguno de ustedes ya había venido antes a México?

Thomas: Yo ya había venido antes, pero nunca había estado en Puebla.

Jorge: ¿Alguien más?

Varios estudiantes responden a la vez: Yo, yo, yo

Jorge: Muy bien.

Anna: Tengo una pregunta

Jorge: Dígame.

Anna: ¿Hay algún libro que describa la catedral, que cuente su historia?

Jorge: Sí, hay muchos libros que cuentan el proceso de construcción y la importancia de la catedral dentro de la historia del catolicismo en México.

John: ¿Puede darnos algo de información general?

Jorge: ¡Sí, por supuesto! Por ejemplo, se dice que esta catedral es la más aventurera de México porque se tardaron muchos años construirla.

Thomas: Y, ¿por qué pasó eso?

Jorge: Bueno porque, no siempre había dinero para continuar la construcción, pero además por la política interna de la iglesia católica, es decir hubo muchos cambios en el liderazgo del arzobispado.

Kevin: Y, ¿cuándo se inició la construcción?

Jorge: La catedral se comenzó a construir en noviembre de 1575.

John: Y, ¿cuándo se terminó?

Jorge: No se terminó sino hasta 1690.

Thomas: ¡Vaya, más de cien años!

Jorge: Así es, un poco más de cien años.

Thomas: Y, ¿qué más nos puede decir?

Jorge: Bueno, la catedral está dedicada a la Virgen de la Inmaculada Concepción y su festividad se celebra el ocho de diciembre.

Jesse: Ese es también el día de mi cumpleaños.

Jorge: Felicidades entonces. Si usted hubiera nacido en México se llamaría Concepción y le dirían Conchita.

Jesse: ¡Su atención, por favor! De ahora en adelante mi nombre es Concepción o Conchita, como ustedes prefieran.

Thomas: ¿Hay algo más sobre la catedral?

Jorge: En el interior de la catedral hay diversas muestras del arte novo hispano.

John: Y, ¿cuál es la distribución interna?

Jorge: La catedral tiene cinco naves; una central, dos laterales y dos para capillas especiales. Al entrar pongan mucha atención al coro; es uno de los coros más hermosos del país, con sillas que datan de principios del siglo XVIII.

Preguntas

1. ¿Dónde está ubicada la catedral?
2. ¿Cuál es la altura de sus torres?
3. ¿Cuántas naves tiene?
4. ¿Es que la catedral tiene una colección rica de arte novo hispano?
5. ¿Cuánto duró su construcción?
6. ¿A quién está consagrada?
7. ¿Cuándo es su festividad?
8. ¿Quién en el grupo cumple años ese día?
9. ¿Qué estudiante ya había estado en México antes?
10. ¿Alguno de ustedes ha visitado México?

NOTA CULTURAL: LAS RELIGIONES EN MÉXICO.

There is no official religion in Mexico, as the constitution guarantees separation of the church and the state. However, around 89% of the population is at least nominally affiliated with the Catholic Church. The Basilica of Guadalupe, the shrine of the Virgin of Guadalupe, Mexico's patron saint, is located in the northern part of Mexico City and is the site of an annual pilgrimage of hundreds of thousands of people.

But Mexican Catholicism is very special because it has a syncretic form, meaning that many pre-hispanic practices have been added to Catholic ones. This syncretism is particularly visible in many village fiestas where ancestors, mountain spirits, and other spiritual forces may be honored alongside Catholic saints. Moreover, the identities of many saints and spirits have been blended together since the early colonial period. At times, however, belief systems still come into conflict.

Protestants, on the other hand, account for a tiny but rapidly growing segment of the population. Their, missionaries have been especially successful in converting the urban poor. According to the INEGI (National Institute of Statistics and Geography) the second largest religious group in Mexico are that of the Jehovah's Witnesses with more than a million people. In third place is the church la **Luz del Mundo**, with its hub in Guadalajara. But the religious group that is growing faster than any other group is the Pentecostal movement with close to a million and a half members. They have a large influence in native towns and communities, and in the border cities and towns. In fact, the Pentecostals are the second largest denomination in Mexico.

When it comes to religion in Mexico, most religious denominations can find a place to worship in the Capital city, although some complain about the lack of Muslim services. Jews and Christians are well catered to, given that as there are plenty of synagogues and Catholic and Protestant churches in Mexico. However, there are also a surprisingly large number of Tibetan Buddhists in Mexico, thanks to the fact that Mexico City has one of only six Tibetan Houses in the entire world.

Dichos

Roma no fue construida en un día.	Rome was not built in a day.
Cuando a Roma fueres has lo que vieres.	When in Rome do as the Romans do.
Estar entre la espada y la pared.	Your back is against the wall.

VOCABULARIO:UN POCO DE GEOGRAFÍA

EJERCICIOS PRÁCTICOS

A. Complete the sentences using the map.
   Modelo: El país más largo es.
                    El país más largo es Chile.

   1.   El país más pequeño de América Latina es _____.
   2.   El país que está al sur de Estados Unidos es _____.
   3.   El ecuador pasa por qué países _____ _____

   _____

4. Panamá está entre _____ y_____.
5. Argentina limita con _____

_____.
6. Brasil tiene frontera con al menos _____ países.
7. República Dominicana comparte la isla con _____.
8. ¿Cuál es la isla más grande del caribe? _____.
9. ¿Qué país está al norte de Costa Rica? _____.
10. ¿Qué países no tienen salida al mar? _____.

☺ ☺

B. In the map, identify each country's capital.

☺ ☺

C. Each member of the class represents a country at a committee meeting at the United Nations. Each person stands, introduces himself or herself, and names the country that he or she represents, its capital, its main language, the continent on which it is located, its population, and its general climate.
Modelo: Yo me llamo Miguel Romero, yo vengo de Quito, la capital de Ecuador. La lengua oficial de Ecuador es el español. Ecuador está en Sudamérica y tiene una población de catorce millones de habitantes y su clima es de tipo ecuatorial, influido por la altitud del terreno y la influencia de la corriente de Humboldt, que provoca una mayor cantidad de lluvia durante todo el año.

Más vocabulario: Las vacaciones

libre	free	el resto	the rest
tiempo libre	free time	un turista	a tourist
feriado	holiday	números	numbers
es difícil	it's difficult	lleno	crowded
tener suerte	to be lucky	ocio	leisure
vacaciones	vacation	un seguidor	a fan
en alta mar	on the high seas	Ir de pesca	go fishing

EJERCICIOS PRÁCTICOS

☺ ☺

A. Escuche y comprenda

Thomas no comprende bien las expresiones "ocio", "vacaciones" "Días feriados".Como José está hoy en casa, pues es un día feriado, aprovecha
para hacerle algunas preguntas.

Thomas: José, ¿qué diría usted que es el ocio?

José: Primero recuerda que ya nos tuteamos. Así que háblame de tú. Ahora
voy a contestar tu pregunta; el ocio es el tiempo fuera del trabajo, un
tiempo para el disfrute personal, para leer, para divertirse, para estar con la
familia, el tiempo ideal para salir de vacaciones.

Thomas: La ley en México, ¿otorga vacaciones a los mexicanos?

José: Sí la ley Federal del Trabajo de 1970, otorga hasta un máximo de dos
semanas de vacaciones al año, con goce de sueldo, para los trabajadores
de tiempo completo.

Thomas: ¡Sólo dos semanas!

José: Sí, más los días feriados obligatorios como el primero de enero, el primer lunes de febrero, el tercer lunes de marzo, etc.

Thomas: Y, ¿tienen feriados por razones religiosas?

José: Sí, por ejemplo, jueves y viernes santos son feriados y, en algunos
lugares como las escuelas, toda la semana santa es de vacaciones, pero
eso depende del tipo de trabajo que uno tenga.

Thomas: Y, ¿ustedes cuándo toman vacaciones como familia?

José:Nosotros solemos tomarlas en julio.

Thomas: Y, ¿a dónde van?

José: Si podemos vamos a la playa. Ya sabes que México tiene playas muy
hermosas.

Thomas: Pero, ¿no es julio mala época para ir a la playa?

José: Depende, hay mucha gente es cierto, pero hay tantas playas, que
puedes encontrar lugares sin tanto turismo, como las playas de Nayarit.

Thomas: Pero, ¿hay en estos lugares buenos hoteles?

José: Hay hoteles limpios y cómodos y lo mejor de todo no tan caros. Es cosa
de saber buscar. Pero lo mejor de México son las playas, algunas de ellas
son verdaderamente paradisíacas. No tienes idea lo bonitas que son.

Thomas: Y, ¿la comida?

José: ¡Cómo en todo México, la comida es magnífica!Y ustedes, ¿tienen
muchas semanas de vacaciones?

Thomas: Nosotros sólo tenemos quince días, más los feriados obligatorios.

José: Ahí está, ¡están igual que nosotros de fregados!

Thomas: ¡Pues sí!

Preguntas

1. ¿Qué es lo primero que le dice José a Thomas antes de contestarle la pregunta?
2. ¿Qué es lo que José entiende por ocio?
3. ¿De qué año es la Ley Federal del Trabajo en México?
4. ¿A cuántos días de vacaciones tiene derecho un trabajador mexicano?
5. ¿Qué hace la familia de José durante ese tiempo?
6. ¿Es julio una mala temporada para ir a la playa en México?
7. ¿Qué playa recomienda José visitar?
8. ¿Cómo son los hoteles en esa zona?
9. ¿Cómo son las playas en esa zona?
10. Y, la comida, ¿cómo es?

APUNTES GRAMATICALES
46. LOS PARTICIPIOS PASADOS

1. Past participles in Spanish can be used as adjectives.

2. In combination with the auxiliary verb **haber,** a past participle forms a perfect tense.

3. The past participle of regular **—ar** verbs is formed by adding **—ado** to the stem: hablar ⇒ habl + **ado** = **hablado**

4. The past participle of regular **—er** and **—ir** verbs is formed by adding **—ido** to the stem: comer ⇒com + **ido** = **comido**

   vivir ⇒viv + **ido** =**vivido**

5. The past participle doesn't change when used with the auxiliary verb **haber** to form perfect tenses.

6. In perfect tenses the object pronouns always precede the verb **haber,** and they are never attached to the past participle:
   ¿Has visto la película? Sí, **la** he visto.

7. The following verbs have irregular past participles:

abrir	**abierto**	hacer	**hecho**	soltar	**suelto**
cubrir	**cubierto**	morir	**muerto**	ver	**visto**
decir	**dicho**	poner	**puesto**	volver	**vuelto**
escribir	**escrito**	resolver	**resuelto**	revolver	**revuelto**
freír	**frito**	romper	**roto**	envolver	**envuelto**

8. —**er** and —**ir** verbs that verbs that have double vowel have a written accent mark on the -**í**- in the past participle:

caer	**caído**	leer	**leído**	reír	**reído**
creer	**creído**	oír	**oído**	traer	**traído**
poseer	**poseído**				

EJERCICIOS PRÁCTICOS

Write answers to the questions using the verb in parentheses to create the correct adjective.

Modelo: ¿Cómo está la tienda? (cerrar)
La tienda está cerrada.

1. ¿Cómo está la puerta? (abrir)
2. ¿Cómo está el libro? (manchar)
3. ¿Cómo está la farmacia? (clausurar)
4. ¿Cómo está el coche? (cubrir de nieve)
5. ¿Cómo está la ventana? (romper)
6. ¿Cómo está la carta? (firmar)
7. ¿Cómo está el sobre? (sellar)
8. ¿Cómo está el hombre? (morir)

47. EL PRESENTE PERFECTO

1. The present perfect is used in Spanish, as in English, to mark or describe past events whose influence still continues on the present:
Nosotros **no hemos ganado** la lotería todavía.
We **haven't won** the lottery yet.

2. The present perfect consists of a conjugated form of the auxiliary verb **haber** + a past participle:
yo **he**   nosotros **hemos**

tú **has**	*vosotros* **habéis**
vos **has**	*vosotros* **habéis**
usted **ha**	ustedes **han**
él **ha**	ellos **han**
ella **ha**	ellas **han**

3. Questions are formed as usual:

    ¿**Has terminado** de leer el libro?   **Have you finished** the book?

    ¿Es que tú ya **has terminado** de leer el libro?

    Has terminado de leer el libro, ¿verdad?

    Has terminado de leer el libro, ¿no?

4. Negations are formed placing the **no** before the auxiliary verb **haber**:

    Yolanda **no ha comprado** las cervezas. Yolanda **has not bought** the
                                                                                                      beer.

5. Sometimes the speaker may add the adverb "ya" to the sentence to emphasize the time (already):

    Ella **ya** ha tomado su primera clase   She has **already** taken her first
    de manejo.   driving lesson.

6. In negative sentences the speaker may use the adverb **todavía** to tell us that the action did not occur yet:

    Martín, ¿Ya fuiste por el pan?   No, no he ido **todavía**.

EJERCICIOS PRÁCTICOS

☺ ☺

A. Interview a classmate, asking the following questions.
    1.   ¿Has estudiado para el examen?
    2.   ¿Te has aprendido los verbos de memoria?
    3.   ¿Te has aprendido el vocabulario?
    4.   ¿Has practicado las preposiciones?
    5.   ¿Has entendido la explicación del maestro?
    6.   ¿Has tomado ya la prueba?
    7.   ¿Has pasado el examen?
    8.   ¿Qué calificación has sacado?
    9.   ¿Qué te ha dicho el profesor?

B. Follow the model and change the following sentences to the negative.

Modelo: Nosotros hemos ido a Costa Rica.

Nosotros no hemos ido a Costa Rica todavía.

1.   Ellas han ido a Perú.
2.   Los estudiantes han ido a Nicaragua.
3.   El profesor ha ido a Bolivia.
4.   Yolanda y José han ido a Uruguay.
5.   Yolanda, Cecilia y Martín han ido a Ecuador.
6.   El presidente ha ido a Cuba.

C. Answer the following questions using the present perfect.

Modelo: ¿Ya has reservado la mesa?

No, no lo he hecho.

1.   ¿Han traído el menú?
2.   ¿Has decidido lo que quieres comer?
3.   ¿Han elegido las bebidas?
4.   ¿Has visto a las personas de la mesa del fondo?
5.   ¿Te ha gustado la comida?
6.   ¿Ya has pedido la cuenta?

D. Answer in the negative form.

Modelo: ¿Has estudiado la lección?

No la he estudiado.

1.   ¿Has visto a la profesora de español?
2.   ¿Te has comprado un coche?
3.   ¿Has visto al doctor?
4.   ¿Has abierto la ventana?
5.   ¿Has leído la carta?
6.   ¿Has visto la película?
7.   ¿Has hecho la tarea?
8.   ¿Han cambiado las lámparas de la casa?
9.   ¿Has arreglado las bicicletas?
10. ¿Te has roto la mano?

48. EL PASADO PERFECTO

1. The past perfect tense is formed by the imperfect of the auxiliary verb **haber** + a past participle.

2. The conjugation of the verb **haber** in the imperfect is:

yo **había**	nosotros **habíamos**
tú **habías**	*vosotros* **habíais**
vos **habías**	*vosotros* **habíais**
usted **había**	ustedes **habían**
él **había**	ellos **habían**
ella **había**	ellas **habían**

3. The past perfect tense in Spanish, as in English, designates an event or action that happened before another event or action in the past, that may or may not be further removed:

Thomas ya se **había despertado** cuando sonó el despertador.	Thomas **had** already **woken up** when the alarm went off.
Ya se **había hablado** de eso.	It already **had been** discussed.

    It's customary to use the adverb **ya** in the formation of past perfect:
    Ya habíamos visto todo Puebla.

    In negative sentences the speaker may use the adverb **todavía**:
    No había terminado la película **todavía** cuando me llamó mi mamá.

    It's customary to use **cuando** before the second action, when that second action or event remains as part of the sentence:
    Ya había terminado la clase **cuando** se fue la luz.

EJERCICIOS PRÁCTICOS

A. Use the past perfect to talk about things that had taken place before another event.

    Modelo: Yolanda **ya había servido** la cena (Thomas llegar).
    Yolanda **ya había servido** la cena cuando llegó Thomas.

    1.   Los padres ya se habían desesperado (llegar el autobús).

2. José ya había puesto la mesa (Martín llamar).
3. Thomas ya había regresado a Estados Unidos (Casarse su hermana).
4. Ya había llegado la pizza (los estudiantes empezar la fiesta).
5. Ya había terminado el partido (regresar la luz).

B. Complete the sentences using past perfect tense.
1. La señora ya _____ _____ (haber/limpiar) la cocina cuando entró el gerente.
2. José ya se_____ _____ (haber/levantar) cuando empezó el incendio.
3. Los estudiantes ya _____ _____ (haber/terminar) el examen cuando sonó la campana.
4. Cuando Thomas llegó a casa Yolanda ya _____ _____ (haber/servir) la cena.
5. Cuando John y Anna llegaron al African Safari ya _____ (haber/cerrar) el parque.

☺ ☺
C. Ask your classmate the following questions:
1. ¿Por qué no habías llamado a tus padres?
2. ¿Por qué no le habías dado de comer al perro?
3. ¿Por qué no le habían puesto gasolina al coche?
4. ¿Por qué no habías venido a clase?
5. ¿Por qué no había entregado el examen?
6. ¿Por qué no habían entregado la tarea?
7. ¿Por qué no había ido al baño?
8. ¿Por qué no había pagado la colegiatura?
9. ¿Por qué no habías cenado?
10. ¿Por qué ya te habías ido?

D. Complete using pasado perfecto, pretérito and imperfecto.
El profesor ya _____ (haberse) despertado cuando _____ (oír) la alarma de incendios sonar. Entonces ___ _____ (levantarse) de prisa, ____ _____ (vestirse) y _____ (salir) al jardín. Desde allí _____ (poder) ver a los bomberos que ya _____ (estar) evacuando a las personas de sus casas. Los vecinos no _____ (haber) salido porque _____ (creer) que _____ (ser) un simulacro.

49. OTRAS PREPOSICIONES

In other chapters, you have already studied prepositions like **a, de, con, en** (Chapter 3) and **por** and **para** (Chapter 7). Here you will be introduced to other prepositions.

A. Other common simple prepositions:

desde	from/since	durante	during
entre	between	mediante	by means of
hacia	toward	hasta	until
según	according to	sin	without
sobre	above/about/on	encima (de)	on/above
debajo (de)	under	abajo (de)	under/below
delante (de)	in front of	detrás (de)	behind
atrás (de)	behind		

1. **Desde** is more specific than **de** in labeling the starting point:

   Desde que Thomas llegó ha aprendido mucho español.
   Since Thomas arrived he has learned a lot of Spanish.

   José lo oyó **desde** adentro.
   Jose heard him from inside.

2. **Hacia** refers to attitudes and feelings, as well as direction:

   Voy **hacia** el sur.
   I am going south.

   Sienten mucho amor **hacia** los animales.
   They feel deep affection for the animals.

   Hacia can be used in combination with adverbs of place, such as: **abajo, arriba, atrás, adelante, derecha, izquierda.**

   ¡Vaya **hacia abajo**!
   Go downward!

   El viene hacia ti.
   He is coming toward you.

3. **Hasta** has two meanings: even, and until. The meaning is clarified by the context of the sentence:

   Hasta yo entendí la explicación.
   Even I understood the explanation.

   Hasta aquí llega el autobús.
   This is the last bus stop.

4. **Sin** can be used with verbs or nouns:

   Voy **sin prisa.**
   I am not in a hurry.

   El profesor habla **sin parar.**
   The professor speaks without pause.

5. **Sobre** has a different meaning, it may mean above, about or around a certain time:

Pase **sobre** el puente.	Cross over the bridge.
El autobús va a llegar **sobre** las 4.	The bus will arrive around four.
La maleta está **sobre** la cama.	The suitcase is on (above) the bed.
John discutió **sobre** motos.	John discussed motorcycles.

Note that with the preposition **entre** the pronouns **yo** and tú **do** not change:
Livia está sentada entre **tú** y yo.

B. Preposiciones compuestas.

1. In Spanish, it is common to use compound prepositions. But most of the time, they are equivalent to simple prepositions and don't add any new to the meaning of those simple prepositions.

2. Some common compound prepositions are:

antes de	before	acerca de	about
al lado de	next to	a lo largo de	along
a pesar de	in spite of	a través (de)	through
cerca de	close to	con respecto a	concerning to
debajo de	under	delante de	in front of.
dentro de	inside of/within	después de	after
atrás de	behind	detrás de	behind
en contra de	against	encima de	on top of
enfrente de	across from	frente a	in front of
fuera de	out of/outside of	lejos de	far from
para con	for/with	por medio de	by means of
por encima de	over	junto a	right next to/
por causa de	because of		close to
adelantede	ahead of		

3. **Antes de** is used to describe an immediate past action or a physical location:

Antes de venir a México Thomas ya hablaba español.	**Before** coming to Mexico Thomas already spoke Spanish.
En la fila, **antes de** Thomas está John.	John is before Thomas in line.

4. **Delante de** is used to express a physical location:

Thomas está **delante de** José.	Thomas is **in front of** José.

257

5. **Atrás de** is also used to express a physical location:
Atrás de Thomas está Anna.   Anna is behind Thomas.

6. **Debajo de** is used to express a literal location:
La maleta está **debajo de** la cama.   The suitcase is **under** the bed.

7. **En contra de** usually expresses an ideological perspective that goes against somebody's ideas, policies, perspectives, etc.:
John está **en contra del** maltrato   John is **against** animal cruelty.
a los animales.

8. **En frente de** is used to express a spatial location either face to face or in front of:
Thomas está **en frente del** profesor.   Thomas is **in front of** the teacher.

9. **Al lado de** is used to express a literal location:
Al lado de Thomas está una señora.   Next to Thomas, there is a lady.

EJERCICIOS PRÁCTICOS

☺☺

A. Ask a classmate the following questions.
1.   ¿Desde cuándo estudias español?
2.   ¿Hasta qué capítulo llegaste?
3.   ¿Sobre qué es tu presentación?
4.   ¿La hiciste sin computadora?
5.   ¿Entre quiénes te sientas tú?
6.   ¿Según tú cuál ha sido la mejor película del siglo XXI?
7.   ¿Durante cuánto tiempo viviste en Montevideo?
8.   ¿Hacia quién tienes mayor afecto; tu hermana o tu hermano?
9.   Ella hizo su trabajo durante las vacaciones, ¿verdad?

✎

B. Complete the following sentences using the best compound prepositions:
1.   El avión no pudo despegar _____(because of) el mal tiempo.
2.   Lo que sé lo supe _____ (by means of) las noticias del Internet.
3.   Thomas está sentado _____ (next to) Carmen.
4.   Yo había puesto mi bolsa _____ (under) la silla.

5. La señorita está _____ (out of) sí.
6. El profesor está _____ (behind) los estudiantes.
7. John se sienta _____ (in front of) Lisa.
8. El avión vuela _____ (on top of) las nubes.
9. Yo aprendo _____ (in spite of) mi torpeza.
10. Los estudiantes caminan _____ (right next to) la carretera.

50. EL INFINITIVO DESPUÉS DE UNA PREPOSICIÓN.

1. In Spanish, one must always put the verb in the infinitive after a preposition:

Antes de partir no te olvides telefonearme.

Before leaving, don't forget to call me.

Sin decir nada se ha ido.
Para aprender ella habla todos los días.

He/she has left **without saying** anything.
In order to learn, she speaks daily.

He comenzado **a hablar.**

I have begun **to speak.**

He terminado **de hacer** la tarea.

I have finished **doing** my homework.

Note that the verb after the preposition is sometimes equivalent to an English verb form ending in -ing and sometimes to: to + verb.

EJERCICIOS PRÁCTICOS

A. Complete these sentences using a verb that matches in the infinitive form.
1. Yolanda va a _____.
2. El profesor viene de _____.
3. Los estudiantes están a punto de _____.
4. En México la gente trabaja para _____.
5. Jorge viene para _____ de la catedral de Puebla.
6. La familia Zurita está a punto de _____ a comer.
7. La señora Marín no va a _____ a los chicos a México.
8. El chofer sale para _____.
9. El policía llega para _____ orden.
10. José usó su teléfono celular para _____ al agente de seguros.

MINIRELATO: LA BASÍLICA (*BASÍLICA*) DE LA VIRGEN DE GUADALUPE.

Sin lugar a dudas, la Basílica de Guadalupe, la Villa de Guadalupe o simplemente "la Villita", es un santuario visitado por millones de **peregrinos** (*pilgrims*) cada año, especialmente el 12 de diciembre, día dedicado a honrar a la Virgen de Guadalupe.

La Villa de Guadalupe se encuentra al norte de la ciudad de México. La nueva Basílica tiene un diseño circular, de modo que la imagen de la Virgen pueda verse desde cualquier punto de la iglesia. Al frente, el templo tiene siete puertas que sirven no sólo para entrar y salir sino también para que circule el aire.

La Basílica tiene capacidad para recibir 100,000 **fieles** (*believers*). La nueva Basílica recibe cada año hasta 10 millones de peregrinos y es el templo más visitado después de la Basílica de San Pedro en el Vaticano.

El santuario de la Villa de Guadalupe, se remonta a la época prehispánica. En este lugar, El cerro del Tepeyac, se rendía culto a Tonantzin, **la deidad** (*Goddess*) azteca de la maternidad, cuya celebración se relacionaba con el solsticio de invierno.

En 1531, en plena conquista española, se afirma que la Virgen de Guadalupe se le apareció al indio Juan Diego y en el lugar de la aparición se construyó una **ermita** (*hermitage*), pero debido a la gran cantidad de peregrinaciones tuvo que ser demolida y se levantó un templo más grande, así como varias capillas que aún existen como el convento de las Capuchinas, el Templo del Pocito, la Capilla de Indios y la iglesia del Cerrito en lo alto del Cerro del Tepeyac.

En 1709, se comenzó con la construcción de la primera Basílica de Guadalupe, pero debido al hundimiento de sus cimientos se volvió riesgosa y ahora sirve como museo de arte religioso; a su lado se construyó la nueva Basílica que fue **diseñada** (*designed*) por el arquitecto mexicano Pedro Ramírez Vásquez, y se terminó de construir en 1976.

Preguntas

1. ¿Por qué la Basílica de Guadalupe es tan importante en México?
2. ¿Dónde está ubicada la Basílica?
3. ¿Con qué otros nombres se le conoce a la Basílica de Guadalupe?
4. ¿Cuántas puertas tiene el templo?

5.   ¿A qué divinidad los indígenas adoraban en el cerro del Tepeyac?
6.   ¿En qué año se apareció la Virgen de Guadalupe?
7.   ¿A quién se le apareció?
8.   ¿Qué se construyó en ese lugar?
9.   ¿Cuándo se empezó la construcción de la primera Basílica?
10. ¿Quién diseño la nueva Basílica?

CONVERSACIÓN: LA FAMILIA (CONTINUACIÓN)

John: Y cuando uno va de compras, ¿qué nos recomienda?

El profesor:Lo mejor sería que la primera vez fueran con alguien de la familia.Ahora bien, no tienen que preocuparse demasiado **sino** (*otherwise*) se van a arruinar la existencia.Hay que partir del hecho que los **comerciantes** (*shopkeepers*) siempre le suben los precios a los **extranjeros** (*foreigners*) por lo menos en un 35 **por ciento más** (*per cent above the price*) por ello, es importante aprender a **regatear** (*to bargain*).

Phillip: ¿Y cómo lo hacemos?

El profesor: Fíjate bien cómo lo hace tu hermana, o tu mamá o tu hermano o quien sea que te acompañe. Lo más seguro es que, esa persona ofrezca **la mitad del precio** (*half price*) para empezar a negociar.

David: ¡Guau, la mitad del precio!

El profesor: Sí, la mitad.No estoy diciendo que lo que quieren comprar lo van a obtener a mitad de precio, pero es **un punto de partida** (*a starting point*); si logran que les bajen un 25 o 30 por ciento habrán comprado **casi** (*almost*) como un **nativo** (*native*).

Andrew: Profesor, ¿qué es lo que los mexicanos piensan de nosotros?

El profesor: ¡Ah.!

Jesse (Concepción):Perdón profesor, yo creo que los mexicanos piensan que somos ricos, trabajadores, pero muy **ingenuos** (*naïve*).

El profesor: Ciertamente, quizá más que trabajadores que **nos gusta trabajar** (*workaholics*), puede ser que muchos crean que los estadounidenses son ricos; ingenuos **sin duda** (*no doubt*), generosos también, francos, honestos, desorganizados, inteligentes pero increíblemente **ignorantes** (*ignorant*) de lo que pasa en el mundo, modestos pero complicados, un poco **descontrolados** (*without control*) para beber, aunque esto es una **paradoja** (*paradox*) pues los mexicanos suelen tomar mucho también.

Andrew: ¿Tanto como nosotros?

Preguntas

1. ¿Qué piensa usted de los estereotipos?
2. ¿Cree que los estadounidenses son todos ricos?
3. ¿Cree usted que los estadounidenses son todos honestos?
4. ¿Cree usted que los estadounidenses beben mucho?
5. ¿Cree que los estadounidenses ignoran mucho de lo que pasa en otras partes?
6. ¿Cree que en verdad les gusta trabajar en exceso?
7. ¿Por qué los negociantes les suben los precios a los turistas?
8. ¿Ha regateado usted alguna vez al comprar?
9. ¿Qué hace si el precio le parece muy alto?
10. ¿Usted cree que a los mexicanos les gusta tomar tanto como a los estadounidenses o más?

VOCABULARIO

VERBOS

comenzar	construir	terminar
diseñar	regatear	comprar
escribir	detestar	gustar
beber	trabajar	haber
rogar	freír	escribir
salir	despertarse	sonar
llover	empezar	ser
tomar	pensar	subir
adorar	aparecer	

NOMBRES

la catedral	la basílica	el templo
la ermita	la capilla	el santuario
la iglesia	la sinagoga	la mezquita
el mercado	la ciudad	los albañiles
la paz	el/la taxista	millas
la hora	los bomberos	los incendios
un simulacro	el profesor	los vecinos
un hermano	la paradoja	la intolerancia
la Villita	una divinidad	

ADJETIVOS

ingenuos/as	ricos/as	trabajadores/as
generosos/as	francos/as	honestos/as
ignorantes	modestos	complicados/as
desordenados/as	seis	descontrolados/as
nueve	dos	tres
cuatro	mexicanos/as	nativo/a
negociantes	ingenuos	tanto/a

ADVERBIOS

ciertamente	increíblemente	muy
ya	todavía	cuando
verdaderamente	alegremente	ahora

PREPOSICIONES

por	para	sin
entre	debajo de	a dento
junto	hacia	a pesar de
al lado de	antes de	en contra de
en frente de	frente a	atrás de
junto a	sobre	sobre de

EXPRESIONES UTILES

por cierto	a mitad de precio	una paradoja
para variar	para siempre	para que
por favor	por suerte	

CAPÍTULO 11: UN PEQUEÑO ACCIDENTE

En este capítulo...

You'll learn more about Mexican driving habits, how to express anger, and how to deal with a difficult situation when you are abroad. You'll study the uses of demonstrative pronouns, the adverbs, a variety of command forms in Spanish, including the informal commands, the uses of "se" impersonal and how to use comparatives and superlatives.

Contexto

José y Thomas van en el coche al centro de la ciudad para recoger un material que necesita Yolanda cuando, de pronto se oye el rechinar de unos frenos y sienten un leve golpe en la parte posterior de su coche.

El chofer del otro coche (un joven), abre la puerta y sale de su coche irritado, gesticulando y gritando: ¿Qué pasó señor?, ¿por qué se frenó tan de repente? Usted tiene la culpa de que le haya pegado. Yo no pensé que se fuera a parar así tan de pronto y ya ve lo que sucedió.

José (ya fuera del coche y viendo el daño leve hecho a su carro): Espérate mano, vamos por partes y no te exaltes que somos gente educada. Y este problema lo vamos a resolver como personas civilizadas que somos. ¿Estamos? Así es que no grites, ni te alteres.

El otro chofer (ya más tranquilo): Bueno si, discúlpeme señor, es que...

Un agente de policía llega a la escena en su motocicleta.

Policía: Vamos a ver señores, ¿qué fue lo que pasó aquí?

El otro chofer: Es que aquí el señor que se frenó de repente y yo ya no me pude detener a tiempo para evitar pegarle.

Policía (viendo el daño al coche de José): Y, usted, ¿por qué se frenó señor?

José: Bueno, lo que pasó oficial, es que frente a mí, un niño empezó a bajar de la banqueta y pensé que se me iba a atravesar.

Policía: ¡Me muestran sus licencias de manejo, la tarjeta de circulación de los vehículos y su póliza de seguro, por favor!

José (dirigiéndose a Thomas): Pásame el sobre con documentos que está en ese compartimento.

Thomas: ¿Éste?

José: Sí, ése. Gracias Thomas.

José (dirigiéndose al policía): Aquí tiene los documentos, oficial.

Policía: Gracias señor. Y usted joven, ¿sus papeles?

El otro chofer: Es que no tengo licencia de manejo, oficial.

Policía: ¡Cómo que no tienes licencia!

El otro chofer: No, yo no tengo ningún documento y no sé si el coche tiene seguro.

El policía: ¡Dame al menos la tarjeta de circulación!

El otro chofer: Y, ¿dónde puede estar eso?

El policía: Búscala en la guantera del auto. Si no la encuentras tendrás que acompañarme a la delegación.

José (dirigiéndose al joven): ¿Cómo puedes manejar sin papeles muchacho?

En ese momento, llega el agente de la compañía de seguros, a quien José ha llamado desde su teléfono celular.

Preguntas

1. ¿Cómo ocurrió el accidente?
2. ¿Es que es un accidente grave con heridos?
3. ¿Hace falta que lleguen las ambulancias?
4. ¿Cómo se baja de su coche el chofer joven?
5. ¿Qué le dice José?
6. ¿Qué les pide el policía?
7. ¿Qué le pide José a Thomas que le pase?
8. ¿Tiene el joven sus documentos en regla?
9. ¿Quién cree usted que tiene la culpa?
10. ¿Le parece justo que quien pega pague?

NOTA CULTURAL: PEDIR AVENTÓN Y EL TÉRMINO ARREGLARSE.

1. **Pedir aventón** (*to hitchhike*) nunca ha sido común en México y ahora lo es menos. Pero para aquellos que se aventuran a hacerlo, se usa el mismo gesto que en los Estados Unidos, el dedo pulgar (el dedo gordo) de la mano derecha señalando en la misma dirección del tráfico. Por la situación de inseguridad que actualmente vive el país, no es recomendable pedir aventón en México, pues puede resultar muy peligroso.

2. **Arreglarse.** Es una palabra que se emplea en México en caso de un accidente menor, para tratar de evitar la intervención de la policía y no complicar más las cosas. Arreglarse significa, llegar a un acuerdo entre las personas involucradas en un accidente menor, donde no hay heridos ni daños graves.

3. After an accident, you may say that the two drivers: "**que se insultan** como peseros" ("They swear like troopers" -literally, bus drivers). You can also say that both drivers "se dan hasta con la cubeta" ("are up the creek without a paddle").

EJERCICIOS PRÁCTICOS

☺ ☺

A. Ask the following questions to a classmate.

1. ¿Ha pedido alguna vez aventón? (*hitch a lift*)
2. Si la respuesta es afirmativa, ¿qué experiencias ha tenido?
3. Si la respuesta es negativa, ¿por qué no ha pedido aventón nunca?
4. ¿Ha estado alguna vez involucrado en un accidente de tránsito?
5. Si la respuesta es afirmativa, conteste las siguientes preguntas:
6. ¿en qué circunstancias?
7. ¿qué ha hecho?
8. ¿se han arreglado entre ustedes o ha intervenido la policía?
9. Si la respuesta es negativa, ¿sabe de alguien que haya estado involucrado en un accidente?
10. ¿Sabe usted cómo contactar a la policía en caso de una emergencia?
11. ¿Sabe usted cómo contactar a su compañía de seguros?

Dichos

Del dicho al hecho hay mucho trecho.	There's many a slip twixt the cup and the lip.
El camino al infierno está lleno de buenas intenciones.	The road to hell is paved with good intentions.

VOCABULARIO: ¡UN ARRESTO!

La policía[92]	The police
Procuraduría General de la República (PGR)	Mexican FBI
Escuadrón de asaltos	SWAT squad
Delegación de Policía	Police Commissioner
Oficial de Policía	Police Officer
Un detective	a detective
Un criminal	a criminal
Un ratero	a thief
Un ladrón	a burglar
Un robo	a burglary
Un asalto	an assault
El reclusorio	federal prison

[92] Recuerde que en México la población, en general, desconfía de la policía y muy rara vez solicita su ayuda.

Las huellas digitales	fingerprints

Un incendio/un fuego — **Fire**

llamas	flames
humo	smoke
bomberos	fire fighters
el hidrante	hydrant
la manguera	fire hose
un extinguidor	fire extinguisher
sistema de alarmas	alarm system

El hospital — **The hospital**

la ambulancia	the ambulance
un/a doctor/a	a doctor
un/a enfermero/a	a nurse
el encargado de la farmacia	a pharmacist
una clínica	a clinic
la sala de urgencias	(ER) emergency room

SERVICIOS DE EMERGENCIA A NIVEL NACIONAL (México)

Seguridad Pública: 911
Policía Judicial: 117
Policía Federal De Caminos: 062
Radio Patrullas: 066
Cruz Roja: 065
Información General: 040
Bomberos: 068
Reportes de Fallas en el servicio de Luz: 071
Quejas de Servidores Públicos (SACTEL): 072
RESCATEL: 100
Ángeles Verdes (Auxilio Turístico): 120
PROFECO (Procuraduría Federal del Consumidor): 079
Policía Federal Preventiva: *112
LOCATEL: 119
Dirección General de Protección Civil: 56 83 11 42

Escuadrón de Rescate y Urgencias Médicas: 57 22 88 05

Here is an **interactive link** with a list of emergency numbers in Mexico:

Preguntas

INTERACTIVE LINK

bookstudio.pro/nq9

1. Cuando ocurre un incendio, ¿a quién hay que llamar?
2. Cuando ocurre un asalto, ¿a quién hay que llamar?
3. Cuando ocurre un accidente, ¿a quién hay que llamar?

EJERCICIOS PRÁCTICOS

☺☺

A. Emplee el vocabulario ilustrado para las siguientes situaciones.

1. Hay un asalto en un banco.¿Qué se debe hacer?
   Modelo: El empleado toca, con suma discreción, el botón de la alarma. Inmediatamente la delegación de policía va a enviar

2. Usted pasa delante de una casa y de pronto ve humo saliendo de esa casa, ¿qué hay que hacer?
   Modelo: Yo marco el número *080 de emergencias y notifico el lugar del incendio con la esperanza de que lleguen los bomberos...

3. Usted va manejando por la autopista y ve un accidente muy grave, ¿qué hace?
   Modelo: Estaciono el coche, a la orilla de la autopista, llamo al teléfono de emergencias para reportar el accidente y veo si puedo ayudar en algo...

Más vocabulario: Los proyectos

encontrarse	to meet	porque	because
el ballet	the ballet	regresar	to go back/to return
la limonada	the lemonade	el mesero	the waiter/waitress
entusiasmados	excited	a casa	going home
en poco tiempo	in a little while	los boletos	tickets

una cerveza	a beer	la terraza	the deck/the terrace
la cuenta	the bill/the check	la propina	the tip
la caja	the cashier/the box	el cambio	the change

EJERCICIOS PRÁCTICOS

A. Escuche y comprenda.

Anna le telefonea a Thomas y a John para encontrarse en la terraza del Café Macondo. La señora Bernal le ha regalado cuatro boletos para ir al Palacio de Bellas Artes, en la Ciudad de México, el sábado próximo para ver el Ballet Folclórico de Amalia Hernández. Ella quiere que se reúnan para planear el viaje y hacer un proyecto para la clase de Cultura de México.

Como Anna tiene cuatro boletos, ella pregunta a sus amigos ¿quién les gustaría que fuera con ellos? Los dos piensan que Lisa sería la indicada y Anna está de acuerdo. Anna le telefonea y Lisa acepta juntarse con ellos en poco tiempo en la terraza del café.

Cuando llega Lisa, uno de los meseros se acerca a su mesa y les pregunta "¿Si desean tomar algo?"

Anna pide una naranjada con agua mineral, Lisa pide una limonada con agua natural, Thomas pide una Coca Cola y John una cerveza. Un instante después el mesero sirve lo ordenado.

Un instante después los jóvenes discuten las posibilidades del viaje a México. De pronto Lisa dice: "Mi madre tiene un Jetta nuevo, del año. Le voy a preguntar si ella nos puede llevar a México. Le voy a decir que ella necesita probar su nuevo coche en la carretera". Todos ellos están entusiasmados con la idea. Si falla, tendrán que irse en autobús.

Es hora de regresar a casa y Thomas le hace una señal al mesero para que se acerque. ¿Cuánto le debemos? pregunta. El mesero, hace la cuenta y les da el recibo diciendo: "son novecientos pesos". John le pregunta, "¿la propina está incluida?" "No señor", responde el mesero un poco sorprendido por la pregunta.

Después de que Thomas le da el dinero, el mesero va a la caja y regresa con el cambio y el recibo.

☺☺
B. Ahora es su turno. Haga estas preguntas a otro estudiante.
1. ¿Por qué Anna telefonea a sus compañeros?
2. ¿Qué van a ver en el Palacio de Bellas Artes?
3. ¿Dónde está el Palacio de Bellas Artes?
4. ¿Dónde se reúnen los amigos?
5. ¿A quién llama Anna después?
6. ¿Es que Lisa acepta ir con ellos?
7. ¿Qué les pregunta el mesero?
8. ¿Qué le responden ellos?
9. ¿Qué propone Lisa?
10. ¿Cuál es la excusa que va a usar Lisa?

☺☺
C. Si usted decidiera ir al teatro, ¿qué tipo de obra le gustaría ver? Si tuviera que ir a otra ciudad, ¿qué medio de transporte usaría? ¿iría solo o invitaría a otros amigos?. ¡Haga sus propios proyectos!

APUNTES GRAMATICALES
51. LOS PRONOMBRES DEMOSTRATIVOS

1. A demonstrative pronoun may replace a noun preceded by a demonstrative adjective. The pronoun agrees in gender and number with the noun replaced. The forms of the demonstrative pronouns are as follows:

	MASCULINE	FEMININE
SINGULAR	este ese aquel	esta esa aquella
PLURAL	estos esos aquellos	estas esas aquellas

2. There is also a neuter set of demonstrative pronouns: **esto, eso, aquello**
¿Qué es **esto**?   ¿Qué es **eso**?   ¿Qué es **aquello**?

Note that you do not have to write an accent mark on the demonstrative pronouns. If you want to know more about the new rules you can check the web site of the Real Academia de la Lengua Española: http://www.rae.es

3. Neuter pronouns are used to refer to situations, ideas, or things that are

general or unidentified. This neuter pronoun is equivalent to the English "this" or "that" referring to matter, business, stuff, things:

¿Qué piensa Yolanda de **eso**?   What does Yolanda think about **that?**

4. On certain occasions, a demonstrative pronoun needs to be with an adverb of place to clarify the object:

No quiero esta bolsa, quiero **esa**   I don't want this bag, I want **that**
que está **allá**.   **one over there.**

5. A demonstrative pronoun may be followed by **que** and a relative clause:

Aquellos que comen poco duermen   **Those who** eat little sleep well.
bien.

Aquellos que ríen mucho viven más.   **Those who** laugh a lot live longer.

EJERCICIOS PRÁCTICOS

A. Complete the sentences with the correct demonstrative pronoun.
    1.   Yolanda no quiere este coche, quiere _____.
    2.   A los estudiantes no les gusta este maestro prefieren _____.
    3.   A los niños no les gusta esta comida, prefieren _____.
    4.   Yo no quiero este sombrero, quiero _____.
    5.   A Thomas no le gusta esa chica, le gusta _____.
    6.   ¿Va a llevarse esta camisa o _____?
    7.   ¿Vas a ponerte esta falda o _____?
    8.   Prefieres este color o _____?
    9.   Gustas de estos muebles o de _____?
    10.   A los jóvenes no les gusta este barrio o prefieren _____.

☺ ☺

B. Help your classmate make the following decisions by answering the questions with the correct demonstrative pronoun.
    1.   ¿Quieres este automóvil o ese?
    2.   ¿Prefieres este suéter de color verde o aquel?
    3.   ¿Te gusta esta corbata o esa?
    4.   ¿Prefieres estos patines o aquellos?
    5.   ¿Quieres comprar estos zapatos o esos?
    6.   ¿Me queda mejor esta camisa o esa?
    7.   ¿Cuál es más bonito este reloj o ese?

52. LOS ADVERBIOS

1. Adverbs modify verbs, adjectives, or other adverbs:

   Él habla **bien** español.　　　　He speaks Spanish **well.**

   Ella habla **lentamente.**　　　　She speaks **slowly.**

2. An adverb may appear in several places in a sentence:

   a. An adverb is usually placed immediately after the verb in a simple tense:
   Ellos hablan **rápidamente.**　　　They speak **quickly.**

   b. Sometimes an adverb may appear at the beginning of a sentence especially when it is being emphasized:
   Desafortunadamente él no comprendió.　　　　**Unfortunately**, he did not understand.

   c. An adverb of time or place may either begin or end a sentence[93]:
   Ayer, José tuvo un accidente.　　**Yesterday**, Jose had an accident.
   José tuvo un accidente **ayer.**　　Jose had an accident **yesterday.**

3. Many adjectives can be made into adverbs:
   a. If the masculine singular form of an adjective ends in the **−o**, make the adjective feminine and then add the ending **−mente**:

   absolut**o**　⇒ absolut**a**　　⇒ absolut**amente**

   b. If the masculine singular form of an adjective ends in any other vowel or consonant, simply add the ending **-mente**:

   fuerte⇒ fuert**emente**

   cruel ⇒cruel**mente**

---

[93] The rule for the position of the adverb is not rigorous. As you use Spanish more and more, you will develop a natural feeling for the placement of adverbs.

4. If the adjective already has a written accent mark keep it. If it doesn't have it, do not add it:

    fácil⇒ fácilmente

    gentil ⇒ gentilmente

5. In Spanish you cannot use two adverbs ending in **—mente** in the same sentence, as you can in English:
    Él actuó cruel**mente** y despiadad**amente. (incorrect in Spanish)**
    Él actuó **cruel** y despiadad**amente.**

    Note that **cruel** is here an adverb, and has dropped the suffix —mente.

6. But remember that if the first adjective ends in an **—o** it has to be changed into the feminine form in order to become an adverb, and only the second adverb gets the suffix **—mente**:
    Ella actuó tiern**a** y amigable**mente.**

7. You have already seen many common adverbs, such as **hoy, todos los días, más, muy, casi, bien, mal, allá.** Here you have other common adverbs:

ADVERBIOS DE TIEMPO

pronto	soon
desde	since
tarde	late
temprano	early
mañana	tomorrow

ADVERBIOS DE CANTIDAD

suficiente	enough
tanto	so much/ so many
poco	little
demasiado	too much/ too many
otro tanto	another bit

ADVERBIOS DE LUGAR

cerca	near
lejos	far
allá	there
aquí	here
allí/ahí	there
más allá	over there

ADVERBIOS DE PROBABILIDAD

probablemente	probably
quizá (s)	perhaps
acaso	maybe
sin duda	without any doubt
seguramente	possibly
tal vez	maybe

EJERCICIOS PRÁCTICOS

A. Form sentences with two adverbs.

Modelo: Ella le habla (serio) (apasionado)

Ella le habla seriamente.

Ella le habla seria y apasionadamente.

1. Ellos se rehusan a trabajar. (arduo) (correcto)
2. Él le responde. (apasionado) (valiente)
3. Nosotros repetimos. (lento) (torpe)
4. *Vosotros gastáis* dinero. (tonto) (indiscriminado)
5. Ella baila. (elegante) (rítmico)
6. Yolanda maneja. (agresivo) (intrépido)

B. Change the adjective in parentheses into an adverb.

Modelo: Eso es divertido. (profundo)

Eso es profundamente divertido.

1. Él está solo. (virtual)
2. Ellos están felices. (loco)
3. Nosotros emprendemos el regreso. (paciente)
4. *Vosotros pensáis* en ella. (constante)
5. Martín ha respondido. (seco)
6. José hace su trabajo. (mecánico)
7. Los Zurita viven. (alegre)

☺ ☺

C. Complete las frases con el adverbio adecuado.

1. Ella canta _____.
2. Yolanda conduce _____ y _____.
3. José trabaja _____ y _____.
4. Martín estudia _____.
5. El profesor enseña _____ y _____.
6. Los alumnos se comportan _____.
7. Thomas ayuda _____.
8. Anna llama _____.
9. Lisa y su novio se aman _____ y _____.

53. LOS MANDATOS INFORMALES Y OTRAS FORMAS DE MANDATOS

A. AFFIRMATIVE INFORMAL COMMANDS

1. Singular affirmative informal commands have the same conjugation as the third person singular in the present tense:

Indicativo tercera persona:	Ella **vende** casas.	She **sells** houses.
Mandato informal (tú):	**¡Vende la casa!**	**Sell** the house!

2. The following verbs have irregular informal commands:

decir	**di**	hacer	**haz**	ir	**ve**
poner	**pon**	salir	**sal**	ser	**sé**
tener	**ten**	venir	**ven**		

   Note that in some cases the command is formed by dropping the family ending of the infinitive of the verb. For example the verb **tener, you** drop the **–er** of the family and what you get is the informal command **ten**.

   Note also that the affirmative command for **ir** and **ver** is the same ¡**ve**! Only the context will clarify the meaning.

3. Affirmative informal commands for the first person plural **nosotros**, often take the form of **ir** + **a** + a place or a verb in infinitive. This type of command has two forms, the one that has the Direct Object Pronoun attached to the verb **ir**, and the other one without the Direct Object Pronoun. Both mean *let's go*, and it is a matter of preferences to use one or the other:

¡Vámonos **al partido**!	Let's go to the game!
¡Vamos **a trabajar**!	Let's go to work!

4. The Informal affirmative command for the second person plural *vosotros* is made by replacing the **–r** of the infinitive by **–d**, for example, the verb **cerrar**:
   ¡Cerra**d** la puerta!

   Note that when the infinitive is a reflexive verb the **–d** is never placed:
   Verbo reflexivo en infinitivo. Take for example the verb **bañarse**:
   ¡Bañaos rápido!
   The only exception to this rule is the reflexive form of the verb **ir (irse)**, this verb retains the **–d**:
   ¡**idos** pronto!

EJERCICIOS PRÁCTICOS

A. We are all on edge. Change the verbs form in the infinitive into informal tú commands.

Modelo: Salir a dar un paseo!

¡**Sal** a dar un paseo!

1. Ir a la discoteca.
2. Hacer ejercicio.
3. Tomarse un té de tila.
4. Ver a los amigos.
5. Comprarse un coche.
6. Dormir la siesta.
7. Venir al parque.

B. Write the correct command to complete the sentences.

1. Thomas, ¡_____(comerse) toda la comida!
2. John, ¡_____ (ponerle) gasolina a la moto!
3. Anna, ¡_____ (sacar) la basura!
4. Martín, ¡_____ (comprar) el pan!
5. Concepción, ¡_____ (hacer) la tarea!
6. David, ¡_____ (ir) al mercado!
7. Yolanda, ¡_____ (contarnos) un cuento!
8. Jorge, ¡_____ (encender) la luz!
9. Lisa, ¡_____ (tener cuidado) al cruzar la calle!

B. MANDATOS USANDO VERBOS EN INFINITIVO

1. Very often Spanish newspaper ads for employment, recipes, and instructions use the infinitive of the verb as imperative:
   Interesados favor de **enviar** Curriculum Vitae (CV).
   Interested candidates, please send your resume.
   Después de un rato, **freír** el arroz en el sartén con el aceite caliente.
   After awhile, fry the rice in hot oil.

2. The infinitive of a verb is used in phrases that express or suggest

formality and politeness. Those expressions convey the use of "**please**" in English:

¡Favor de no **fumar**!   **Don't smoke**, please!

¡**Firmar** el documento, por favor!   S**ign** the document, please!

EJERCICIOS PRÁCTICOS

A. Change the verbs from the imperative to the infinitive.
   Modelo: ¡Estudien el capítulo preliminar!
                 ¡Estudiar el capítulo preliminar!
   1.   ¡Vayan al laboratorio para practicar!
   2.   ¡Hagan la tarea en grupos!
   3.   ¡Entréguensela al profesor asistente!
   4.   ¡No olviden ver el capítulo de la telenovela esta noche!
   5.   Mañana, por favor, ¡traigan un diccionario!

B. Change the verbs from the infinitive to the imperative.
   Modelo: ¡Cortar el pollo!
                 ¡Corte el pollo!
   1.   ¡Poner un chorro de vino blanco!
   2.   ¡Añadir una pizca de sal!
   3.   ¡Poner la mesa!
   4.   ¡Servir la comida!
   5.   ¡Retirar la mesa!

C. MANDATOS INDIRECTOS

1. Indirect commands in Spanish are formed by the relative pronoun **que** +
   a formal command that you studied those commands in **Chapter 8**. The English equivalents are **let** or **have somebody do something**:

   ¡**Que pase**!   Have him/her come in!

2. When using indirect commands, direct and indirect objects as well as reflexive pronouns are placed before the verb:

   ¡**Que se sienten**!   Please take a seat!/Let them sit!

   ¡**Que les den de comer**!   Let them be fed!

3. It is common to add a pronoun to indirect commands to clarify who has to obey the command:

   ¡**Que lo traiga él**!   Let him bring it.

4. Indirect commands are commonly used with impersonal expressions using **se** and indirect object pronouns. However, they are usually translated by using regular commands in English:

¡Que no se les vaya a olvidar el pan!   Don't forget to bring the bread!

EJERCICIOS PRÁCTICOS

A. Use que + a formal command to form indirect commands.
   Modelo: Yo no quiero ir. (ellas)
                ¡Que vayan ellas!
   1.   No quiero leer. (él)
   2.   No tengo ganas de jugar. (los demás)
   3.   No pienso sentarme a esperar. (mi mamá)
   4.   No deseo hacer la tarea. (mis hermanas)
   5.   No quiero ir al banco. (mi papá)

54. LOS USOS DE "SE" IMPERSONAL

1. Spanish uses **se** + a verb in third person, singular or plural. The number depends on whether the grammatical subject is singular or plural. The agent of the sentence is not used in this type of construction in order to deemphasize the subject:

Se venden coches usados.   Used cars are sold here.

Note that in English, these sentences are translated in many different ways.

2. For intransitive verbs (verbs that do not have a direct object) the verb is always in the third person singular form:

¡Se come bien en España!   One eats well in Spain.

3. If the verb is reflexive, the only way to use **se** with a deemphasized subject is by adding **uno** or **una** (if the reference is feminine) to a third person singular verb:

Uno se despierta más tarde cuando **está** de vacaciones.
One wakes up later when one is on vacation.

4. In Spanish we use **se** in sentences where someone is trying to "save face":
El coche **se arruinó.**   **The car was ruined.**

5. In Spanish we use **se** in questions that are looking for a single word translation:

¿Cómo **se dice** "enthusiastically" en español?	How does one say "enthusiastically" in Spanish?
Se dice ...	One says…
No sé cómo se dice...	I don't know how to say that…

6. In Spanish we use **se** in asking for directions:
¿Cómo **se llega** al aeropuerto JF Kennedy?
How does one go to JFK airport?

7. In Spanish we use **se** in announcements or ads:

Se venden libros usados.	Used books are sold here.

8. In Spanish we use **se** in sentences to advise that another language is spoken in a particular place:

Se habla español.	Spanish is spoken.

9. In Spanish we also use **se** in recipes:

¿Cómo **se hace** una ensalada?	How does one make a salad?
Se lava la lechuga,	One washes the lettuce,
S**e cortan** los tomates...	One cuts the tomatoes…

EJERCICIOS PRÁCTICOS

A. We are still getting acquainted with our new surroundings. Use the impersonal 'se' to talk about what is sold in each neighborhood store.
   Modelo: En una pollería...
                     Se venden pollos.
   1.   En una tienda de electrodomésticos...
   2.   En una librería...
   3.   En una tienda de telas...
   4.   En una licorería...
   5.   En una zapatería

   ☺ ☺

B. Ask a classmate the following questions.
   1.   ¿Cómo se hace una hamburguesa?

2. ¿Cómo se llega al Ángel de la Independencia?
3. ¿Cómo se dice "collar" en inglés?
4. ¿Cómo se prepara una margarita?
5. ¿Cómo se va al Gran Cañón?
6. ¿Cómo se dice "Wolf" en español?
7. ¿Cómo se vive en España?
8. ¿Cómo se comunica la gente ahora?

55. COMPARATIVOS DE DESIGUALDAD, IGUALDAD Y EL USO DE LOS SUPERLATIVOS

1. **Comparatives of inequality**. Adjectives adverbs, verbs, or nouns may be compared by using the forms: **más ... que** or **menos ... que**:

a. **más... que** and **menos... que** are comparisons that express inequality:

Thomas es **más** alto **que** Martín.	Thomas is **taller than** Martin.
Martín tiene **menos** dinero **que** Thomas.	Martin has **less** money **than** Thomas.
John escribe **menos** seguido **que** Lisa.	John writes **less often than** Lisa
Thomas corre **más que** el profesor.	Thomas runs **more than** the professor.

b. The form **más... que**, **menos... que** may also used to contrast ideas:

Yo tengo **más** dinero **que** sentido común.	I have **more** money **than** common sense.

Note that **más bueno** and **más malo** express moral qualities:

El profesor es **más bueno que** el pan.	The professor is a very good guy.
Ese hombre es **más** malo **que** el mismo diablo.	That man is worse than the evil.

c. **que** is followed by subject pronouns unless the pronoun is a direct or an indirect object. In that case, it is followed by the preposition "a" that makes explicit the indirect object:

Thomas escribe **más que** nadie en clase.
A ella le gusta escribir **más que** a Thomas.

d. **que** is replaced by **de** before a numeral:
José gana **más de** 300 pesos al día.

e. **que** is also replaced by **de** before **el que, lo que, la que, los que, las que**. The article replaces the noun:
El profesor tiene **menos** libros **de lo que** yo esperaba.
Nuestra clase es **la que** estudia más.

2. **Comparatives of equality.**
a. **tan... como** is a comparison of equality that works with adjectives and adverbs:

John es **tan** inteligente **como** Jesse.	John is as intelligent as Jesse.
Thomas escribe **tan** a menudo **como** John.	Thomas writes **as often as** John.

b. **tanto/tanta... como** is a comparison of equality used with verbs or qualitative nouns:

José camina **tanto como** el profesor.	Jose walks **as much as** the professor.
Ella tiene **tanta** libertad **como** yo.	She has **as much** freedom **as** I do.
Bill Gates tiene **tanto** dinero **como** Jeff Bezos.	Bill Gates has **as much** money **as** Jeff Bezos.

c. **tantos/tantas... como** as a comparison of equality is used for quantitative nouns, and they always agree with the gender of the noun that follow it:

Usted tiene **tantos** coches **como** él.	You have **as many** cars **as** he does.
Ella tiene **tantas** bolsas **como** tú.	She has **as many** bags **as** you do.

Note that if you place the word "no" before the verb you are making an inequality comparison in a very unusual form:

Yo **no** soy tan inteligente como él.	I am not as smart as he is.
John **no** trabaja tanto como Thomas.	John does not work as much as Thomas.
Ella **no** tiene tanto dinero como ellos.	She does not have as much money as they do.
Tú **no** tienes tantos hermanos como yo.	You do not have as many brothers as I do.

3. **To form the superlative of an adjective use:el, la, los, las más... de:**
Lisa es **la más** inteligente **de** todos.   Lisa is **the smartest** of all.
el, la, los, las menos de:
Thomas y John son **los menos** tímidos **de** la clase.
Thomas and John are **the least** shy of the class.

4. **To form the superlative of a noun use**: el, la, los, las que más... de:
Andrés es **el que más** hermanos tiene **de** toda la clase.
Andrés has **the most** siblings of the entire class.

   el, la, los, las que menos... de:
Andrea es **la que menos** dinero tiene **de** todos mis alumnos.
Andrea has **the least** money out of all my students.

   Note that in this construction, **de** is used to mean "in" or "of".

   Note also than in a superlative construction, the adjective or noun remains in its usual position:
La catedral de Puebla tiene **las** torres **más altas de** México.
The cathedral in Puebla has **the highest** towers **in** Mexico.

   Los Zurita son **los que menos** hijos tienen en su colonia.
The Zurita have the **least** children in the neighborhood.

5. **Some adjectives have irregular comparative and superlative forms**:
   bueno/a (s)   good
   mejor (es)... que   better than
   el mejor, la mejor, los mejores, las mejores... de   best of/in
   Examples:
   Es una **buena** idea.   It is a **good** idea.
   Esta camisa es **mejor que** aquella.   This shirt is **better than** that one.

   Note that in Spanish you never use the expression "más mejor... que", you only can say "mejor... que":
   Ella es mejor que él.   She is better than him.

6. **Other irregular adjectives are**:

malo	peor... que	el, la, los las peor (es)... de
grande	mayor... que	el, la, los, las mayor (es)... de
pequeño	menor... que	el, la, los, las menor (es)... de

Mi hermana es **la menor de** la familia.
My sister is **the youngest** in the family.

7. The superlative of an adverb is rarely used in Spanish except for the adverbs **bien** and **mal**, which have the same irregular comparisons and superlatives as the adjectives:

bien ⇒ mejor... que ⇒   el, la, los, las que mejor (es)... de:

Jesse escribe **bien**.	Jesse writes **well**.
Jesse escribe **mejor que** yo.	Jesse writes **better than** me.
Jesse es **la que mejor** escribe **de** la clase.	Jesse is **the best** writer in the class.

Mal⇒ peor que⇒   el, la, los, las peor (es)... de:

Yo vivo **mal**.	**I live badly**.
Él vive **peor que** yo.	He lives **worse than** me.
Ellos son **los que peor** viven **de** todos nosotros.	They live the worst out of all of us.

Note these two frequently used idiomatic expressions with the adverbs **mejor** and **peor**:

tanto mejor: Thomas va a México por un semestre. **Tanto mejor** para él.
Thomas goes to Mexico for a semester.Good for him.

tanto peor: Yo no pude ir a México. **Tanto peor** para mí.
I could not go to Mexico. Too bad for me.

EJERCICIOS PRÁCTICOS

A. Transform these sentences by using superlatives.

Modelo: Es un buen estudiante.   He is a good student.
                  Es el mejor estudiante de todos.   He is the best student of all.

1.   Es un mal chofer.

2. Es un buen empleado.
3. Yolanda es la más vieja de la familia.
4. Martín es el más joven.
5. Es un buen médico.
6. Es un mal hospital.

B. Create sentences using comparatives with the information provided.
   Modelo: Jesse tiene 20 años/David 19. (mayor)
   Jesse es mayor que David.
   1. John tiene un BMW/José un Ford. (rico)
   2. Thomas reprueba los exámenes. Anna los pasa. (inteligente)
   3. Paul perdió su dinero. María perdió su lápiz. (descuidado)
   4. Jim escucha con atención. Roberto no se concentra. (impaciente)
   5. Elena viste a la moda. Sonia no. (moderna)

C. Change the sentences to practice all of the comparative phrases.
   Modelo: Ella tiene más hermanos que hermanas. (menos) (tantos)
   Ella tiene menos hermanas que hermanos.
   Ella tiene tantos hermanos como hermanas.
   1. Ella tiene tantos zapatos como su hermana. (menos) (más)
   2. Tú tienes menos maletas que tu mamá. (más) (tantas)
   3. El gato come tanto como el perro. (menos) (más)
   4. Thomas maneja mejor que Kevin. (peor) (tan)
   5. Jim tiene tanta libertad como su sobrina. (menos) (más)
   6. John bebe más vino que su hija. (tanto) (menos)

D. Complete these sentences using the correct formula to establish comparatives.
   Modelo: Supermán es _____ fuerte _____ un león. (desigualdad)
   Supermán es **más** fuerte **que** un león.
   1. Un elefante es _____ grande _____ un ratón.(desigualdad)
   2. El profesor es _____viejo _____ Ryan. (desigualdad)
   3. Un Ferrari es _____ caro _____un Toyota. (desigualdad)
   4. Un abogado gana _____ _____ un barrendero.(desigualdad)
   5. Yo tengo _____ hijos _____ Brad Pitt.

E. Complete using the correct formula to establish comparatives.
   Modelo: Supermán es _____ guapo _____ el capitán América. (igualdad)

Supermán es **tan** guapo **como** el capitán América.

1. Un toro es _____ fuerte_____ un búfalo. (igualdad)
2. Yo tengo _____ dinero _____ tú. (igualdad)
3. Los franceses tienen _____ libertad _____ los estadounidenses. (igualdad)
4. Livia tiene _____ hermanos _____ Sofía. (igualdad)
5. Brittany es _____ inteligente _____ Jane. (igualdad)

MINIRELATO: UNA FARMACIA EN MÉXICO.

Una farmacia en México, es relativamente fácil de distinguir desde lejos (*to recognize from far away*) pues todas ellas tienen anuncios luminosos, o el nombre de la farmacia desplegado en un lugar muy visible. También muchas farmacias se ubican cerca de las clínicas y hospitales.

En una farmacia uno puede encontrar medicina que se despacha sólo con receta médica (*prescription*) o medicina ordinaria que no requiere de la receta de un doctor, como pastillas o jarabes (*lozenges or syrup*) para la tos (*cough*). También en la farmacia se pueden conseguir productos para la higiene: cepillos de dientes, toallas sanitarias, limas para las uñas (*nail files*), champús, rasuradoras, y cremas para rasurarse (*shaving creams*). Igualmente se pueden conseguir productos de belleza, productos para bebés, lociones y aceites para la piel y comida para bebé (*baby food*).

Los mexicanos confían (trust) en quienes trabajan en las farmacias. Algunas veces la gente los consulta y les piden consejos (*advice*) sobre molestias y dolencias que puedan tener o sentir y de esta forma evitar el tener que pagar por una consulta con el doctor, quien muy probablemente les recetará lo mismo que el farmacéutico.

Preguntas

1. ¿Cómo se reconoce una farmacia en México?
2. ¿Qué tipo de medicamentos se pueden comprar en ellas?
3. ¿Qué otro tipo de productos se pueden adquirir en una farmacia?
4. ¿Es que los mexicanos confían en los farmacéuticos?
5. ¿Sobre qué les pide consejos la gente?
6. ¿En qué lugares suelen estar ubicadas la mayoría de farmacias?

LECTURA: "LA CIUDAD MÁS CARA Y ESTRESANTE AL VOLANTE[94]"

La Ciudad de México y Pekín son las peores urbes para usar auto, de acuerdo con **una encuesta** (opinion poll) de IBM. Conducir en la Ciudad de México es una de las **peores experiencias** (worst experiences) del mundo, de acuerdo con este estudio. Según la encuesta, manejar en la Ciudad de México es emocionalmente **desgastante** (stressful) y económicamente costoso.

Los resultados de la encuesta hecha a ocho mil ciento noventa y dos **automovilistas** (drivers) en veinte ciudades alrededor del mundo, revelan que la ciudad de México y Pekín, China, son las más demandantes para manejar. En una **escala** (scale) del 1 a 100, siendo cien la peor calificación, el Distrito Federal y Pekín, obtuvieron 99 puntos cada una.

El índice (indicator) toma en cuenta el tiempo de traslado, el tiempo perdido en **congestionamientos** (traffic jams) el precio del combustible, la velocidad del avance y el empeoramiento de las condiciones de tráfico con el paso del tiempo.

La encuesta analiza en qué medida se estresa el conductor, si el conducir le causa **enojo** (anger) si ha afectado su vida, si ha dejado de manejar por lo pesado del tráfico.

De acuerdo con el estudio, 56 **por ciento** (per cent) de los habitantes de la Ciudad de México aseguran que el tráfico ha afectado negativamente su trabajo o estudios. Y un 62 por ciento piensa que el tráfico es "**algo peor**" (somewhat worse) o "**mucho peor**" (much worse) que en años previos. De acuerdo con el estudio, el tráfico impacta en todos los ámbitos y obliga a todos, gobierno, empresa privada y ciudadanos, a buscar soluciones que vayan más allá de la construcción de carreteras y del uso del **transporte público** (public transportation). Según esta encuesta, cada año se suman 200 mil autos a la circulación en la Ciudad de México.

Preguntas:

1. ¿Quién realizó esta encuesta?
2. ¿Cuáles son las peores ciudades para manejar según la misma?
3. ¿Cuál fue la calificación obtenida por estas dos ciudades?
4. ¿Cuál fue la escala usada?

---

[94] Retrieved from the Internet on July 11, 2010. The report by Arturo Páramo was published in the Mexican newspaper *Excélsior*, and was published on July 2nd, 2010.

5. ¿Qué factores midió la encuesta?
6. ¿Por qué piensa que es importante medir el enojo de los conductores?
7. ¿Qué porcentaje de mexicanos piensa que el tráfico ha afectado su trabajo?
8. ¿Qué porcentaje piensa que el tráfico ha empeorado?
9. ¿Quiénes tienen que buscar las soluciones al problema?
10. ¿Cuántos vehículos ingresan a la circulación anualmente en México?

VOCABULARIO

VERBOS

arreglar(se)	servir(se)	lavar(se)
confiar(se)	tener	decir
venir	hacer	querer
matar	robar	desear
construir	borrar	tomar
entregar	haber	hacer

NOMBRES}

los papeles	el compartimento	el sobre
la guantera	la naranjada	la limonada
el cambio	el recibo	la propina
los trajes	la bufanda	la falda
las pastillas	los jarabes	la tos
el tráfico	el enojo	el conductor
el congestionamiento	la ambulancia	las emergencias
los pantalones	la tintorería	la lavadora
la voz	los edificios	las cartas
los puentes	el pizarrón	el hospital
el/la arquitecto	el albañil	los/las ingenieros/as
el índice	los puntos	la vida
las carreteras	el transporte	la encuesta

ADJETIVOS

folclórico/a	tranquilo/a	próximo/a
desgastante	peor	mucho/a
estresante	pasivo/a	público/a
bueno/a	malo/a	mejor
peor	inteligente	fuerte

ADVERBIOS

así	ya	después
allá	allí/ahí	sólo
emocionalmente	económicamente	más
fuertemente	ocasionalmente	torpemente

EXPRESIONES UTILES

pico de cera	arreglarse	licencia de manejo
tarjeta de circulación	teléfono celular	compañía de seguros
entre la espada y la pared	pedir aventón	receta médica

CAPÍTULO 12: VIVIENDO EN FAMILIA

En este capítulo...

In this chapter, you will learn how to use the future tense, as well as the conditional tense. Besides these 2 new tenses, you will learn the use of relative pronouns, the use of the gerund form, and some verbs beside **estar** than can be used with verbs in the gerund form. You will continue reading the story of the **Farmacia en México** that you started in chapter 11, and finally you will read an extract of a short story by the Mexican writer José Emilio Pacheco.

Contexto

Es tarde y por fin, José, está regresando de su trabajo en la florería. Al llegar su padre, Martín le pide a Thomas que le ayude a poner la mesa para merendar.

Martín: Recuerda que primero se ponen los vasos, después las servilletas y por último se ponen los cubiertos.

Thomas: OK. Mientras yo voy poniendo las servilletas, tú ve poniendo los cubiertos, ¿qué te parece?

Martín: Perfecto.

José (después de que han terminado de merendar): Muchas gracias. Estaré viendo las noticias. Si me necesitan, ya saben donde encontrarme. Por cierto, ¿alguien gusta acompañarme? (Dirigiéndose a Thomas) ¿a ti te gusta ver la televisión, Thomas?

Thomas: La veo muy poco, muy de vez en cuando. Únicamente cuando hay algún deporte que me interesa.

José: ¿Y por qué es eso?

Thomas: Porque en general, me parecen muy malos los programas, todo falso y de mala calidad sus contenidos. Como bien la llama Pedro Almodóvar: "La telebasura".

José: Bueno sí, pero al menos verás las noticias. Ahora mismo son las diez y es hora del noticiero. Vamos a sentarnos en la sala, ya verás que te ayudará a mejorar tu español.

José pone las noticias nacionales del canal dos de Televisa con Joaquín López Doriga. En ese momento entra Yolanda a la sala.

Yolanda: Hola jóvenes. ¿Qué están mirando?

José: La noticias. Por cierto, nos gustaría no ser interrumpidos.

Yolanda (pretendiendo estar ofendida): ¡Perdón!

José: Por cierto Yolanda, Thomas te contará lo que hizo hoy.

Yolanda: Me encantaría escucharlo todo con pelos y señales.

Thomas: Martín y yo, y algunos de mis compañeros de clase, fuimos al teatro Principal para oír un recital de poesía del escritor José Emilio Pacheco que acaba de ganar el premio Cervantes de Literatura.

Yolanda: ¡Qué bien!

Martín: Yo lo convencí de que fuéramos.

José (dirigiéndose a Martín): Préstale uno de sus libros para que lo conozca mejor.

Martín: ¡Qué buena idea! Se lo pondré en el buró, junto a su cama.

Thomas: Muchas gracias, me encantaría conocer más de él, de su obra.

Yolanda: ¿Y te ha gustado la velada literaria?

Thomas: Sí mucho. Yo no conocía a este escritor, pero me ha gustado muchísimo. Como dicen ustedes, "es muy sobrio".

Martín: Lo cual es muy raro en un escritor mexicano, pues somos dados a la verborrea.

Thomas: Lo sé, he leído mucho a Carlos Fuentes y él peca de eso.

José: Por eso no le dieron nunca el Nobel de Literatura.

Thomas: ¡Seguramente! Pues es muy bueno, ideológicamente es muy coherente, pero casi siempre le sobran páginas a sus textos literarios, sobre todo en sus últimos libros.

Yolanda: ¡Qué interesante observación! ¿No la hemos oído ya antes de algunos críticos?

José: Yo no estoy de acuerdo, yo creo que Fuentes es el mejor escritor mexicano de la actualidad.

Martín: Será el más prolijo, ¿cómo calificarías a Sergio Pitol?

José: Me gusta sí, pero creo que Fuentes es superior; es ¿cómo decirlo?, más universal.

Preguntas

1. ¿Quién regresó tarde a la casa de los Zurita?
2. ¿Qué le pide Martín a Thomas que haga?
3. ¿Qué le pregunta José a Thomas?
4. ¿Por qué Thomas casi no ve la televisión?
5. ¿Qué programa pone José?
6. ¿A dónde fueron los jóvenes hoy?
7. ¿A quién escucharon?
8. ¿Qué premio ganó recientemente ese escritor?
9. ¿Cómo lo define Thomas?
10. ¿Qué le sugiere José hacer a Martín?

NOTA CULTURAL: LOS HERMANOS SERDÁN.

De los tres hermanos Serdán, Aquiles es el más conocido. Este revolucionario mexicano nació en Puebla el dos de noviembre de 1876. Proveniente de una familia acomodada de comerciantes, fomentó las ideas revolucionarias en Puebla, su ciudad natal, con la ayuda de sus hermanos Carmen y Máximo.

1909 se afilió, junto con sus hermanos, al Partido Anti-Reeleccionista despúes de la visita a Puebla del candidato Francisco I. Madero, lo cual le costó a Aquiles que lo metieran a la cárcel.

Cuando Madero perdió las elecciones frente al dictador Porfirio Díaz en una elección fraudulenta, Madero se exilió en los Estados Unidos y hasta aquí vinieron a verlo Aquiles y su hermana Carmen. Recibieron de Madero veinte mil pesos para empezar la lucha armada en Puebla el día 20 de noviembre.

La policía comenzó a sospechar de las actividades de los hermanos Serdán y pensaban catear la casa la mañana del 18 de noviembre; los hermanos Serdán se enteraron de los planes de la policía y se les adelantaron distribuyendo las armas entre los amigos que vinieron a su casa para resistir el cateo de la policía.

Cuando la policía llegó la mañana del 18 de noviembre, los revolucionarios ya los estaban esperando. Después de muchas horas de combate la policía y el ejército tomaron la casa y Aquiles Serdán fue asesinado en su escondite, dentro de la casa. Así se dio inicio a uno de los momentos más importantes de la Historia de México: la Revolución Mexicana.

Dichos

En un abrir y cerrar de ojos.	In the blink of an eye.
En gustos se rompen géneros.	Everyone has their own taste.
Con pelos y señales.	In minute detail.

VOCABULARIO: LA TELEGUÍA.

Here are two **interactive links** to the most important TV Stations in Mexico:

INTERACTIVE LINK

bookstudio.pro/gui
bookstudio.pro/bar

EJERCICIOS PRÁCTICOS

☺ ☺

Estudie bien el vocabulario ilustrado de las televisoras y conteste las siguientes preguntas.

1.   ¿Qué tipo de programación tienen en común las dos televisoras?
2.   ¿Cuántas telenovelas al día transmiten en sus canales?
3.   ¿Cuántos programas noticiosos tiene cada televisora?
4.   ¿Cuál es la oferta deportiva?
5.   ¿Qué otro tipo de programación tienen?
6.   ¿Hay alguna diferencia fundamental en la programación de ambas televisoras o es más de lo mismo?
7.   ¿Ofrecen las televisoras algún programa cultural?
8.   ¿De ser así a qué horas se transmite?
9.   ¿Cuál es la apariencia de los conductores?
10. ¿Hay alguna diferencia con los conductores de los Estados Unidos?

Más vocabulario: ¡Vamos a comprar un disco!

qué le gustará a ella	what would she like...?
todo tipo de...	all kinds of
una videograbadora	VCR
una grabadora	a tape recorder
cámara de video	digital camcorder
cámara digital	digital camera
una cámara para filmar	film camera
discos compactos	CD's
un iPod	iPod
un teléfono celular	a cell phone

video juegos	video games
entrar	to walk in
regalar	to give
computadora portátil	laptop

EJERCICIOS PRÁCTICOS

Escuche y comprenda.

Este fin de semana es el cumpleaños de Julia, la hija mayor de la señora Marín, y Jesse se pregunta qué le puede regalar. Ella va al Centro Comercial Angelópolis para ver que le puede comprar. Estando allí, se decide a entrar a una tienda que se especializa en todo tipo de aparatos electrónicos. En la tienda hay una gran variedad de televisores, estéreos, computadoras portátiles, cámaras digitales, grabadoras y videograbadoras y hasta cámaras para filmar, pero todo es muy caro. Más allá está la sección de teléfonos celulares, pero Julia ya tiene uno.

Después ella se va a la sección de video juegos y discos compactos y allí mismo ve una sección nueva de iPods. Eso es lo que le va a regalar. Entonces ella llama al empleado para que se los muestre pues están bajo llave.

Jesse: Señor, ¿me puede mostrar los iPods, por favor?
Empleado: Por supuesto señorita. ¿Qué es lo que está buscando exactamente?
Jesse: Uno que sea versátil, que se pueda usar cuando se hace ejercicio o cuando se sale a correr o caminar, que se pueda llevar a la escuela, etc.
Empleado: Entonces le conviene el nano.
Jesse: ¿Y cuánto cuesta?
Empleado: Esta semana tienen un 10% de descuento, así que le sale en 2699 pesos.
Jesse: ¡Guau! sí que son caros en México!
Empleado: Cuestan más o menos el doble que en Estados Unidos. ¿Por qué no lo compra allá?
Jesse: Porque es para dar un regalo.
Empleado: Entiendo.
Jesse: Bueno ni modo, ¡me da el de color rosita, por favor!

Empleado: Con el mayor gusto. De pronto, el empleado la tutea y le dice: Con esto mi cielo, ve a la caja, allí te cobran y te entregan la mercancía.

Jesse (quien a propósito enfatiza lo formal): ¡Muchas gracias, señor!

Empleado: De nada, preciosa.

☺ ☺

B. Haga estas preguntas a otro estudiante.
1. ¿Qué celebra Julia este fin de semana?
2. ¿A dónde va Jesse para comprar un regalo?
3. ¿A qué tipo de tienda entra?
4. ¿Qué productos ve?
5. ¿Cuál es el primer comentario de Jesse?
6. ¿Por qué no le compra un teléfono celular?
7. ¿Dónde ve los iPods?
8. ¿Cuál es el descuento que tienen hoy?
9. ¿Cuánto cuesta el iPod que le gusta para Julia?
10. ¿Qué le pregunta el empleado?

APUNTES GRAMATICALES
56. EL TIEMPO FUTURO

1. The future tense of most verbs is formed by adding the future tense endings to the infinitive. The future tense endings are: **—é, —ás, —á, —emos, —éis, —án**:

hablar	comer	vivir
hablar**é**	comer**é**	vivir**é**
hablar**ás**	comer**ás**	vivir**ás**
hablar**á**	comer**á**	vivir**á**
hablar**emos**	comer**emos**	vivir**emos**
hablar**éis**	comer**éis**	vivir**éis**
hablar**án**	comer**án**	vivir**án**

2. Some verbs have an irregular future stem. The future endings, however, remain the same:

caber   **cabr—**   Thomas **cabrá** en el coche de los Zurita.

decir	**dir—**	Yo le **diré** la verdad al profesor cuando lo vea.
haber	**habr—**	**Habrá** muchos estudiantes en Puebla en el verano.
hacer	**har—**	Ellos **harán** la tarea esta noche.
querer	**querr—**	Anna **querrá** comprarse una moto.
poder	**podr—**	*Vosotros* **podréis** ir a Cuba.
poner	**pondr—**	Nosotros **pondremos** la mesa.
saber	**sabr—**	Tú te **sabrás** las conjugaciones mañana.
salir	**saldr—**	Ellas **saldrán** temprano para México.
satisfacer	**satisfar—**	Yo **satisfaré** mi apetito.
tener	**tendr—**	**Tendremos** una fiesta el fin de semana.
valer	**valdr—**	Las casas **valdrán** más en diez años.
venir	**vendr—**	Ella **vendrá** a casa tarde.

Note that the future tense stem always ends in **—r**.

3. Compound verbs of irregular future tense verbs maintain the same irregularities:

deshacer	**deshar—**	Ellas **desharán** el tejido.
reponer	**repondr—**	Tú **repondrás** las cosas dañadas.
detener	**detendr—**	El policía **detendrá** al ladrón.
convenir	**convendr—**	Yo **convendré** con la policía.
contradecir	**contradir—**	Nosotros **contradiremos** al profesor.
desdecir	**desdir—**	Ellos se **desdirán** de lo dicho.

4. All other compound forms of **decir** have regular conjugations:

bendecir	**bendecir—**	El Papa **bendecirá** a los feligreses.
predecir	**predecir—**	Los meteorólogos **predecirán** buen tiempo.
maldecir	**maldecir—**	El hombre **maldecirá** su suerte.

5. In general, Spanish usage of the future is like the usage in English in that it expresses something that is going to happen after a present reference point:

Yo la **veré** mañana.	I **will see** her tomorrow.
Nosotros **hablaremos** en clase.	We **will speak** in class.

6. The future tense in Spanish is used to express a goal, a project, an aspiration, a dream or a stronger commitment or purpose:

Esta noche **cenaré** con mis padres.

Tonight I **will** have dinner with my parents.

7. The future tense in Spanish is also used with the force of an imperative:

No **matarás**   You **will** not kill.
Usted **volverá** a casa cuando amanezca.
You **will** go back home when the dawn breaks.

8. The future tense in Spanish is quite often replaced by the immediate future form **ir** + **a** + infinitive:

Voy a estar en Puebla todo el   I will be in Puebla the whole semester.
semestre.

9. In Spanish, the future tense is often replaced by the present tense when there is a clue in the sentence that implies the future:

Te **hablo** en la noche.   **I will call** you tonight.

10. The present tense is also used for asking instructions; in situations where we use "should" or "may" in English:

¿Me **salgo** en la próxima salida?   **Should** I take the next exit?

11. Future tense is often used in sentences where the "if" clause is in the present tense:
Si Anna va, John irá.   **If Anna goes,** John will go.
John irá, **si Anna va.**   John will go, **if Anna goes.**

12. The future tense is used in Spanish when there is probability, conjecture or wonder expressed in present tense:

Let's say that somebody knocks at your door and you are wondering:
¿Quién será?   Who could that be?

Let's say you don't have a watch and you are wondering:
¿Qué horas **serán**?   What time could it be?

Let's say you see a girl for the first time and you wonder:
¿Quién será esa chica?   Who will that girl be?

EJERCICIOS PRÁCTICOS

A. Change the sentences from present tense to future tense.
   Modelo: Ella tiene un hijo.
                Ella **tendrá** un hijo.
   1.   Yo no recuerdo su nombre.
   2.   Él prefiere helado.
   3.   Ellas quieren ir de compras.
   4.   Mi mamá aprende a bailar.
   5.   El profesor nos perdona.
   6.   Los estudiantes compran regalos.

B. Change the sentences from informal future to regular future.
   Modelo: John va a probar el motor.
                John probará el motor.
   1.   José va a caminar muy rápido.
   2.   Él va a tomar el examen de manejo.
   3.   Anna va a recibir su primera lección.
   4.   Los jóvenes van a regresar tarde.
   5.   John va a ver si es seguro manejar en México.

   ☺☺
C. Fill in the blank using the future tense for the verbs in parentheses.
   1.   ¿Qué le _____(llevar) a tu mamá cuando vuelvas a casa?
   2.   2. ¿Quién _____ (ganar) el campeonato de fútbol?
   3.   ¿Cómo _____ (ir) nosotros a Oaxaca?
   4.   ¿Quiénes _____ (manejar) el carro?
   5.   ¿Dónde _____ (tener) la cabeza John?
   6.   ¿Quiénes _____ (atrapar) al ladrón?
   7.   ¿Quién _____ (tener) que hacer la comida?
   8.   ¿Qué _____ (ser) tú cuando seas adulto?
   9.   ¿Dónde _____ (poner) los estudiantes sus maletas?
   10. 10. ¿De dónde _____ (venir) ese autobús?

57. EL TIEMPO CONDICIONAL

1. As in English, the conditional is used to indicate an eventuality.

2. The conditional of regular verbs is formed by adding the —**er**/—**ir** imperfect ending to the infinitive:

Stems		endings
—**ar** verbs	**trabajar-**	
—**er** verbs	**comer-**	—**ía**, —**ías**, —**ía**, —**íamos**, —**íais**, —**ían**
—**ir** verbs	**vivir-**	

Note that the first person singular and the third person singular have the same conjugation (similar to the imperfect tense).

3. Irregular verbs follow the same pattern as regular verbs. The verbs that are irregular in the future tense, are irregular in the conditional tense:
De ser posible, Thomas le **diría** la verdad.
If possible, Thomas **would tell** him/her the truth.

4. Irregular compound verbs have the same irregularities as the basic verb:
componer ⇒ compondría
El mecánico **compondría** el coche si yo tuviera dinero
The mechanic **would fix** the car if I had money.

5. Many times conditional is used to translate "**would**" (Haría, sería), "**should**" (debería) and "**could**" (podría):

Deberías estudiar más.	You **should** study more.
Podrías estudiar más.	You **Could** study more.
Sería mejor si estudiaras más.	It **would** be better if you studied more.
Haría bien en acostarme.	It **would** do me good to lie down.

Note that when **would** means **used to**, the imperfect tense (and not the conditional tense) is used in Spanish:
Cuando vivíamos en Puebla **íbamos** a misa todos los domingos.
When we used to live in Puebla, we **would go** to mass every Sunday.

6. The conditional is used in Spanish in dependent clauses after a verb of communication like **decir**, or knowledge or belief like **saber** or **creer**, when the main verb is in the past tense (past ⇒ conditional):
   Thomas **supo** que Cecilia **vendría** a ver a sus padres.

7. The conditional is used in Spanish when there is probability, conjecture or wonder in the past:
   Let's say that somebody knocked at your door this morning, but you did not go answer the door to see who it was, and now you are wondering:
   ¿Quién **sería**?   Who was it?
   Or somebody called you but did not leave a message:
   ¿Quién me **llamaría**?   Who could have called me?

8. The conditional also express an action that will take place sometime in the future, after a past reference point:
   Thomas dijo que **regresaría** a México. Thomas said that he would return to Mexico.
   ¿Qué te dijo el doctor? Me dijo que **sanaría** en tres días si me tomo las medicinas.
   What did the doctor say? He told me that I **would** heal in three days if I take the medicine.

9. In Spanish we use the conditional to make polite requests:
   ¿Me **podría** dar una caja de chocolates, por favor?
   Could you give me a box of chocolates, please?

10. The conditional is used in Spanish, as well as in English, in if clauses contrary to fact. You will study this in detail in Chapter 19:
   Si yo fuera rico, **tendría** un apartamento en Manhattan.

11. In sentences where the situation is impossible to achieve because of the restriction of the conjunction pero (but):
   Ella dijo que **vendría** pero tiene que trabajar.
   She said she would come but she has to work.

EJERCICIOS PRÁCTICOS

A. Change the verb from the future to the conditional tense.
   Modelo: Nosotros podremos elegir mejor.

Nosotros podríamos elegir mejor.
1. Yo iré al club.
2. Yo nadaré en la alberca/ piscina.
3. Nosotros podremos descansar.
4. Ella jugará tenis.
5. Ellas darán un paseo.
6. Tú irás en bicicleta al trabajo.

B. Finish the statements by adding a question to the end using the conditional tense.

Modelo: Alguien tocó a la puerta, pero no abrí... (un rato después me pregunto): ¿Quién **tocaría**?

1. Vi pasar a un grupo con sus esquíes...
2. Una mujer entró a su casa corriendo...
1. En mi teléfono (había un mensaje de voz...
2. Esta tarde llegó una carta sin remitente...
3. Vi pasar las ambulancias, la policía y los bomberos...

C. Form a negative response to each statement using the conditional.

Modelo: José va a llevar su coche a ese taller mecánico. (Yo)
Yo no lo **llevaría**.

1. José piensa cambiarle las cuatro llantas.
2. Martín le aconseja que sólo le cambie la batería.
3. José va a gastar unos tres mil pesos en el coche.
4. José quiere darle su coche a Martín.
5. Yolanda se opone a que le dé el coche.

D. Fill in the blank using the conditional.

1. Lisa nos dijo que le _____ (gustar) tener una fiesta en su casa.
2. Pero a nosotros nos preocupaba lo qué _____ (pensar) él.
3. Lisa nos dijo que no _____ (haber) problema con su familia.
4. Yolanda nos dijo que ella _____ (hacer) unas pizzas.
5. José nos dijo que él nos _____ (recoger) en su coche.
6. El profesor dijo que no se _____. (oponer)
7. El grupo entero le prometió a Lisa que la _____. (ayudar)
8. Además yo le dije que _____ (llegar) temprano.
9. Lisa me pidió si yo _____ (poder) comprar unas sodas.
10. Le contesté que con gusto las _____. (llevar)

58. El uso de los pronombres relativos.

1. A relative pronoun connects a clause to a noun or a pronoun that precedes it. A relative pronoun is also used to join two sentences together.

2. The relative pronoun **que** replaces the direct object in a relative clause. Consider the following two separate but related thoughts:

   El estudiante se llama Thomas.
   Tú lo conoces.
   El estudiante **que** tú conoces se llama Thomas.
   The student **whom** you know is named Thomas.

3. The relative pronoun **quien** (*who or whom*) or **quienes** in the plural form acts as the subject of a verb in a relative clause:

   Yo tengo una hermana.
   Ella es muy bonita.
   Yo tengo una hermana **quien** es muy bonita.
   I have a sister **who** is very beautiful.

   Note that the pronoun **quien** replaces the subject of the second sentence (**ella**) and directly follows its antecedent (**una hermana**)

   Note also that it is very common that in conversational Spanish people use **que** instead of **quien**: Yo tengo una hermana **que** es muy bonita.

4. **Quien** is used only used with people but **que** may refer to either people or things. The key difference is that **quien** is the **subject** of the relative clause:

ANTECEDENT	RELATIVE CLAUSE	MAIN CLAUSE
La chica,	**quien** llega	es mi novia.

   Whereas **que** is the **object** of a relative clause:

ANTECEDENT	RELATIVE CLAUSE	MAIN CLAUSE
La chica	**que** ves	es mi novia.

5. **Que** and **quien** are usually used without a preposition but in some situations they may be used after the prepositions **a, de, en, con**:

No me sorprende la contundencia **con que** el profesor expone sus temas.

a. **Que** is used with a preposition when the antecedent is not a person:
Este es el pueblo **de que** te hablé. This is the town **that** I told you about.

b. **Que** is commonly used with the preposition **en** in sentences that express imprecise places, and it is also used as means of discussing transportation:
El coche **en que** viajaban estaba viejo.   The car they used to travel in was old.

c. When **que** is the direct object of the verb and has an antecedent that is a person, it can be replaced by **a quien** or **a quienes** if the antecedent is plural:

Busqué a las personas **a quienes** vi ayer.	I looked for the people that I saw yesterday.

d. express possession:
Este es el libro del profesor **de quien** te hablé.
This book belongs to the teacher that I told you about.

e. The preposition **con** and the relative pronoun **quien** express relations:
El profesor **con quien** hablé es muy fina persona.
The teacher with whom I spoke is a very nice person.

f. The preposition **a** and the relative pronoun **quien** when the relative pronoun is the object of a verb can be replaced by **al que**:
El plomero **a quien** he llamado no ha llegado aún.
The plumber that I called has not arrived yet.
El plomero **al que** he llamado no ha llegado aún.

6. The relative pronoun **lo que** refers to a situation:
Lo que ella necesita es practicar más español.

7. The relative pronoun **donde** refers to a place:
El no sabe **donde** ellos han ido   He doesn't know **where** they have gone
El cajero automático está en el supermercado **donde** mi madre trabaja. The automated teller machine is in the supermarket **where** my mom works.

8. **El que** or **el cual** have four possible forms depending the gender and number of the pronoun, el, la, los, las:
Los chicos **a los cuales** hemos atendido son muy simpáticos.
Those boys that we served are nice guys.

a. **El que** or **el cual**, since they agree with gender and number may be used to avoid confusion when there is more than one possible antecedent for que or quien:
El amigo de mi hermana, **el que** trabaja en la universidad, llegó hoy.
El amigo de mi hermana, **la que** trabaja en la universidad, llegó hoy.

b. In general, **el cual** is a more formal form than **el que**. Use **el cual** after **según** when it means "according to":
La afirmación según **la cual** los blancos son más inteligentes que los demás seres humanos es poco menos que desafortunada.

c. Also use **el cual** after long prepositions or prepositional phrases with a masculine noun:
Ofrecemos un curso mediante **el cual** los futuros médicos tendrán la oportunidad de aprender español.

9. The relative pronoun **cuyo** means whose. **Cuyo** is often an elegant alternative for a tortuous relative clause. It agrees in gender and number with the noun that follows it:
Ellos son los profesores **cuyas** clases tomamos en México.
Those are the teachers **whose** classes we took in Mexico.

Note that if there is more than one noun, the **relative pronoun** only agrees with the first one:
La mujer **cuya blusa y falda** eran ridículas.

EJERCICIOS PRÁCTICOS

A. Use relative pronouns to combine the two sentences.
   Modelo: Las entradas cuestan mucho. Yo las compro.
   Las entradas que yo compro cuestan mucho.
   1.   La presentación fue espectacular. Nosotros la vimos.
   2.   Los bailarines son profesionales. Nosotros los admiramos.
   3.   Amalia Hernández tiene mucha imaginación. Nosotros la aplaudimos.

4. Los bailarines son entusiastas. Nosotros los conocimos.
5. El periódico hizo una buena crítica del ballet. Nosotros la leímos.

B. Use relative pronouns with prepositions in order to make one sentence.
Modelo: El autor es fantástico. Yo te hable de él.
El autor de quien te hablé es fantástico.
1. El panadero ya no trabaja aquí. Yo ya te hablé de él.
2. Esta chica es farmacéutica. Yo escucho sus consejos
3. Él es un compositor fabuloso. *Vosotros conocéis* su música.
4. El futbolista es muy famoso. Ustedes lo conocen.
5. El profesor es muy profesional. Yo le hablé a Yolanda de él.

C. Use relative pronouns to combine the two sentences.
Modelo: El lápiz es amarillo. Yo escribo con él.
El lápiz con el que/cual escribo es amarillo.
1. La tinta de mi pluma es verde. Me gusta escribir con ella.
2. El papel es fino. Yo escribo sobre ese papel.
3. El sobre es grande. Yo meto la carta dentro.
4. El sobre es rectangular. Yo le pongo el timbre.
5. El cartero llega ahora. Yo estaba pensando en él.

D. Write the proper form of the relative pronoun **cuyo** in the blank.
1. Este es el nuevo estudiante _____ padres vienen del campo.
2. Este es el taxista _____ modales dan mucho que hablar.
3. Ellas son las nuevas empleadas _____ esposos perdieron el
4. trabajo en la crisis del 2008.
5. México es un país _____ historia es interesantísima.
6. Se cuenta que el escritor _____ libros son populares, es un arrogante.

59. Diversos usos del gerundio

1. As you may remember from the preliminary chapter, the gerund is always invariable in form:

El profesor **está hablando**.   The professor is **speaking**.

2. Some verbs have irregular gerund forms:
decir   diciendo   preferir   prefiriendo

dormir	durmiendo	reír	riendo
hervir	hirviendo	seguir	siguiendo
mentir	mintiendo	sentir	sintiendo
morir	muriendo	servir	sirviendo
pedir	pidiendo	venir	viniendo
poder	pudiendo	vestir	vistiendo

3. A gerund may also be used to indicate simultaneous actions:
El hombre se **fue gritando** de dolor.   The man left **screaming** in pain.

4. Gerunds are also used to indicate a method by which an action is performed:
José hizo su casa **trabajando** de sol a sol.
José made his house **working** from sunrise to sunset.

5. Gerunds are used to express a purpose, especially with verbs of communication:
Me escribió **pidiéndome** dinero.
He/she wrote me **asking** for money.

6. Gerunds are also used to indicate a reason for doing something:
No **teniendo** nada que hacer, me fui del trabajo.
Not **having** anything left to do, I left work.

7. A gerund is used instead of **como si** when it is preceded by **como**:
Yolanda se quedó como **sopesando** sus palabras.
Yolanda stayed as if **weighing** her words.

8. The verb **ser** can only be used in its gerund form in phrases that express the passive voice:
Los expedientes **están siendo** analizados por el FBI.
The files are being analyzed by the FBI.

9. The verb ser can also be used to make a prediction:
Siendo tan atrevido como es, Thomas aprenderá español rápido.
Being as daring as he is, Thomas will learn Spanish fast.

EJERCICIOS PRÁCTICOS

A. Complete these sentences using the correct form of the irregular gerunds.
Modelo:　José está trabajando (dormir)
　　　　　José está **durmiendo**.

1.　El profesor se está levantando. (vestirse)
2.　Las chicas están nadando. (pedir dinero)
3.　Mis compañeros de clase están jugando. (reírse)
4.　El abogado está saliendo a la corte. (mentir)
5.　Superman está cocinando una hamburguesa. (servir)

B.　Organize these sentences using gerund forms.
Modelo:　El/hombre/irse/doblar/de/dolor.
　　　　　El hombre **se va doblando** de dolor.

1.　José/estar/trabajar/mucho.
2.　Yo/le/andar/pensar/en/escribir/una/carta/a/mi/hermana.
3.　Ellas/continuar/hablar/de/sus/amigas.
4.　Thomas/salir/gritar/de/alegría.
5.　El/juez/seguir/sentar/como/sopesar/su/decisión.

60. OTROS VERBOS QUE PUEDEN SER USADOS CON GERUNDIOS

1.　In addition to **estar**, gerunds can be used with other verbs:
a.　Verbs that imply the action of a direct object like **pillar, agarrar, dejar, sorprender, arrestar**: La policía lo **agarró durmiendo**.

b.　Verbs of representation **describir, pintar, imaginar**:
　El pintor la **imaginó nadando** en el mar azul.

c.　Verbs of perception, when the gerund is used to qualify the object of the main verb like **oír, ver, recordar, olvidar**:　La **recuerdo bailando** siempre.

2.　Other verbs that can be used as auxiliaries with progressive include:
a.　The verb **andar** can be translated as "to stroll":
　Ella **anda paseando** por el parque.

b. The verb **ir** tends to express a slow or gradual action. It may also mean to leave a place or to progress towards a goal:
El hombre **se fue doblando** hasta quedar en el suelo.
El ladrón **se fue corriendo**.
Los albañiles **van avanzando** en la construcción del edificio.

c. The verb **llevar** expresses a period of time:
El profesor **lleva viviendo** en México más de diez años.

d. The verb **quedarse** or **vivir** express the idea of continuing to do something:
Me **quedé esperándola** para siempre.
Vivo sufriendo tu ausencia.

e. The verb **salir** often suggests the idea of going out or running away:
El ladrón **salió corriendo.**

f. The verb **seguir** or **continuar** suggest the idea of "still" doing, or to keep on doing something:
José **continúa trabajando** en la florería.
José **sigue trabajando** en la florería.

g. The verb **venir** suggests the idea that something increases with time or expresses mounting exasperations:
Hace tiempo que **viene diciendo** eso.
Con este gobierno, la violencia **viene siendo** imposible de resolver.

h. The verbs **acabar** or **terminar, to** mean to "end by" or "end up":
Con su mal temperamento John siempre **acaba peleándose** con todos.
Por sus malos modales los taxistas **terminan teniendo** mala fama.

i. The verb llegar means to arrive:
Él **llegó corriendo** a su clase.

EJERCICIOS PRÁCTICOS

Transform these sentences to practice the gerund.
Modelo: Él se fue saltando de alegría. (salir)
           Él salió saltando de alegría.
1.   Él se fue corriendo. (continuar)

2. Él se fue riendo. (entrar)
3. Él se fue destruyendo las cosas a su paso. (salir)
4. Él se fue gritando de alegría. (correr)
5. Él se fue disparado. (salir)

☺ ☺

B. Finish this dialogue using verbs in the gerund form.
1. ¿Qué estás _____ ? (hacer)
2. Estoy _____. (comer)
3. ¿Por qué estás comiendo y no estás _____ (hacer) la tarea?
4. Porque la estuve _____ (hacer) en la escuela mientras tú estabas _____. (dormir)
5. ¡Qué dices! Yo no estaba _____ (dormir), sólo estaba _____ (descansar) los ojos.
6. ¡Qué cinismo el tuyo! deberías de estar _____ (trabajar) ahora mismo y mira andas _____ (pasearse) como si nada.
7. No te preocupes que para esta noche, sin duda, estaré _____ (terminar) toda la tarea.
8. Eso espero, pues si no lo haces te estarás _____ (lamentar) todo el fin de semana.
9. Ya verás que no. La voy a terminar antes de lo que estás _____ (pensar) ¡palabra de honor!
10. Bueno pues, ahora ya vete a trabajar. Y su amigo salió _____ (correr) a su casa, pero por el camino se le fue _____ (olvidar) lo prometido.

C. Complete this exercise choosing the correct conjugation.

1. Martín está_____ (estudiar)
    a. dormir   b. estudiado   c. estudiando

2. Los estudiantes van _____ del examen.
    a. saliendo   b. platicar   c. a y b

3. José se fue _____ dormido en el sofá.
    a. quedar   b. quedando   c. estado

4. Nosotros andamos _____ en comprar una casa.

      a. pensando   b. durmiendo   c. a y b

5. Yo estoy _____ arduamente.
     a. trabajar   b. tristemente   c. trabajando

6. Usted salió _____ de alegría.
     a. gritando   b. cantando   c. a y b

MINIRELATO: UNA FARMACIA EN MÉXICO (CONTINUACIÓN).

Al igual que las farmacias estadounidenses, en las farmacias mexicanas también se pueden comprar **dulces** (sweets), **tarjetas de felicitación** (greeting cards), perfumes (perfumes), cremas y lociones (creams and lotions), y muchos otros productos. Algunas farmacias son parte de un **establecimiento comercial** mucho más grande, como el caso de Sanborn's. En ellas se pueden encontrar **periódicos**, (newspapers) libros, revistas, agua mineral, y todavía en algunas farmacias se pueden usar **básculas** (scale) para **poder pesarse uno mismo** (weigh oneself) depositando una moneda.

Ahora, como en los Estados Unidos, en las farmacias mexicanas ya no se pueden comprar **medicamentos** (medicines) sin receta médica, aunque (although) en algunas se puede consultar al farmacéutico sobre qué medicina se puede comprar **para curar** (to cure) malestares leves, como **catarros** (colds), gripes, dolores de cabeza, **comezón** (itch) en la piel, etc.

En las ciudades grandes, es posible todavía encontrar farmacias que están abiertas toda la noche; a estas farmacias se les llama **de turno** es decir, que siempre hay un farmacéutico que está **de guardia** (on duty) para atender las urgencias que se puedan presentar.

Preguntas

1. ¿Qué cosas se pueden comprar en una farmacia mexicana, que
2. también se pueden comprar en las farmacias de los Estados Unidos?
3. ¿Qué otras cosas hay en las farmacias mexicanas?
4. ¿Es que se pueden comprar medicamentos sin receta médica?
5. ¿Es todavía posible usar básculas para pesarse uno mismo?
6. ¿Qué se tiene que hacer para pesarse?
7. ¿Hay farmacias que están abiertas toda la noche?

8.   ¿En qué lugares es posible todavía encontrar este tipo de farmacia?
9.   ¿Es que el farmacéutico le puede ayudar con malestares menores?
10. ¿Hay máquinas para tomarse la presión arterial?

LECTURA: EL MUNDO ANTIGUO, JOSÉ EMILIO PACHECO.

José Emilio Pacheco nació en la ciudad de México en 1939 y murió en enero del año 2014. Es uno de los escritores latinoamericanos más conocidos y leídos. Su obra es muy amplia y diversa y va del ensayo a la novela breve pasando por la poesía que es, sin duda alguna, su mejor arte, sin demeritar el resto de su obra.

José Emilio Pacheco ha recibido muchos premios, pero sin duda el premio más importante que ha recibido es el premio Cervantes, el premio más importante que se da en español, y que él recibió en el 2009.

Además de su actividad literaria, José Emilio Pacheco también ha dado clases en México, los Estados Unidos, Inglaterra y Canadá.

He aquí un fragmento breve de su texto "El mundo antiguo" que está en uno de sus mejores libros: *Las Batallas en el Desierto*.

Me acuerdo, no me acuerdo: ¿qué año era aquél? Ya había supermercados pero no televisión, radio tan **sólo** (*only*): Las aventuras de Carlos Lacroix, Tarzán, **El Llanero Solitario** (*The Lone Ranger*), La Legión de los Madrugadores, Los Niños Catedráticos, Leyendas de las Calles de México, Panseco, El Doctor I.Q., La Doctora Corazón desde su clínica de **Almas** (*souls*), Paco Malgesto narraba las corridas de toros, Carlos Albert era el cronista de fútbol, el Mago Septién transmitía el beisbol. Circulaban los primeros coches producidos después de la guerra: Packard, Cadillac, Buick, Chrysler, Mercury, Hudson, Pontiac, Dodge, Plymouth, De Soto. Ibamos a ver **películas** (*films*) de Errol Flynn y Tyrone Power, a matinées con una serie de episodios completa: La invasión de Mongo era mi predilecta. Estaban de moda Sin ti, La rondalla, La burrita, La múcura, Amorcito Corazón. Volvía a sonar en todas partes un antiguo bolero puertorriqueño: Por alto que esté el cielo en el mundo, por hondo que sea el mar profundo, no habrá una barrera en el mundo que mi amor profundo no rompa por ti.

Fue el año de la poliomielitis: escuelas llenas de niños con aparatos ortopédicos: de la fiebre aftosa: en todo el país **fusilaban** (*shot*) por decenas de miles **reses** (*cows*) enfermas; de las inundaciones: el centro de la ciudad se convertía otra vez en laguna, la gente iba por las calles en **lancha** (*kayaks*). Dicen que con la próxima tormenta estallará el Canal del Desagüe y anegará la capital. Qué importa, contestaba mi hermano, si bajo el régimen de Miguel Alemán ya vivimos en la mierda.

La cara del Señor presidente en donde quiera: dibujos inmensos, retratos idealizados, fotos **ubicuas** (*ubiquitous*), alegorías del progreso con Miguel Alemán como dios Padre, caricaturas laudatorias, monumentos. Adulación pública, insaciable maledicencia privada. Escribíamos mil veces en el cuaderno de castigos: Debo ser obediente, debo ser obediente, debo ser obediente con mis padres y con mis maestros. Nos enseñaban historia patria, lengua nacional, geografía del DF: los ríos (aún quedaban ríos), las montañas (se veían las montañas). Era el mundo antiguo. Los mayores se quejaban de la inflación, los cambios, el tránsito, la inmoralidad, el ruido, la delincuencia, el exceso de gente, la mendicidad, los extranjeros, la corrupción, el enriquecimiento sin límite de unos cuantos y la miseria de casi todos.

Preguntas

1.   ¿Cuándo nació José Emilio Pacheco?
2.   ¿En qué año murió?
3.   ¿Qué época refleja el fragmento?
4.   ¿Quién era el presidente de México?
5.   ¿De qué se quejaba la gente de aquel entonces?
6.   ¿De qué se queja la gente hoy en día?
7.   ¿Quién es el narrador?
8.   ¿Qué edad puede tener el narrador?
9.   ¿Dónde pasan las cosas?
10. ¿Qué tipo de coches describe el narrador?

VOCABULARIO

VERBOS

ver	oír	nacer	llegar
comprar	tener	fusilar	ser
decir	poner	ir	vender
sacrificar	hablar	comer	vivir
caber	venir	tener	valer
hacer	saber		

NOMBRES

la verborrea	las noticias	la televisión	el día
el buró	el escritor	el premio	los ríos
los puercos	la mercancía	las reses	la mujer
los/las radios	el béisbol	la guerra	el hombre
las montañas	las anchas	la báscula	la farmacia
el aeropuerto	la ensalada	las casas	la cabeza
el Palacio Nacional	la motocicleta	las vacas	el/la capital
las batallas	el desierto	las maletas	el autobús
una caja sorpresa	Tarzán	la computadora portátil	

ADJETIVOS

prolijo/a	muy caros/as	grato/a	alto/a
bueno/a	ubicuas	cruel	fuerte
fácil	gentil	loco/a	tonto/a
torpe	rápido/a	solitario/a	

ADVERBIOS

solamente	seguramente	ideológicamente
bien	lentamente	rápidamente
ayer	anteanoche	mañana
fuertemente	simplemente	decididamente
elegantemente	formalmente	seriamente
despiadadamente	tristemente	ayer

EXPRESIONES UTILES

bajo llave	¡muchas gracias!	¡de nada!
de segunda mano		

CAPÍTULO 13: UNA COINCIDENCIA

En este capítulo...

You will learn a little bit about free time activities, and about Mexican currency, and at the end of the chapter you will read about Mexican newspapers and the press. In this chapter, you will study the use of other progressive tenses. You will learn about diminutives and augmentatives, adjectives of nationality, and the use of the neutral gender.

Contexto

Los estudiantes están de visita en la Ciudad de México. Al día siguiente de su llegada, los cuatro amigos deciden ver un poco la ciudad. Ellos se han hospedado en un hotel modesto cerca de la Embajada de los Estados Unidos. Después de desayunar, ellos van a la zona Rosa, que les queda a unas cinco cuadras del hotel, y se sientan en la terraza de un café para planear el resto de su día en la ciudad. De pronto ven que un hombre grandote ataca a otro hombre y ellos deciden ir a ver en qué pueden ayudar y cómo está la víctima. El atacante ha salido corriendo y se ha llevado el portafolio de la víctima.

Thomas: ¿Está bien señor?

El hombre: Sí, pero ese desgraciado se fue huyendo con mi portafolio.

Thomas: ¡Espero que no haya perdido cosas de mucho valor!

El hombre: ¡Le diré!

Thomas: ¿Quiere que llame a la policía?

El hombre: No, no. A la policía no; además de nada serviría. El ladrón ya estará vendiendo lo que se ha llevado y la verdad no voy a recuperar nada de lo perdido.

Thomas: ¿Quiere que le pida un té para el susto? Yo acabo de pedir un té chino muy bueno.

El hombre: No se preocupen jóvenes, en esta ciudad vivimos con el Jesús en la boca todos los días. Hasta ya nos estamos acostumbrando a la violencia.

Lisa: Pero, ¿se siente bien?

Anna: ¿Por qué no se sienta acá en esta silla?

Uno de los meseros les acerca una silla.

John: Siéntese. Mire los muchachos le trajeron una silla.

El hombre: ¡Muchas gracias! Pero no deberían de molestarse.

La policía turística llega al lugar.

Uno de los policías: ¿Qué pasó aquí?

El hombre: ¡Que va a pasar! lo de siempre, que los ladrones nos viven fregando a todas horas.

El otro policía: Pero, ¿qué le robaron?

El hombre: Mi portafolio.

El primer policía: Acompáñenos a la delegación para poner la denuncia. Estos jóvenes pueden servirle de testigos. ¿Verdad muchachos?

Thomas: Si el señor así lo desea, nosotros vamos.

El hombre: ¿Y de qué serviría?

El segundo policía: Al menos queda registrada la denuncia. Sirve al menos para las estadísticas sobre la delincuencia en la ciudad.

El hombre: Y yo, ¿qué gano con eso? Además tengo que regresar a Puebla.

John: ¿A Puebla?

El hombre: Sí. Yo vivo en Puebla, yo sólo estaba terminando de hacer unas cuantas cositas aquí en el DF.

John: ¡Qué coincidencia! Nosotros también estamos viviendo en Puebla y estamos pasando el fin de semana en la ciudad. En un hotelito muy bonito, aquí cerquitita.

El hombre: Pues tengan mucho cuidado no los vayan a desvalijar como a mí.

Anna: ¡Lo tendremos, se lo prometemos!

Preguntas

1. ¿Qué es lo que los amigos deciden hacer?
2. ¿A dónde van?
3. ¿Es que la Zona Rosa está cerca del Hotel Casa González?
4. ¿A qué se sientan en la terraza del café?
5. ¿De qué son testigos?
6. ¿Por qué el hombre no quiere que llamen a la policía?
7. ¿Qué estaba haciendo el hombre en la Ciudad de México?
8. ¿Qué tipo de policía llega al lugar del robo?
9. ¿Para qué serviría al menos la denuncia en la delegación?
10. ¿Por qué John exclama ¡qué coincidencia!?

NOTA CULTURAL: LA DIVISA MEXICANA

El peso mexicano es la moneda oficial de México. Pero por un breve periodo de tiempo entre 1993 y 1995 se le cambió el nombre a la moneda y se le llamó **Nuevo Peso** pero, a partir del primero de enero de 1996 se volvió a denominar simplemente **peso**.

En 1997 se imprimió por última vez un billete de $10 pesos, ya que era un gasto muy grande e innecesaria su producción pues ya existían las monedas de la misma denominación y como se sabe las monedas duran más en circulación.

En el año 2000, el Banco de México lanzó unas monedas conmemorativas de cuño corriente (veinte pesos) para celebrar el inicio del milenio: una con la efigie del poeta Octavio Paz y la otra con el Señor del Fuego (Xiuhtecutli).

El Banco de México decidió experimentar con la emisión de billetes impresos en polímero con el fin de extender la vida útil de los billetes de mayor circulación y dificultar su falsificación. El primer billete en imprimirse con este material fue el de $20 pesos.

En septiembre de 2005 salió a la circulación la moneda de cien pesos conmemorativa de los cuatrocientos años de la primera edición de la obra literaria *El Ingenioso Hidalgo Don Quijote de la Mancha* de Miguel de Cervantes Saavedra.

En el 2006 se diseñó un nuevo tipo de billetes para facilitar la identificación del valor del billete a las personas invidentes y para dificultar su falsificación. Se comenzó con el billete de $50 pesos en noviembre del 2006, después se siguió con el de $20, en agosto del 2007, el de $200, en septiembre del 2008 y el de $1,000, en abril del 2009. Los billetes de $100 y $500 entraron en circulación en el 2010 y 2011 respectivamente.

Para celebrar el Bicentenario del inicio del movimiento de Independencia y el centenario del inicio de la Revolución Mexicana, a partir del 29 de octubre del 2008 se comenzaron a poner en circulación monedas conmemorativas de cinco pesos.

VOCABULARIO: LOS BILLETES Y LAS MONEDAS

INTERACTIVE LINK

This **interactive link** provides the images of Mexicans bills and coins

booksitudio.pro/u8r

Dichos

Dar el primer paso es lo más difícil.	The first step is the most difficult.
Hay pájaros en el alambre.	Walls have ears.
Con el Jesús en la boca	Be with one's heart in one's mouth.

Más vocabulario: ¿A qué dedican el tiempo libre los mexicanos?

preparar alimentos	to cook	hacer deportes	to play sports
cocinar	to cook	ver telenovelas	watch soap operas
pasear	to take a walk		
leer	to read	celebrar	to celebrate
Ir a fiestas	go to parties	andar en bicicleta	riding a bicycle
ir al teatro	go to the theater	ir al cine	go to the movies
ver la tele	watch TV	ir al estadio	go to the stadium
hacer trabajo voluntario		to volunteer	

EJERCICIOS PRÁCTICOS

A. Escuche y comprenda.

José (hablando con Thomas): El otro día tú me preguntaste sobre el uso del tiempo libre en México. Hace poco leí sobre un estudio de unos investigadores que afirman que, hoy en día en México la gente gasta un 14% de sus ingresos en educación, cultura y actividades de recreación.

José: Después leí en una encuesta sobre el uso del tiempo, hecha en el 2009, que las mujeres mexicanas dedican 23.6% de su tiempo a tareas domésticas, unas quince horas a la semana se la pasan en la cocina preparando alimentos, mientras los hombres apenas dedican cuatro horas, un 7.3% de su tiempo.

Los jóvenes de entre 16 a 20 años de edad dedican más tiempo a ver televisión y usar el Internet, alrededor de 15 horas a la semana.

En actividades relacionadas con el estudio, las mujeres invierten 6.1% de su tiempo semanal y los hombres el 7.1%.

En cuanto a la convivencia social, la recreación, el juego, la cultura, el deporte y la utilización de medios masivos de comunicación, las mexicanas asignan 13.9% de su tiempo y los hombres el 18.6%, la diferencia está en que los hombres ven más deportes por televisión, mientras que las mujeres tienden a ver más telenovelas.

Sin embargo, hay expertos que señalan que en promedio los mexicanos ven cuatro horas al día de televisión, y que los mayores de 50 años ven hasta 5 horas diarias. Y las horas en que más se ve televisión es de las 6 a las 9 de la noche.

En actividades relacionadas con el cuidado a otras personas, el apoyo para otros hogares, el trabajo comunitario o de voluntariado, las mujeres dedican 8 horas a la semana en promedio y los hombres 5.4 horas.

Thomas: Y con respecto a las actividades al aire libre, ¿qué tanto tiempo invierten los mexicanos?

José: Bueno, según datos de la Comisión Nacional del Deporte, el 80% de los niños y jóvenes no realizan suficientes actividades físicas para alcanzar un desarrollo óptimo. Sólo el 7% de las personas mayores de 15 años realiza algún tipo de actividad física o deporte que sea significativa para su estado de salud.

La práctica de algún deporte o actividad física no es de más de una hora a la semana. Por si fuera poco, no existen programas que favorezcan la integración de la familia en torno a la actividad física y tampoco hay espacios suficientes para dar cabida a toda la población ni la calidad del aire lo permite, sobre todo en la capital.

Thomas: Es decir que México debe tener un problema grande de obesidad.

José: En efecto, se afirma que al menos 44 millones de personas tienen algún tipo de sobrepeso u obesidad, lo que equivale al 42% de la población. México ocupa el segundo lugar en el mundo, sólo después de los Estados Unidos, mientras que el Ciudad de México es la ciudad con mayor número de obesos a nivel mundial, según la propia Secretaría de Salud. Según estos datos, un 30% de la población infantil mexicana también presenta un cuadro de sobrepeso.

B. Ahora, responda las siguientes preguntas
1. ¿Qué porcentaje de dinero invierten los mexicanos en la educación, la cultura y el ocio?
2. ¿Cuántas horas a la semana dedican las mujeres a cocinar?
3. ¿Cuántas dedican los hombres?
4. ¿Cuántas horas a la semana invierten las mujeres en el estudio?
5. Según los expertos, ¿cuántas horas de televisión al día ven los mexicanos?
6. ¿Cuántas horas ven las personas mayores de 50 años?
7. ¿A qué horas se ve más televisión?
8. ¿Cuántas horas dedican las mujeres al trabajo comunitario?
9. ¿Qué tipo de programas prefieren ver los hombres en la tele?
10. ¿Qué tipo de programas prefieren las mujeres?

APUNTES GRAMATICALES
61. OTROS TIEMPOS PROGRESIVOS

1. Like the present progressive tense that expresses events in progress or repeated events, in Spanish we also use the preterite, imperfect, perfect tenses or the informal future to denote prolonged events over a period of time:
Estuvimos bailando toda la noche.
We were dancing all night.
Ellos **han estado viviendo** con la angustia de no saber de ti.
They have been living with the anguish of not knowing about you.
Voy a estar esperándola hasta que vuelva.
I'll be waiting for her until she comes back.

2. In Spanish we use the future progressive to describe continuous events which will be in progress, or to advise about the consequences of certain actions:
Esta noche **estaré llegando** a mi casa en México.
Tonight I will be arriving at my house in Mexico.
¡Hazlo y **estarás maldiciendo** tu suerte!
Do it and you will be cursing your luck!

3. The future perfect can also be used in Spanish to express conjecture in the future:

¿Me **habrán estado esperando**?
Have they **been waiting** for me?

4. In Spanish we also use the progressive conditional as in English to express "would be —ing", and to speculate about an event that may have been happening:

Era el día de su cumpleaños, y su familia la **estaría recordando.**
It was her birthday, and her family **would be remembering** her.

¿Por qué él no abrió la puerta? **Estaría durmiendo.**
Why didn't he open the door? He must have been **sleeping**.

5. The progressive tense is not commonly used in Spanish with verbs that express inner mental activities like: **amar, odiar, aborrecer**. However, you may find that some verbs like **creer or temer** can be used:

Estoy creyéndome lo que dices.
Estaba temiendo que no llegaras.

6. In Spanish, the progressive is not used to describe a state. This is contrary to English, where the progressive is quite often used to express states, such as "I am sitting." In Spanish, that phrase is expressed as:

Estoy sentado.   I am sitting.

7. The gerund form is not frequently used with the verbs like **estar** or **haber**. Here you have some rare examples that are quite literary and not very common in Spanish:

Habiendo vivido tanto tiempo decidió poner fin a su existencia.
Estando cansado de sufrir puso fin a sus días.

EJERCICIOS PRÁCTICOS

A. Change the sentences from the present to the imperfect tense while practicing the gerunds

Modelo: El profesor está corriendo.
El profesor estaba corriendo.

1. Los estudiantes están estudiando.
2. La policía está investigando.

3.   El ladrón anda huyendo.

4.   Los estudiantes están ayudando al hombre.

5.   El hombre está levantándose.

B. Form questions using the answers provided. Try to surmise about the situation by using the conditional and a gerund.

Modelo: Anna no abrió la puerta.

¿Estaría durmiendo?

1.   El profesor no oyó el teléfono.

2.   Yolanda no contestó la llamada.

3.   José no atendió al timbre.

4.   Martín no se asomó a la puerta.

5.   Thomas no vino a la cita.

C. Change the sentences from the simple future to the future progressive tense while practicing the use of the gerund.

Modelo: John va a estar de viaje.

John estará viajando.

1.   Los chicos van a estar en México hasta el fin de año.

2.   El profesor va a estar en clases hasta navidad.

3.   José va a estar trabajando en la florería hoy.

4.   Yolanda va a manejar al supermercado.

5.   Martín va a presentar un examen.

62. EL USO DE LOS DIMINUTIVOS

1. Diminutives are widely used in Spanish. To express the idea of small in size or to denote affection in Spanish we employ diminutives. The most common diminutive suffixes are —**ito/—ita.** They are added to nouns or personal names, except those ending in -n like Martín or Carmen when the ending will be cito/cita:

Luis	Luis +**ito**	**Luisito**
Pedro	Pedr+**ito**	**Pedrito**
Carmen	Carmen+**cita**	**Carmencita**

2. Most nouns ending in —**o** or —**a** drop the vowel and get the suffix –**ito/—ita:**

| piso | pis+**ito** | **pisito** |
| casa | cas + **ita** | **casita** |

mamá	mam+ita	mamita
papâ	pap+ito	papito

3. The following spelling changes occur when **−ito/−ita** is added to a noun or a name with a syllable that has either consonant, **−c−** or **−g−**:

Paco	**paqu** + ito	**Paquito**
tango	**tangu** + ito	**tanguito**

4. The suffixes **−ito/−ita** change into **−cito/−cita** if the noun or name ends with **−n**, **−r**, **−e**, and has more than one syllable:

joven	+ cita	**jovencita**
dolor	+ cito	**dolorcito**
café	+ cito	**cafecito**

5. There is a spelling change for nouns like **panza** or the adjective **panzón**:

panza	**pan** + cita	**pancita**
panzón	panzón+ cito	panzoncito

Note that in Spanish, adding a diminutive to a pejorative adjective like panzón (big belly) detoxifies the word and gives it an ironic and humorous twist.

6. Nouns ending in **−os, −oz**, or **−uz** get the suffix **−ecita**:

tos	+ecita	**tosecita**
voz	+ ecita	**vocecita**
luz	+ ecita	**lucecita**

7. Nouns with at least two syllables whose first syllable includes **−ie−** or **−ue−** and ends in **−a** or **−o** drop the vowel and get **−ecito** or **−ecita**. The same is true of one syllable nouns ending with a consonant:

piedra	piedr+ ecita	**piedrecita**
fiesta	fiest+ecita	**fiestecita**
cuerpo	cuerp+ ecito	**cuerpecito**

8. In some countries, diminutives are expressed with **−in** or **−ina**:

chiquito	**chiquitín**	The little one

9. In rare situations a word can have a "double diminutive" by changing the diminutive into a second diminutive:

chico	chiquito	chiquit + **ito**	**chiquitito**

10. Other diminutive endings are **—illo, —ucho, —(e)zuelo/a, —ete,** and **—eta,** but quite often they convey a pejorative meaning or downgrade importance:

abogado	abogad + illo	**abogadillo**	(a third rate lawyer)
abogado	abogad + ucho	**abogaducho**	(a third rate lawyer)
escritor	+ zuelo	**escritorzuelo**	(a bad writer)
mujer	+zuela	**mujerzuela**	(a woman with a very bad reputation)
rey	+ezuelo	**reyezuelo**	(a weak king)
amigo	amig + uete	**amiguete**	(an irrelevant pal/not a close friend)

11. Sometimes a word with a diminutive takes on a new meaning:

avión	(airplane)	**avioneta**	(a Cessna/small plane)
tesis	(thesis)	**tesina**	(dissertation)
zapato	(shoe)	**zapatilla**	(slipper)
mano	(hand)	**manecilla**	(hand of watch or clock)
bolsa	(bag)	**bolsillo**	(pocket)
paño	(cloth)	**pañuelo**	(handkerchief)
viola	(viola)	**violín**	(violin)
peluca	(wig)	**peluquín**	(hairpiece/toupee)

12. In Mexico, in particular, diminutive forms pervade everyday speech:

Ya **merito** llego.	(I'll be there in a second).
Ahorita mismo.	(Right now).
Clarito que lo recuerdo.	(I remember it clearly).
Espérate **tantito.**	(Wait a second).
Son **todititas igualitas.**	(They are all the same).
Hazte a un **ladito.**	(Would you please move a little bit).
Espérate un **poquito** más.	(Wait a little bit longer).

EJERCICIOS PRÁCTICOS

A. Practice using diminutives!

Modelo: ¡Buenos días amor!
  ¡Buenos días amorcito!

1. ¿Te duele la cabeza?
2. ¿Quieres que te prepare un té?
3. ¿O, prefieres un café?

4.   ¿Quieres que te traiga las pastillas?

5.   ¿Quieres que te caliente tu comida?

B.   More practice using diminutives!
   Modelo: Hola Carmen, ¿cómo estás?
                Hola **Carmencita**, ¿cómo estás?

1.   Buenos días mamá.

2.   Hola papá. ¿cómo amaneciste?

3.   ¿Qué tal Irma?

4.   ¿Dónde andas Martín?

5.   ¿Qué pasa contigo hija?

C.   Escriba el diminutivo de las siguientes palabras.

voz	traje
Pedro	Raúl
Carmen	caballo
luz	jugo
viento	Adán
dolor	coche
lago	puerta
fiesta	mujer
poco	tanto
todo	ahora

63. ADJETIVOS DE NACIONALIDAD

1.   There is no formal rule for the adjectives of nationality, but in general if the masculine adjective ends in **—o,--l**, **—n**, or **—s** the feminine form will end in **—a**:

COUNTRY	ADJECTIVE MASCULINE	FEMININE
Alemania	alemán[95]	alemana
Argentina	argentino	argentina
Austria	austríaco	austríaca

---

[95] For plural adjectives follow the plural rule: **—s** for nouns ending in a vowel, **—es** for nouns ending in a consonant.

Bolivia	boliviano	boliviana
Brasil	brasileño	brasileña
China	chino	china
Chile	chileno	chilena
Colombia	colombiano	colombiana
Corea	coreano	coreana
Dinamarca	danés	danesa
Ecuador	ecuatoriano	ecuatoriana
Egipto	egipcio	egipcia
Escocia	escocés	escocesa
España	español	española
Francia	francés	francesa
Grecia	griego	griega
Guatemala	guatemalteco	guatemalteca
Holanda	holandés	holandesa
Honduras	hondureño	hondureña
India	indio	india
Inglaterra	inglés	inglesa
Irlanda	irlandés	irlandesa
Italia	italiano	italiana
Líbano	libanés	libanesa
Luxemburgo	luxemburgués	luxemburguesa
México	mexicano	mexicana
Noruega	noruego	noruega
Nueva Zelanda	neocelandés	neocelandesa
Panamá	panameño	panameña
Paraguay	paraguayo	paraguaya
Perú	peruano	peruana
Polonia	polaco	polaca
Portugal	portugués	portuguesa
Rusia	ruso	rusa
El Salvador	salvadoreño	salvadoreña
Suecia	sueco	sueca
Suiza	suizo	suiza
Turquía	turco	turca
Uruguay	uruguayo	uruguaya
Venezuela	venezolano	venezolana

Note that in Spanish we do not capitalize the adjective of nationality.

2. If the masculine adjective of nationality ends in a vowel other that **-o**, there is no difference in the feminine adjective:

COUNTRY	ADJECTIVE MASCULINE	AND FEMININE
Canadá	canadiense	
Bélgica	belga	
Costa Rica	costarricense	
Estados Unidos	estadounidense	
Kuwait	kuwaití	
Irán	iraní	
Irak	iraquí	
Israel	israelí/israelita	
Marruecos	marroquí	
Nicaragua	nicaragüense	
Yemen	yemenita/yemení	

3. You can derive an adjective of identity from a continent:

CONTINENT	ADJECTIVE MASCULINE	FEMININE
Africa	africano	africana
Asia	asiático	asiática
Europa	europeo	europea
Australia	australiano	australiana
América	americano	americana[96]

4. You can also derive an adjective of identity from an island:

ISLAND	ADJECTIVE MASCULINE	FEMININE
Las Antillas	antillano	antillana
Mallorca	mallorquín	mallorquina
Las Canarias	canario	canaria
Filipinas	filipino	filipina
Cuba	cubano	cubana
Rep. Dominicana	dominicano	dominicana
Haití	haitiano	haitiana

---

[96] Note that America here means the whole continent and not only the United States.

Puerto Rico	puertorriqueño	puertorriqueña
Jamaica	jamaiquino/jamaicano	jamaiquina/jamaicana
Japón	japonés	japonesa

EJERCICIOS PRÁCTICOS

A. Change the sentences from nation to nationality.
   Modelo: Mi amigo es de Cuba.
               Mi amigo es cubano.
   1.   ...de Puerto Rico.
   2.   ...de Polonia.
   3.   ...de Argentina.
   4.   ...de El Salvador.
   5.   ...de Nicaragua
   6.   ...de Chile

B. **Modelo:**   La novia de mi hermano es de Uruguay.
               La novia de mi hermano es uruguaya.
   1.   ...de China.
   2.   ...de Honduras.
   3.   ...de las Islas Canarias.
   4.   ...de Holanda.
   5.   ...de Escocia.
   6.   ...de Portugal.

C. **Modelo:**   El presidente de Estados Unidos...
               El presidente de los Estados Unidos es estadounidense.
   1.   ... de Panamá.
   2.   ... de Bolivia.
   3.   ... de Venezuela.
   4.   ... de República Dominicana.
   5.   ... de Perú.
   6.   ... de Guatemala.

D. **Modelo:**   Yo soy de México, pero...
               Me gustaría ser colombiana.
   1.   Yo soy de Nicaragua, pero...
   2.   Yo soy de Costa Rica, pero...
   3.   Yo soy de Australia, pero...

4.   Yo soy de Dinamarca, pero...
5.   Yo soy de Alemania, pero...
6.   Yo soy de Nueva Zelanda, pero...

64. EL GÉNERO NEUTRO

1. In Spanish some form of the neuter gender still survives, like the neuter article **lo**, the neuter pronoun **ello**, and the neuter demonstrative pronouns **esto**, **eso** and **aquello**.

2. Neuter pronouns are necessary in Spanish to refer to concepts, ideas or statements that have no gender, or when somebody doesn't know it or has not identified the name of an object:
   ¡Páseme eso, por favor!   Pass me that, please!

3. The neuter article **lo** can be used either with adjectives or adverbs to express an abstract idea or a quality. **Lo** is always invariable and is used with feminine or masculine, singular or plural.

   a. With adjectives:
      El vio **lo** lista que es Lisa.   He saw how clever Lisa is.
      Lo bueno es que pensamos **lo** mismo.   The good thing is that we think the
                                               same way.

      Haz**lo lo** más rápido que puedas.   Do it as fast as you can.

   b. With adverbs:
      Llegaré **lo** antes posible.   I will arrive as soon as possible.
      Lo demás es **lo** de menos.   The rest is irrelevant.

4. **Lo** as a neuter pronoun refers to an idea, clause or sentence to some unspecific thing that has no gender, or something not mentioned before:

   Lo siento.   I am sorry.
   Se **lo** están poniendo difícil.   They are making things difficult for him/her.
   Mi fe me **lo** impide.   My faith prevents me from doing that.

5. The neuter third person pronoun **ello** is invariable in form, and can be translated as "it" when it doesn't refer to any specific noun. **Ello** can be combined with a preposition:

Prefiero no hablar de **ello.**   I'd rather not talk about it.

6. **Ello** can also be used as a subject pronoun:
Los arquitectos sugirieron comenzar de nuevo y **ello,** no debería sorprender-nos.
The architects recommended that we start over and that should not surprise us.

7. Neuter demonstrative pronouns **esto, eso, aquello** never have a written accent mark because they don't refer to any noun in particular. The difference between them is a matter of distance:

¿Quién ha hecho **esto**?	Who has done this?
¡De **eso** ni hablar!	Not a single word about that!
¿Qué hay de **aquello** que te dije?	What about that business that I told you about?

EJERCICIOS PRÁCTICOS

A. Complete las oraciones usando las formas del género neutro.
 1.   Todo _____ que sea arte nos interesa.
 2.   _____ bonito de vivir junto al mar es la vista.
 3.   Mi madre me aconsejó que gaste _____ menos posible.
 4.   Es bueno ahorrar por _____ del futuro incierto en que vivimos.
 5.   _____ de salir a correr a las seis de la mañana ni pensarlo.
 6.   De verdad siento _____ de tu hermano.
 7.   Estoy pensando en _____ bien que la van a pasar.
 8.   ¿Qué es _____ de que te vas de la casa?
 9.   _____ me pasó por dármelas de genio.
 10. Por _____ te digo, ¡ten mucho cuidado con ____ que haces!

65. EL USO DE LOS AUMENTATIVOS

1. The most common augmentative suffixes are: **−ón, −azo, −ote,** and **−udo**:

rico	**ricachón**	(loaded/extremely wealthy)
puerta	**portazo**	(the loud sound made when closing a door when somebody is angry or does it in a rude manner)

grande	**grandote**	(really big)
fuerte	**forzudo**	(very strong)

2. These augmentatives are used in general to express intensity or big in size, but they are not as common as diminutives:

pata	**patota**	(big leg)
cuerpo	**cuerpazo**	(great body, in good shape)
pie	**piesezote**	(big foot)

3. In some contexts **—azo** can express admiration:

¡Eres un	**buenazo**!	You are a good person!
¡Fue un	**exitazo**!	It was a success!

4. Some suffixes like **—aco, —astro, —ucho** form pejorative expressions:

pájaro	**pajarraco**	(sinister bird)
poeta	**poetastro**	(poetaster/inferior poet)
cuarto	**cuartucho**	(miserable room)

5. Some augmentative suffixes create a new set of words:

soltero	**solterón**	(old bachelor)
silla	**sillón**	(arm chair)
caja	**cajón**	(drawer)
rata	**ratón**	(mouse)
bolsa	bolsón	(sac/big bag)

6. Some verbs can be used as adjectives in their augmentative forms:

dormir	dormilón/dormilona
mirar	mirón/ mirona
gritar	gritón/gritona
fisgonear	fisgón/ fisgona

EJERCICIOS PRÁCTICOS

A. Use the appropriate augmentative suffixes.

   Modelo: Eres bueno.

   ¡Eres un **buenazo**!

   1.   Esto es un éxito.
   2.   Ese es un muchacho.
   3.   Aquel es un hotel.

4. Tienes un carro.
5. Vives en una casa.
6. ¡Mira qué cuerpo tiene el salvavidas!

B. Escriba los aumentativos de las siguientes palabras.

contestar	pobre
llorar	casa
gritar	hotel
comer	palabra
dormir	animal
preguntar	flaco
mirar	carro
responder	carta
mujer	cabeza
perro	fácil

MINIRELATO: LA PRENSA EN MÉXICO

Los periódicos mexicanos se parecen mucho a los periódicos estadounidenses. En México se usan tanto el formato asabanado, que es el formato tradicional como el del periódico Reforma o El Universal y el formato tabloide como el del periódico La Jornada.

En general, todos los periódicos tienen la misma estructura. Las planas: primera plana es la cara del periódico donde se destacan las noticias más importantes y la última plana que cierra el periódico; las secciones que incluyen: local, nacional, internacional, policíaca, política, deportes, espectáculos, cultura, viajes; la línea editorial y artículos de opinión; los clasificados (classified ads), el clima, y algunos tienen una sección de obituarios.

Hoy en día todos los periódicos tienen sus páginas en Internet, algunos son de consulta gratuita como la Jornada, otros, como el periódico Reforma o El Norte, requieren de un pago de suscripción para consultar sus contenidos.

He aquí algunas direcciones electrónicas de periódicos en español que pueden ser de interés para usted: http://www.prensaescrita.com/

Preguntas

1. ¿Es que los periódicos mexicanos y estadounidenses se parecen?
2. ¿Cuáles son los dos tipos de formatos de los periódicos?
3. ¿Cuál es la parte más importante del periódico?
4. ¿Cómo se llama la sección donde se puede encontrar información de otros países?
5. ¿Dónde se encuentra la opinión del periódico como tal?
6. ¿Dónde puede uno encontrar información sobre servicios o ventas?
7. ¿Todos los periódicos cobran por las consultas en Internet?
8. En México, ¿qué periódico cobra?
9. En México, ¿qué periódico tiene formato tabloide?
10. ¿Qué periódico tiene formato asabanado?

LECTURA: LOS PERIÓDICOS EN MÉXICO

Según una encuesta sobre hábitos de lectura hecha en México por el INEGI en el 2006, 92.1% de la población mayor de doce años sabe leer y escribir.

En cuanto a lectura de periódicos, los hombres suelen leer más (47.5%) que las mujeres (37.5%).

Los periódicos son más leídos en la Ciudad de México (55.6%), seguido de la región noroeste (52.2%) y por último la región sur con 35.5%.

La lectura de periódicos se da más en quienes cuentan con educación universitaria o superior (59.9%).

Un 55.8% de los entrevistados prefiere los periódicos regionales, o locales después los nacionales con 54.6% y los deportivos con 26.4%.

En la actualidad hay más de un centenar de periódicos en México, pero de ellos unos quince son los más importantes por su historia, circulación nacional o regional, algunas veces internacional, tiraje, la calidad de sus articulistas y el respeto y credibilidad que el público les tiene. Sin embargo, ninguno de los periódicos, salvo tal vez La Jornada, que es claramente un periódico de izquierda, tiene una línea editorial definida y todos juegan a mostrarse imparciales, con una tendencia a presentarse como periódicos de centro, tendencia que está de moda no sólo en México.

He aquí, algunos de los periódicos mexicanos más importantes:

El Universal, de circulación nacional, periódico de centro a veces tirando hacia la derecha, pero mucha de su información es frívola y tiende a presentar noticias del mundo del espectáculo.

Reforma y El Norte (editado este último en Monterrey), de mayor presencia nacional y de referencia internacional. Periódicos de centro izquierda con muy buenos articulistas y editorialistas.

Milenio, también de circulación nacional. Muy buenos articulistas y buena sección política. Su línea es de centro izquierda, pero más de izquierda que Reforma.

El Financiero, periódico de centro un poco cargado a la derecha, más enfocado en los aspectos económicos del país. Con una línea que intenta imitar al WSJ, pero que se queda lejos de la calidad de los análisis económicos y financieros del periódico estadounidense.

La Jornada, es el único periódico abiertamente de izquierda, respetado internacionalmente. Es el periódico que lee la clase política e intelectual de México y los universitarios, especialmente los de la UNAM.

La Crónica de Hoy, es un periódico de centro, que tiene un discurso más para la clase política, especialmente de tendencia priísta (Partido Revolucionario Institucional)

La Prensa, es sin duda el periódico más popular de México, es un periódico de nota roja que a la gente más sencilla le encanta por el morbo de los asesinatos y violaciones de que están rellenas sus páginas.

Excélsior, es uno de los periódicos más viejos de México, tuvo un peso político importante, pero todo acabó cuando hubo una intervención del Gobierno del Presidente Echeverría en 1975. Desde entonces el periódico no ha logrado recuperar su lugar de primer periódico de México que le arrebató El Uno Más Uno, primero y después La Jornada.

El Sol de México, un periódico con ediciones en todas las ciudades grandes del país, un periódico de centro derecha, completamente irrelevante desde el punto de vista político; es un periódico que está pensado más para hacer negocio con las ventas de publicidad.

Esto, es un periódico deportivo Periódico muy popular pues es un periódico de la chismografía deportiva.

Ovaciones, otro periódico deportivo que publica dos tiradas diarias, la Primera y la Segunda. También es muy popular por sus notas deportivas y por que en sus páginas aparecen fotos de chicas con poca ropa y encabezados sensacionalistas.

Preguntas

1. Según el INEGI ¿qué porcentaje de mexicanos sabe leer y escribir?
2. ¿Por qué los hombres leen más periódicos que las mujeres?
3. ¿Por qué se leen más periódicos en la Ciudad de México?
4. ¿Cuál es la relación nivel de escolaridad y lectura de periódicos?
5. ¿Por qué los periódicos deportivos gustan tanto?
6. ¿Qué factores hacen que un periódico sea importante?
7. ¿Cuál es la tendencia de los periódicos mexicanos?
8. ¿Qué periódico es abiertamente de izquierda?
9. ¿En qué periódico se pueden encontrar noticias relacionadas con la economía y las finanzas?

VOCABULARIO

VERBOS

salir	asaltar	soplar	leer
acabar	terminar	seguir	continuar
venir	quedarse	llevar	andar
examinar	pintar	ir	ser
estar	oír	ver	recordar

NOMBRES

las diligencias	el consejo	la terraza	el café
la rabia	la fama	la florería	el temperamento
el periódico	el norte	el país	la portada
el suelo	pintores	estudiantes	profesores
el centro	el ladrón	el formato	el/la encargado/a
el/la recepcionista	el sol	el pasaporte	el gobierno
un/una periodista	el nivel	el centro	la semana
el fin	el suelo	un hotel	el parque
el edificio	el mar	el/la policía	el hombre
el teléfono	las mujeres	las chicas	la muchacha

ADJETIVOS

mucho/a	fuerte	malo/a	injusto/a
cruel	superficial	descarado/a	ingrato/a
atrevido/a	mismo/a	azul	bonito/a
mexicano/a	chino/a	argentino/a	chileno/a
estadounidense	coreano/a	guatemalteco/a	colombiano/a
boliviano/a	uruguayo/a	cubano/a	dominicano/a
chiquito/a	grandecito/a	grandote/a	canadiense

ADVERBIOS

simplemente   mal

EXPRESIONES UTILES

de sol a sol	malos modales	mal temperamento
echar pestes	¡qué cinismo!	palabra de honor
con el Jesús en la boca		

CAPÍTULO 14: LAS PROFESIONES Y LOS OFICIOS

En este capítulo...

You'll learn about professions and about the challenges many Mexicans face while finding a job in Mexico, leading them to have to immigrate to the US. You will also learn about how other immigrants cross Mexico on their way to the US, and how dangerous this experience can be for them.

You'll learn how to express necessity, will, judgment, emotion, doubt, uncertainty and other situations that trigger the subjunctive. In this chapter you'll be introduced to the present subjunctive in its regular and irregular forms and uses, and you will contrast the indicative with the subjunctive to have a better sense of each.

Contexto

José, Thomas y Martín están en la sala conversando. De pronto, José orienta la conversación hacia lo que Thomas quiere ser cuando sea un profesional y tenga que trabajar.

José: ¿Cuál es la profesión de tu padre, Thomas?

Thomas: Mi padre es un abogado en Nueva York.

José: Y tu mamá, ¿dónde trabaja?

Thomas: Ella es médico cirujano en un hospital en Manhattan.

José: Cuando yo tenía tu edad yo quería ser ingeniero mecánico, pero no teníamos los recursos, así que me puse a trabajar y aprendí el oficio de los arreglos florales y aquí me tienes ateniendo el negocio.

Thomas: ¿De verdad querías ser ingeniero?

José: Sí, pero y tus padres que quieren que tú seas cuando te gradúes.

Thomas: Están indecisos.

José: Y tú, ¿qué querrías ser?

Thomas: Me gustaría ser doctor como mi mamá.

Martín: Yo no me haría doctor nunca. ¡Ni loco!

Thomas: ¿Por qué? ¿No te agrada la medicina?

Martín: Tengo por lo menos una docena de razones para que no me guste la medicina. Además, con solo ver sangre siento que me voy a desmayar

José (haciendo caso omiso del comentario de Martín): En serio, Thomas, ¿quieres estudiar medicina cuando termines la licenciatura?

Thomas: Bueno, primero me gustaría trabajar como voluntario en el Cuerpo de Paz, ganar experiencia y después estudiar en la escuela de medicina.

José: ¿Y eres bueno en biología y química?

Thomas: Siempre se puede mejorar.

Martín: Yo quiero ser arquitecto.

Thomas: Muy bien. ¿Y eres bueno con las matemáticas y el dibujo?

Martín: ¡Soy el mejor!

José: ¡Caray qué modesto!

Thomas: Si eres tan bueno, hasta te voy a pedir que diseñes mi casa, ¡claro, cuando tenga con qué pagarte!

Martín: Por ser tú, te daré un precio especial. ¡Una verdadera ganga! Así sea una casona lo que quieras.

Preguntas

1. ¿Cuál es la profesión del padre de Thomas?
2. ¿Dónde trabaja la madre?
3. ¿Qué quiere ser Thomas?
4. Pero antes de estudiar medicina, ¿qué piensa hacer?
5. ¿Qué quería ser José cuando era joven?
6. ¿Qué le impidió lograr su meta?
7. ¿Es que Martín querría ser doctor?
8. ¿Cuántas razones tiene Martín para no querer ser médico?
9. ¿Qué le pasa cuando ve la sangre?
10. ¿Qué quiere ser Martín?

NOTA CULTURAL: LA MIGRACIÓN DE MEXICANOS A LOS ESTADOS UNIDOS

Durante las dos últimas décadas del siglo XIX y las dos primeras del XX, los migrantes mexicanos jugaron un papel importante en la construcción de las vías férreas en el suroeste de Estados Unidos. Los trabajadores mexicanos llegaron a representar el 70% de las cuadrillas y tan sólo en 1908 fueron contratados más de 16 mil trabajadores mexicanos para trabajar en los ferrocarriles.

Poco tiempo después, cuando Estados Unidos entró en la Primera Guerra Mundial, la industria y el campo estadounidenses necesitaron suplir a sus trabajadores que habían marchado a la guerra. Los migrantes mexicanos resolvieron su problema. El gobierno de los Estados Unidas legalizó el flujo en 1917 estableciendo un programa especial para admitir temporalmente la mano de obra mexicana; este programa finalizó en 1921.

La crisis de 1929 propició que surgieran y se desarrollaran algunos grupos que proponían restricciones a la migración y por lo tanto que se oponían al empleo de mano de obra mexicana, aduciendo, exactamente como ahora, que los mexicanos ocupaban puestos que deberían corresponder a los ciudadanos estadounidenses agobiados por los altos índices de desempleo. ¡Una vez más la historia se repite!

Cuando los Estados Unidos entraron en la Segunda Guerra Mundial, los Estados Unidos y México firmaron un acuerdo mediante el cual los trabajadores mexicanos podían ingresar a los Estados Unidos con la finalidad de suplir temporalmente a los obreros estadounidenses. Este acuerdo, que se conoce con el nombre de **Programa Bracero**, se mantuvo vigente desde 1942 hasta 1964.

En 1986 se implementó la Ley Simpson-Rodino, que buscaba ejercer un mayor control sobre las empresas que contratan indocumentados de todas las nacionalidades.

Durante todos estos años, los Estados Unidos han tratado de contener el flujo de mano de obra a través de la frontera, sin embargo, todos sus esfuerzos han fracasado.

Hoy en día se estima que entre 12 y 14 millones de personas viven en los Estados Unidos sin documentos legales, y cada año el número aumenta en un estimado de 400.000; aunque hay quienes afirman que la actual crisis económica está obligando a algunos a regresar a sus países de origen.

Hasta ahora, se cree que más de **cinco mil** migrantes han perecido tratando de cruzar la frontera entre México y Estados Unidos.

Dichos

Cuando a Roma fueres haz lo que vieres.
No hay peor ciego que quien no quiere ver.

When in Rome do as the Romans do.
There are none so blind as those who will not see.

A lo hecho pecho.   There's no use crying over spilled
                                           milk.

VOCABULARIO: LAS PROFESIONES Y LOS OFICIOS

(The professions and trades)

Yo me especialicé en …

filosofía	ciencias (biología/química/física)	ciencias políticas
mate (matemáticas)	psicología	computación/ informática
bellas artes.	(pintura/arquitectura/ escultura/música)	
historia	idiomas	lingüística
arquitectura	ingeniería	diplomacia
contabilidad	trabajador/a social	enfermería
medicina	farmacéutica	

Preguntas

1.   ¿Cuántas clases toma usted?
2.   ¿Cómo son sus clases, grandes, pequeñas?
3.   ¿Cuáles son las clases más difíciles?
4.   ¿Cuáles son las más fáciles?
5.   ¿Les dejan mucha tarea en cada clase?
6.   ¿En su clase de inglés, escribe composiciones?
7.   ¿En la clase de español, usa el laboratorio?
8.   ¿Suele sacar buenas calificaciones?
9.   ¿Ha tomado usted recientemente algún examen?
10.   ¿Lo preparó bien?
11.   ¿Aprobó o reprobó usted ese examen?

Más vocabulario: Las profesiones y los oficios

Usted ya ha aprendido algunas profesiones, ahora veremos otras más y cómo referirse a ellas cuando es una mujer quien las desempeña. Por ejemplo **el profesor/la profesora**; en otros casos la forma de referirse a la profesión cambia como por ejemplo: **el actor/la actriz**. Otras veces, la profesión se mantiene invariable aunque se tiene que usar el artículo masculino o femenino, según sea el caso: **el juez/la juez.**

un agente/una agente: de viajes, inmobiliario, de policía, de seguros

un asistente/una asistente[97]: social, médico, dental, limpieza

el representante/la representante: político, de ventas, deportivo

un policía/una policía	un arquitecto/una arquitecto
un artista/una artista	un dentista/una dentista
un médico/una médico[98]	el cantante/la cantante (singer)
un psiquiatra/una psiquiatra	un periodista/una periodista
un oculista/una oculista	un deportista/una deportista
un poeta/una poeta	un astronauta/una astronauta
el atleta/la atleta	el guía/la guía[99]
el chofer/la chofer	el modelo/la modelo
el piloto/la piloto	el soldado/la soldado
el soprano/la soprano	el intérprete/la intérprete
un economista/una economista	un músico/una músico
un ingeniero/una ingeniero	el gerente/la gerente (manager)
el conductor/la conductora (TV anchor)	el reportero/la reportera
el presidente/la presidente[100]	el abogado/la abogada
un funcionario/una funcionaria (civil worker)	el director/la directora
un banquero/una banquera	un doctor/una doctora
un contador/una contadora	un escritor/una escritora (writer)
el cocinero/la cocinera	un fotógrafo/una fotógrafa
el asesor/la asesora	el enfermero/la enfermera
el programador/la programadora	el vendedor/la vendedora

---

[97] In some countries, the feminine form **una asistenta** is accepted.

[98] In some countries. like Cuba, the expression **una médica** is used. But in general you will hear **una médico,** or more often, **una doctora.**

[99] This is also used to mean guide book.

[100] In some countries like Chile, it is acceptable to say "**la presidenta**".

el catedrático/la catedrática

el camarero/la camarera

un diplomático/una diplomática

un trabajador/una trabajadora

el editor/la editora

el mago/la maga

el bailarín/la bailarina

el poeta/la poetisa[101]

el rector/la rectora (president of a college/university)

el mesero/la mesera

el sirviente/la sirvienta

un obrero/una obrera (worker)

el ministro/la ministra

el decano/la decana

el monje/la monja

el actor/la actriz

el abad/la abadesa

EJERCICIOS PRÁCTICOS

☺ ☺

A. Ahora vamos a contestar estas preguntas.
1. ¿Quién trabaja en un hospital?
2. ¿Quién es el líder en una compañía?
3. Si tiene un accidente, ¿quiénes lo pueden ayudar?
4. Si piensa construir una casa, ¿a quién va a contratar?
5. Si piensa hacer un viaje, ¿a quién va a consultar?
6. Si piensa invertir dinero, ¿a quién va a ver?
7. Si se siente mal, ¿a quién recurre?
8. Si quiere saber qué va a pasar en el futuro, ¿a quién va a ver?
9. ¿Cómo se llaman los empleados que ayudan al patrón?
10. Cuando va a un restaurante, ¿quién lo atiende?
11. ¿Para qué profesión es importante estudiar un idioma?
12. Cuando va a una embajada ¿con quién habla?
13. ¿Que profesión le gustaría ejercer?
14. ¿Qué profesiones dejan mucho dinero?
15. ¿Qué profesiones requieren un título universitario?

☺ ☺

B. En general, un buen profesor posee las cualidades siguientes:

la sinceridad	el entusiasmo	la curiosidad
la integridad	la paciencia	la inteligencia
la imaginación	la generosidad	la comprensión

---

[101] This expression has become derogatory, so many women prefer the expression **una poeta** instead.

el respeto por los estudiantes   conocimiento de su materia

C. Hable de las características que usted admira más en sus profesores.
    ¿Por qué valora más esas características?

APUNTES GRAMATICALES
66. EL PRESENTE DEL SUBJUNTIVO

Note that you already have practiced this tense in **chapter 8** when you
learned formal commands.

1. The subjunctive stem of regular verbs can be found by dropping the **-o**
    ending from the first person singular form (**yo**) of the present tense:

	FIRST PERSON	STEM FOF SUBJUNCTIVE
—ar verbs	yo **habl**o	**habl**—

Add the following subjunctive endings to the stem of **—ar** verbs: **—e, —es,—
e, —emos, —éis, —en**

hablar
Ella quiere que yo habl**e**.
Ella quiere que tú habl**es**.
Ella quiere que vos habl**és**
Ella quiere que él habl**e**.
Ella quiere que usted habl**e**.
Ella quiere que nosotros habl**emos**.
Ella quiere que *vosotros habléis*.
Ella quiere que ellas habl**en**.
Ella quiere que ustedes habl**en**.

Add the following subjunctive endings to the stem of **-er/-ir** verbs: **—a, —as,
—a, —amos, —áis, —an**

comer	**vivir**
... que yo com**a**.	...que yo viv**a**.
... que tú com**as**.	... que tú viv**as**.
... que vos com**ás**	...que vos viv**ás**
... que ella com**a**.	... que ella viv**a**.
... que usted com**a**.	... que usted viv**a**.
... que nosotros com**amos**.	... que nosotros viv**amos**.

346

... que *vosotros com**áis**.*
... que ellos com**an**.
... que ustedes com**an** .

... que *vosotros viv**áis**.*
... que ellos viv**an**.
... que ustedes viv**an**.

Note that the first person singular **yo**, and the third person singular (**él, ella, usted**) have the same conjugation, the context is responsible for clarifying the meaning.

2. The subjunctive is used in a subordinate clause when the main clause expresses judgment, wishes, demands, advice, persuasion or any other type of will or influence (**querer, prohibir, exigir, aconsejar, desear, demandar, rogar, pedir**):
Él **quiere que** tú **estudies.**   He wants you to study.

    Note that the subject of the subordinate clause differs from the subject of the main clause.

3. The subjunctive is required in a subordinate clause when a verb expresses an emotional state (**estar contento, esperar, sentir, alegrarse, apenarse, odiar, estar triste, sorprenderse, arrepentirse**):
Estoy **triste de** que ustedes no **vengan.**   I'm sad that you're not coming.

4. The subjunctive is used in subordinate clauses when a verb expresses doubt, uncertainty, disbelief, denial or negates facts (**dudar, no es cierto, no pensar, no es posible, no puede ser cierto, no es verdad, no creer**):
Tu padre **no cree** que tú **vayas** a escoger un buen coche.
Your father doesn't believe that you will choose a good car.

    Note that verbs like **creer, pensar, parecer** are never triggers for the subjunctive unless you use them to pose a question that suggests an action in the future:
¿Crees que ella me **entienda**?   Do you think she understands me?

5. The subjunctive is required in a subordinate clause when the main clause expresses unreality, expectations, indefiniteness or nonexistence (**buscar, hay alguien aquí, existe alguien que**):
La universidad de Harvard busca un robot que **sepa** hablar español.
Harvard University is looking for a robot that can speak Spanish.

6. The subjunctive is required in a subordinate clause when the main clause uses impersonal expressions that convey urgency, necessity, emotion, unreality, uncertainty or an indirect or implied command (**es necesario, es urgente, es importante, es bueno, es malo, es saludable, ojalá**[102]**, es mejor, es deseable, es aconsejable, qué triste, qué malo, qué pena**):
Es importante que llegues a tiempo. It's important that you arrive on time.

7. The subjunctive is required in a subordinate clause with some expressions that suggest future time, commands, temporal conjunctions or adverbs of probability in the main clause[103]:
Llámanos **en cuanto** llegues. Call us as soon as you arrive.
Comeremos **tan pronto** lleguen. We will eat as soon as they get here.

8. Nowadays, the use of the future subjunctive in Spanish is obsolete. The present subjunctive is used when a future time is indicated or implied:
Me apena que ella no **pueda** venir mañana. I feel sad that she can't come tomorrow.

9. In sentences that have the final conjunction, para que:
Ellos preparan todo para que no se vaya a ir la luz.
They are preparing everything so the lights do not go off.

10. In sentences that establish a condition: **en caso**, **a menos que**, **a no ser que**:
No vengas a no ser que estés libre. Do not come unless you are free.

11. In sentences that establish concessions using **aunque**, **aun cuando**:
Aunque tenga que ir al fin del mundo lo haré.
Even if I have to go to the end of the world, I will do it.

12. In sentences that express probability, using **tal vez**, **quizá**:
Tal vez llueva esta noche. It may rain tonight.

13. In relative sentences:

---

[102] **Ojalá** can be translated as "May God grant".
[103] You will study this in more detail in Apunte gramatical # 79 in this chapter.

Necesitamos estudiantes que les guste estudiar.
We need students that like to study.

14. In sentences that express desires:
Que todos sepan que tengo hambre.
Everybody should now that I am hungry.

EJERCICIOS PRÁCTICOS

A. Use the clue in parentheses to write a new sentence using the subjunctive.
Modelo: Él no tiene acento al hablar. (me alegro)
Me alegro que él no tenga acento al hablar.
1. Usted habla suavemente. (yo quiero que)
2. Ustedes se besan mucho al saludar. (no es verdad que)
3. Tú respondes correctamente. (Es importante que)
4. Hablas elocuentemente. (ojalá que)
5. Salúdame sin pena al llegar. (espero que)

B. Use the clue in parentheses to write a new sentence using the subjunctive.
Modelo: Nosotros lavamos los cobertores. (es deseable que)
Es deseable que nosotros lavemos los cobertores.
1. Ustedes pasan la aspiradora. (Estoy contento de que)
2. Ellas tiran la basura. (Es urgente que)
3. Ella encera el piso. (Me sorprende que)
4. Yo lavo los baños. (Es encomiable que)
5. Nosotros renovamos la cocina. (Es increíble que)

C. Use the clue in parentheses to write a new sentence using the subjunctive.
Modelo: Usted ama tocar la guitarra. (su amiga no cree)
Su amiga no cree que usted ame tocar la guitarra.
1. Nosotros tomamos clases de piano. (Me alegra que)
2. Ellos aprenden por muchas horas. (Es necesario que)
3. *Vosotros tenéis* mucha paciencia. (Es imprescindible que)
4. Ellas adoran el violín. (Usted quiere que)
5. Ustedes escogen un buen maestro. (Es una sorpresa que)

D. Use the clue in parentheses to write a new sentence using the subjunctive.
Modelo: Usted olvida el nombre de sus amigos. (Es una pena)
Es una pena que usted olvide el nombre de sus amigos.

1. El profesor olvida el nombre de sus alumnos. (Es una vergüenza que)
2. Usted no trabaja bien. (Estamos desolados de que)
3. Tú no cuidas de tus amigos. (Es una lástima que)
4. Ellos se quedan hasta tarde. (El jefe quiere que)
5. Nosotros respondemos bien a todas las preguntas. (Ellas dudan que)

67. SUBJUNTIVOS IRREGULARES EN EL PRESENTE

1. **—ar, —er** verbs that have a stem change in the present tense also have the same change in the subjunctive:

INFINITIVE		FIRST PERSON	SUBJUNCTIVE FORM	
Pensar	(e: ie)	pienso	**piense**	**pensemos**
mostrar	(o:ue)	muestro	**muestre**	**mostremos**
entender	(e:ie)	entiendo	**entienda**	**entendamos**
volver	(o:ue)	vuelvo	**vuelva**	**volvamos**
torcer	(o:ue)	tuerzo	**tuerza**	**torzamos**
poder	(o:ue)	puedo	**pueda**	**podamos**

Ella quiere que yo le **muestre** el apartamento.
Ella quiere que nosotros le **mostr**emos el apartamento.

Note that all these changes come from the "yo" form in the present tense: p**ie**nso, m**ue**stro, ent**ie**ndo, etc.

2. **—ir** verbs that have a stem change in the present tense also have changes in the subjunctive. However, there are two main types of stem changes:

pedir	(e:i)	pido	**pida**
sentir	(e:ie)	siento	**sienta**
dormir	(o:ue)	duermo	**duerma**

a. Verbs like **pedir**, (-**e** to -**i**) that keep the same change for all subjects including **nosotros** and *vosotros*: **pida, pidas, pidás, pida, pidamos, pidáis, pidan**:
El profesor espera que nosotros **pidamos** el libro.
El profesor quiere que ella **pida** el libro.

Similar verbs to **pedir** are: **competir, concebir, despedir(se), elegir, impe-dir, reír, reñir, repetir, seguir, servir, vestir(se)**

b. Verbs like **dormir (—o to –ue)** or **sentir (—e to –ie)** that have a slightly **differ-ent stem-change** in **nosotros** and *vosotros,* and for the form *vos* used in some countries of South and Central America:

dormir	**sentir**
que yo d**ue**rma	que yo s**ie**nta
que tú d**ue**rmas	que tú s**ie**ntas
que **vos durmás**	que **vos sintás**
que él d**ue**rma	que él s**ie**nta
que nosotros **durmamos**	que nosotros **sintamos**
que *vosotros* **durmáis**	que *vosotros* **sintáis**
que ustedes d**ue**rman	que ustedes s**ie**ntan

El doctor me sugiere que **duerma** más.
El doctor nos sugiere que nosotros **durmamos** más.

Mi abuela desea que me **sienta** bien en su casa.
Mi abuela desea que nos **sintamos** bien en su casa.

The other verb like **dormir** is: **morir**

Similar verbs to **sentir** are: **advertir, divertir(se), arrepentirse, consentir, disentir, convertir(se), discernir, herir, hervir, mentir, desmentir, preferir, referir, sugerir.**

3. There are five verbs that do not follow the **yo** form rule because they are irregular in the present subjunctive: **dar, estar, ir, saber,** and **ser**:
   dar: dé, des, dé, demos, deis, den
   estar: esté, estés, esté, estemos, estéis, estén
   ir: vaya, vayas, vaya, vayamos, vayáis, vayan
   saber: sepa, sepas, sepa, sepamos, sepáis, sepan
   ser: sea, seas, sea, seamos, seáis, sean

   La mamá se alegra de que su hijo **dé** dinero a los pobres.
   El profesor espera que Thomas **esté** haciendo la tarea.
   Lisa quiere que Allan **vaya** mañana al gimnasio.
   Me alegra que John **sepa** la respuesta.

Es importante que tú **seas** responsable.

4. Verbs whose infinitives end in **—car, —gar, —zar** undergo spelling changes in the yo form for phonetic reasons (as they do in the preterite yo form):

INFINITIVE	FIRST PERSON PRETERIT	STEM FOF SUBJUNCTIVE
sacar	saqué	**saque**
pagar	pagué	**pague**
abrazar	abracé	**abrace**

Es urgente que nosotros **paguemos** la colegiatura.
Es urgente que él **saque** la basura.
Yo quiero que mi madre me **abrace**.

Note that if a verb also is a stem-change verb in present tense like the verb **almorzar** or the verb **colgar**, this verb will have a double transformation the one coming from the stem-change and the one coming from the **—zar** ending:

Alm**uerce**	almor**ce**mos	**cuelgue**	col**gue**mos
Alm**uerce**s	almor**cé**is	**cuelgue**s	col**gué**is
Alm**uerce**	alm**uerce**n	**cuelgue**	cuel**gue**n

Es importante que ellas **almuercen** temprano.
Quiero que **cuelgues** la ropa en el armario.

5. The verbs **enviar, actuar** and **continuar** have an accent mark in the **-í** or the **—ú** of all forms except for **vos, nosotros** and *vosotros*:
enviar: envíe, envíes, **enviés**, envíe, **enviemos, enviéis**, envíen
continuar: continúe, continúes, continués, continúe, **continuemos, conti-nuéis**, continúen.
La gente quiere que **continúe** el concierto.
Los fanáticos quieren que **continuemos** el concierto.

6. Verbs like **jugar, oler** and **inquirir** also have a change in their stem. They return to regular conjugation in the **vos, nosotros** and *vosotros* forms, as we have studied in the present tense:
jugar: juegue, juegues, **jugués**, juegue, **juguemos, juguéis**, jueguen
oler: huela, huelas, **olás**, huela, **olamos**, oláis, **huelan**
inquirir: inquiera, inquieras, **inquirás**, inquiera, **inquiramos, inquiráis**, inquieran.

EJERCICIOS PRÁCTICOS

A. Practice using the present tense subjunctive by conjugating the verb according to the subject given in parenthesis.

Modelo:　Ella quiere que yo saque la basura. (tú)

　　　　　Ella quiere que (tú) saques la basura.

1. La mamá desea que su hija apague la luz. (sus hijas)
2. El director quiere que los alumnos almuercen temprano. (Thomas)
3. El profesor quiere que Yolanda cuelgue el teléfono. (las familias)
4. El presidente quiere que los ciudadanos paguen los impuestos. (tú)
5. Ustedes quieren que ellos toquen sus instrumentos. (nosotros)

B. Practice using the present tense subjunctive by conjugating the verb according to the subject given in parenthesis.

Modelo:　La mamá desea que su hijo almuerce. (nosotros)

　　　　　La mamá desea que nosotros almorcemos.

1. El entrenador quiere que tu juegues. (*vosotros*)
2. El profesor quiere que ustedes traigan sus libros. (nosotros)
3. El cura pide que los feligreses vuelvan pronto. (*vosotros*)
4. José quiere que Thomas piense en español. (nosotros)
5. La profesora no quiere que los niños se caigan. (nosotros)

C. Practice using the present tense subjunctive by conjugating the verb according to the subject given in parenthesis.

Modelo:　Los padres esperan que su hijo escoja chino. (ellas)

　　　　　Los padres esperan que ellas escojan chino.

1. Yo espero que tú prefieras el español. (*vosotros*)
2. El profesor espera que los estudiantes no mientan. (nosotros)
3. Los Zurita quieren que yo hierva las verduras. (nosotros)
4. La señora Bernal quiere que su hija duerma más. (*vosotros*)
5. El director quiere que la soprano sienta la música. (nosotros)

D. Escriba la forma correcta del subjuntivo para completar las oraciones.

1. La madre espera que el bebé _____ (nacer) bien.
2. ¡Es una lástima que _____ (comenzar) a llover!
3. El entrenador quiere que todos nosotros _____ (jugar).
4. El jefe quiere que la secretaria _____ (enviar) las cartas.
5. Mi madre quiere que yo _____ (hacer) la tarea.
6. José quiere que Martín _____ (convencer) a Thomas de ir al paseo.

7. Yolanda espera que Thomas _____ (caber) en el coche.
8. El profesor duda que todos _____ (concluir) el examen final.
9. Santa quiere que los niños _____ (elegir) sus regalos.
10. Yo no creo que _____ (ir) a llover.
11. La niñera no cree que el niño se _____ (torcer) el pie si brinca.
12. Mi padre quiere que nosotros _____ (pedir) una ensalada.
13. El profesor demanda que le _____ (explicar) lo que pasó.
14. Mi madre me ruega que yo no le _____. (mentir)
15. El alcalde ordena que todos lo _____. (seguir)
16. La chica quiere que nosotros _____ (oler) el perfume.
17. El juez ordena que la policía _____ (inquirir) sobre el crimen.
18. Me apena que nosotros _____ (empezar) a estudiar tan tarde.

E. Con un compañero de clase escuche y descubra los verbos en subjuntivo de las siguientes canciones:

INTERACTIVE LINK

booksstudio.pro/8vx
booksstudio.pro/l9u

68. ¿INDICATIVO O SUBJUNTIVO?

1. It is necessary to distinguish between impersonal expressions that need the subjunctive in the subordinate clause and those that do not.

TAKE SUBJUNCTIVE	DO NOT TAKE SUBJUNCTIVE
Es posible...	Es verdad...
Es probable...	Es evidente...
Es imposible...	Es cierto...
Es bueno...	Existe la certeza...
Es justo...	Parece que...
Conviene...	Es seguro...
Es difícil...	Es positivo...
Es útil...	Es absolutamente cierto...
Es deseable...	Es indudable...

Es conveniente...
Es mejor...
Es necesario...
Puede ser...
Es importante...
Es una lástima...
Ojalá...

Note that the expressions that require the subjunctive suggest that something may happen, and the expressions that do not require the subjunctive indicate that something is definitely going to happen.

2. When used in negative statements the verbs **creer, pensar, parecer** suggest uncertainty. Consequently, the verb in the subordinate clause that follows these must be in the subjunctive:
No creo que él **esté** diciendo la verdad.
No pienso que él **venga** mañana.
No espero que él **traiga** dinero.
¿No crees que él **tenga** razón?

Note that interrogative and negative sentences with these verbs require the indicative:
¿Piensas tú que él **no** va a decir la verdad?
¿Crees tú que ella **no** puede hacerlo mejor?
Parece que ella **no** puede hacerlo.

3. The verb **esperar** suggests uncertainty in negative sentences, and also in interrogative phrases. Therefore, the verb in the subordinate clause must be in the subjunctive:
¿Esperas que nosotros **podamos** pasar la materia?
No esperas que ella **venga** temprano ¿verdad?

EJERCICIOS PRÁCTICOS

A. Practice using the present subjunctive.
   Modelo: Esta actriz puede hacerlo. (Es posible)
                  Es posible que esta actriz pueda hacerlo.
   1.   La sesión estará terminando ya. (Es probable)
   2.   Esta película será un éxito. (Es difícil)

3. Él escribe a menudo la crítica del cine. (Es natural)
4. Él conoce a todos los directores. (Es mejor)
5. Ella ama estar en el escenario. (Es imposible)
6. El promotor envía las invitaciones. (Puede ser)

B. Practice using an impersonal phrase to replace the underlined part of the sentence.

Modelo: El doctor pide que lo veas. (es necesario)
              Es necesario que lo veas.

1. El farmacéutico quiere que te tomes las pastillas. (es importante)
2. Él necesita tomarte unos rayos X. (es urgente que)
3. La enfermera necesita ponerte la inyección. (es mejor que)
4. El doctor está en la sala de emergencia. (ojalá que)
5. El niño necesita usar las muletas. (es conveniente que el niño)

69. EL SUBJUNTIVO CON CIERTAS CONJUNCIONES DE TIEMPO

1. A subordinate clauses that contains an expression that suggests a future time, a command, a temporal conjunction or an adverb of probability in the main clause warrants the subjunctives:

apenas:
Llámame **apenas** llegues.   Call me as soon as you arrive.

nada más:
Avísame **nada más** aterrices.   Tell me as soon as you have landed.

siempre que:
Siempre que vengas avísame.   Always let me know any time you want
                                      to come over.

tan pronto (como):
Dímelo **tan pronto** lo sepas.   Tell me as soon as you know it.
Avísame **tan pronto como**   Let me know as soon as he calls you.
él te llame.

en cuanto:
Llámame **en cuanto** llegues.   Call me as soon as you arrive.

hasta que:
Llámame **hasta que estés** aquí.   Call me when you get here.

cuando:
Ven **cuando quieras.**   Come whenever you want.

después (de) que:
Mándame un mensaje **después (de) que** llegues.   Send me a message after you arrive.

2. The subjunctive is used with conjunctions when these express contingency or purpose:
a menos que: (unless)
No me llames **a menos que** tengas tiempo.
Don't call me unless you have time.

antes (de) que (before)
Escríbeme **antes (de) que** vengas.   Write me before you come.

con tal (de) que: (as/provided that)
Con tal (de) que estudies yo te pago la colegiatura.   As long as you study, I will pay your tuition.

en caso (de) que: (if/in case)
En caso (de) que llueva lleva tu paraguas.   Take your umbrella in case it rains.

sin que: (without/unless)
No vengas **sin que** se lo digas a tu madre.   Do not come without telling your mother.

para que: (so that)
Sal temprano **para que** estés a tiempo.   Leave early in order to be on time.

3. There are other conjunctions that inherently imply uncertainty or an unfulfilled condition, thus they always require the use of the subjunctive:
aunque (although)
Aunque me digas la verdad, no te creeré.   Even if you tell me the truth, I won't believe you.

por temor a que (For fear of):
Por temor a que te vayas, esconderé las llaves del coche.

For fear of you leaving, I'll hide the car's keys.

siempre que (whenever /as long as):
Siempre que pagues te darán un recibo.

Whenever you pay they will give you a receipt.

mientras (While):
Mientras estés bien, lo demás no importa.

As long as you're fine, the rest doesn't matter.

a la espera (de) que (waiting for that):
Estamos **a la espera (de) que** ella lo haga.

We're waiting for her to do it.

salvo que (unless):
Salvo que sigas las instrucciones no armarás el mueble.

Unless you follow the instructions, you won't put the cabinet together.

a no ser que (unless):
A no ser que vengas, no tendrás tu regalo.

Unless you come, you won't get your gift.

a menos que (unless):
A menos que estudies no entenderás el subjuntivo.

Unless you study you won't understand the subjunctive.

como no (if/as not):
Como no vengas, no sé lo que haré.

If you do not come, I don't know what I'll do.

EJERCICIOS PRÁCTICOS

☺ ☺

A. Ordene las frases con las conjunciones aprendidas.

Modelo: Llámale por teléfono (aunque/ir/trabajar).
          Aunque tengas que ir a trabajar llámale por teléfono.

1.   Haz la tarea (para que/ poder/salir).

2. Escríbele (a la espera de que/te/comentar/las novedades).
3. Escucha música (mientras/estar/volando).
4. Comeremos juntos (cuando/tú/tener/tiempo libre).
5. No te enfades (para que/lo/hacer/bien).
6. Vístete bien (en caso de que/ella/venir/a verte).

B. Escriba la forma correcta del verbo para completar las oraciones.
1. Ella pone sal en su leche sin que lo _____. (saber)
2. Estaré allí aunque no lo _____. (querer)
3. Este vino es malo a menos que tú _____ (decir) lo contrario.
4. Estaré en la estación cuando ella _____. (llegar)
5. Jugaremos tenis antes de que _____. (llover)
6. No comeremos juntos a menos que tú _____ (regresar) a tiempo.
7. No hará mucho dinero hasta que _____ (conocer) mucha gente.

C. Escoja indicativo o subjuntivo.
Modelo: La profesora López quiere que yo _____. (estudiar)
               La profesora López quiere que yo estudie.
1. No me sentiré tranquila hasta que él _____. (llegar)
2. Nos podremos reunir por la mañana a menos que tú no _____. (ir)
3. Yo me levanto todos los días antes de que tú lo _____ (hacer).
4. Él hará hasta lo imposible para que tú lo _____. (obtener)
5. Creo que _____ (ser) muy listo.
6. El sol _____ (salir) todos los días.
7. El _____ (venir) en su propio coche.

☺ ☺
D. Traduzca la conjunción indicada y use el subjuntivo.
Modelo: No te hablaré. Pedirme disculpas. (until)
               No te hablaré **hasta que** me pidas disculpas.
1. No pasarás el examen **a menos** que _____ (comprender) la materia. (unless)
2. No iré al campamento **hasta que** _____ (prometer) que vendrás a verme. (until)
3. No haremos la mudanza **a menos que** todo _____ (estar) correcto. (unless)
4. Debo decírtelo **antes de que** tú _____ (irse). (before)

5. Intento sonreír **aunque** _____ (estar) de mal humor. (although)

6. No le podremos llamar **hasta que** _____(encontrar) mi teléfono (until)

7. Te sugiero leer un libro **para que** _____ (aprender) más. (so that/In order to)

8. Que no se vaya Roberto **sin que** me _____ (decir) adiós. (without)

70. RECAPITULACIÓN DEL PRESENTE SUBJUNTIVO

1. The subjunctive is mainly used in subordinate clauses introduced by **que**.

2. The subjunctive is used when an expression of urgency or necessity precedes the subordinate clause:
Es **necesario que leas** el libro inmediatamente.
Es urgente **que los niños vuelvan** pronto.

3. The subjunctive is used when a verb expressing judgment, any type of will or an indirect command precedes the subordinate clause:
Mi padre **quiere que** yo **estudie.**

4. The subjunctive is used when an expression of emotion precedes the subordinate clause:
Ella **teme que** sus amigos no **vengan** a la fiesta.

5. The subjunctive is used when an expression of doubt, denial or uncertainty precedes the subordinate clause:
El profesor **duda que** todos los estudiantes **pasen** el examen final.

6. The subjunctive is used when phrases expressing unreality or non-existence precede the subordinate clause:
Busco a un doctor que **sepa** español.

7. The subjunctive is used for certain impersonal expressions:
Es importante que te **bañes.**
Es mejor que te **acuestes.**

Note that there are certain impersonal expressions that express that something is going to happen, but that do not require the subjunctive:
¿**Es cierto que** te **vas** a casar?

8. The subjunctive is used after certain conjunctions of time when they suggest the future or a command:
Llámanos **en cuanto** el avión **aterrice.**

9. In Spanish we do not use the future subjunctive any more. The present subjunctive is used when a future time is indicated or implied:
Me entristece que no **puedas** venir **mañana.**
Ahora que yo **sea** presidente **terminaré** la guerra.

EJERCICIOS PRÁCTICOS

☺ ☺

A. Complete las oraciones usando el presente subjuntivo
Modelo: Usted está cansado, y sus amigos lo invitan a una fiesta.
Es necesario que se **disculpe** con ellos y les **diga** que está cansado y no puede ir.

1. Su suegra ha llegado sin avisar, pero usted ha quedado con unos amigos para ir al cine.
Es necesario que…

2. Un amigo lo invita a tomar un trago, pero usted no tiene dinero.
Es mejor que…

3. Usted dona parte de su salario para una causa justa.
Que bueno que usted…

4. Sus hijos quieren que usted vaya al parque.
Dudo que…

5. Su padre les pide a sus hijos que ellos estudien más.
Es importante que…

6. Tu esposa piensa que estás trabajando demasiado.
No creo que…

MINIRELATO: LA MIGRACIÓN DE LAS MUJERES DE GUATEMALA A MÉXICO

Las mujeres guatemaltecas conocen las temporadas en las cuales se requiere de su trabajo en el estado de Chiapas, México. Llegan a estas tierras, que alguna vez fueron de Guatemala, en pequeños grupos. Cuando están trabajando se ponen en la cabeza un pañuelo o un sombrero, para cubrirse del sol. Por su trabajo, obtendrán un salario que no tienen en su país. Hablan poco, no importa sin son casadas o no.

Todas están trabajando después de romper ataduras sociales y culturales de todo tipo. Regresarán a sus lugares de origen y transmitirán sus experiencias a otras amigas y familiares. Este indicador forma parte de las redes sociales de la migración.

Los factores culturales de identidad, a nivel individual y de grupo, así como el sentimiento de pertenencia a una comunidad, también se expresan en otro tipo de flujo migratorio; el de las trabajadoras domésticas. Su origen se localiza en los departamentos de San Marcos y Huehuetenango. Al iniciar el viaje a Chiapas se acompañan de amigas. Con ellas y sus familiares han decidido trabajar. Por esta razón, saben como evitar problemas en el camino y ninguna ignora el lugar donde serán contratadas: en el parque **Miguel Hidalgo** de Tapachula. No ignoran el salario que van a recibir que es de entre 600 a 1200 pesos mensuales, según sea la experiencia que tengan. Es decir, ganarán poco más o menos, entre 60 y 120 dólares al mes.

La decisión de dejar su hogar ha sido meditada y empiezan a trasladarse con la autorización y bendición de sus padres. En conversaciones con amistades que también se desempeñan como trabajadoras domésticas, han sido considerados los factores positivos y de esta forma, han asumido viajar a Chiapas. En un reducido número de casos, a las muy menores las acompaña su padre, lo cual le permitirá conocer las condiciones económicas y la casa donde trabajarán. La inmensa mayoría son menores de edad, de entre 13 y 18 años. Van en busca de un ingreso económico, pues en sus casas hay pobreza. Su identidad cultural se mantiene, pues continuarán utilizando el traje indígena y se comunicarán con sus amigas en el idioma maya natal.

Al permanecer fuera de sus casas, las jóvenes guatemaltecas se integran a un proceso de adaptación social lento. Se trata de vivir en otro país donde deben comprender nuevas pautas culturales. Su presencia en Tapachula, en forma inicial es de treinta días y, posteriormente, se incrementará con base a su experiencia. No firman contratos de trabajo. El arreglo con la contratista es verbal y aunque no ignoran que pueden resolver problemas en el consulado guatemalteco en Tapachula y en la Junta de Conciliación y Arbitraje de esa ciudad, prefieren evitar a toda costa los problemas. Todas tienen muy claro que al terminar su contrato, de no ser renovado van a regresar a sus casas y con el dinero ganado, van a ayudar a sus padres y, también, van a participar en las diferentes actividades culturales en sus lugares de origen.

La amplia presencia de mujeres guatemaltecas trabajando como parte de la migración laboral de carácter internacional, tiene el especial significado de anular expresiones de intolerancia y ocupar diferentes espacios sociales y económicos en un país como Guatemala. Esta es la nueva realidad que se vive en ese país centroamericano. Cabe recordar aquí lo dicho por la escritora chiapaneca Rosario Castellanos: "Las mujeres estamos en proceso, no sólo de descubrirnos, sino de inventarnos."

LECTURA: LOS ADIOSES

Quisimos aprender la despedida
y rompimos la alianza
que juntaba al amigo con la amiga.
Y alzamos la distancia
entre las amistades divididas.

Para aprender a irnos, caminamos.
Fuimos dejando atrás las colinas, los valles,
los verdeantes prados.
Miramos su hermosura
pero no nos quedamos.

Llevamos nuestros pies
donde la soledad tiene su casa
y allí nos detuvimos para siempre.
En silencio aguardamos
hasta aprender la muerte.

Rosario Castellanos

Preguntas

1. ¿De qué trata el poema?
2. ¿Quién es Rosario Castellanos?
3. ¿Por qué piensa usted que la autora usó ese título?
4. ¿Qué significa "alzamos la distancia"
5. ¿Qué se gana cuando se emigra?
6. ¿Qué se pierde?
7. ¿Por qué emigra la gente?
8. ¿De dónde es su familia?
9. ¿En su clase hay personas de otros países?
10. Algunas personas afirman que el cambio climático va a la huerta a migraciones masivas en los próximos años, ¿qué piensa usted de eso?

Here you have a video by Ricardo Arjona, a singer and a composer from Guatemala, about the undocumented immigrants that travel from our counties trying to enter into the US.

INTERACTIVE LINK

bookstudio.pro/crm

VOCABULARIO

VERBOS

presentar	jugar	practicar	tocar
llamar	presentar	dirigir	querer
nacer	avergonzar	poder	saber
colgar	almorzar	querer	dudar
pasar	temer	pagar	sacar
pintar	pasar	estudiar	haber
aguardar	aprender		

NOMBRES

el cirujano	el abogado	el voluntario	el arquitecto
el pañuelo	el sombrero	los dólares	el título
la mayoría	los contratos	la experiencia	la florería
las migraciones	el sillón	el pájaro	el cuerpo
la puerta	la pata	el éxito	el poema
las mujeres	la clase	la imagen	la frontera
México	Estados Unidos	Guatemala	Rosario
el hombre	la talavera	la familia	el plato
la muerte	el silencio	los pies	la soledad
la alianza	la despedida	un/a amigo/a	la distancia

ADJETIVOS

imprevisto/a	fluido/a	moderno/a	obsoleto/a
imprescindible	alicaído/a	autóctonos/as	nuevo/a
preocupado/a	verdeantes		

ADVERBIOS

después	poco	también	económicamente
nunca	jamás	menos	mañana

EXPRESIONES UTILES

¡caray!   ¡una ganga!   ¡ni loco!   ¡lo demás es lo de menos!

CAPÍTULO 15: A LA SALIDA DEL GIMNASIO

En este capítulo...

You will learn more about the types of activities the students do during their free time while they are in Puebla. You will study the future and the conditional perfect tenses, and you will learn how to form the absolute superlative. You will also learn the present perfect subjunctive and the uses of the imperfect subjunctive, which you will continue studying in Chapter 16. Finally you'll read a poem by Rubén Darío.

Contexto

Thomas está un poco preocupado pues Yolanda lo llamó y le pidió si podía regresar a casa, por un momento. Antes de salir del gimnasio Thomas habla con John.

Thomas: Es necesario que vuelva a casa, Yolanda necesita que regrese pero, los veré en el café tan pronto como me haya desocupado. Es posible que llegue un poquito tarde, si no puedo venir yo te hablo por teléfono para que no me esperen.

John: ¡De acuerdo!

David y Jesse salen del gimnasio.

David: ¿Por qué Thomas salió disparado como una flecha?

Jesse: Habrá pasado algo en su casa, tal vez.

John: Sí, hubo un imprevisto y tuvo que regresar, pero me prometió que tan pronto como se desocupara irá al café.

David: Pero ha pasado algo grave.

David: No se preocupen no es nada grave. ¡Vámonos al café! Que los demás nos deben de estar esperando.

John, Jesse y David, de salida se encuentran con Allan, un estudiante de otro programa que también está por un semestre en Puebla, y lo invitan a venir con ellos al café. En el café David le presenta a Anna y a Lisa que ya están esperándolos allí.

Jesse: Pensé que Henry y Sylvia ya estaban acá. No las vi allá dentro.

Anna: Pensé que vendrían con ustedes, pero ya veo que no.

Uno de los meseros se acerca para saber si están listos para ordenar.

Lisa: Todavía faltan otros por llegar, vamos a seguir esperando un poco más.

John (muy entusiasmado se pone a hablar de deportes): Ustedes se acuerdan en el partido aquel cuando Tom Brady ...

Lisa: Escucha John esas historias carecen de interés, estamos en Puebla, aquí se respira pasión por el fútbol, el verdadero, el que se juega con los pies.

Anna: ¿No hay otro tema del que puedan hablar que no sea de ustedes mismos o de los deportes? Todo el tiempo es la misma cosa.

John: Y a ustedes, ¿qué mosca les ha picado?

Lisa: Nada, es que siempre es lo mismo; ustedes y los deportes.

John: Bueno, ¿de qué tema les agradaría a las señoritas conversar?

Lisa y Anna (en coro): De cualquiera, menos de deportes.

Allan: Las chicas tienen razón. Quizá les gustaría que hablásemos de... música, por ejemplo.

John: Eso es lo que tú quisieras, pues tú estudias música.

Lisa: ¿Estudias música?

Allan: Sí. Ahora estoy aprendiendo sobre los sonidos de los instrumentos autóctonos en la música mexicana.

Anna: ¡Interesantísimo!

Allan: ¿Te parece?

Anna: Claro que sí. Y ¿qué nos puedes decir de ellos?

Allan: Bueno pues, por ejemplo entre los Aztecas había muchos instrumentos, pero los más comunes eran los tambores, las flautas, las ocarinas, el caracol marino y el raspador.

Lisa: ¡Guau! Me sorprende que en tan poco tiempo hayas aprendido tanto.

Allan: Bueno es que el tema me interesa muchísimo.

Lisa y Anna (en coro): ¡Qué bueno! Te felicitamos.

Preguntas

1. ¿Por qué regresa a casa Thomas?
2. ¿Con quién habla antes de salir?
3. ¿Cómo sabrán si regresa o no?
4. ¿Qué le pregunta David?
5. ¿Con quién se encuentran a la salida del gimnasio?
6. ¿A quién le presentan al llegar al café?
7. ¿Qué le dice Lisa al mesero?
8. ¿Quién pregunta por Henry y Sylvie?
9. ¿Por qué están molestas Lisa y Anna?

NOTA CULTURAL: LOS DEPORTES Y LOS SONIDOS

Si a usted le gustan los deportes acuáticos, usted puede practicar natación, clavados, esquí acuático, surf, submarinismo, pesca, navegación, remo.

Si a usted le gusta disfrutar del aire libre, puede practicar el atletismo, la caminata, los paseos por el campo, el ciclismo, el alpinismo, el esquí de montaña, la equitación, el golf y por supuesto el tenis.

Si le gustan las cuevas puede hacer espeleología, descendimientos con sogas y cuerdas, caminatas e incluso natación en ríos subterráneos o en cenotes.

Si le gustan los deportes en grupo puede practicar fútbol, fútbol de playa, fútbol americano, baloncesto, voleibol, voleibol de playa, béisbol.

Si le gusta usar la fuerza puede practicar boxeo, lucha libre, lucha grecorromana, judo, karate.

Allan nos va a enseñar algunos de los sonidos que se hacen en México:

mmm	duda
jajaja	risa sonora, abierta
zzzz	dormir
uooooaaay	bostezo
brrrr	cuando se está enfadado
bang	disparo
buaaah	llanto de niño
crack	cuando se rompe algo
glup, glup, glup	cuando se bebe un líquido
snif	el ruido de la nariz cuando se llora
mua	el sonido de un beso
achú	estornudo
tic tac, tic tac	el sonido del reloj
bum	sonido de un golpe seco como una bomba
din don	sonido del timbre
toc, toc	sonido cuando se toca la puerta con los nudillos
roammm	arranque de motor
ñieeeec	frenado de un coche
ratatata	sonido de metralleta disparando
riiiiin	sonido de teléfono sonando
ráas	rasgamiento de tela o ropa
eeeeeeeh	sirena de una ambulancia
tilín tilín	sonido de campana
umph	sorpresa
pssssst	llamado de atención

Dichos

Más vale pájaro en mano que ciento volando.	A bird in the hand is worth two in the bush.
A otro perro con ese hueso.	Tell me another one/Try to giving another dog with that bone.

Estar en la luna.   To have one's head in the clouds.

VOCABULARIO: LOS DEPORTES Y LOS INSTRUMENTOS MUSICALES

Allan toca...

el piano	la guitarra	el violín
la trompeta	el clarinete	el saxofón
el tambor	el acordeón	los platillos

John juega:

baloncesto	tenis	béisbol
cartas	fútbol	golf

Preguntas

1. ¿Prefiere usted nadar en la piscina (pool) o en el mar?
2. ¿Le gusta ir de pesca o navegar?
3. ¿Le gusta correr o caminar?
4. ¿Sabe usted montar a caballo?
5. ¿Ha descendido alguna vez a una cueva?
6. ¿Sabe usted jugar tenis?
7. ¿Cuál es su deporte favorito?
8. ¿Ha jugado alguna vez voleibol de playa?
9. ¿Le gusta el béisbol?
10. ¿Por qué razón practica usted deportes?

EJERCICIOS PRÁCTICOS

A. Describa las cualidades más importantes de un atleta, de un músico o de un director de cine.

B. ¡Vamos a hacer un poco de ejercicio! A usted le toca dirigir el ejercicio en frente de la clase; algo así como: Simón dice... Sus compañeros harán lo que usted les diga que hagan. Por ejemplo, usted puede indicarles Simón dice que se levanten de sus sillas/caminen hacia adelante/regresen caminando de espaldas/estiren (stretch) los brazos y piernas/doblen (bend) las rodillas/den tres pasos a la derecha/dos pasos a la izquierda/troten alrededor del salón de clase/ respiren profundo (breathe deep)/ suelten el aire (breathe out)/ etc.

Más vocabulario: ¿Cómo hacer una llamada telefónica desde un teléfono público?

descolgar	to pick up	colgar	to hang up
marcar	to dial	contestadora	answering machine
está sonando	it's ringing	está ocupado	It's busy
¿quién llama?	who is calling	oigo un ruido	I hear a noise
no cuelgue	don't hang up	dejar recado	leave a message
número equivocado	wrong number	perdón	I'm sorry
operadora	operator	la ranura	slot
me equivoqué	I made a mistake	vuelva a marcar	dial again
teléfono público	public telephone	una moneda	a coin
el tono	dial tone	hacer una llamada	to make a pone call
larga distancia	long distance	nadie contesta	nobody answers
llamada local	local call	llamada internacional	International call
Llamada por cobrar	collect call	está sonando	It's ringing

EJERCICIOS PRÁCTICOS

Escuche y comprenda.

Hace años si usted deseaba llamar a una persona y no tenía teléfono en casa, usted necesitaba ir a la calle para usar un teléfono público, tenía que depositar una moneda en la ranura, descolgar, esperar el tono y marcar el número deseado. Ahora es más fácil, si usted tiene teléfono en casa o si tiene un celular.

Pero siempre que se hace una llamada tiene siete posibilidades:

1.   La línea a la que llama está ocupada. Usted puede volver a marcar.

2.   El teléfono llama y llama y no contestan. Necesitará intentarlo de nuevo.
3.   Nadie contesta, pero puede usted dejar un recado en la contestadora automática o en el buzón del teléfono. Ojalá, la persona le devuelva la llamada más tarde, si usted tiene teléfono en casa o celular.
4.   Alguien responde: ¡Aló!, ¿con quién desea hablar? No, aquí no vive nadie con ese nombre. Número equivocado.
5.   Alguien responde: ¡Aló!, Buenos días ¿con quién desea hablar? Si, un momentito por favor.
6.   Alguien responde: ¡Aló!, Buenos días ¿con quién desea hablar? Verá, él/ella no se encuentra, ¿gusta dejar recado o prefiere llamar más tarde?
7.   Si la persona que contesta es la persona con quien usted desea hablar esa persona dirá: Él/ella habla.

Ahora bien, si usted llama a un número equivocado es necesario que pida disculpas por el error. Así que usted puede decir: **perdone, disculpe** o simplemente **lo siento**.

Si la comunicación no es fluida y hay muchos ruidos, avise a la otra persona que va a colgar y vuelva a marcar, quizá tenga mejor suerte la siguiente vez.

Si va a hacer una llamada internacional, puede hacerla por cobrar, para lo cual se necesita de la ayuda de una operadora; también puede comprar una tarjeta prepagada de las que venden en tiendas o kioscos de periódicos. Hay dos tipos de tarjeta, las que tienen un número al cual llamar y un código y las que se deben de introducir en la ranura del teléfono para que este lea la información del microchip. Si lo prefiere puede hacer una llamada con cargo a su tarjeta de crédito.

Si usted está viajando con su teléfono celular y planea usarlo mientras esté en el extranjero, antes de salir hable con su compañía telefónica para que le habiliten un plan internacional, asegúrese de que le den los costos por minutos de dicho plan y de que su teléfono funcione en el país al que va a viajar.

Es verdad que hoy día casi todo mundo usa sus propios teléfonos celulares/móviles, pero si no tiene un plan internacional o su plan es demasiado caro, algunos teléfonos le permiten hacer FaceTime, usar WhatsApp o también puede usar *Skype* en su propia computadora portátil.

APUNTES GRAMATICALES
71. EL FUTURO PERFECTO

1. The future perfect indicates that an action will have taken place in the future before another action will take place:

   Habré terminado para cuando ellas lleguen.

   I will have finished by the time they arrive.

2. The future perfect is formed by using the future of the auxiliary verb **haber** + a verb in past participle:

   Tú **habrás terminado** la tarea para esta noche.

   You **will have finished** the homework by tonight.

   Ellos se **habrán ido** al terminar el partido.

   They **will have left** by the end of the match.

   Note that a speaker may decide to use the present subjunctive to complete the sentence, in this particular case the reason to use subjunctive in the second clause is because **tan pronto como** triggers the subjunctive:

   Ellos se **habrán ido** tan pronto como **termine** el partido.

   They **will have gone** by the end of the match.

3. Note the differences between the following two sentences:

   Lo **harás** cuando lleguemos.

   You'll **do** it when we arrive.

   Tú lo **habrás hecho** en cuanto lleguemos.

   You **will have done** it by the time we arrive.

   In the first sentence **the future** is used in the first clause because the second action will be done as soon as the people arrive. In the second sentence, the **future perfect** is used in the first clause because that action (something being done before the subject arrives) will precede the action in the second clause.

Both sentences use the subjunctive in the second clause because both have the time clause **cuando**, and **en cuanto**.

4. The future perfect is also used to express conjecture, form questions or show perplexity:

¿Dónde **habré puesto** los lentes?   Where **might I have put** the glass es?

¡No sé si ya se lo **habrán dicho**!   I do not know if **they've already told** him.

EJERCICIOS PRÁCTICOS

A. ¡**Ya**! Plus the Future Perfect Tense.
   Modelo: Cuando llegue Thomas. (Yolanda/servir la cena)
                  Cuando llegue Thomas Yolanda ya habrá servido la cena.
   1.   Cuando llegue Navidad. (los estudiantes/regresar a los Estados Unidos)
   2.   Cuando llegue José. (Thomas/ver visto las noticias)
   3.   Cuando regrese del cine. (la mamá de Anna/dormirse)
   4.   Cuando se vaya de México. (Thomas/hacer muchos amigos)
   5.   Cuando vuelva del gimnasio. (Yolanda/olvidarse de sus problemas)

B. Complete las oraciones usando futuro perfecto y los siguientes verbos: terminar, cambiar, salir, decir, ordenar, traducir, graduarse, poner, revisar, depositar.
   1.   Me pregunto si Yolanda, ya le _____.
   2.   La secretaria, ¿ya _____ en orden el archivo?
   3.   ¿Ya _____ los dólares por pesos?
   4.   Para cuando mi mujer vuelva, ya _____.
   5.   Los trabajadores ya _____ los cheques.
   6.   Para el año entrante, yo ya me_____.
   7.   Para mañana, mi madre ya _____.
   8.   Para el lunes, el traductor ya _____ los documentos.
   9.   Para cuando salgan del aeropuerto, el agente de aduanas
         _____ los documentos.
   10.   Para diciembre del 2026 el presidente de México
         _____ su mandato.

72. EL CONDICIONAL PERFECTO (POTENCIAL COMPUESTO)

1. The Conditional Perfect is formed with the conditional of the verb **haber** + the past participle of the main verb:

   A mi padre, le **habría gustado** verte antes de morir.

   My dad **would have liked** to see you before he died.

2. The Conditional Perfect expresses both in Spanish and in English an action that you would have done if something else had happened:

   Habríamos lamentado que no vinieras.

   We would have regretted it if you had not come.

3. In Spanish the Conditional Perfect is used to indicate probability or conjecture in the past:

   Si hubiera estado en Mexico, él **habría votado** por el presidente.

   If he stayed in Mexico, he **would have voted** for the president.

   Habrían sido las tres cuando mi madre llamó por teléfono.

   It **would have been** three o'clock when my Mother called.

4. The Conditional Perfect may be used to express an unfulfilled condition in the past. In this type of situations, the verb in the if clause is expressed in the pluperfect subjunctive and the main clause is usually in Conditional Perfect, but also the Pluperfect Subjunctive can also be used:

   Si hubiera tenido dinero, **habría pagado** todas mis deudas.

   If I had had money, **I would have paid** all my debts.

   Si **hubiera** tenido dinero, **hubiera pagado** todas mis deudas.

   If I had had money, **I would have paid** all my debts.

EJERCICIOS PRÁCTICOS

A. Complete las oraciones usando el condicional perfecto
   1. Me pregunté si Yolanda, ya le _____ _____. (avisar)
   2. De ser posible, ella ya _____ _____ (poner) orden en el archivo.
   3. Si todo estuviera bien, ya le _____ _____ (llegar) los dólares que le mandé.
   4. Si pudiera, ella ya ___ _____ _____ (olvidarse) de mí.

5. Si el patrón les pagara a tiempo, los trabajadores ya _____ _____ (recibir) sus cheques.

73. EL SUPERLATIVO ABSOLUTO

1. To form the absolute superlative, many Spanish adjectives add the suffix **—ísimo/a/os/as**. When the suffix is used, it intensifies the meaning of the adjective.

2. When an adjective ends in a vowel, it is dropped but gender is maintained by the ending vowel of the suffix:

   linda   **lind—**   **lindísima**

3. If the adjective ends in —co or —go, it changes to qu— and gu—. If it ends in —z it changes to c—:

   rico   **riqu—**   **riquísimo**
   largo   **largu—**   **larguísimo**
   feliz   **felic—**   **felicísimo**

4. If the adjective ends in another consonant, the suffix is added to the adjective as is:

   singular   singular**ísimo**

5. Note that the written accent mark have to be moved when using the absolute superlative, because absolute superlatives always have the the written accent mark on the suffix:

   lentos   lent**ísimos**
   fácil   facilísimo

6. The following adjectives have irregular forms:

amable	amabilísimo	afable	afabilísimo
antiguo	antiquísimo	apacible	apacibilísimo
bueno	bonísimo	cierto	certísimo
confiable	confiabilísimo	cruel	crudelísimo
cursi	cursilísimo	fiel	fidelísimo
inferior	ínfimo	joven	jovencísimo
lejos	lejísimo (adverb)	mayor	máximo
menor	mínimo	mejor	óptimo

miserable	miserabilísimo	peor	pésimo
superior	supremo	venerable	venerabilísimo

7. Some adjectives **do not have** an absolute superlative, especially those whose meaning cannot be intensified: **baladí, bonita, arduo, espontáneo, homogéneo, carnívoro, desmontable, fantástico, ideal, infinito, inmortal.**

EJERCICIOS PRÁCTICOS

A. Transforme los adjetivos en superlativos absolutos.
   Modelo: Thomas es muy atento. (atento)
                  Thomas es **atentísimo**.
   1.   Yolanda es cariñosa.
   2.   Los Zurita están encantados con Thomas.
   3.   El profesor está cansado.
   4.   Los estudiantes viven lejos unos de los otros.
   5.   Las familias compran muchas cosas.

B. Cambie el adjetivo usando un superlativo absoluto en las siguientes oraciones.
   1.   Mi casa es grande.
   2.   Mis padres son ricos.
   3.   Mi hermana es guapa.
   4.   Tengo muchos amigos.
   5.   El profesor es una excelente persona.
   6.   Mis clases son aburridas.
   7.   Mi coche es rápido.
   8.   Mi hermano es cursi.
   9.   Mi perro es cruel.
   10.   Mi novia es linda.

74 EL PRESENTE PERFECTO DEL SUBJUNTIVO

1. The present perfect of the subjunctive is formed with the present subjunctive of the verb **haber** and a past participle of the main verb:

yo **haya**	nosotros **hayamos**
tú **hayas**	vosotros **hayáis**
vos **hayás**	vosotros **hayáis**
él **haya**	ellos **hayan**

ella **haya**   ellas **hayan**
usted **haya**   ustedes **hayan**

Note that the first and third person singular have the same conjugation.

2. The present perfect subjunctive is used in the same type of dependent clauses as the present subjunctive, with the exception of it indicating that the action in the dependent clause happens before the action in the main clause:

Ojalá que a los estudiantes les   I hope that the students enjoyed the
haya gustado la película.   movie.

Note that the action in the dependent clause occurred (went to the cinema) prior to the action of the main clause (I hope).

EJERCICIOS PRÁCTICOS

A. Cambie las oraciones del ejercicio usando el presente perfecto del subjuntivo.
Modelo: Las hijas de Yolanda llegaron temprano. (es bueno)
                Es bueno que las hijas de Yolanda **hayan llegado** temprano.
1.   No vieron el accidente en la autopista. (es una lástima)
2.   Thomas pasó el examen final. (es importante)
3.   Anna y Lisa pasaron el año nuevo en México. (me alegro)
4.   Los estudiantes vieron la película en español. (ojalá)
5.   El profesor regresó a los Estados Unidos. (dudo)

☺ ☺
B. Con un compañero de clase complete las oraciones usando el presente perfecto del subjuntivo.
Modelo: Me alegro de que tu hermana... (llegar bien a Madrid)
                Me alegro que tu hermana haya llegado bien a Madrid.
1.   Qué bueno que nosotros... (tomado los exámenes ya)
2.   Dudo que la profesora de español... (ver la película)
3.   Es increíble que los Boston Bruins... (ganar la Copa)
4.   Es una lástima que tu papá... (no ir al paseo)
5.   No es cierto que yo... (comprar un Ferrari)
6.   Es admirable que tú... (estudiar para médico)
7.   El director afirma que es imposible que... (filmar en Afganistán)

8. Nadie cree que el doctor... (irse de viaje)
9. La policía busca a un testigo que... (ver el robo)
10. Andrea espera que el vuelo de Antonio.... (llegar a tiempo)

☺ ☺

C. Complete las preguntas y su compañero de clase que complete las respuestas usando siempre el presente perfecto del subjuntivo.
1. ¿Dudo que los estudiantes _____ _____ (ver) la película en español?
1. Y también dudo que la profesora la _____ _____ .
2. Ojalá que nosotros _____ _____ (pasar) el examen de
3. química.
4. No creo que yo lo _____ _____.
5. ¿Consideras necesario que tu madre _____ _____ (ir) al hospital?
6. Sí, y espero que ya la _____ atendido y ya _____ regresado a casa.
7. Ellas esperan que sus padres ya _____ _____
8. (solucionar) sus múltiples problemas legales, aunque no es seguro que esto ya _____ ocurrido.
9. Es probable que algunos de ustedes ya _____ _____ (viajar) a
10. México, pero no es posible que lo _____ publicado en el New York Times.

75. EL IMPERFECTO DEL SUBJUNTIVO

1. The imperfect subjunctive is the past tense of the subjunctive.

2. The forms of the imperfect subjunctive are derived from the conjugation in the preterite of the third person plural (**ustedes, ellos, ellas**).

3. The endings of the imperfect subjunctive are: **—ra,--ras, —ra, —ramos, —rais, —ran**:

| hablaron | habla[104]— | habla**ra** |
| comieron | comie— | comie**ras** |

_____

[104] Note that the stem of all **–ar** verbs is the same informal command that you studied in **chapter 11**.

| vivieron | vivie— | vivie**ran** |

4. There is an alternative ending form **—se**, for the imperfect subjunctive that is less common, but which is perfectly interchangeable: **—se, —ses, —se, —semos, —seis, —sen**

hablaron	habla—	habla**se**
comieron	comie—	comie**se**
vivieron	vivie—	vivie**se**

5. The **nosotros** form of the imperfect subjunctive always has a written accent mark:
    Ella quería que nosotros **fuésemos**.
    Ella quería que nosotros **fuéramos**.

6. Any irregularity that occurs with the third person form in the preterit will occur in the imperfect subjunctive:

durmieron	durmie—	d**u**rmiera/d**u**rmiese
pidieron	pidie—	p**i**diera/p**i**diese
trajeron	traje—	tra**j**era/tra**j**ese

7. The imperfect subjunctive is used in a subordinate clause when the verb in the main clause is in the past and demands the subjunctive because it is expressing judgment or will, emotions, doubt, disbelief, denial, uncertainty, non-existence, or impersonal expressions that require the subjunctive:

Era importante que **fueras** a clase.	It was important that you go to class.
Fue imposible que John **pasara** el examen.	It was impossible that John [**would**] pass the exam.
Mi madre **habría preferido** que la casa se **pintara** de blanco.	My mother **would have preferred** that the house be **painted** white.

EJERCICIOS PRÁCTICOS

A. Practique usando el imperfecto del subjuntivo.
    Modelo: José deseaba que Thomas. (hablar en español)
                    José deseaba que Thomas **hablara** en español.
    1.   El rector quería que el profesor. (vivir en Puebla)
    2.   Yolanda no esperaba que Martín. (casarse tan pronto)
    3.   Los estudiantes dudaban que el profesor. (darles un examen fácil)

4. El profesor les dijo a los estudiantes que. (estudiar mucho)
5. Thomas quería que los Zurita encontraran una playa donde (poder
6. descansar en sus vacaciones)

B. Practique usando el imperfecto del subjuntivo.
   Modelo: Tus padres dudaban que tu hermana (pasar de grado)
   Tus padres dudaban que tu hermana **pasase** de grado.
   1. La policía dudaba que nosotros (haber atrapado al ladrón)
   2. El entrenador quería que (practicar dos veces al día)
   3. La mamá se alegró de que su hijo (pasar el año)
   4. Las familias esperaban que los estudiantes (volver pronto)
   5. Yolanda no creía que Thomas (regresar a México antes de un año)

☺ ☺
C. Con su compañero de clase tomen turno para completar las oraciones
   usando imperfecto del subjuntivo.
   1. Yolanda le pidió a Thomas que _____ (ir) a la farmacia y le
      _____ (comprar) unas pastillas para el dolor de cabeza.
   2. Thomas le contestó que iría tan pronto como _____ (terminar)
      la tarea que tenía que entregar mañana.
   3. Yolanda le pidió que _____ (apurarse) pues sentía que la ca-
      beza le iba a explotar
   4. Thomas decidió entonces ir a la farmacia antes de que Yolanda
      _____ (enojarse) con él o peor aún _____ (volverse) loca.
   5. Yolanda se disculpó por forzarlo y le dijo que era una lástima que José
      no _____ (estar) pues sino le pediría a él que _____ (ir).
   6. Thomas le contestó que no _____ (preocuparse) que él iría con
      gusto y que le agradaba que ella lo _____ (necesitar) para
      algo.
   7. Yolanda le prometió a Thomas prepararle su comida favorita cuando
      _____ (sentirse) mejor.
   8. Thomas se fue a la farmacia y le pidió al encargado que le _____
      (surtir) las medicinas que Yolanda necesitaba.
   9. El encargado le dio lo que quería y le dijo que le _____ (saludar)
      a Yolanda.
   10. Thomas le prometió hacerlo tan pronto como _____ (llegar) a
       casa.

✎

D. Complete las oraciones con la conjugación correcta de los verbos usando imperfecto del subjuntivo.

1. Los estudiantes esperaban que el ladrón no _____ (huir) de la policía.
2. Anna se alegró de que el hombre _____ (estar) bien pese al asalto.
3. El policía insistió en que nosotros _____ (ir) a la delegación para levantar el acta.
4. Nosotros le dijimos que no era posible que _____ (poder) ir pues no habíamos visto lo que pasó.
5. No fue posible que lo _____ (convencer) y tuvimos que ir con él.
6. El encargado nos dijo que le gustaría que le _____ (decir) la verdad.
7. El no creyó nuestra versión y nos pidió que _____ (colaborar) con la justicia para atrapar al ladrón.
8. Yo pensé, "cómo me gustaría que José _____ (estar) aquí".
9. Después de un rato los policías nos dijeron que _____ (irse) que ya habíamos hecho bastante.
10. Antes de salir los policías nos aconsejaron que no _____ (decir) nada de esto a nadie.

✎

E. Complete las oraciones con la conjugación correcta del los verbos usando el imperfecto del subjuntivo.

1. La madre esperaba que el bebé _____ (nacer) bien.
2. El juez ordenó que la policía _____ (inquirir) sobre el crimen.
3. El entrenador quería que _____ (jugar) todos nosotros.
4. El jefe ordenó que la secretaria _____ (enviar) las cartas.
5. Mi madre me pidió que _____ (hacer) la tarea.
6. José quería que Martín _____ (convencerme) de ir al paseo.
7. El profesor dudó que todos _____ (concluir) el examen final.
8. Santa les dijo a los niños que _____ (elegir) sus regalos.
9. Yo no pensé que _____ (ir) a llover.
10. Mi padre nos demandó que no le _____. (mentir)

MINIRELATO: IR AL ESTADIO EN MÉXICO

En México, cuando se va a un estadio (*stadium*) de fútbol, en general se va con un grupo de amigos, con la familia o con la pareja; es muy raro que alguien vaya al estadio solo.

Antes de llegar a la **taquilla** (*ticket counter*) uno puede encontrarse con muchos revendedores (*scalpers*) que tratan de hacer negocio con los aficionados. Algunas veces, si el partido es importante, uno se puede encontrar con una fila muy larga.

Por lo general, la gente llega temprano a los estadios para comer afuera, en los muchos puestos de comida que se ponen en las afueras, también es común que haya muchos vendedores de banderas y playeras de los equipos que van a jugar, algunas veces se pueden comprar trompetas de plástico para hacer ruido dentro del estadio.

Hoy en día también ya se pueden comprar los boletos por adelantado, y al llegar al estadio se recogen las entradas en una taquilla especial. Obviamente existen distintos precios de las entradas, dependiendo que tan cerca se quiere estar de la cancha. Al llegar a la entrada del estadio, el revisor, cortará su boleto a la mitad.

Dentro del estadio abundan los vendedores de refrescos, cervezas y comida. Conviene sentarse siempre del lado de la barra (**fans**) del equipo al que uno apoya.

Por último, todavía en México muchos juegos son al mediodía y por ello es conveniente llevar un sombrero o una gorra (**hat**) para protegerse del sol.

Preguntas

1. ¿Cómo evitar la reventa de las entradas al estadio?
2. En México, cuando se va al estadio, ¿cómo se va?
3. ¿De qué otras formas se pueden comprar los boletos?
4. ¿Qué tipo de cosas se venden afuera de los estadios?
5. ¿Dónde conviene sentarse cuando se va al estadio?
6. ¿Qué tipo de cosas se pueden comprar dentro de los estadios?
7. ¿Qué conviene llevar a los estadios?
8. ¿Por qué la gente suele llegar temprano a los estadios?
9. ¿En dónde le rompen el boleto a la mitad?
10. ¿De qué depende el precio del boleto?

LECTURA: UN POEMA DE RUBÉN DARÍO

Rubén Darío, poeta nicaragüense nacido en el pueblo de Metapa, en el departamento de Matagalpa, en 1867, murió en la ciudad de León en 1916. Rubén Darío es considerado en América Latina como el padre del modernismo latinoamericano, movimiento que le dio carta de identidad a la literatura latinoamericana en el siglo XIX. Entre sus libros están *Azul*, *Prosas Profanas*, *Cantos de Vida y Esperanza*:

SONATINA

La princesa está triste... ¿qué tendrá la princesa?
Los suspiros se escapan de su boca de fresa,
que ha perdido la risa, que ha perdido el color.
La princesa está pálida en su silla de oro,
está mudo el teclado de su clave sonoro,
y en un vaso, olvidada, se desmaya una flor.

El jardín puebla el triunfo de los pavos reales.
Parlanchina, la dueña dice cosas banales,
y vestido de rojo piruetea el bufón.
La princesa no ríe, la princesa no siente;
la princesa persigue por el cielo de Oriente
la libélula vaga de una vaga ilusión.

¿Piensa, acaso, en el príncipe de Golconda o de China,
o en el que ha detenido su carroza argentina
para ver de sus ojos la dulzura de luz?
¿O en el rey de las islas de las rosas fragantes,
o en el que es soberano de los claros diamantes,
o en el dueño orgulloso de las perlas de Ormuz?

¡Ay!, la pobre princesa de la boca de rosa
quiere ser golondrina, quiere ser mariposa,
tener alas ligeras, bajo el cielo volar;
ir al sol por la escala luminosa de un rayo,
saludar a los lirios con los versos de mayo
o perderse en el viento sobre el trueno del mar.

Ya no quiere el palacio, ni la rueca de plata,
ni el halcón encantado, ni el bufón escarlata,
ni los cisnes unánimes en el lago de azur.
Y están tristes las flores por la flor de la corte,

los jazmines de Oriente, los nelumbos del Norte,
de Occidente las dalias y las rosas del Sur.
¡Pobrecita princesa de los ojos azules!
Está presa en sus oros, está presa en sus tules,
en la jaula de mármol del palacio real;
el palacio soberbio que vigilan los guardas,
que custodian cien negros con sus cien alabardas,
un lebrel que no duerme y un dragón colosal.
¡Oh, quién fuera hipsipila que dejó la crisálida!
(La princesa está triste, la princesa está pálida)
¡Oh visión adorada de oro, rosa y marfil!
¡Quién volara a la tierra donde un príncipe existe,
—la princesa está pálida, la princesa está triste—,
más brillante que el alba, más hermoso que abril!
—«Calla, calla, princesa —dice el hada madrina—;
en caballo, con alas, hacia acá se encamina,
en el cinto la espada y en la mano el azor,
el feliz caballero que te adora sin verte,
y que llega de lejos, vencedor de la Muerte,
a encenderte los labios con un beso de amor».

Preguntas

1.   ¿Dónde nació Rubén Darío?
2.   ¿Cuándo nació?
3.   ¿Cuándo murió?
4.   Mencione algunos de sus libros.
5.   ¿Por qué se dice que él es el padre del modernismo latinoamericano?
6.   ¿De qué trata el poema "Sonatina"?
7.   ¿Considera usted que es un poema infantil?
8.   ¿Por qué está triste la princesa?
9.   ¿Cómo tiene los ojos la princesa?
10. ¿Por qué el poeta dice que la princesa es pobrecita?

En la siguiente página hay un video con el poema de Rubén Darío:

INTERACTIVE LINK

booktudio.pro/ywa

VOCABULARIO

VERBOS

Haber	ir	entrar	comprar
ser	querer	hablar	comer
vivir	esperar	disfrutar	tener
regresar	hacer	llamar	dormir
callar	decir	mencionar	considerar
tratar	nacer	volar	llegar

NOMBRES

el rato	la cantaleta	el tema	la cueva
los cantos	una vez	la operadora	la llamada
la limosna	los remedios	las muletas	los rayos X
los libros	el jardín	las prosas	la princesa
la niña	las perlas	los aficionados	la tribuna
el estadio	los deportes	el/la revisor/a	el boleto
el padre	el salón	la taquilla	un sombrero
la clase	el aire	el reporte	profesor
el gimnasio	la esperanza	las trompetas	un poema
el cheque	el patrón	la cancha	las cervezas
los refrescos	la comida	el revendedor	las playeras
las banderas	la llamada	la ranura	el poeta
el príncipe	el oro	la rosa	la literatura
abril	el marfil	el alba	el hada
la madrina	los jazmines	el palacio	los precios

ADJETIVOS

facilísimo/a	larguísimo/a	buenísimo/a	pálido/a
mudo/a	orgulloso/a	solo/a	triste
nicaragüense	fácil	rico/a	feliz
guapo/a	hermoso/a	latinoamericano/a	
azul			

ADVERBIOS

muy	bien	recientemente	todavía
especialmente	lejos	frecuentemente	ya

EXPRESIONES UTILES

¡salir disparado como una flecha!	¿qué mosca te picó?
tener mejor suerte	hoy por hoy
la misma cantaleta	

CAPÍTULO 16: EN EL CINE

En este capítulo...

You'll learn a bit about going to the movies in Mexico. You'll also have the opportunity to read part of the Letter of Jamaica written by Simón Bolívar, the leader of the Independence movement in South America. To help you in your journey, you'll learn more about the imperfect subjunctive, the if clauses contrary to fact, and expressions "**como si**" and "**cual si**" that always trigger the imperfect subjunctive. You'll also study the past perfect (pluperfect) subjunctive.

Contexto

Anna se entera que la semana pasada estuvieron pasando en los cines de Angelópolis una película de animación. A Anna le encantan estas películas y lamenta no haber visto la cartelera a tiempo.

Anna: Qué lástima que no supe a tiempo que estaban pasando una película de animación. Me hubiera encantado ir, pues a mí me encantan las películas para niños, especialmente las que hace Pixar.

Lisa: Bueno pues, ¡hoy es tu día de suerte!

Anna: ¿Por qué?

Lisa: Pues, hoy vuelven a exhibir Toy Story 3. Parece que tuvo tal demanda que la volvieron a poner en cartelera.

Anna: ¿No?

Lisa: Sí. ¿Quieres ir?

Anna: ¿Qué si quiero ir? ¿Qué clase de pregunta es esa?

Lisa: Deberíamos preguntarles a los muchachos si quieren ir ellos también.

Anna: Muy bien, hay que llamarlos ahoritita mismo.

Lisa: Manos a la obra.

Anna llama a Thomas, mientras Lisa llama a John.

Thomas: ¡Claro que voy! Faltaba más. Pero me gustaría que la viéramos en español como si fuéramos nativos.

John: Si fuera un niño iría, pero como ya soy adulto… La verdad, no me gustan las películas para niños, pero por estar con mis amigos me apunto a ir.

Anna: ¿A quién más llamamos?

Lisa: Hay que llamar a Jesse y a David.

Anna: ¿No crees que debamos preguntarles a los demás chicos del grupo?

Lisa: Quizá tengas razón...

Frente al cine.

Anna: Bueno, ¿quiénes querrían ver la película doblada al español?

John: A mí me da lo mismo, porque no me gustan las películas infantiles, vine por estar con ustedes.

Thomas: A mí me encantaría muchísimo si la pudiéramos ver en español sirve que seguimos aprendiendo más.

Jesse: A David y a mí también nos gustaría verla en español.

Lisa: Pues no se diga más y compremos los boletos para la función en español.

Thomas: Mientras, yo voy a comprar unas palomitas grandes y seis sodas con poco hielo.

John: Si te alcanzara el dinero podrías comprarme un "perro caliente".

Lisa: John, tú comes como si estuvieras en los Estados Unidos.

Thomas: No lo creo John, estoy en la lona.

Anna: Jajaja, eso ¡me pareció genial!

Preguntas sobre el escenario

1. ¿Qué tipo de películas le gustan a Anna?
2. ¿De quién fue la idea de ir al cine?
3. ¿Qué película se está estrenando en los cines de Puebla?
4. ¿Quién llama a quién?
5. ¿Qué es lo que sugiere Thomas?
6. ¿Es que a John le gustan las películas para niños?
7. Entonces, ¿por qué va al cine?
8. ¿A quiénes más invitan para ir al cine?
9. ¿Quiénes quieren ver la película doblada al español?
10. ¿Qué va a hacer Thomas, mientras los otros compran los boletos?

NOTA CULTURAL: Divertirse en el cine

Una película puede ser un drama psicológico, de acción, policíaca, cómica, de horror, de **espionaje** (espionage movie), de ciencia ficción, o infantil. Para hacer una película se requiere mucho dinero. En nuestros días hacer una película puede costar muchos millones de dólares. Las personas encargadas de financiar la película se llaman **productores** (producers), pero también se requiere un buen **guión** (screenplay). Quien hace el guión se llama **guionista** (screenwriter). Pero, para hacer una buena puesta en escena se necesita **un director** o **una directora** (director) que es el responsable último de toda la película. Están además el encargado de la decoración, de la fotografía y de **la banda sonora** (sound track) que incluye la música apropiada, así como el encargado de la **iluminación** (lighting). Todos forman parte de la distribución y sus nombres pueden ser leídos en los **créditos** (credits) que aparecen al final de la película.

La publicidad es organizada, algunas veces, mucho antes de que la película esté completamente terminada; es un proceso largo, complicado y costoso. Si la película no logra una buena crítica se corre el riesgo de perder mucho dinero, pues la película no tendrá el éxito deseado; sin embargo, muchas veces las películas **terminan siendo taquilleras** (are a hit), pese a las críticas negativas de los expertos.

Los Oscar premian las siguientes categorías:
Mejor película

Mejor director
Mejor actor masculino
Mejor actriz
Mejor actor secundario
Mejor actriz secundaria
Mejor guión
Mejor adaptación
Mejor película **extranjera** (foreign film)
Mejor película de animación
Mejor fotografía
Mejores efectos visuales
Montaje (editing)
Música original
Maquillaje (makeup)
Mejor documental
Mejor **cortometraje** (short film)

EJERCICIOS PRÁCTICOS

☺ ☺

A. Con un compañero de clase, siéntese a describir un aspecto de una película que hayan visto
recientemente. Puede enfocarse en la dirección, la fotografía, los efectos visuales, la
banda sonora, o las actuaciones.

Here you have a video clip of one of the most
recent movies produced in Mexico that describes a difficult situation that Mexico is facing
today.

INTERACTIVE LINK

bookstudio.pro/16f

Dichos

Entre más tienes más quieres.   The more you get, the more you want.
Estar en la lona.   To be broke.
Hay que echarle ganas.   Throw yourself into it/to apply oneself.

EJERCICIOS PRÁCTICOS

☺ ☺

Vea la cartelera cinematográfica o de teatro. Vea que películas se están exhibiendo en este momento y cuál de ellas le gustaría ver. Fíjese si la película está doblada al español o si se presenta con subtítulos. Fíjese también en el número de funciones, las horas y si pueden comprar las entradas por adelantado.

Aquí tiene la página electrónica en la que puede consultar la información actualizada sobre la cartelera cinematográfica en Puebla.

INTERACTIVE LINK

bookstudio.pro/cine

Aquí tiene la página electrónica en la que puede consultar la información sobre las obras de teatro que se están presentando en Puebla

INTERACTIVE LINK

bookstudio.pro/egt

VOCABULARIO: EL SUEÑO BOLIVARIANO DE FORMAR UNA PATRIA GRANDE EN AMÉRICA LATINA.

anales	annals	yugo	yoke
igualdad	equality	gloria	glory
virtudes	virtues	unión	union
equilibrio	balance	nación	nation
felicidad	happiness	persuadido	persuaded

EJERCICIOS PRÁCTICOS

☺ ☺

A. Escuche y comprenda. (fragmentos de la Carta de Jamaica, 1815)

(...) Es más difícil, dice Montesquieu, sacar un pueblo de la servidumbre, que subyugar uno libre. Esta verdad está comprobada por los anales de todos los tiempos, que nos muestran las más de las naciones libres, sometidas al yugo, y muy pocas de las esclavas recobrar su libertad. A pesar de este convencimiento, los meridionales de este continente han manifestado el conato de conseguir instituciones liberales, y aun perfectas; sin duda, por efecto del instinto que tienen todos los hombres de aspirar a su mejor felicidad posible; la que se alcanza infaliblemente en las sociedades civiles, cuando ellas están fundadas sobre las bases de la justicia, de la libertad y de la igualdad. Pero ¿seremos nosotros capaces de mantener en su verdadero equilibrio la difícil carga de una República? ¿Se puede concebir que un pueblo recientemente desencadenado, se lance a la esfera de la libertad, sin que, como a Ícaro, se le deshagan las alas, y recaiga en el abismo? Tal prodigio es inconcebible, nunca visto. Por consiguiente, no hay un raciocinio verosímil, que nos halague con esta esperanza.

Yo deseo más que otro alguno ver formar en América la más grande nación del mundo, menos por su extensión y riquezas que por su libertad y gloria. Aunque aspiro a la perfección del gobierno de mi patria, no puedo persuadirme que el Nuevo Mundo sea por el momento regido por una gran república; como es imposible, no me atrevo a desearlo; y menos deseo aún una monarquía universal de América, porque este proyecto sin ser útil, es también imposible. Los abusos que actualmente existen no se reformarían, y nuestra regeneración sería infructuosa. Los Estados Americanos han menester de los cuidados de gobiernos paternales que curen las llagas y las heridas del despotismo y la guerra. La metrópoli, por ejemplo, sería México, que es la única que puede serlo por su poder intrínseco, sin el cual no hay metrópoli. Supongamos que fuese el istmo de Panamá punto céntrico para todos los extremos de este vasto continente, ¿no continuarían éstos en la languidez, y aún en el desorden actual? Para que un solo gobierno dé vida, anime, ponga en acción todos los resortes de la prosperidad pública, corrija, ilustre y perfeccione al Nuevo Mundo sería necesario que tuviese las facultades de un Dios y, cuando menos, las luces y virtudes de todos los hombres.

(...) Es una idea grandiosa pretender formar de todo el mundo nuevo una sola nación con un solo vínculo que ligue sus partes entre sí y con el todo. Ya que tiene un origen, una lengua, unas costumbres y una religión debería, por consiguiente, tener un solo gobierno que confederase los diferentes Estados que hayan de formarse; mas no es posible porque climas remotos, situaciones diversas, intereses opuestos, caracteres desemejantes dividen a la América. ¡Qué bello sería que el istmo de Panamá fuese para nosotros lo que el de Corinto para los griegos! Ojalá que algún día tengamos la fortuna de instalar allí un augusto Congreso de los representantes de las repúblicas, reinos e imperios a tratar y discutir sobre los altos intereses de la paz y de la guerra, con las naciones de las otras tres partes del mundo.

(...) Seguramente la unión es la que nos falta para completar la obra de nuestra regeneración. Sin embargo, nuestra división no es extraña, porque tal es el distintivo de las guerras civiles formadas generalmente entre dos partidos: conservadores y reformadores. Los primeros son, por lo común, más numerosos, porque el imperio de la costumbre produce el efecto de la obediencia a las potestades establecidas; los últimos son siempre menos numerosos aunque más vehementes e ilustrados. De este modo la masa física se equilibra con la fuerza moral, y la contienda se prolonga, siendo sus resultados muy inciertos. Por fortuna entre nosotros, la masa ha seguido a la inteligencia.

Yo diré a usted lo que puede ponernos en aptitud de expulsar a los españoles, y de fundar un gobierno libre. Es la unión, ciertamente; mas esta unión no nos vendrá por prodigios divinos, sino por efectos sensibles y esfuerzos bien dirigidos. América está encontrada entre sí, porque se halla abandonada de todas las naciones, aislada en medio del universo, sin relaciones diplomáticas ni auxilios militares y combatida por España que posee más elementos para la guerra, que cuantos furtivamente podemos adquirir.

Cuando los sucesos no están asegurados, cuando el Estado es débil, y cuando las empresas son remotas, todos los hombres vacilan; las opiniones se dividen, las pasiones las agitan y los enemigos las animan para triunfar por este fácil medio. Luego que seamos fuertes, bajo los auspicios de una nación liberal que nos preste su protección, se nos verá de acuerdo cultivar las virtudes y los talentos que conducen a la gloria; entonces seguiremos la marcha majestuosa hacia las grandes prosperidades a que está destinada la América meridional; entonces las ciencias y las artes que nacieron en el Oriente y han ilustrado a Europa, volarán a Colombia libre que las convidará con un asilo (...)

Simón Bolívar

Kingston, 6 de septiembre de 1815.

☺ ☺

B. Ahora haga las siguientes preguntas a su compañero de clase.
1. ¿A quién cita Simón Bolívar en esta carta?
2. ¿Cuál es la tesis de este pensador francés?
3. ¿Qué significa la idea de mejor felicidad posible?
4. ¿Cuáles son las bases para que se de esa felicidad?
5. ¿Qué deseaba Simón Bolívar?
6. Pero, ¿de qué estaba persuadido el general Bolívar?
7. ¿Qué facultades tendría que tener el Nuevo Mundo para poder tener un gobierno único?
8. ¿Qué cosas ya tenemos en común que podrían favorecer un gobierno único?
9. ¿Qué es lo que nos falta para completar la obra de nuestra regeneración?
10. 10. Sin embargo, ¿qué es lo que tenemos?

APUNTES GRAMATICALES
76. EL IMPERFECTO DEL SUBJUNTIVO PARA PETICIONES DE CORTESÍA

1. Spanish uses the imperfect of the subjunctive, as well as the conditional (as you may remember from the **Capítulo 12**) to make polite requests or to soften a suggestion.

2. The imperfect subjunctive is used more commonly with the verbs **querer**, **poder**, **deber**:

   ¡**Quisiera** un kilo de zanahorias, por favor!
   ¡**Pudiera** darme un poco más de café, por favor!
   ¡**Debieras** poner más atención en clase!

3. Sometimes the verbs **tener** and **ser** are also used in the imperfect subjunctive:
   ¡**Fuera** tan amable de traerme más café, por favor!
   ¡**Tuviera** la amabilidad de darme más café, por favor!

4. But it is also very common to use the conditional form of some verbs like **deber**, **gustar**, **poder**, **querer**, **desear,** and the expressions **tener la amabilidad de**, **ser tan amable de**, instead of the imperfect subjunctive:
   Me **gustaría** un café con leche, por favor.
   I would like a coffee with milk, please.
   Podría darme dos hamburguesas, por favor.
   May I have two hamburgers, please.
   Querría un vaso de vino tinto.
   I would like to have a glass of red wine.
   Sería tan amable de darme un vaso de agua, por favor.
   May I have a glass of water, please.
   Tendría la amabilidad de darme un vaso con agua, por favor.
   Would you be so kind to bring me a glass of water, please.
   Deberías estudiar más.
   You should study more.

EJERCICIOS PRÁCTICOS

A. El uso del tiempo pretérito o imperfecto en la cláusula principal supone el uso del imperfecto del subjuntivo.

Modelo: John les sugiere a sus amigas que **vayan** a una discoteca. (sugerir/ir)

John les sugirió a sus amigas que **fueran** a una discoteca.

1. José le dice a Martín que salga. (dijo)
2. Yolanda espera que Thomas hable con ella. (esperaba)
3. Anna quiere que el chico baile con ella. (quería)
4. Lisa duda que ella vaya al cine con Allan. (dudaba)
5. Thomas espera que con su reporte pasar la materia. (esperaba)

B. Cambie estas oraciones del presente subjuntivo al imperfecto del subjuntivo.

Modelo: Thomas desea que la casa **esté** cerca de la universidad.

Thomas deseaba que la casa **estuviera** cerca de la universidad.

1. Thomas quiere que los Zurita tengan un hijo de su edad.
2. Thomas lamenta que su mamá no venga a verlo.
3. Thomas teme que nadie lo entienda.
4. Thomas tiene miedo que no le guste la comida.
5. Thomas duda que su profesor lo estime.

C. Conteste las preguntas usando imperfecto del subjuntivo.

Modelo: Martín, ¿qué te pedí que hicieras? (cortar el pasto)

Me pediste que cortara el pasto.

1. Emilia, ¿qué te dijo tu madre que hicieras? (lavar los trastes)
2. Yolanda ¿qué quería la secretaria que hicieras? (ir pronto)
3. Thomas, ¿qué quería Anna que hicieras? (acompañarla al cine)
4. Profesor, ¿qué esperaba que hiciéramos? (estudiar más)
5. Señor policía, ¿qué esperaba que hiciéramos nosotros? (decir la verdad)
6. Sargento García, ¿qué quería el Zorro? (ir nosotros tras él)

☺ ☺

D. Usted está con su amigo en un restaurante y están listos para ordenar. Recuerde usar el imperfecto del subjuntivo o condicional para hacer sus peticiones.

1. Señorita, primero que nada, ¡_____ (querer) un vaso con agua, sin hielo por favor! Después me _____ (poder) traer la sopa azteca, y las enchiladas suizas. Y de postre me _____ (gustar) un <u>pastel de tres leches y una taza de café.</u>

2. Para mí, primero la taza de café, después _____ (querer) la carne asada a la tampiqueña y de primer plato _____ (desear) el consomé de pollo. Y no quiero postre.

3. A lo que la señorita responde: con todo respeto joven, pero _____ (deber) de probar las crepas con Nutella, están riquísimas, mejor que las de París.

4. Está bien, entonces por favor, _____ (ser) tan amable de traerme unas crepas con Nutella y que conste que es por sugerencia suya.

5. De pronto usted nota que se le está acabando el agua y a su amigo el café y llama a la señorita para pedir más. Señorita, por favor _____ (poder) servirme más agua y más café para mi amigo.

6. Y, después ¿_____ (poder) traerme la cuenta, por favor?

77. CLÁUSULAS SI

1. In Spanish, as well as in English, the conditional is used in sentences with two clauses when one is an "if" clause.

2. To express a condition that is contrary to a fact in Spanish, the imperfect subjunctive in the "if" clause is used, and the conditional in the main clause: Si **tuviera** dinero, **iría** a Nueva York.
    If I had money, I **would** go to New York.

3. In Spanish, as in English, it's possible to begin the sentence with the clause that expresses the condition (main clause):
    Iría a Nueva York, **si tuviera** dinero.
    I **would** go to New York, If I had money.

EJERCICIOS PRÁCTICOS

A. Complete las oraciones usando el imperfecto del subjuntivo.
    Modelo: Yo iría si... (tener los medios).
                    Yo iría si tuviera los medios.
    1.   Yo compraría un coche si... (tener dinero).
    2.   Ella lavaría los trastes si... (pedírselo su mamá).

3.   Nosotros iríamos a Moscú si... (tener un motivo).
4.   *Vosotros serías* espías si... (ser audaces).
5.   Ellos trabajarían para el gobierno si... (pasar el examen)

☺ ☺
B. Con su compañero de clase, escoja la cláusula dependiente que mejor responda a las cláusulas independientes.

A	B
1. Si fuera muy joven	sería bicicleta.
2. Si tuviera dinero	vendería seguros.
3. Si tuviera valor	compraría un bote.
4. Si fuera inteligente	no saldría con otros chicos.
5. Si fuera guapo	estudiaría en una buena universidad.
6. Si estuviera casada	les traería juguetes a todos los niños.
7. Si supiera bailar	tendría muchas admiradoras.
8. Si tuviera ocho años	ganaría mucho dinero.
9. Si fuera el presidente	no usaría zapatos de tacones.
10. Si tuviera ruedas	no tendría licencia de manejo.
11. Si pudiera	iría a muchas fiestas.
12. Si fuera convincente	impulsaría una reforma energética.
13. Si fuera deportista	viajaría a muchos países.
14. Si fuera alta	me alistaría en el ejército.
15. Si fuera Santa Claus	jugaría mucho.

✎
C. Complete las oraciones usando el imperfecto del subjuntivo y condicional.
1.   Los _____ (visitar), si _____ (poder).
2.   Ella _____ (aceptar) el trabajo, si se lo _____ (ofrecer).
3.   Si Thomas la _____ (llamar), Anna _____ (ir).
4.   Mis padres _____ (salir) de vacaciones, si _____ (tener) dinero.
5.   Si Martín _____ (poner) la mesa, Thomas _____ (servir) el agua.
6.   Si ustedes _____ (saber), no _____ (hablar) de esa forma.
7.   Todos _____ (sacar) buenas calificaciones, si _____ (estudiar).
8.   El profesor nos _____ (dar) una buena nota, si _____ (depender) de él.
9.   José _____ (ir) a Londres, si _____ (ser) necesario.
10.   Yo _____ (cantar) mejor, si _____ (tener) un profesor de canto.

78. IMPERFECTO DEL SUBJUNTIVO DESPUÉS DE "COMO SI..." Y "CUAL SI"

1. The expression **como si** (as if) and the more literary **cual si** (as if) always trigger the imperfect subjunctive:

   Me madre me miró **como si** no me conociera.

   La chica pasó **cual si** él no existiese.

EJERCICIOS PRÁCTICOS

A. Complete las oraciones usando imperfecto del subjuntivo.
   Modelo: Thomas habla español como si... (ser nativo).
                Thomas habla español como si fuera nativo.
   1.   Mi mujer gasta dinero como si... (ser millonaria).
   2.   De todas formas, debiste decírselo como si... (ser amigos).
   3.   Se siente como si... (no poder respirar).
   4.   Ellos hablan como si... (saber lo que decían).
   5.   Nosotros fuimos a la fiesta como si... (ser de la familia).

B. Complete las oraciones usando imperfecto del subjuntivo.
   Modelo: Anna abrazó a Thomas cual si... (no haberlo visto en años).
                Anna abrazó a Thomas cual si no lo hubiera visto en años.
   1.   José protestó cual si... (estar enojado).
   2.   El profesor reprobó a los alumnos cual si... (no le importar).
   3.   El niño lo trató con familiaridad cual si... (ser amigos).
   4.   El policía siguió su camino cual si... (no pasar nada).
   5.   La mujer atiende al esposo cual si... (este ser bueno).

79. RECAPITULACIÓN DEL IMPERFECTO DEL SUBJUNTIVO

1. The imperfect subjunctive is used:
 a. In the same situations as the present subjunctive, (except the expression of time that suggest future). Remember that the verb in the main clause is in the past:

   Se **alegró** de que llegaran.

   Esperaba que la llamaran.

Le **había dicho** que dudaba que fuese/fuera[105].

b. In situations when the main clause is in the conditional and the dependent clause is an "if" clause contrary to fact:
Iría con gusto, si **pudiera.**

c. With expressions like **como si** and **cual si**:
José trabaja **como si** quisiera hacerse millonario.

2. The past subjunctive is commonly used to make polite requests with the verbs **querer** and **poder, tener**, or to soften a suggestion with the verb **deber**:
¿**Pudieras** ayudarme?
Debieran estudiar si quieren pasar las materias y graduarse a tiempo.

EJERCICIOS PRÁCTICOS

☺ ☺

A. Responda a cada situación usando el imperfecto del subjuntivo o el condicional cuando sea posible.

Modelo: Usted estaba enamorado y deseando que su novia lo llamara
¿Qué fue lo que hizo usted?
Me puse a pensar en ella para que me **llamara.**

1.   Usted estaba cansado y deseaba que su mamá lo consintiera.
¿Qué fue lo que hizo usted?

2.   Su novia gasta dinero como si se fueran a acabar las mercancías.
¿Qué fue lo que usted le dijo?

3.   El profesor dijo que si él fuera más joven... (usted no alcanzó a oír)
¿Cómo completó usted la frase?

4.   Su padre dijo que era necesario que usted fuera a estudiar a México
¿Qué fue lo que dijo usted?

5.   Usted y sus amigos llegan a la cafetería ¿Cómo ordena usted?

6.   Sus amigos se sentían tristes ¿Qué fue lo que hizo usted?

7.   Según su jefe, era necesario que usted trabajara más ¿Qué fue lo que dijo usted?

8.   Si usted tuviera diez años menos, ¿Qué haría usted?

---

[105] Remember that there are two possible endings for the imperfect subjunctive —ra, and —se.

9. Thomas los saludó cual si no los conociera ¿Qué pensó usted?
10. Querían que usted diera su dinero para una causa justa ¿Qué fue lo que hizo usted?

80. EL PASADO PERFECTO (PLUSCUAMPERFECTO) DEL SUBJUNTIVO

1. The past perfect (pluperfect) subjunctive consists of the imperfect subjunctive of the verb **haber** + the past participle:
Fue muy bueno que Thomas **hubiera vivido** con los Zurita.
It was great that Thomas **had lived** with the Zuritas.

2. The most common use of the past perfect subjunctive occurs in conditional sentences:
Si yo lo **hubiera sabido**, no **habría** tomado la clase.
If I **had known**, I **would** not have taken the class.

3. The past perfect subjunctive is used after **ojalá** (**que**) to express a wish that is in the past and contrary to fact:
Ojalá (que) **hubieras ido**.   I wish you **had gone**.

4. The past perfect subjunctive is used instead of the present perfect subjunctive to indicate that the action of the dependent clause occurred before the action of the main clause when this action is in the past tense:
En Boston, todos celebraron que los Medias Rojas **hubieran ganado el campeonato**.
Everyone in Boston **celebrated** that The Red Sox **had won the cup**.

5. When a sentence indicates a condition in the past that was not fulfilled, the verb in the "if" clause is in the pluperfect subjunctive and the verb in the main clause is usually in the perfect conditional:
Si Andrea **hubiera ido** a México, Yolanda la **habría conocido**.
If Andrea **had gone** to Mexico, Yolanda **would have met** her.

6. Quite often in conversational Spanish people use pluperfect subjunctive in both clauses:
Hubiera sido bueno que te **hubieras puesto** un suéter.   It would have **been** good for you to **put on a sweater**. (literal translation)
It **was good** you put on a sweater. (common translation)

Note that the correct form should be Pluscuamperfecto del subjuntivo plus the imperfect subjunctive:

Hubiera sido bueno que te **pusieras** un suéter.

It **would have been** good if you **had used** a sweater. (literal translation)
It **was good** you put on a sweater. (common translation)

7. As a cultural note, is very common to joke in Spanish about **hubiera** because it represents an unfulfilled condition in the past that obviously can not be changed. We tend to say that **hubiera** doesn't exist because you cannot change the fact that something already happened or did not happen:

Ojalá que el profesor no **hubiera muerto.**

I wish that the teacher **had not died.**

Ojalá que **hubiera pasado el examen.**

I wish that I **had passed** the exam.

EJERCICIOS PRÁCTICOS

A. Practice new sentences using the verbs in parentheses to form the past perfect subjunctive.

Modelo: Si lo hubiera conocido no lo habría olvidado. (saber)
Si lo hubiera sabido no lo habría olvidado.

1. Si yo hubiera sabido bailar habría sido famoso. (aprender a)
2. Si ella no se hubiera enamorado, estaría soltera. (casarse)
3. Si nosotros no hubiéramos reprobado el examen nos habríamos graduado. (fallar)
4. Si el presidente hubiera dicho la verdad, lo habríamos apoyado. (expresar)
5. Si los colombianos no hubieran tenido una guerra, estarían mucho más felices. (sufrir)

B. Cambie las oraciones del imperfecto del subjuntivo al pasado perfecto del subjuntivo.

Modelo: Si yo fuera rico compraría un Ferrari.
Si yo hubiera sido rico habría comprado un Ferrari.

1. Si yo fuera una chica sexy sería una monja.
2. Si yo fuera el presidente, yo sería muy poderoso.
3. Si tú fueras gordo, tendrías un trabajo como Santa Claus.

4. Si nosotros viviéramos en China, hablaríamos mandarín.
5. Si ellas se fueran a Hollywood serían muy famosas.

C. Complete las oraciones usando pasado perfecto del subjuntivo.
Modelo: **Hubiera sido** bueno que.... (estudiar)
Hubiera sido bueno que **estudiaras**.
1. Hubiera sido saludable que... (hacer ejercicio)
2. Hubiera sido práctico que... (conseguir trabajo)
3. Hubiera sido maravilloso que mi hermana... (casarse)
4. Hubiese sido recomendable que... (ir al baile)
5. Hubiese sido deseable que... (tener seguro médico)

D. Fill in the blank, using pluperfect subjunctive to complete the sentences.
1. _____ sido mejor que te quedaras en Boston y no _____ (haber) regresado a este país que está tan peligroso.
2. Mamá. Si _____ sabido que me ibas a rechazar me _____ (haber) quedado en Boston.
3. No es que te rechace, es solo que si me _____ llamado aunque sea una sola vez en todos estos años, te _____ (haber) enterado de lo difícil que es vivir en nuestro país.
4. Te garantizo que si tú _____ estado en mi lugar, _____ (haber) hecho lo mismo.
5. No creo que yo _____ hecho lo mismo, pues yo tengo una sensibilidad más fina. Pero como bien dicen en mi pueblo, el _____ no existe así que déjame que te dé un abrazo y que te diga que eres bienvenido.

MINIRELATO: EL NUEVO CINE MEXICANO

A partir del año 2000 se comenzó a hablar en los medios de comunicación que había en México un nuevo grupo de cineastas y actores que estaban dándole nueva vida al alicaído (crestfallen) cine mexicano y creando lo que se conoce como el Nuevo Cine Mexicano. Se hablaba de la realización de nuevas películas que estaban llevando a la gente, de nuevo, a las salas de cine. Películas como, Sexo, pudor y lágrimas, Amores Perros, De la calle, El crimen del Padre Amaro, La Ley de Herodes impactaron a las audiencias no sólo en México sino también en el extranjero.

Esta nueva propuesta cinematográfica, está creando películas que tienen historias alejadas de lo convencional y que están enmarcadas en la problemática que vive el país. Todas ellas constituyen una propuesta diferente a lo antes visto, donde dependiendo de la época deambulaban por la pantalla charros cantores, enmascarados luchando contra monstruos.

Este que se conoce hoy como el nuevo cine mexicano tiene una nueva propuesta: el retratar la actualidad mexicana sin maquillajes, sin falsos romanticismos, sin ambages (plainly) sin olvidar que es, a la vez, un artificio.

La última película de éxito de este nuevo cine se titula Roma, del director Alfonso Cuarón; esta película ganó el Oscar a la mejor película extranjera en el 2019.

LECTURA: ALFONSO CUARÓN OROZCO

Alfonso Cuarón nació el 28 de noviembre de 1961 en Ciudad de Mexico. Cuarón se ha convertido en un director de mucho éxito y su mayor éxito es la película Roma, con la que ganó el Oscar al mejor director, a mejor fotografía y además ganó el Oscar a la mejor película extranjera en el 2019 y un Globo de Oro como mejor director.

Cuarón inició su carrera a inicios de los años 80.

Su primer largometraje fue *Sólo Con Tu Pareja* (1991); esta película le abrió las puertas de Hollywood, Sidney Pollack en 1983 lo invitó a participar del proyecto televisivo *Ángeles Caídos*. En 1995 debutó en el cine estadounidense, sin mayor éxito comercial, con la película *La Princesita*.

Su revelación como director se produjo en el 2001 con la película *Y Tu Mamá También*, protagonizada por Maribel Verdú, Diego Luna y Gael García Bernal. El film fue un éxito internacional notable.

Su siguiente éxito comercial ocurrió en el 2004 con la adaptación cinematográfica de uno de los libros de la saga de Harry Potter. En el 2013 filmó *Gravity* que tuvo como protagonistas a Sandra Bullock y a George Clooney; por esta película consiguió el Oscar al mejor director, además de un Globo de Oro.

En el 2018 estrenó la que ha sido hasta ahora su mejor película *Roma*, ambientada en la Ciudad de México de comienzos de los años 70.

Preguntas

1. ¿Dónde y cuándo nació Alfonso Cuarón?
2. ¿Con cuál película se dio a conocer internacionalmente?
3. Mencione dos Oscares recibidos por la película Roma.
4. Mencione el premio que recibió por la película Gravity.
5. ¿Dónde ocurre Roma y qué época refleja?
6. ¿En cuál de sus películas actúa Sandra Bullock?
7. ¿En cuál película actúan Diego Luna, Maribel Verdú y Gael García?

EJERCICIOS PRÁCTICOS

A. En México, las películas estadounidenses son frecuentemente subtituladas. Sin embargo, algunas veces éstas son dobladas al español especialmente cuando se trata de películas para niños. Un caso muy notable por el doblaje al español fue la película *Buscando a Nemo* (Finding Nemo).

Aquí tiene una lista de títulos de cómo se presentaron algunas de las películas estadounidenses en México:

El secreto de la montaña. (Brokeback Mountain)
La marca de la horca. (Hang'em high)
Lo que el viento se llevó. (Gone with the Wind)
Son como niños. (Grown Ups)
Shrek para siempre. (Shrek Forever After)
Atrapado sin salida. (One Flew Over the Cuckoo's Nest)
Antes de partir. (The Bucket List)
El gran escape. (The Great Escape)
Dos tontos muy tontos. (Dumb and Dumber)
Los hombres de negro. (Men in black)
Socios y sabuesos. (Turner & Hooch)
Algo pasa en Hollywood. (What just happened?)
La sombra del poder. (State of Play)

B. Ahora su tarea es tomar los títulos de las películas que a usted le gustan y trate de traducir esos títulos al español; después haga lo contrario, tome algunas películas en español y póngalos en inglés, veremos que resulta del ejercicio.

C. En una página de papel escriba, sin dudar, lo que se le viene a la cabeza cuando su compañero de clase le diga:

Si tú vivieras en el año 2420, _____.
Si usted fuera elegido por la NASA para ir a Marte, _____.
Si usted fuera una chica/chico, _____.
Si sus padres fueran mexicanos, _____.
Si la profesora le pidiera dar la clase, _____.
Si el presidente Kennedy no hubiera muerto _____.

VOCABULARIO

VERBOS

ver	ir	llamar	comprar
visitar	vender	encontrar	escribir
comprometerse	saber	haber	sentir
querer	deber	poder	tener
alegrarse	morir	ganar	celebrar
venir			

NOMBRES

la función	la princesa	las películas	el teatro
el cine	las palomitas	las sodas	el director
las entradas	el actor	la actriz	el guionista
la taquilla	el boleto	el guión	la cámara
las perlas	el poema	la lectura	la boca
la fresa	el príncipe	el oriente	la locación
el poeta	los libros	la hora	el oficial
Marte	el presidente	el profesor	la bicicleta
la abuelita	la NASA	la tarea	el poder
los amores	los perros	la marca	la horca
el maquinista	las entradas	los subtítulos	la página

ADJETIVOS

público/a	piratas	grave	sexy
nuevo/a	alicaído/a	mexicano/a	

ADVERBIOS

particularmente	bien	ciertamente	actualmente
inmediatamente	muy		

EXPRESIONES UTILES

faltaba más	¡me parece genial!	para nada
manos a la obra	como si	cual si
ojalá que...	para variar	para siempre
por favor	para que	

CAPÍTULO INFORMATIVO

En este capítulo...

You'll find information about when to omit the use of the definite and indefinite articles, as well as some other uses of the infinitive. You'll also discuss how to use negative expressions in conversations, the differences between **dejar** vs **salir**, and the uses of conjunctions and interjections.

By now, you, like the four American students, have enough knowledge of structure and vocabulary and enough cultural awareness to communicate with the vast majority of people in the Spanish-speaking World.

APUNTE GRAMATICAL A

Usos del infinitivo

1. In Spanish the infinitive may act as a verb (**-ar,-er,-ir**) or a noun. When the infinitive acts as a noun it tends to be singular and masculine:
   Manejar borracho es peligroso.

2. The infinitive often requires personal pronouns; remember that the position of the pronoun may change depending upon the type of sentence:
   Vamos a comprar**lo.**
   Lo vamos a comprar.

3. Do not forget that after a preposition if you need a verb it has to be in the infinitive: Trataré **de comprar** la leche.

4. The infinitive can be use in impersonal commands but is definitely more common with negative commands:
   ¡A **callar**!
   ¡Favor de **no sacar** las manos por la ventanilla!
   ¡Prohibido **fumar**!

5. **De** + infinitive can be use instead of **si** in an "if clause", but the subject in the first clause has to appear in the second clause directly or indirectly:
   De haberlo visto le habría dicho que se escondiera.
   Si lo hubiera visto le habría dicho que se escondiera.

6. When two verbs are part of the same construction in a sentence, the first one is conjugated and the second is in infinitive: Ella **sabe nadar.**

7. In Spanish the infinitive is often preceded by the pronoun **que**:
   A José le queda mucho **que hacer** todavía.
   Los estudiantes compran algo **que llevarles** a sus familias.
   Dame algo **que ponerme.**

8. In some cases the infinite article can be used before the infinitive:
   a. Al + infinitive: Se hace camino **al andar.** (a verse from a poem by Antonio Machado)
   b. el + infinitive: Con **el pasar** de los años.
   c. un + infinitive: En **un abrir** y **cerrar** de ojos.

9. The infinitive can be used to give short answers:
   Y ahora, ¿qué vamos a hacer?   ¡**Esperar**!

10. The Infinitive is used after expressions like **más que, menos**:
    No nos queda **más que decir**le la verdad.
    Todo **menos decir**le la verdad.

11. The infinitive is used in sentences with a verb already conjugated when they are listing actions:
    Después me voy a **bañar, vestir y salir** a la calle.

12. The infinitive is also used to express passive meaning, especially after prepositions like **sin, por** and **para**:
    Las maletas estaban **sin hacerse.**

13. The infinitive can be used in rhetorical questions or to express disbelief or indignation:

¿**Manejar** cuatro horas para esto?

¡Parece mentira, **pasarse** la vida esperando este momento!

APUNTE GRAMATICAL B

Perífrasis en español.

1. The periphrasis in Spanish serves to refer indirectly to other things that sometimes can not be referred to in any other way or that we wish to refer more extensively. Its syntactic construction involves two or more verbs that function as the core of the predicate. They are widely used in daily conversations and tend to include colloquial forms of the language. Here is an example:

María lee hasta altas horas de la noche.

En vez de: María lee hasta tarde.

2. There are different types of periphrasis:

A. Periphrasis "modales". They are those that inform about the attitude of the speaking subject before the verbal action and there are three types:

a. Of obligation: Tenemos que trabajar.

b. Of assumption: Esa camisa debe (de) costar un ojo de la cara.

c. Of possibility: Es posible realizar los sueños.

B. Periphrasis "aspectuales" that inform about the very development of verbal action, that is, about the moment of action in which the speaker is setting:

a. Of imminent action: Estaba a punto de llamarte, pero me leíste el pensamiento.

b. Of those to refer the beginning of the action: De pronto empezó a llover.

c. Of habitual action: Los policías suelen tener un temperamento áspero.

d. Of repetitive action: Volveremos a vernos muchas veces.

e. Of progressive action: Mi hermano lleva quejándose de las clases desde que entró a la escuela.

f. Of final action: La chica nos ha pedido que la dejemos en paz.

APUNTE GRAMATICAL C

Dejar vs. salir

1. **Dejar** and **salir** both can be translated as to leave, but they are not interchangeable.

2. **Dejar** as a transitive verb means to leave something or someone behind:
   Thomas **dejó** a su familia en Chappaqua.

3. As a reflexive verb **dejarse** means stop behaving as a certain way... or to put your past behind you and move on:
   ¡Hay que **dejarse** de niñerías y tomar al toro por los cuernos!

4. **Dejar de** + infinitive means to stop doing something:
   Saldremos tan pronto **deje de llover.**

5. **Dejar** + infinitive means to let:
   ¿Cuándo **dejarán salir** a los niños a recreo?

6. **Salir** is an intransitive verb that means to go out or leave. The preposition **de** follows the verb before the location that is being left:
   Thomas y los demás estudiantes **salieron de** Nueva York.

7. The preposition **a** follows **salir** before a certain time is expressed:
   Nuestro avión **sale a** las tres y cuarto.

8. The preposition **a** or **para** is used to express destination:
   Thomas salió **para** México.

9. The preposition **con** is used to express in the company of people:
   Thomas salió **con** los Zurita.

10. **Salir** + an adjective or adverb means to turn out/ turn out. An indirect object is often added:
    Comprar la casa **nos salió muy caro.**
    Comprar la casa **le** salió **mal.**

APUNTE GRAMATICAL D

Las conjunciones
1. Conjunctions link sentences and create relations between them:
En el avión hay un piloto.   El piloto se llama Jesús.
En el avión hay un piloto **y** se llama Jesús.

Another possibility is to use the relative pronoun **que** instead of the co junction **y** since **que** is also a conjunction that establishes a relationship be- tween two sentences creating a new sentence with less information. For example:
En el avión hay un piloto.   El piloto se llama Jesús.
En el avión hay un piloto **que** se llama Jesús.

2. Some common conjunctions are:
a. las **copulativas:** y (e), ni.   Ex. Maricruz **y** Daniel van al cine.

b. las **disyuntivas:** o (u). Ex. El niño tendría doce o trece años.

c. las **adversativas:** pero, sino. Ex. Pedro come poco, **pero** Andrés come mucho.

d. las **ilativas:** pues, luego, por consiguiente. Ex. El padre salió temprano, la madre salió temprano, los niños salieron temprano, **por consiguiente** todos salieron temprano.

e. las **causales:** porque, puesto que. Ex. Anna estudia español **porque** le gusta.

f. las **condicionales:** si, con tal que. Ex. Lisa irá a México **si** Anna va.

g. las **consecutivas:** que. Ex. Yolanda tiene un hijo **que** se llama Martín.

3.   For phonetic reasons the conjunction "**y**" changes into "**e**" before words that begin with "**i**" or words that starts with the syllable "**hi**":
Thomas **e** Ignacio son amigos.
Necesito una aguja **e** hilo.

4.   Sometimes Spanish omits the conjunction in coordinated sentences because this creates a sense of elegance:

Ansiedad, sufrimientos y quebrantos son el pan nuestro de cada día en muchos de los hogares pobres latinoamericanos.

5.   In other cases, the conjunction is repeated in order to emphasize the relation between the parts:
Hubo en la fiesta mucha comida y bebidas y música y jolgorio.

APUNTE GRAMATICAL E

Las interjecciones
1. An interjection (**interjección**) is a word or a phrase that expresses emotion or affection, and it tends to be spontaneous. Interjections keep their independence from other parts of the sentence.

2. There are different types of interjections:
 a. **Interjecciones propias**, are those words that have no other value or meaning but to express emotion or affection:
¡Ay! me duele la cabeza.
¡Bah!, eso no es nada.
¡Hola! ¿Cómo está?

 b. **Interjecciones impropias**, are those words that have other functions in a sentence:
¡Qué cosa tan horrible!
¡Auxilio! ¡Socorro! ¡Me están asaltando!

 c. adjectives used as **interjecciones**:
¡alto! ¡bravo! ¡abusado!

 d. verbs used as **interjecciones**:
¡anda! ¡mira! ¡dale! ¡viva! ¡calla! ¡oiga! ¡vaya! ¡muera!

 e. adverbs used as **interjecciones**:
¡abajo! ¡fuera! ¡adelante! ¡arriba!

 f. nouns used as **interjecciones**:
¡ojo! ¡silencio! ¡hombre! ¡aguas!

 g. phrases used as **interjecciones**:

¡Pobre hombre!
¡Señor mío!
¡Ay de mí!
¡No, hombre, no!

h. there are **interjecciones** of sorrow, pain or pity:
¡Ay!, ¡huy!

i. there are **interjecciones** that express surprise:
¡Ah! ¡oh! ¡caramba! ¡híjole!

j. there are **interjecciones** that express warning:
¡eh! ¡cuidado! ¡ey!

APUNTE GRAMATICAL F

La voz pasiva
1. In the active voice, the subject of the sentence performs the action of the verb. But in the passive voice, the subject receives the action of the verb:
ACTIVE: Thomas halaga a Yolanda.
PASIVE: Yolanda es halagada por Thomas.
2. In Spanish we use the passive voice to deemphasize the agent of the action, therefore the speaker can focus on the direct object by transforming it into the subject of a passive sentence:
Los exámenes **fueron contestados por** los alumnos.

3. As in English, the passive voice in Spanish is formed by using a past participle of any transitive verb, and the appropriate form of the verb **ser:**
Los edificios **fueron construidos** por los albañiles.
Las cartas **serán entregadas** por el cartero esta tarde.
La solicitud ya **ha sido hecha por** la secretaria.

4. The past participle agrees in gender and number with the subject because it is used as an adjective:
La puerta está cerrada.   The door is closed.
El libro está abierto.   The book is open.

5. In the passive voice, the performer of the action (the agent) is usually introduced by **por**:

John fue castigado **por** el profesor.

6. When there is no agent expressed, the passive voice may be replaced by **se impersonal**, as you learned in **Chapter 11**:
   Se habla inglés.   English spoken.

7. In some cases the verb **ser** can be replaced by other verbs to suggest a passive voice:
   a. **quedar**: La plaza **quedará** abierta por varios motivos.

   Note here that **quedar** is suggesting a condition that has arisen from some event that will occur in the future.

   b. **verse**: Los derechos de autor **se vieron** reducidos por la piratería.

   c. **venir**: Como viene diciéndose desde hace años.

   Note that the verb **venir** also emphasizes that a condition has arisen from some previous event.

APUNTE GRAMATICAL G

Casos en que no se usan los artículos definidos e indefinidos
1. The definite article should be omitted:
a. Before a proper noun:
   El es Roberto.

   b. Before quantitative and qualitative nouns that do not refer to the whole of their class:
   Los Zurita tienen mucha paciencia.
   Martín compró sesenta pesos de pan.

c. After the verb **haber**:
   Hay gente en el comedor.

d. When two nouns are joined by the preposition **de** to form a compound noun, the definite article is omitted before the second noun:
   Martín olvidó comprar el pan de dulce.

e. Before ordinal numbers with dignitaries, and other rulers:
Luis Catorce.

f. Many adverbial phrases do not demand the use of the article in Spanish (contrary to English):
Vamos cuesta abajo.   We are going down **the** hill.

g. The definite article may not be before partitive nouns[106] (qualitative or quantitative):
No hay comida.
Yolanda les dio (las) flores a las alumnas.

   Note that certain verbs that suggest consuming, desiring or producing tend to be partitive so the definitive article is not required:
   Las ranas comen moscas.

h. The definite article is omitted at the beginning of titles of works of literature or headlines in newspapers:
Selección de poemas.
Un clérigo iraní afirma que los divorcios producen (los) temblores.

i. The indefinite article is omitted before predicative nouns that denote social status in general (profession, occupation, nationality, gender):
Anna es estudiante.
Los estudiantes son estadounidenses.

j. The indefinite article is omitted after verbs like **usar, llevar** (to wear), **comprar**:
Jesse lleva anteojos.

2. The indefinite article is omitted:
A In phrases with ¡**qué**...! and before **otro, cierto, tal, medio, ciento**, and **mil**:
¡Qué calor!
John tiene otro estilo.

---

[106] In linguistics, the **partitive** is a word, phrase, or case that indicates partialness.

b. The indefinite article is often omitted in appositive phrases:
José es ferviente admirador de los Estados Unidos.

c. The indefinite article is not used after expressions that include **como, a modo/manera de**:
Yolanda citó como ejemplo a Thomas.

d. When referring to **casa** as space and not the building:
Cuando estoy en casa duermo bien.

APUNTE GRAMATICAL H

Las paráfrasis

a. The paraphrase expresses the meaning of (something written or spoken) using different words, especially to achieve greater clarity. Paraphrases are coming from the middle of the 16th century (as a noun): via Latin from Greek "paraphrazein", from para- (expressing modification) + phrazein 'tell'.

b. Paraphrasing is a discourse or a text that aims to explain and expand information, with the aim of making the data easier to understand and assimilate by the receiver:
Dadme un prejuicio y moveré el mundo.
Give me a prejudice and I will move the world.

c. At the end, what the paraphrase seeks is to clarify the different dimensions of a message. For this he develops a kind of imitation of the original discourse, although appealing to a different language.

d. There are two fundamental types of paraphrasing:
Mechanics: This consists fundamentally in carrying out the substitution of expressions by other phrases or synonyms, which suppose, however, a minimum syntactic change:
La irrupción del febo alumbró la morada. = La salida del sol iluminó la casa.
The irruption of Febo illuminated the dwelling. = The sunrise illuminated the house.

Note that at the school stunts tends to use this form of paraphrasing especially when a teacher as then to express with their own words what they read.

Constructive: This type of paraphrase is more difficult and requieres much more control of the language, because this type consists of maintaining completely its meaning, reworking any text to get another that is totally different.

EL MUNDO DE HABLA HISPANA

La hispanidad
El español es una de las lenguas oficiales de la **Organización de las Naciones Unidas** (ONU) de la **Organización de Estados Americanos** (OEA) y de la **Unión Europea** (UE).

En su conjunto el español es uno de los cuatro idiomas internacionales más grandes que se usa como una de las lenguas oficiales en muchos organismos internacionales. Además de los arriba mencionados, también se usa como lengua oficial en la **Organización de las Naciones Unidas para la Educación, la Ciencia y la Cultura** (UNESCO), en la **Organización de las Naciones Unidas para la Agricultura y la Alimentación** (FAO), en la **Organización Mundial del Comercio** (OMC).

La hispanidad es también la producción cultural que se da a través de una multitud de periódicos, revistas, canales de televisión, radiodifusoras, sitios de Internet, libros y revistas que emplean diariamente el español en varias partes del mundo.

Pero sobre todo la hispanidad o el mundo de habla hispana son los pueblos y culturas que hablan español en América Latina, España, Guinea Ecuatorial, Estados Unidos, Filipinas, Belice, Andorra y otros lugares.

¿Qué es un hispanohablante?
Es ante todo una persona que emplea el español de forma regular. Existen actualmente cerca de 500 millones de personas que hablan español, siendo el español la cuarta lengua más hablada después del mandarín, el inglés, y el hindi.

Sólo en América Latina, de los 19 países (incluyendo a Puerto Rico) donde el español es la lengua oficial, existen al menos cuatro variedades distintivas del español: el andino, el ríoplatense, el caribe y el mexicano; y en España se pueden detectar al menos tres: el castellano, el andaluz y el canario.

Se estima que en América Latina unos trescientos veinte millones de personas hablan español, mientras unos 44 millones lo hablan en España y unos 50 millones en los Estados Unidos.

Orígenes del español

El castellano, dialecto románico surgido en Castilla y origen de la lengua española, nació en una franja montañosa, mal y tardíamente romanizada, inculta y con fuertes raíces prerromanas (Burgos, Iria Flavia, Oviedo, Amaya, Pamplona), en la cual surgieron los condados y reinos medievales españoles, y en torno a esos nuevos centros fueron desarrollándose las variedades dialectales. El castellano, dialecto de los montañeses, que en el siglo IX estaban a cargo de defender la frontera oriental del reino astur- leonés, de los árabes (en la península desde el año 711), toma su nombre de castilla —del latín *castella,* plural de *castellum*— que en el período visigótico significó 'pequeño campamento militar' (diminutivo de *castrum*) y luego 'tierra de castillos'.

La consolidación del castellano

El primer texto literario escrito íntegramente en castellano fue el anónimo *Cantar del mío Cid*, cuya versión original data del siglo XII (1140 aproximadamente) aunque la versión que hoy se conoce data de 1307, copiada por Per Abatt. También del siglo XIII es la *Grande e General Estoria* de España de Alfonso X, apodado el Sabio, que fue rey de Castilla entre 1252 y 1284. Fue justamente, a partir de los textos de Alfonso X, quien publicó sus obras en castellano en vez de latín, que es posible detectar una cierta uniformidad naciente en la lengua castellana. Con los trabajos en prosa de Alfonso X, El Sabio, este nuevo idioma comienza a adquirir el prestigio de lengua nacional.

En la historia lingüística del castellano se pueden distinguir dos etapas: la primera, denominada "romance", en la que se escriben las primeras muestras de esta nueva lengua y cuyas variedades se van nivelando en torno al habla de Burgos, primer centro de nivelación del idioma, y la segunda, denominada "castellana", que comienza a partir de la obra de Alfonso X.

Durante esta época, el castellano se volvió la lengua en que se tradujeron las grandes obras históricas, jurídicas, literarias y científicas. En este proceso también tuvo suma importancia la visión de Alfonso X y su corte de intelectuales agrupados en la Escuela de traductores de Toledo, integrada, entre otros, por judíos conocedores del hebreo y el árabe.

Por otro lado, en el ámbito histórico, Castilla se consolidó como la monarquía más poderosa del centro peninsular, lo cual le permitió, en el siglo XIII, gracias al dominio ejercido sobre los reinos vecinos, convertirse en el único reino ibérico capaz de lograr la recuperación de los territorios bajo el dominio musulmán, lo que en términos prácticos también supuso la expansión de la lengua.

Poco más tarde, en el siglo XIV, aparece otro libro importante para la consolidación de esta lengua: el *Libro de Buen Amor, de* Juan Ruiz, el arcipreste de Hita.

El castellano como lengua unificadora

Con la boda en 1469 de Fernando II de Aragón e Isabel I, reina de Castilla y de León, los llamados reyes Católicos, se dio, al menos en términos prácticos, la unión monárquica de Castilla y Aragón. El advenimiento de los reyes Católicos fue un paso fundamental para terminar el proceso de la reconquista contra el domino musulmán en la península Ibérica que concluyó con la recuperación del reino de Granada, el 2 de enero de 1492, el mismo año del descubrimiento de América y de la expulsión de los judíos de España.

De esta forma el castellano, ensanchó cada vez más su acción de norte a sur hasta terminar por implantarse en esa parte de la península ibérica. A su paso, el castellano se fue enriqueciendo gracias a los regionalismos peninsulares.

El castellano unificó rápidamente a gran parte de la península, desplazó las hablas leonesas y aragonesas y se convirtió en la lengua romance propia de Navarra, en lengua única de Castilla, de Andalucía y del reconquistado reino de Granada. Tuvo tal fuerza que no sólo se consolidó como lengua de unidad, sino que también se vio consagrada de forma definitiva con la aparición de la primera gramática de una lengua romance: la *Gramática de la lengua castellana* de Elio Antonio de Nebrija, publicada en 1492. Veinticinco años después, en 1517, el mismo autor publicó su libro *Reglas de ortografía castellana.*

La llegada del español a América

El castellano, en un avance histórico continuo, alcanzó todos los rincones de la geografía española, cruzó los mares y se alojó en lugares muy lejanos de la Península Ibérica, especialmente en América, donde creció con vigor enriquecido por la cultura y las tradiciones de los nativos. Esta lengua castellana o española, los dos nombres responden hoy en día al mismo idioma, se realiza gracias a una gran riqueza de dialectos y variedades tanto en España como en Iberoamérica.

En 1492, cuando Cristóbal Colón llegó a América, el castellano se encontraba consolidado en la península, pero durante los siglos XV y XVI se produjo una verdadera revolución consonántica que afectó especialmente a las llamadas sibilantes, las cuales se redujeron, y ésa fue la variedad que llegó al Nuevo Mundo, generalmente conocida como español de América. Esta lengua se extendió con la colonización, pero no hay que olvidar que los colonizadores eran personas de diferente nivel cultural, y que además el español americano se enriqueció con el aporte de las lenguas aborígenes del nuevo mundo. Esta diversidad de las lenguas indígenas, algunas ya extintas y otras en uso, fue un factor clave de diferenciación en el español americano.

Entre los muchos vocablos que han enriquecido el español están:
a. el de los Caribes que aportaron palabras como: *canoa, caribe, caníbal, manatí, caimán, piragua...*
b. *el del* Náhuatl *petate, tiza, chocolate, tomate, cacao, coyote, chicle...*
c. *el del* Quechua y Aymará *choclo* (mazorca), papa, *chacra (*terreno pequeño para cultivar), *pisco* (aguardiente de uva), *mate, pucho* (residuo, colilla), *chirimoya, coca, quena, llama...*
d. el del Guaraní tenemos *maraca, tucán, tapioca, mandioca, guaraná* (planta frutal)

Como resultado de estas fusiones, tenemos una variedad dialectal del español que es enormemente rica. Esa riqueza no respeta fronteras entre países, ni divergencias geográficas o culturales dentro de un mismo país, como es el caso de México donde en la península de Yucatán se observan fenómenos que pueden ser desconocidos en el resto del país y que pueden estar más cercanos a formas culturales de algunas zonas de Centro América.

Hasta hoy ha sido la norma estudiar la diversidad y complejidad del español de América distribuyéndolo por zonas geográficas: El español de México y el sur de los Estados Unidos, el español caribeño, el español andino, y el español ríoplatense. Pero este criterio responde más a la geografía que a la lingüística. Aunque existe consenso entre los estudiosos de la lengua que el español culto es bastante uniforme en toda la región de Hispanoamérica.

Por ello, algunos investigadores piensan que para estudiar el fenómeno del español en América de una mejor manera no sólo hay que tener en cuenta las diferencias lingüísticas de los distintos países y regiones sino que es preciso observar diferencias que tienen que ver con el nivel sociocultural de los hablantes, el tipo de población, las distintas zonas ya sea rurales, urbanas, de la provincia o de las capitales, si se trata de hablantes monolingües o bilingües, pues todos estos factores inciden en la variación lingüística.

También hay que considerar los factores históricos como la procedencia de los contingentes de población que colonizaron el continente americano y su distribución regional. Es innegable que el español meridional peninsular y el habla de las zonas costeras de América y de las Antillas comparten muchos rasgos lingüísticos. Sin embargo, esta influencia del español meridional no se dio por igual en las distintas regiones de América, pues hay grandes áreas lingüísticas como el altiplano mexicano, el interior de Colombia y Venezuela, la serranía de Ecuador, Perú o Bolivia, en las que no aparecen este tipo de rasgos de debilitamiento articulatorio propios de las variedades meridionales.

Los rasgos lingüísticos más aceptados para estudiar la riqueza del español americano en la actualidad son:

a. Los rasgos fonéticos
Se suele aceptar la existencia de algunas áreas dialectales, como la mencionada andina, el español caribeño (Antillas y costa atlántica de México, Centroamérica, Venezuela y Colombia) o el español del Río de la Plata (Argentina, Uruguay).

Sin duda alguna, se puede afirmar que el rasgo fonético que caracteriza el español americano por excelencia es el seseo. Otro de los rasgos que se suelen citar como identificadores del español americano es el yeísmo y también la neutralización de la letra "r" y "l" que se extiende fundamentalmente por el Caribe y Las Antillas, aunque este fenómeno también se documenta en los estratos sociales sin instrucción en lugares como Chile, Perú, Paraguay o Ecuador.

Otro rasgo común en el Caribe es la pérdida del sonido de la letra "s", al final de las palabras, pero el sonido se mantiene en las tierras altas como en la meseta mexicana.

b. Los rasgos morfosintácticos

Uno de estos rasgos es el uso generalizado de "*se los*" por "*se lo*" (*se los dije* 'les dije esto a ellos), esto es, dado que la forma de objeto indirecto "*se*" es invariable y no puede llevar la marca de plural, es la forma pronominal de objeto directo, "*lo*", la que lleva los rasgos de número; de esta manera el hablante explicita la pluralidad del referente indirecto. Este uso está extendido a los hablantes de todas las clases sociales y se puede localizar incluso en la lengua escrita, sobre todo en los medios de comunicación.

Otro rasgo tiene que ver con el orden sujeto-verbo en oraciones interrogativas del tipo *¿qué tú quieres?* similar al de las oraciones enunciativas; este rasgo es típico del habla del Caribe y Panamá.

Otro rasgo es el voseo o empleo de la forma **vos** como segunda persona del singular está bastante generalizado en muchas áreas, si bien las desinencias verbales que acompañan esta forma pueden ser tanto diptongadas (*vos cantáis*) como no diptongadas (*vos cantás*). Se documenta el voseo en la mayoría de los países hispanoamericanos, a excepción de Panamá, la mayor parte de México y las Antillas.

Sin embargo, la generalización del voseo en estos países depende del nivel de prestigio que este rasgo haya alcanzado en esos países. Así, se ha convertido en un uso prestigioso en Argentina, Paraguay o Uruguay, se está generalizando, pero es poco prestigioso en Colombia, Venezuela o Ecuador, pues se asimila a las formas de hablar de las clases con poca instrucción.

Otro rasgo muy notable en Hispanoamérica, ya existente en el español peninsular, pero cuya explosión se volvió excesiva es el uso de los diminutivos y aumentativos, especialmente en países como México: ranchito, ahorita, suavecito, momentito; amigazo, cuerpazo, guamazo, etc. son palabras de uso muy frecuente en el habla cotidiana.

c. Los rasgos léxicos

Entre los rasgos léxicos están el uso generalizado de *carro* por "coche", al igual que *cuadra* por "manzana", *departamento* por "piso", *computadora* por "ordenador", *camioneta* o *camión* por "autobús" funciona en México y Centroamérica, *ómnibus* se restringe más bien a los países del cono sur americano, *jugo* por "zumo", *cachetes* por "mejillas", *durazno* por "melocotón", *tanque* por "depósito de gasolina", *boleto* por "billete", *pizarrón* por "pizarra", *manejar por* "conducir", *tomar por* "beber", *botar por* "echar". Otros de esos rasgos léxicos son los llamados arcaísmos léxicos, esto es, voces que han dejado de utilizarse en el español peninsular estándar de manera general, como *pararse* por "ponerse derecho, de pie", *cobija por* "manta", *enojarse por* "enfadarse".

Otros, por el contrario, son voces de nueva creación como *balear,* (tirotear), *lonchar* (del inglés *lunch,* comer a mediodía), *timbrar (*llamar al timbre).

Otras voces son específicas de ciertos países como México: *ejote* (vaina del frijol tierna), *bolsa de dormir* (saco de dormir), *elote* (maíz tierno), *pesero* (autobús), *chueco* (que está torcido, fig.: persona falsa), *checar* (verificar, comprobar la validez de algo, por la influencia del inglés), *pilón (*pequeña cosa que se añade como regalo). O en Venezuela: *arepa* (especie de empanadilla), *catire* (persona rubia, de tez blanca), *gafo* (estúpido, torpe), *guachafa* (broma pesada), *embarcar a alguien* (dejarle plantado, no cumplir lo prometido); en Argentina, Paraguay y Uruguay: *vereda* (acera), *pollera* (falda), *remedios* (medicinas), morocho (de piel morena), *gaucho* (campesino), *chacra* (huerta, sembrado).

El español moderno

En el año 1713 se fundó la Real Academia Española. Su primera tarea fue la de fijar el idioma y sancionar los cambios que del idioma habían hecho los hablantes a lo largo de los siglos, siguiendo unos criterios de autoridad. En esta época ya se había terminado el cambio fonético y morfológico y el sistema verbal de tiempos simples y compuestos fue el mismo que estuvo vigente hasta la primera mitad del siglo XX.

Los pronombres átonos ya no se combinaban con las formas de participio y, gracias a la variación morfológica, los elementos de la oración se pueden ordenar de formas muy diversas con una gran variedad de estilos literarios, desde la mayor violación sintáctica que representan el barroco del siglo XVII y los poetas de la generación del 27, así como la versatilidad de que dispone el lenguaje publicitario, hasta la imitación de los cánones clásicos que incorporaron los neoclásicos o los primeros renacentistas.

Coincidiendo con otro momento de esplendor literario, el primer tercio del siglo XX, aparecieron las nuevas modificaciones gramaticales que aún hoy están en proceso de asentamiento.

De ellas cabe citar: la reducción del paradigma verbal en sus formas compuestas de indicativo y subjuntivo, la sustitución de los futuros por perífrasis verbales del tipo "tengo que ir" por "iré", la práctica desaparición del futuro subjuntivo, la reduplicación de los pronombres átonos en muchas estructuras oracionales y con verbos de significación pasiva, que están desarrollando una conjugación en voz media como en "le debo dinero a María"; la posposición casi sistemática de los calificativos, la reducción de los pronombres relativos, prácticamente limitados a "que" y "quien" en la lengua hablada.

La irrupción continua de neologismos, que por lo general se refieren a las innovaciones técnicas y avances científicos y que tiene dos momentos: los de la primera mitad del siglo XX, que contienen raíces clásicas como termómetro, televisión, átomo, psicoanálisis o morfema, y los neologismos recientemente castellanizados, siglas y calcos del inglés y fruto de la difusión que de ellos hacen las revistas especializadas, la publicidad o la prensa, como filmar, radar, módem, casete, anticongelante, compacto, PC, spot, o Internet, Ipod, que siguen entrando en la lengua.

España e Iberoamérica
Iberoamérica es una parte sustancial de la identidad de España, que no se entiende sin la historia que nos vincula y sin el presente que compartimos con los pueblos y naciones de la región. Por ello Iberoamérica es una prioridad permanente de la política exterior española y el Gobierno ha puesto en marcha iniciativas en distintos ámbitos para situar las relaciones entre España y América Latina en el nivel privilegiado que se merecen.

España es hoy uno de los principales países inversores en América Latina y hay una presencia decisiva de empresas y capital español en sectores como la banca, las comunicaciones, la energía y los servicios públicos en general. Además, España apoya los diferentes procesos subregionales de integración económica y comercial como el MERCOSUR, la Comunidad Andina, el Sistema Centroamericano y la Unión de Naciones Suramericanas (UNASUR).

España, además, ha experimentado en los últimos años un significativo flujo de inmigración procedente de América Latina, especialmente de países como Ecuador y Colombia. En España se valora este fenómeno desde una óptica positiva y se aprecia la contribución que hace la migración iberoamericana al desarrollo cultural, social y económico de España.

España y los Estados Unidos

Existe en los Estados Unidos, un enorme interés por la lengua y la cultura española: el 60% de los estudiantes universitarios estadounidenses que estudian un idioma extranjero eligen el español, y España es el segundo destino de los estadounidenses que estudian en el extranjero, después del Reino Unido. El Gobierno impulsa la difusión de la lengua y la cultura española en los Estados Unidos a través de un amplio programa de profesor- es visitantes, al amparo del cual unos 1.200 profesores titulares españoles imparten diversas materias en centros de enseñanza media de todo el territorio estadounidense. A hacer una labor muy similar se consagran las cinco sedes del Instituto Cervantes y el Aula Virtual Cervantes que existen en los Estados Unidos.

El español en Estados Unidos

La lengua española ha tenido una larga historia en lo que es hoy Estados Unidos. Fue llevada primero a La Florida, en 1513, por Juan Ponce de León. Gradualmente, los conquistadores españoles ocuparon lo que llegaría a denominarse *Spanish Borderlands* (Territorios Españoles Fronterizos), que incluían La Florida, Luisiana y el Suroeste (Craddock, 1992), donde el español pasó a ser la lengua de prestigio y continuó siéndolo por un período de entre dos y tres siglos (desde mediados del siglo XVII hasta la primera mitad del siglo XIX).

El período colonial español fue más largo en Texas y Nuevo México, territorios que fueron explorados por españoles a partir de 1536. Los primeros asentamientos permanentes fueron establecidos en Nuevo México en 1598, y en Texas en 1659. En Colorado, por otro lado, el primer asentamiento permanente fue establecido por campesinos en 1851.

Los españoles ya habían comenzado a explorar Arizona desde la década de 1530, pero no sería hasta 1700 cuando los misioneros jesuitas que ejercían su labor en el sur de la región fundaron la primera misión. El primer presidio permanente fue fundado en 1752.

California fue la última de las regiones colonizadas por España en el Suroeste. La primera misión en Alta California se fundó en San Diego en 1769. En la década de 1840 había 21 misiones de San Diego a Sonoma, 4 presidios y 3 pueblos, pero la población que no era indígena tan sólo llegó a alcanzar una cifra máxima de siete mil personas.

México se independizó de España en 1821, pero la administración mexicana de las regiones del Suroeste de Estados Unidos duraría poco. Texas se declaró independiente quince años después, y la subsiguiente guerra entre Estados Unidos y México (1846-1848) terminó con la firma del tratado de Guadalupe Hidalgo de 1848, por el cual se cedía a los Estados Unidos, la nación victoriosa, todo el territorio al oeste de Texas. Texas y California pasaron a ser estados de la Unión en 1845 y 1850, respectivamente, seguidos de Colorado en 1876.

Una vez que se constituyeron como nuevos estados, el inglés fue declarado inmediatamente como lengua única en la enseñanza en las escuelas públicas, así como la lengua de uso en los tribunales y en la administración. Arizona y Nuevo México, por el contrario, tuvieron que esperar mucho más tiempo, hasta 1912, para que se les admitiera como estados, posiblemente porque la mayoría de la población era hispana y básicamente hispanohablante, lo cual hacía difícil imponer el inglés como lengua única en la enseñanza y en la administración.

Los colonos anglos no pudieron sustraerse a la influencia de la lengua y la cultura de los que les habían precedido en la colonización del Suroeste. En el siglo XVIII, la vida en el Suroeste tenía un sabor rural; se desarrollaba principalmente en pequeñas poblaciones, y en ranchos en los que la cría de ganado era vital. Por entonces, los españoles y mexicanos ya estaban familiarizados con la flora y fauna de la región y con las prácticas de los vaqueros que el cine mitificaría más adelante. Los recién llegados pronto aprendieron muchas de las palabras españolas características del medio y las adaptaron a las reglas fonéticas y morfológicas del inglés: *canyon* (de cañón), 'mesa', 'sierra', 'arroyo', 'adobe', 'chaparral', 'saguaro', 'patio', 'hacienda', *ranch* (de rancho), 'sombrero', 'vaquero', 'rodeo', 'vigilante', *desperado* (de desesperado), 'burro', 'bronco', y muchas otras que pasaron a formar parte del inglés.

Además, los nombres de los estados y de muchas ciudades, pueblos, ríos y montañas son también españoles: las ciudades de El Paso, Amarillo, Santa Fe, San Diego, Los Ángeles, Florida, San Antonio, San Francisco, Palo Alto, los ríos Colorado, Brazos, Río Grande, las «Montañas Sandía» en Albuquerque, la «Sierra Nevada» en California, las «Montañas Sangre de Cristo» en Colorado y Nuevo México.

Hacia el final del siglo XIX el número de hispanos en el Suroeste posible-mente alcanzó los cien mil, concentrados principalmente en Texas (Mc. Wi-lliams, 1990: 152). Esta situación cambió en el siglo XX: dos olas masivas de migración desde México, la una a partir del comienzo de la Revolución mexi-cana en 1910, la otra, después del comienzo de la Segunda Guerra Mundial, así como un número significativo de migrantes de Centro y Suramérica han vuelto a hispanizar el Suroeste de los Estados Unidos, lo que Carlos Fuentes denomina la reconquista "cromosomática" de lo que fueron territorios mexi-canos.

La inmigración desde Cuba y Puerto Rico ha tenido un efecto similar en Flor-ida y el Noreste (García & Otheguy, 1988; Zentella, 1988). Hoy día, está claro que los hispanos han extendido su lengua y cultura a casi todos los estados de los Estados Unidos.

La influencia mutua del español y el inglés, especialmente en Nueva York, Florida y el Suroeste, es, por otro lado, una realidad ininterrumpida, aunque la dirección de la influencia ha cambiado: en los primeros momentos de con-tacto el inglés tomó más préstamos del español, mientras que durante el siglo XX y lo que va del presente siglo, el español ha tomado prestado mucho más del inglés, como sería de esperar en una situación en la que una lengua está subordinada a la otra tanto política como tecnológica y socialmente.

Otro tipo de préstamo que penetró en el inglés antes del siglo XX es lo que Hill (1993) denomina «Nouvelle Southwest Anglo Spanish», usado para promover comercialmente el Suroeste como la tierra del «déjalo para ma-ñana», relajada, despreocupada. Estos préstamos están relacionados con la industria turística, sobre todo en Nuevo México, Arizona y la costa del sur de California, y han experimentado un considerable incremento en los últimos cincuenta años.

Nota, esta parte ha sido tomada y ligeramente modificada a partir del texto del Centro Virtual Cervantes, 2000. Usted puede consultar el Centro Virtual Cervantes en la siguiente direc-ción electrónica:

INTERACTIVE LINK

booksstudio.pro/rfb

APÉNDICE 1

APÉNDICE A: LOS VERBOS

Verbos regulares:		Primer modelo de conjugación: -AR	

AMAR (to love)   Gerundio: amando   Participio: amado

simple tenses		compound tenses	
singular	plural	singular	plural

Presente de indicativo		presente perfecto de indicativo	
amo	amamos	he amado	hemos amado
amas	amáis	has amado	habéis amado
ama	aman	ha amado	han amado

Imperfecto de indicativo		pasado perfecto de indicativo	
amaba	amábamos	había amado	habíamos amado
amabas	amabais	habías amado	habíais amado
amaba	amaban	había amado	habían amado

pretérito		pretérito anterior	
amé	amamos	hube amado	hubimos amado
amaste	amasteis	hubiste amado	hubisteis amado
amó	amaron	hubo amado	hubieron amado

futuro		futuro perfecto	
amaré	amaremos	habré amado	habremos amado
amarás	amaréis	habrás amado	habréis amado
amará	amarán	habrá amado	habrán amado

condicional (potencial simple)		condicional perfecto (potencial compuesto)	
amaría	amaríamos	habría amado	habríamos amado
amarías	amaríais	habrías amado	habríais amado
amaría	amarían	habría amado	habrían amado

presente de subjuntivo		perfecto de subjuntivo	
ame	amemos	haya amado	hayamos amado
ames	améis	hayas amado	hayáis amado

| ame | amen | haya amado | hayan amado |

Imperfecto de subjuntivo

pluscuamperfecto del subjuntivo

amara	amáramos	hubiera amado	hubiéramos amado
amaras	amarais	hubieras amado	hubierais amado
amara	amaran	hubiera amado	hubieran amado

OR

amase	amásemos	hubiese amado	hubiésemos amado
amases	amaseis	hubieses amado	hubieseis amado
amase	amasen	hubiese amado	hubiesen amado

Imperativo

imperativo negativo

-	amemos	-	no amemos
ama	amad	no ames	no améis
ame	amen	no ame	no amen

Words related with this verb:

nombre (noun):	amor (love)
	amabilidad (kindness, amiability)
adjetivo (adjective)	amable (kind)
adverbio (adverb)	amablemente (kindly, amiably)

Some Common -ar verbs:

abrazar	to hug	aceptar	to accept
acompañar	to go with, accompany	aconsejar	to advise
ahorrar	to save	alquilar/rentar	to rent
apagar	to turn off, shut off	arreglar	to fix up, to arrange
aumentar	to increase	averiguar	to find out
ayudar	to help	bailar	to dance
bajar	to go down, lower	besar	to kiss
borrar	to erase	buscar	to look for
cambiar	to change, to exchange	caminar	to walk
cantar	to sing	celebrar	to celebrate
cenar	to have supper	cocinar	to cook
colocar	to put, place	comprar	to buy
contestar	to answer	cortar	to cut
cruzar	to cross	dejar	to let, leave
desear	to want	dibujar	to draw
disfrutar	to enjoy	doblar	to turn, fold
durar	to last	echar	to throw
empujar	to push	entrar	to enter, come in
entregar	to hand in/over	escuchar	to listen (to)
esperar	to hope, to wait, expect	esquiar	to ski
estacionar	to park	estudiar	to study

explicar	to explain		felicitar	to congratulate
firmar	to sign		ganar	to win, earn
gastar	to spend, waste		grabar	to record
gritar	to shout		hablar	to talk
invitar	to invite		llamar	to call, to name
llegar	to arrive		llevar	to carry, wear
llorar	to cry		mandar	to send, order
manejar	to drive, manage		marcar	to dial, mark
mirar	to look at		nadar	to swim
necesitar	to need		pagar	to pay
parar	to stop		pasar	to pass, spend (time)
patinar	to skate		pintar	to paint
practicar	to practice		preguntar	to ask (a question)
preparar	to prepare		presentar	to introduce, present
quitar	to take away		regresar	to return, come back
repasar	to review		sacar	to take out
saludar	to greet		tardar	to be late
terminar	to finish, end		tirar	to throw
tocar	to play (an instrument) to touch, knock (at door)		tomar	to take, drink
			trabajar	to work
trotar	to jog		usar	to use, wear
viajar	to travel			

Segundo modelo de conjugación: -ER

TEMER (to fear, to dread)
simple tenses

Gerundio: temiendo   Participio: temido
compound tenses

singular	plural		singular	plural
Presente de indicativo			presente perfecto de indicativo	
temo	tememos		he temido	hemos temido
temes	teméis		has temido	habéis temido
teme	temen		ha temido	han temido
Imperfecto de indicativo			pasado perfecto de indicativo	
temía	temíamos		había temido	habíamos temido
temías	temíais		habías temido	habíais temido
temía	temían		había temido	habían temido
pretérito			pretérito anterior	
temí	temimos		hube temido	hubimos temido
temiste	temisteis		hubiste temido	hubisteis temido te-
mió	temieron		hubo temido	hubieron temido

futuro

temeré	temeremos
temerás	temeréis
temerá	temerán

futuro perfecto

habré temido	habremos temido
habrás temido	habréis temido
habrá temido	habrán temido

condicional (potencial simple)

temería	temeríamos
temerías	temeríais
temería	temerían

condicional perfecto (potencial compuesto)

habría temido	habríamos temido
habrías temido	habríais temido
habría temido	habrían temido

presente de subjuntivo

tema	temamos
temas	temáis
tema	teman

perfecto de subjuntivo

haya temido	hayamos temido
hayas temido	hayáis temido
haya temido	hayan temido

Imperfecto de subjuntivo

temiera	temiéramos
temieras	temierais
temiera	temieran

pluscuamperfecto del subjuntivo

hubiera temido	hubiéramos temido
hubieras temido	hubierais temido
hubiera temido	hubieran temido

OR

temiese	temiésemos
temieses	temieseis
temiese	temiesen

hubiese temido	hubiésemos temido
hubieses temido	hubieseis temido
hubiese temido	hubiesen temido

Imperativo

-	temamos
teme	temed
tema	teman

imperativo negativo

-	no temamos
no temas	no temáis
no tema	no teman

Words related with this verb:

nombre (noun):	temor (fear)
	temeridad (daring, temerity)
adjetivo (adjective)	temeroso/a (fearful)
adverbio (adverb)	temerosamente (fearfully)

Some common -er verbs:

aprender	to learn	beber	to drink
comer	to eat	comprender	to understand
correr	to run	deber	to ought, must
leer	to read	meter	to put in
prender	to turn on/to light up	romper	to break
toser	to cough	vender	to sell

Tercer modelo de conjugación: -IR

PARTIR (to leave, to depart, to divide, to split)
                         Gerundio: partiendo   Participio: partido

simple tenses		compound tenses	
singular	plural	singular	plural

Presente de indicativo		presente perfecto de indicativo	
parto	partimos	he partido	hemos partido
partes	partís	has partido	habéis partido
parte	parten	ha partido	han partido

Imperfecto de indicativo		pasado perfecto de indicativo	
partía	partíamos	había partido	habíamos partido
partías	partíais	habías partido	habíais partido
partía	partían	había partido	habían partido
pretérito	pretérito anterior		
partí	partimos	hube partido	hubimos partido
partiste	partisteis	hubiste partido	hubisteis partido
partió	partieron	hubo partido	hubieron partido

futuro		futuro perfecto	
partiré	partiremos	habré partido	habremos partido
partirás	partiréis	habrás partido	habréis partido
partirá	partirán	habrá partido	habrán partido

condicional (potencial simple)		condicional perfecto (potencial compuesto)	
partiría	partiríamos	habría partido	habríamos partido
partirías	partiríais	habrías partido	habríais partido
partiría	partirían	habría partido	habrían partido

presente de subjuntivo		perfecto de subjuntivo	
parta	partamos	haya partido	hayamos partido
partas	partáis	hayas partido	hayáis partido
parta	partan	haya partido	hayan partido

Imperfecto de subjuntivo		pluscuamperfecto del subjuntivo	
partiera	partiéramos	hubiera partido	hubiéramos partido
partieras	partierais	hubieras partido	hubierais partido
partiera	partieran	hubiera partido	hubieran partido

OR

partiese	partiésemos	hubiese partido	hubiésemos partido

partieses	partieseis	hubieses partido	hubieseis partido
partiese	partiesen	hubiese partido	hubiesen partido

Imperativo	imperativo negativo		
-	partamos	-	no partamos
parte	partid	no partas	no partáis
parta	partan	no parta	no partan

Words related with this verb:
nombre (noun): partida (departure)

Compound verbs with partir:

compartir (to share)
departir (to converse)
repartir (to distribute)
partirse (to become divided)

Some common -ir verbs:

abrir	to open	añadir	to add
asistir	to attend, assist	describir	to describe
discutir	to discuss, argue	escribir	to write
interrumpir	to interrupt	ocurrir	to happen
recibir	to receive, get	subir	to go up, rise
sufrir	to suffer	vivir	to live

APÉNDICE B: STEM-CHANGING VERBS

A. Primer grupo (e ⇒ ie) **pensar** (to think)

presente indicativo	presente subjuntivo	imperativo	gerundio
pienso	piense	-	pensando
piensas	pienses	piensa	
piensa	piense	piense	
pensamos	pensemos	pensemos	
pensáis	penséis	pensad	
piensan	piensen	piensen	

pretérito	imperfecto	subjuntivo	
pensé	pensara	pensase	
pensaste	pensaras	pensases	
pensó	pensara	pensase	

pensamos	pensáramos	pensásemos
pensasteis	pensarais	pensaseis
pensaron	pensaran	pensasen

Verbos como pensar:

acertar	atravesar	cegar	cerrar
comenzar,	confesar	despertar(se)	divertir(se)
empezar	encender	entender	fregar
negar	nevar	perder	querer
regar	sentar(se)	tender	tropezar

B. Segundo grupo (o ⇒ ue) **poder** (to be able to, can)

presente indicativo	presente subjuntivo	imperativo	gerundio
puedo	pueda	_	pudiendo
puedes	puedas	puede	puede
pueda	pueda		
podemos	podamos	podamos	
podéis	podáis	poded	
pueden	puedan	puedan	

pretérito	imperfecto	subjuntivo
pude	pudiera	pudiese
pudiste	pudieras	pudieses
pudo	pudiera	pudiese
pudimos	pudiéramos	pudiésemos
pudisteis	pudierais	pudieseis
pudieron	pudieran	pudiesen

Verbos como poder:

acordar(se)	acostar(se)	almorzar	cocer
colgar	colgar	contar	costar
demostrar	dormir(se)	encontrar	llover
mostrar	mover(se)	probar(se)	recordar
resolver	rogar	soler	sonar
soñar	torcer	volver	

C. Tercer grupo verbos terminados en -ir:
Note that verbs ending in **-ir** are more complex and they can have three type of spelling changes:

a. e ⇒ie like **mentir**

presente indicativo	presente subjuntivo	imperativo	gerundio
miento	mienta	_	mintiendo
mientes	mientas	miente	

miente	mienta	mienta
mentimos	mintamos	mintamos
mentís	mintáis	mentid
mienten	mientan	mientan

pretérito	imperfecto	subjuntivo
mentí	mintiera	mintiese
mentiste	mintieras	mintieses
mintió	mintiera	mintiese
mentimos	mintiéramos	mintiésemos
mentisteis	mintierais	mintieseis
mintieron	mintieran	mintiesen

Verbos como mentir:

preferir	referir(se)	sentir(se)	sugerir

b. o ⇒ ue **dormir**

presente indicativo	presente subjuntivo	imperativo	gerundio
duermo	duerma	_	durmiendo
duermes	duermas	duerme	
duerme	duerma	duerma	
dormimos	durmamos	durmámonos	
dormís	durmáis	dormid	
duermen	duerman	duerman	

pretérito	imperfecto	subjuntivo
dormí	durmiera	durmiese
dormiste	durmieras	durmieses
durmió	durmiera	durmiese
dormimos	durmiéramos	durmiésemos
dormisteis	durmierais	durmieseis
durmieron	durmieran	durmiesen

Verbos como dormir: morir

c. e ⇒ i **pedir** (to ask for)

presente indicativo	presente subjuntivo	imperativo	gerundio
pido	pida	_	pidiendo
pides	pidas	pide	
pide	pida	pida	
pedimos	pidamos	pidamos	
pedís	pidáis	pedid	
piden	pidan	pidan	

pretérito	imperfecto	subjuntivo
pedí	pidiera	pidiese
pediste	pidieras	pidieses
pidió	pidiera	pidiese
pedimos	pidiéramos	pidiésemos
pedisteis	pidierais	pidieseis
pidieron	pidieran	pidiesen

Verbos como pedir:

competir	concebir	despedir(se)	elegir
impedir	medir	perseguir	reír(se)
reñir	repetir	seguir	servir
sonreír	vestir(se)		

Apéndice C: Verbs that have changes in the first person of the present indicative.

a. verbs ending in **-go**, like **caer** ⇒ caigo

decir ⇒ digo	hacer ⇒ hago	poner ⇒ pongo
salir ⇒ salgo	satisfacer ⇒ satisfago	seguir ⇒ sigo
tener ⇒ tengo	traer ⇒ traigo	valer ⇒ valgo
venir ⇒ vengo		

b. verbs ending in **-zco**, like **conocer** ⇒ conozco

conducir ⇒ conduzco	desaparecer ⇒ desaparezco
obedecer ⇒ obedezco	producir ⇒ produzco

c. verbs ending in **-jo** like **dirigir** ⇒ dirijo

corregir ⇒ corrijo	escoger ⇒ escojo	elegir ⇒ elijo
exigir ⇒ exijo	proteger ⇒ protejo	

d. verbs ending in **-cer**, like **convencer** ⇒ convenzo

torcer ⇒ tuerzo	vencer ⇒ venzo

e. verbs ending in **-uir**, like **incluir** ⇒ incluyo

construir ⇒ construyo	destruir ⇒ destruyo	distribuir ⇒ distribuyo

huir ⇒ huyo   influir ⇒ influyo

f. Other verbs like **caber** and **saber** change drastically in the first person:

caber ⇒ quepo

saber ⇒ sé

Apéndice D: Irregular verbs in present tense.
dar: doy, das, da, damos, dais, dan
ser: soy, eres, es, somos, sois, son
decir: digo, dices, dice, decimos, decís, dicen
estar: estoy, estás, está, estamos, estáis, están
ir: voy, vas, va, vamos, vais, van
jugar: juego, juegas, juega, jugamos, jugáis, juegan
oír: oigo, oyes, oye, oímos, oís, oyen
oler: huelo, hueles, huele, olemos, oléis, huelen
inquirir: inquiero, inquieres, inquiere, inquirimos, inquirís, inquieren,
guiar: guío, guías, guía, guiamos, guiáis, guían
continuar: continúo, continúas, continúa, continuamos, continuáis, continúan
huir: huyo, huyes, huye, huimos, huís, huyen.

Apéndice E: Irregular verbs in the preterit, the imperfect, and the past participles.

a. Verbs ending in **-car, -gar, -zar** have a spelling change in the first person singular in preterit.

tocar ⇒ **toqué**.
Verbs like tocar: atacar, buscar, comunicar, explicar, indicar, pescar, sacar

pagar ⇒ **pagué.**
Verbs like pagar: apagar, colgar, jugar, llegar, navegar, negar, regar, rogar

almorzar ⇒ **almorcé.**
Verbs like almorzar: abrazar, alcanzar, comenzar, cruzar, empezar, endulzar, forzar, gozar, rezar

b. The verbs **ser** and **ir** have the same conjugation:
ser/ir: fui, fuiste, fue, fuimos, fuisteis, fueron

c. The verbs **dar** and **ver** have irregular conjugations also:
dar: di, diste, dio, dimos, disteis, dieron

ver: vi, viste, vio, vimos, visteis, vieron

d. Verbs with double vowels have a **-y** in the third person singular and
plural:
caer: caí, caíste, **cayó**, caímos, caísteis, **cayeron**

Verbs like caer: creer, leer, oír, poseer

Note that all the subjects except the third person plural do not have a written accent mark.

e. Verbs ending in **-uir** also have a **-y** in the third person singular and
plural:
huir: huí, huiste, **huyó**, huimos, huisteis, **huyeron**

Verbs like huir: construir, incluir, destruir,

Note that verbs ending in –**uir** are very similar to the verbs with double vowels except for
the different written accent marks.

f. In the preterit only an **-ir** verb can be subject to a stem-change, and that only
occurs in the third person. There are only two forms: **e:i**, and **o:u**.
pedir (e:i): pedí, pediste, **pidió**, pedimos, pedisteis, **pidieron**
Verbs like pedir: conseguir, consentir, despedir(se), hervir, mentir, preferir, reír, repetir,
seguir, sentir(se), servir(se), sonreír, vestir(se)

dormir (o:u): dormí, dormiste, **durmió**, dormimos, dormisteis, **durmieron**
The other verb like dormir is morir.

g. Irregular verbs in the preterit:
andar: anduve, anduviste, anduvo, anduvimos, anduvisteis, anduvieron
estar: estuve, estuviste, estuvo, estuvimos, estuvisteis, estuvieron
haber: hube, hubiste, hubo, hubimos, hubisteis, hubieron
poder: pude, pudiste, pudo, pudimos, pudisteis, pudieron
poner: puse, pusiste, puso, pusimos, pusisteis, pusieron
saber: supe, supiste, supo, supimos, supisteis, supieron
caber: cupe, cupiste, cupo, cupimos, cupisteis, cupieron
tener: tuve, tuviste, tuvo, tuvimos, tuvisteis, tuvieron
hacer: hice, hiciste, hizo, hicimos, hicisteis, hicieron
querer: quise, quisiste, quiso, quisimos, quisisteis, quisieron
venir: vine, viniste, vino, vinimos, vinisteis, vinieron
conducir: conduje, condujiste, condujo, condujimos, condujisteis, condujeron

Note that the following verbs have a **-j** in the stem like **conducir**: decir, deducir, inducir,
producir, reducir, traducir, traer

Apéndice F: Only three verbs only are irregular in the imperfect:

ser: era, eras, era, éramos, erais, eran
ir: iba, ibas, iba, íbamos, ibais, iban
ver: veía, veías, veía, veíamos, veíais, veían

Apéndice G: Verbs that have irregular past participle:

abrir	abierto	absolver	absuelto
adscribir	adscrito	cubrir	cubierto
decir	dicho	describir	descrito
descubrir	descubierto	disolver	disuelto
encubrir	encubierto	entreabrir	entreabierto
escribir	escrito	freír	frito
hacer	hecho	inscribir	inscrito
manuscribir	manuscrito	morir	muerto
poner	puesto	prescribir	prescrito
proscribir	proscrito	pudrir	podrido
resolver	resuelto	romper	roto
satisfacer	satisfecho	soltar	suelto
suscribir	suscrito	transcribir	transcrito
ver	visto	volver	vuelto

Apéndice H: Verbs that are irregular in the future and the conditional.

a. Irregular verbs in the future tense:
   caber: cabré, cabrás, cabrá, cabremos, cabréis, cabrán
   decir: diré, dirás, dirá, diremos, diréis, dirán
   haber: habré, habrás, habrá, habremos, habréis, habrán
   hacer: haré, harás, hará, haremos, haréis, harán
   poder: podré, podrás, podrá, podremos, podréis, podrán
   querer: querré, querrás, querrá, querremos, querréis, querrán
   saber: sabré, sabrás, sabrá, sabremos, sabréis, sabrán
   poner: pondré, pondrás, pondrá, pondremos, pondréis, pondrán
   salir: saldré, saldrás, saldrá, saldremos, saldréis, saldrán
   tener: tendré, tendrás, tendrá, tendremos, tendréis, tendrán
   valer: valdré, valdrás, valdrá, valdremos, valdréis, valdrán

b. irregular in the conditional:
   caber: cabría, cabrías, cabría, cabríamos, cabríais, cabrían
   decir: diría, dirías, diría, diríamos, diríais, dirían
   haber: habría, habrías, habría, habríamos, habríais, habrían
   hacer: haría, harías, haría, haríamos, haríais, harían

poder: podría, podrías, podría, podríamos, podríais, podrían
querer: querría, querrías, querría, querríamos, querríais, querrían
saber: sabría, sabrías, sabría, sabríamos, sabríais, sabrían
poner: pondría, pondrías, pondría, pondríamos, pondríais, pondrían
salir: saldría, saldrías, saldría, saldríamos, saldríais, saldrían
tener: tendría, tendrías, tendría, tendríamos, tendríais, tendrían
valer: valdría, valdrías, valdría, valdríamos, valdríais, valdrían

Apéndice I: Verbs that are irregular in the present subjunctive.

dar: dé, des, dé, demos, deis, den
estar: esté, estés, esté, estemos, estéis, estén
ir: vaya, vayas, vaya, vayamos, vayáis, vayan
saber: sepa, sepas, sepa, sepamos, sepáis, sepan
ser: sea, seas, sea, seamos, seáis, sean

a. The verbs endings in **-car, -gar, -zar** maintain the same phonetic
changes that they have in the preterit in the present subjunctive:
sacar: saque, saques, saque, saquemos, saquéis, saquen
llegar: llegue, llegues, llegue, lleguemos, lleguéis, lleguen
abrazar: abrace, abraces, abrace, abracemos, abracéis, abracen

b. -Ir verbs that are stem-changing verbs in the present tense have the
same stem-change in the present subjunctive. In addition the **nosotros** and **vosotros**
forms undergo a stem-change also but in a slightly different way:
pedir (e:i) pida, pidas, pida, pidamos, pidáis, pidan
Verbs like pedir: competir, concebir, despedir(se), elegir, impedir, reír, reñir, repetir, seguir,
servir, vestir(se)

sentir (e:ie) sienta, sientas, sienta, sintamos, sintáis, sientan
Verbs like sentir: advertir, arrepentirse, consentir, convertir(se), discernir, divertir(se), herir,
hervir, mentir, preferir, referir, sugerir
dormir (o:ue) duerma, duermas, duerma, durmamos, durmáis, duerman
Verbs like **dormir: morir**

c. Verbs like **jugar**, and **almorzar** besides being **-gar, -zar** verbs, also have a
change in the stem, and because they are **-ar** verbs they go back to the regular conjugation in the **nosotros** and **vosotros** forms.
jugar (u:ue) juegue, juegues, juegue, juguemos, juguéis, jueguen
almorzar (u:ue) almuerce, almuerces, almuerce, almorcemos, almorcéis, almuercen

d. The verbs **enviar, actuar** and **continuar** have an accent mark on the **-í** or the
-ú in all forms but **nosotros** and **vosotros**.

enviar: envíe, envíes, envíe, enviemos, enviéis, envíen
continuar: continúe, continúes, continúe, continuemos, continuéis, continúe

Apéndice J: Verbs that need a preposition.

a. Verbs of motion need the preposition **a** + infinitive
apresurarse a (to hurry to, to hasten to)
dirigirse a   (to go to, to go toward)
ir a (to go to)
regresar a (to return to)
salir a (to go out to)
venir a (to come to, to end up by)
volver a (to return to, to do it again)

b. The following verbs are also used with the preposition **a** + infinitive
acertar a (to be right about, to hit on the right idea, to manage to)
acostumbrarse a (to become accustomed to)
aficionarse a (to become fond of)
alcanzar a (to succeed in)
aprender a (to learn to, to learn how to)
aspirar a (to aspire to)
atreverse a (to dare to)
ayudar a (to help to)
comenzar a (to begin to)
condenar a (to condemn to)
convidar a (to invite to)
dar a (to give to)
decidirse a (to decide to)
dedicarse a (to devote oneself to)
detenerse a (to stop to, to pause to)
disponerse a (to get ready to)
echarse a (to lie down to, to start to, to begin to)
empezar a (to begin to, to start to)
enseñar a (to teach to)
exponerse a (to run the risk of)
invitar a (to invite to)
negarse a (to refuse to)
obligar a (to oblige to, to obligate to)
ponerse a (to begin to)
prepararse a (to get ready to, to prepare to)
principiar a (to begin to, to start to)
resignarse a (to resign oneself to)
resolverse a (to make up one's mind to)
someter a (to subdue, to put into consideration)
someterse a (to put oneself under the rule of other person)

c. Verbs with the preposition **a** + a noun
   acercarse a (to approach)
   asemejarse a (to resemble, to look like)
   asistir a (to attend, to be present)
   asomarse a (to appear at, to show up)
   cuidar a (to take care of)
   jugar a (to play...)
   llegar a (to arrive to, to become)
   llevar a (to carry out)
   oler a (to smell like)
   parecerse a (to resemble, to look like)
   querer a (to love, to want)
   saber a (to taste of, to taste like, to have the flavor of)
   sonar a (to sound like)
   subir a (to get on, to get into...)
   tocarle a (to be somebody's turn)

d. Verbs with the preposition **con** + infinitive
   amanecer con   (to wake up with)
   amenazar con (to threaten to)
   contar con (to rely on, to count on)
   contentarse con (to be satisfied with)
   soñar con (to dream about, to dream of)

e. Verbs with the preposition **con** + noun or pronoun
   acabar con (to make an end of, to finish off)
   casarse con (to get married to)
   conformarse con (to put up with)
   cumplir con (to fulfill)
   dar con (to find, to come upon)
   encontrarse con (to run into)
   entenderse con (to come to an understanding with)
   meterse con (to pick a quarrel with)
   quedarse con (to hold on to)
   tropezar con (to run across unexpectedly, to trip over)

f. Verbs with the preposition **de** + infinitive
   acabar de (to have just)
   acordarse de (to remember to)
   alegrarse de (to be glad to/of)
   arrepentirse de (to repent)
   cansarse de (to get tired of)
   cesar de (to stop, to cease)
   dejar de (to stop, to fail to)

encargarse de (to take charge of)
ocuparse de (to take care of, to be busy with)
olvidarse de (to forget to)
tratar de (to try to)
tratarse de (to be a question of, to deal with, to be about)

g. Verbs with the preposition **de** + noun or pronouns
abusar de (to abuse)
alejarse de (to go away from)
apartarse de (to keep away from)
apoderarse de (to take possession of)
aprovecharse de (to take advantage of)
bajar de (to get out of, to get off, to descend from)
burlarse de (to make fun of)
cambiar de (to change)
carecer de (to lack)
compadecerse de (to feel sorry for, to pity)
constar de (to consist of)
cuidar de (to take care of)
depender de (to depend on)
despedirse de (to say good-bye to)
despojarse de (to take off clothing, to get rid of)
disfrutar de (to enjoy)
enamorarse de (to fall in love with)
encogerse de (to shrug)
enterarse de (to find out about)
fiarse de (to put your trust in)
gozar de (to enjoy)
oír de (to hear about)
perderse de (to lose the opportunity of)
ponerse de (to put oneself in a position)
preocuparse de (to worry about, to be concerned about)
quejarse de (to complain about)
reírse de (to laugh at)
saber de (to know about)
salir de (to go out, to leave from)
servir de (to serve as)
servirse de (to make use of/to take advantage of)

h. Verbs with the preposition **en** + infinitive
complacerse en (to be pleased to)
consentir en (to consent to)
convenir en (to agree on)
empeñarse en (to persist in, to insist on)
quedar en (to agree on)

tardar en (to be late in)

i. Verbs with the preposition **en** + noun or pronoun
apoyarse en (to lean on, to lean against)
confiar en (to rely on, to trust in)
consistir en (to consist of)
convertirse en (to become, to convert to)
entrar en (to enter into, to go into)
fijarse en (to stare at, to notice, to observe)
meterse en (to get involved in, to plunge into)
pensar en (to think of, to think about)
ponerse en (to get in/on)
reparar en (to notice)
volver en (to return)

j. Verbs with the preposition **por** + infinitivo, noun, pronoun or adjective
acabar por (to end up)
dar por (to consider)
darse por (to regard as)
estar por (to be in favor of)
interesarse por (to take an interest in)
pasar por (to be considered as)
preguntar por (to inquire about, to ask for)
temer por (to be afraid of/for)
tener por (to have an opinion, to consider something)
tomar por (to take someone for)

k. Verbs that take the preposition **para** + infinitive or noun
salir para (to go to, to leave to)
servir para (to be useful for)
vivir para (to live for)

The uses of "vos"
The form "vos" is used in countries like Argentina, Uruguay, Chile and in all Central American countries.
In general "vos" different from "tú" only in the present tense, the present subjunctive, and the commands, positive and negative as well.

a. The best way to describe the conjugation of the "vos" form in the presente tense is using the infinitive of the verb and then replace the final "-r" to an "-s" and put an acento en the last vowel.
exemples:
Pienso que (vos) trabajás mucho.
(Vos) bebés mucha agua.
¿(Vos) vivís en Costa Rica?

There are only two exceptions this pattern: the verb "ir" and the verb "ser":
(Vos) vas a la escuela.
(Vos) sos inteligente.

b. In the present subjunctive as well as in the negative commands the only difference with "tú" is that you need to put an acento over the last vowel:
Tu papá quiere que vos vayás a Cuba.
Dudo que vos estés enamorado de esa chica.
Me alegro que comprés esa casa.
No es verdad que seas feo.
Llamame en cuanto llegués.

c. In the Negative commands follow the same construction:
No te tomés las cosas tan en serio.
No te vayás a dormir tan tarde.

d. The affirmative commands are easy to do, drop the "-r" of the infinitive and place an acento to the vowel:
Hablá más fuerte
vení a verme.

e. When an affirmative command has to carry a pronoun then the acento is dropped:
Llamame pronto.
vendeme la casa.
Mirala bien.
Venite para acá.

Glosario de términos gramaticales
adjetivo: palabra usada para modificar, describir o limitar un nombre. Ejemplos: bonita, alto.

adjetivo demostrativo: un adjetivo que indica o señala a la persona o cosa referida. Ejemplos: este, esta, estos, estas, ese, esa, esos, esas, aquel, aquella, aquellos, aquellas.

adverbio: palabra usada para modificar un verbo, un adjetivo o otro adverbio. Ejemplos: bien, rápidamente.

antecedente: palabra, frase o cláusula a la que se refiere un pronombre.

artículo: palabra usada para señalar un objeto específico o uno indefinido. Ejemplos: el, la, los, las, un, una, unos, unas.

verbo auxiliar: es un verbo que ayuda al verbo principal a expresar una acción o un estado. Ejemplos: haber, ser, estar, tener, ir, venir.

cláusula: grupo de palabras que contienen un sujeto (nombre o pronombre), y un verbo. Cuando la cláusula principal existe por sí misma se llama cláusula independiente. La cláusula subordinada no puede existir sin otra cláusula y se le llama cláusula dependiente.

cláusula relativa: es una cláusula introducida por un pronombre relativo.
comparación: es el cambio en la forma de un adjetivo o adverbio mostrando así diferentes grados de calidad: positivo (grande, útil) comparativo (mayor, más útil) superlativo (el mayor, el más útil) o superlativo absoluto (grandísimo, utilísimo).

verbos compuestos: un verbo cuya forma consiste en más de una palabra. He hablado.

conjugación: el cambio en el verbo respecto al sujeto, tiempo o modo.

conjunción: una palabra usada para conectar otras palabras, frases o cláusulas. Ejemplos: y, e, o, pero.

género: es la clasificación gramatical de los nombres o pronombres como masculinos, femeninos o neutros.

imperativo: el modo de un verbo para expresar una orden. Ejemplos: ¡cante! ¡no baile! ¡váyanse!

infinitivo: la forma del verbo que expresa su sentido general. Ejemplos: hablar, comer, vivir.

interrogación: el uso de un adjetivo o un pronombre para formular una pregunta. Ejemplos: ¿qué? ¿cuál?

invariable: que no cambia en su forma.

inversión: cambio en el orden normal de las palabras en una frase u oración. Ejemplo: ¿Tiene él una casa?

modo: la forma que asume el verbo para expresar la actitud o sentimientos del hablante hacia lo dicho.

nombre: es la palabra usada para nombrar a una persona, lugar, cosa o cualidad.

número: es la forma de un nombre, pronombre o verbo indicando uno (singular: un libro) o más de uno (plural: libros).

objeto directo: nombre o pronombre que recibe directamente la acción del verbo. Ejemplo: Adán mordió **la manzana.**

objeto indirecto: un nombre o pronombre que recibe el objeto directo, para quien se hace algo, o hacia quien se dirige la acción expresada en el verbo. Ejemplo: Thomas **le** llamó **a Shannon**.

participio: es la forma de un verbo usado como adjetivo o verbo. Como verbo en presente se vuelve un gerundio (andando, comiendo, yendo) como verbo en pasado se torna un pasado participio (caminado, dolido, abierto, roto).

persona: es la característica de un verbo o pronombre indicando si el sujeto es el hablante (primera persona) la persona a quien se habla (segunda persona) o la persona de quien se habla (tercera persona).

posesivos: son los adjetivos para mostrar posesión o pertenencia (mi, tu, su, nuestro/a, vuestro/a, su).

preposición: es la palabra usada para mostrar relación con otra palabra en una frase u oración.

pronombre: es una palabra usada en vez del nombre (yo, tú, usted, él, ella, nosotros, vosotros, ustedes, ellos, ellas).

pronombre relativo: es un pronombre que conecta la cláusula dependiente con la cláusula principal al referir directamente al nombre o pronombre de la cláusula principal.

raíz del verbo: es la parte de un verbo en infinitivo o conjugado que es invariable para cada verbo y que expresa la idea fundamental de éste. La raíz se obtiene al borrar la familia verbal, a la raíz le son añadidas las desinencias de acuerdo a cada sujeto o pronombre, tiempo verbal o modo.

subjuntivo: es el modo que expresa deseos, voluntad, dudas, necesidad, juicios o lo que es posible en lugar de expresar certezas.

sujeto: es la palabra (persona, animal o cosa) que sirve como agente de la acción o situación en la oración. Ejemplo: Ella canta opera.

tiempo: es la forma del verbo mostrando el tiempo de la acción o estado de un ser.

tiempo simple: señala la forma de un verbo usando una sola palabra. Ejemplo: yo hablo español.

verbo: es una palabra que expresa una acción o el estado de un ser.

verbo intransitivo: un verbo que no requiere de un objeto directo para completar su significado.

verbo pronominal: es un verbo que requiere de un pronombre que refiere la acción hacia el sujeto, es decir requiere de dos pronombres de la misma persona.

verbo transitivo: es un verbo que requiere un objeto directo.

voz: la forma del verbo que indica si el sujeto actúa (voz activa) o se actúa sobre él (voz pasiva).

Abreviaciones más comunes en español

a	área		kg.	kilogramos
affmo.	afectísimo		km.	kilómetros
art.	artículo		l.	litros
atto.	atento		m.	metros
cap.	capítulo		M., MM.	Madre, Madres
cf., cfr.	confer (compárese)			(de una orden religiosa)
Cía.	compañía		N.	Norte
cm.	centímetros		N.B.	nota bene
D.	don		NE.	Nordeste
D.ª	doña		NO.	Noroeste
Dr.	doctor		n°., num.	número
dupdo.	duplicado		O.	Oeste
E.	Este		P., PP.	Padre, Padres
etc.	etcétera			(de una orden religiosa)
Excmo.	Excelentísimo		p.a.	por autorización
g.	gramos		p., pág.	página
Gral.	general		Pbro.	presbítero
Ha.	hectáreas		P. D.	posdata
ib., ibíd.	ibídem (en el mismo lugar)		p. ej.	por ejemplo
id.	idem (idéntico)		P. O.	por orden
Ilmo.	Ilustrísimo		P. P.	por poder
J.C.	Jesucristo		pral.	principal
S.	post scriptum		Sr.	señor
q. D. g.	que Dios guarde		Sra.	Señora
q. e. p. d.	que en paz descanse		Srta.	Señorita
R.	reverendo		s. s	seguro servidor
R.I.P.	requiescat in pace		S. S	Su Santidad
	(descanse en paz)		Sto.	Santo
S.	Sur		Sta.	Santa
S. A.	Sociedad Anónima		Ud.	usted
s/c	su casa		Uds.	ustedes
Sdad.	sociedad		V., Vid.,	véase
SE.	Sudeste		Vda.	viuda
S. E.	Su Excelencia		V. E.	Vuestra Excelencia
S. en C.	Sociedad en Comandita			

v. gr.	verbigracia		
s.e.u.o.	salvo error u omisión	V. M.	Vuestra Majestad
S. L.	Sociedad Limitada	V. S.	Vuestra Señoría
S. M.	Su Majestad	V.° B.°	visto bueno
SO.	Sudoeste		

APÉNDICE 2: Vocabulario español/inglés

A

Abarrotería - grocery store

Abad/abadesa - abbot/abbess

Abajo - down, under

Abandonado/a - abandoned, deserted

Abismo - abyss, chasm

Abogado/a - lawyer/attorney

Abrigo - coat, overcoat

Abuelo/a - grandfather/grandmother

Abundancia - abundance

Abundante - abundant

Aburrido/a - boring

Abuso - abuse

Academia - academy

Académico - academic

Acarreo - the act of carrying, what you're hauling (to bring people into a political act)

Acceso - access

Accidente - accident

Acción - action

Aceite - oil

Acelga - chard

Acerca - about, relating to

Aconsejable - advisable

Acontecimiento - event

Acordeón - accordion

Acta - document, certificate

Actitud - attitude

Activo/a - active

Actor/actriz - actor/actress

Actuación - performance

Actualidad - present time, current situation

Actualmente - actually

Acuerdo - agreement

Acusado/a - prominent, marked; defendant

Adecuado/a - adequate

Adelante - ahead, in front, forward, come in

Además - beside, moreover, furthermore

Adentro - inside

Administración - administration

Admirador/a - admirer

Aduana - customs

Advenimiento - advent

Aeropuerto - airport

Afable - affable

Afectuosamente - affectionately

Afectuoso/a - affectionate

Afición - liking, fans

Aficionado - fan

Afirmación - affirmation

Afuera - outside

Agente - agent

Agosto - August

Agroindustria - agribusiness, agro industry

Agrupamientos - groups

Agua - water

Aguacate - avocado

Águila - eagle

Ahora - now

Ahorita - right now

Aire - air

Aislamiento - isolation

Ajedrez - chess

Ajeno/a - of another, strange/foreign

Ajo - garlic

Alambre - wire

Alba - dawn, daybreak

Albañil - bricklayer, mason

Alberca - swimming pool, water tank

Alcalde/sa - mayor

Alcance - within reach, range

Aldea - village

Aledaña - surrounding area, adjacent

Alegre - happy

Alegrón - pleasant surprise

Alejado/a - distant, remote

Algo - something

Algodón - cotton

Alguien - someone

Alguno/a, algún - some, any

Alianza - alliance

Alicaído/a - depressed, discouraged

Alimaña - pest, vermin

Allá - there, over there

Alma - soul

Almohada - pillow

Almuerzo - lunch

Alpinismo - mountain climbing

Alquiler - rent

Altavoz - loudspeaker

Altiplano - high plateau, upland

Alto/a - tall

Altura - height

Alumno/a - student

Amabilidad - kindness

Amable - lovable, kind, nice

Amarillo - yellow

Ambages - hesitation

Ambicioso/a - ambitious

Ambulancia - ambulance

Amigable - friendly

Amigo/a - friend

Amistad - friendship

Amor - love

Amplio/a - broad, wide, ample, large

Anales - annals

Andaluz - Andalusian

Andén - platform, sidewalk

Andino/a - Andean

Anexión - annexation

Angosto/a - narrow

Angustia - anguish, distress

Anónimo - anonymous

Ansiedad - anxiety

Antenoche - the night before last

Anteojos - glasses

Anteriores - previous

Antes de - before

Anticongelante - antifreeze

Antiguo/a - old

Antojitos - traditional snack

Anuncio - announcement, advertisement, notice

Apacible - gentle, mild, calm

Aparición - apparition

Apariencia - appearance, look

Apartamento - apartment

Aperitivo - aperitif, appetizer

Aporte - contribution

Apóstol - apostle

Apoyo - support, backing

Aprendizaje - apprenticeship

Aprobatorio – approving

Aprovecha - advantage

Aptitud - aptitude, capability

Aquí - here

Árabe - Arabic

Aragonés/a - From Aragon (Aragonese)

Árbol - tree

Arca - ark

Arcaico/a - archaic

Arcaísmo -
Archaism, a mixture of ancient words with modern language

Archivo - file

Arduo/a - arduous, grueling, hard, difficult

Arepa - cornmeal bread

Aritmética - arithmetic

Arma - weapon

Armada - armed, navy

Arpa - Harp

Arqueológico/a - archeological

Arquetipo - archetype

Arquitecto - architect

Arquitectura - architecture

Arreglo - repair, arrangement

Arriba - up, upwards

Arrogante - arrogant

Arroz - rice

Arte - art

Artesanal - handmade

Artesanía - craftsmanship; handicrafts

Articulista - columnist

Artístico - artistic

Asado/a - roasted, grilled, broiled

Asalto - assault

Asentamiento - settlement

Asesinato - murder, assassination

Asesino - assassin

Asesor/a - advisor, consultant

Así - so

Asiento - seat

Asistente - assistant

Aspecto - aspect

Aspiradora - vacuum cleaner

Astronauta - astronaut

Asunto - affair, matter

Atacante - assailant, attacker

Atención - attention

Atentamente - attentively

Ático - attic

Atleta - athlete

Atlético/a - athletic

Atletismo - athletics

Atrevido/a - bold, daring

Atrio - atrium

Átomo - atom

Atuendo - attire, costume
Audaz - bold, intrepid
Audiencias - audiences
Aún - yet, still, even
Aunque - although, even though
Auspicios - sponsorship, auspices
Autobús - bus
Autóctonos/as - indigenous, native
Autógrafo - autograph
Automovilista - driver
Autonomía - autonomy
Autopista - expressway, highway
Autor - author
Autoridad - authority
Autorización – authorization
Auxilio - aid, assistance
A veces - sometimes
Avances - advances
Aventura - adventure
Avión - plane
Aviso - advertisement
Ayer - yesterday
Azafata - stewardess, flight attendant
Azar - chance, fate
Azteca -
Aztec
Azúcar - sugar
Azul - blue

B

Bacalao - cod
Bache - pot hole, bad patch
Bachillerato - Same as High School, BachelorshipBailable - danceable

Bailarina - dancer, ballerina
Bajo/a - low
Baladí - trivial, irrelevant
Balcón - balcony
Baloncesto - basketball
Banco - bank
Bancaria - bank/banking
Bandeja - tray
Bandolón - mandolin
Banquero/a - banker
Banqueta - stool, pavement
Barato - cheap
Barrera - barrier, obstacle
Barrio - neighborhood, district
Barroco/a - baroque, ornate
Báscula - scale
Bases - bases, foundations, basis
Básico/a - basic
Basílica - Basilica
Bastante - enough, sufficiently
Bastón - walking stick
Basura - garbage, waste
Basurero - garbage collector, garbage dump
Batalla - battle
Batería - battery
Baúl - chest
Bebida - drink
Beca - grant, scholarship
Béisbol - baseball
Bella - beautiful
Belleza - beauty
Bendición - benediction, blessing
Berenjena - eggplant
Beso - kiss
Biblia - Bible
Biblioteca - library
Bicicleta - bicycle
Bien - good

Bienestar - welfare, well-being
Bilingüe - bilingual
Billete - bill
Biodiversidad - biodiversity
Biología - biology
Bistec - steak
Blanco - white
Boca - mouth
Bocadillo - sandwich
Boda - wedding
Boina - beret
Boleto - ticket
Bolsa - bag, purse
Bomba - bomb
Bomberos - firefighters
Bondad - goodness
Bonito/a - nice, beautiful
Borrón - blot, blemish
Botas - boots
Bote - small boat, jar, can
Boxeo - boxing
Brazo - arm
Breve - brief, short
Brevedad - brevity, shortness
Brillante - bright
Brindis - toast
Brisa - breeze
Broche - brooch, fastener
Broma - joke
Bronceador - suntan lotion
Brusco/a - sharp, brusque
Buey - ox
Bufanda - scarf
Bufón/a - clown, buffoon
Buró - bureau
Burro - donkey, stubborn

C

Caballo - horse
Caballero - gentleman

Cabaret - nightclub, cabaret
Cabello - hair
Cabeza - head
Cacao - cacao, cocoa bean
Cada - each
Cadena - chain
Cadera - hip
Café - cafe, coffee
Caja - box
Cajero/a - cashier, teller
Cajón - drawer
Cajuela - trunk, boot
Cachete - cheek
Caimán - alligator
Calabacín - zucchini, squash
Calabacita - zucchini
Calcetines: socks
Calco - transfer, tracing
Cálculo - calculus
Calidad - quality
Caliente - hot
Calificación - grade; rating, score
Calificativo - qualifying
Callado/a - quiet, silent
Calle - street
Calma - calm
Calor - heat
Calzoncillos - briefs
Cama - bed
Cámara - camera
Camarada - comrade
Camarero/a - waiter/waitress
Camarones - shrimp
Cambio - change
Caminata - hike, long walk
Camino - path, road
Camión - truck, bus (in Mexico City)
Camioneta - small truck, van

Camisa - shirt
Campana - bell
Campeón - champion
Campeonato Mundial - World Cup
Campesino/a - peasant, countryman, countrywoman
Campo - country
Canario - Canarian, canary
Canal - channel
Canastilla - basket
Canción - song
Caníbal - cannibalistic; cannibal
Canoa - canoe
Cánones - canons
Cantaleta - nagging
Cantante - Singer
Cantidad - quantity, sum
Canto - song, singing
Cantor– singer, cantor
Capacidad - capacity
Capaz - capable
Capellán - chaplain
Capilla - chapel
Capítulo - chapter
Capote - cloak
Caprichoso/a - capricious, fickle
Cara - face
Caracol marino - Sea Shell
Cárcel - prison, jail
Carga - loading, freight, cargo
Caribe - Caribbean
Caribeño/a - Caribbean
Cariñoso - affectionate
Carismático/a – charismatic
Carnicería - butcher shop
Carnicero - butcher
Carnívoro/a - carnivorous

Característica - característic
Caro - expensive
Carrera - run, race, major
Carretera - road, highway
Carril - lane
Carro - car
Carrocería - bodywork,
Carroza - carriage
Carta - letter
Cartelera - billboard
Cartera - wallet
Cartero - letter carrier, mailman
Casa - house
Casco - helmet, hull, hoof
Casete - cassette
Caso - case
Castellano - Castilian
Castigo - punishment, penalty
Castillo - castle
Castor - beaver
Catalogado - classify, to catalog, to list
Catarro - cold
Catedral - catedral
Catedrático/a - professor
Causa - cause, reason, motive
Cazuela - pan, saucepan
Cebolla - onion
Cecina - dried salted meat
Celebración - celebration
Célebre - celebrate, famous
Cena - dinner, supper
Cencerro - cowbell
Cenotes - natural deposit of spring water
Centenario - centenary, centennial
Cepillo - brush
Cerámica - ceramic
Cerca - near, close

Certeza - certainty
Cerveza - beer
Cesta - basket
Chabola - shack, shanty
Chacra - small farm
Chaleco - vest
Chamarra - sheepskin jacket, jacket
Champiñón - mushroom
Chancletas - sandals
Chapulín - grasshopper
Charlatán/a - talkative
Chatarra - scrap metal
Cheque - check
Chícharo - pea
Chicle - chewing gum
Chilaquiles - chilaquiles, tortilla dish
Chile - chili pepper
Chiquito - tiny, very little, very small
Chismografía - gossip columnist
Chofer - chauffeur, driver
Choque - impact, crash
Chirimoya - custard apple
Chorizo - sausage
Chorro - stream, jet, spurt
Chueco/a - crooked, bent, twisted
Ciclismo - bicycling
Cielo - sky, heaven
Científico/a - scientist
Ciertamente - truly, certainly
Cierto - true, certain, definite
Cigüeña - stork
Cilantro - coriander,
Cimientos - foundations
Cine - cinema, movies
Cineasta - filmmaker
Cinta - tape (film, audio) strip, ribbon
Cinto - strap, belt
Cinturón - belt

Circulación - circulation
Ciruela - plum
Cirujano/a - surgeon
Cisma - schism, split
Cisne - swan
Ciudad - city
Claridad - clarity
Clarinete - clarinet
Claro - clear
Clases - classes
Clavado - dive; just right, nailed
Clave - key, essential
Clérigo/a - cleric, member of the clergy
Clima - climate
Club - club
Coalición - coalition
Cobertores - bedspread, quilt
Cobija - blanket
Coche - car
Cocido/a - boiled, cooked
Cocina - kitchen
Cocinero/a - cook, chef
Coco - coconut
Codiciadas - coveted
Código - code
Codo - elbow
Cofre - trunk, chest
Coherente - coherent
Coincidencia - coincidence
Col - cabbage
Colaboración - collaboration
Colega - colleague
Colegiatura - tuition
Colegio - school
Coliflor - cauliflower
Colilla - butt (of cigarette)
Colonizador/a - colonizer, colonist
Color - color
Comedia - comedy
Comedor - dining room

Comerciante - shopkeeper, business man
Comercio - business, trade
Cometa - comet
Cómica - comic, comical
Comida - food
Comida Congelada - Frozen food
Comisión - commission
Cómo - how
Cómodo - comfortable
Compacto/a - compact
Compañero - companion
Compañía - company
Competencia - competition
Complejidad - complexity
Comprensión - comprehension, understanding
Complicado - complicated Comprometido - committed
Compuesto/a - fixed, repaired
Común - common
Comunidad - community
Con - with
Conato - attempt, effort
Concepto - concept
Conciencia - conscience, consciousness
Concordia - concord, harmonyCondado - county
Condicional - conditional
Condición - condition
Conducta - conduct, behavior
Confiable - trustworthy, reliable
Confianza - confidence
Congestionamiento - traffic jam
Conjunto - joint, band (music)

Conmemorativo/a - commemorative, memorial
Conocimiento - knowledge
Conquista - conquest
Conquistador/a - conqueror
Consejo - advice, counsel, council
Conservador - conserver, conservative
Construcción - construction
Consulado - consulate
Consulta - consultation
Consultorio - doctor's office
Contador/a - accountant
Contemporáneo/a - contemporary
Contenido - content
Contestadora - answering machine
Continente - continent
Contingente - contingent
Contra - against
Contratista - contractor
Contrato - contract
Contundencia - forcefulness
Conveniente - convenient
Convento - convent
Convertible - convertible
Copiloto - copilot
Corazón - heart
Corbata - tie
Cordero - lamb
Cordialmente - cordially
Coreografía – choreography
Coro - choir
Corta - short, small, little
Corte - cut, length, court
Cortesía - courtesy, politeness
Cortina - curtain

Cortometraje - Short film
Cosa - thing
Cosmología - Cosmology
Costumbre - custom
Cotidiano - daily, everyday, routinely
Coyote - coyote, smuggler
Creación - creation
Credibilidad - credibility
Créditos - credits
Creencia - belief
Crema - cream
Cremería - dairy store
Crepas - crepes (pancake)
Cría - breeding, rearing
Criatura - baby, child, creature
Crimen - crime
Crisálida - chrysalis, pupa
Cristiano/a - Christian
Crítica - criticism
Cruel - cruel
Cruz - cross
Cuadra - city block
Cuadrilla - gang, team, group
Cuál - which/what
Cualidad - quality, trait
Cualquier/a - any
Cuarto - room, fourth
Cubierto - silverware, covered
Cuchara - spoon
Cuchillo - knife
Cuello - neck
Cuentista - storyteller
Cuento
story, tale, short story
Cuerda - cord, rope, string
Cuerno - horn, antler
Cuero - leather, skin
Cuerpo - body
Cueva - cave

Cuidado - care; worry, concern
Culinaria - culinary
Culpa - blame
Culpable - guilty
Cultivo - cultivation, farming
Cumbre - summit, top
Cumpleaños - birthday
Cuna - cot, crib
Cuñada - sister-in-law
Cuñado - brother-in-law
Cuño - die, stamp
Cura - priest, cure, band aid
Curiosidad - curiosity
Curioso/a - curious
Curriculum - curriculum
Cursi - affected, pretentious
Curso - course
Cuyo/a - whose

D

Dalia - dahlia
Dama - lady
Danza - dance
Datos - data
Debajo - under
Débil - weak, feeble
Debilitamiento - debilitation, weakening
Debutante - beginner, newcomer
Década - decade
Decano/a - dean
Decapitados - decapitated
Declive - decline
Dedicado/a - dedicated
Dedo - finger
Defensa - defense
Deidad - deity, goddess
Delante de - in front of
Delegación - delegation

Delgado/a - slim, fine, thin, skinny

Delincuencia - delinquency, crime

Demás - remaining

Demasiado/a - too much, too many

Denominación - name, designation; denomination

Dentado - jagged, serrated, sprocket

Dentista - dentist

Dentro de - Inside of

Denuncia - denunciation, condemnation

Deportes - sports

Deportista - athlete, sportsman, sportswoman, sporty

Depresión - depression

Derecho - right

Desarrollo - development

Desayuno - breakfast

Descarado - brazen, impudent

Descortés - impolite, discourteous

Descubrimiento - discovery

Descuidado - neglected

Desde - from, since

Deseable - desirable

Desembarque - unloading, disembarkation

Desgastante - stressful

Deseosa - willing

Desigual - unequal

Desigualdad - inequality

Desmontable - removable, detachable

Desocupado/a - empty, unemployed

Despacio - slowly

Despedida - farewell, goodbye

Despensa - pantry

Despreocupado/a - carefree, easygoing

Después - after

Detenida - detained

Detrás - behind

Deuda - debt

Día - day

Diagnóstico/a - diagnostic

Diario - everyday, daily, newspaper

Dibujo - drawing

Diccionario - dictionary

Dictador - dictator

Diente - tooth

Diferencia - difference

Difícil - difficult

Difusión - spreading, diffusion

Digno - worthy

Dilataciones - expansion, dilation

Diluvio - flood

Dinámica - dynamics

Dinero - money

Dios - God

Diplomático/a - diplomat; diplomatic

Dirección - address, directing

Director - director, manager

Dirigida - directed

Discapacidades - disabilities

Discriminación - discrimination

Distintivo - distinctive, distinguishing

Distinto/a - different

Distribución - distribution

Divergencia - divergence, difference

Divertido/a - funny

Doblaje - dubbing

Docena - dozen

Doctísima - Wise woman

Doctor - doctor

Doctorado - doctorate

Documento - document

Dólar - dollar

Dolor - pain

Doméstica - domestic

Domingo - Sunday

Dominio - domain

Dónde - where

Dragón - dragon

Dramaturgo - dramatist, playwright

Drogas - drugs

Duda - doubt

Dulces - candies

Dulzura - sweetness

Durante - during

Durazno - peach

E

Economía - economy

Economista - economist

Edad - age

Edición - edition

Edificio - building

Editor/a - editor

Editorialista -Editorial writer

Eficaz - effective, efficient

Efectivo/a - effective

Efigie - effigy

Eje - axis

Ejemplo - example

Ejercicios - exercises

Ejote - green bean

Elecciones - elections

Elefante - elephant

Elegante - elegant

Elevado/a - elevated, lofty

Elote - corncob

Emancipación - emancipation

Embajada - embassy

Embargo - embargo
Embrague - clutch
Emergencia - emergency
Emisión - emission
Empleado - employee
Empresa - company
Empresario/a - entrepreneur
Encabezado - header
Encargado/a - in charge
Encuesta - poll
Enemigo/a - enemy
Enfermero/a - nurse
Enmudecen - silent
Enojado/a - angry
Enormemente - enormously
Ensalada - salad
Enseñanza - teaching, education
Entero - entire, whole
Entrada - entrance
Entre - between
Entrega - delivery, dedication
Entrenador - trainer, coach
Entrevista - interview
Entusiasmo - enthusiasm
Envejecimiento - aging
Envoltura - wrapper, wrapping
Epidemia - epidemic
Epitafio - epitaph
Época - epoch, age, period
Equilibrio - balance
Equipo - team
Equitación - horseback riding
Ermita - hermitage, chapel
Escalera - stairs
Escalón - step, rung
Escena - scene

Escenario - stage; setting, stage
Escénico/a - scenic
Escisión - split, division
Esclavo/a - slave
Escritor/a - writer
Escritorio - desk
Escuela - school
Escultura - sculpture
Esencial - essential
Esfera - sphere
Esfuerzo - effort
Eslabón - link
Esmeralda - emerald
Eso - that
Espada - sword
Espalda - back
Espárrago - asparagus
Especial - special
Espectacular - spectacular
Espectáculo - spectacle, show
Espectador/a - spectator, onlooker
Espejo - mirror
Espejo retrovisor - rearview mirror
Espeleología - speleology
Espera - wait
Esperanza - hope
Espinaca - spinach
Espionaje - espionage
Espontáneo/a - spontaneous
Esposo/a - husband/wife
Esquí - ski
Estación - station, season
Estadística - statistic, figure
Estadio - stadium
Estado - state
Estadounidense– from the United States
Estampilla - stamp
Estancia - stay

Estatutario/a - statutory
Estereotipo - stereotype
Estilo - style
Estimado/a – estimated, dear
Estornudo - sneeze
Estrategia - strategy
Estrato - stratum, layer
Estrella - star
Estreno - debut, premiere
Estricta - strict
Estructura - structure
Estruendoso/a - resounding, thunderous
Estudioso/a - studious
Estufa - heater, stove, oven
Etapa - stage
Ética - ethics
Evento - event
Evolución - evolution
Examen - test, quiz, exam
Excelencia - excellence
Excepto - except
Excesivo - excessive
Excursión - excursion
Excusa - excuse, apology
Existencia - existence
Expectativa - expectancy
Experiencia - experience
Explotación - exploitation
Expresión - expression
Exteriores - exteriors
Extinguidor - fire extinguisher
Extranjero - foreign, foreigner, alien
Extraño/a - strange, odd, stranger, unknown
Extraños - stranger

F

Fabricado - fabricated
Facial - facial

Fácil - easy
Factura - bill, invoice
Falda - skirt
Falsificación - counterfeit, forgery
Falta - lack, foul
Fama - fame
Familia - family
Famoso/a - famous
Fantasma - ghost, phantom
Fantástico - fantastic
Farmacéutico/a - pharmacist
Farmacia - drugstore, pharmacy
Faro - lighthouse
Fatalidad - fatality
Fatiga - tired
Fauna - fauna
Favor - favor
Fayuca - contraband; black market
Fe - faith
Fecha - date
Fecundidad - fertility, fruitfulness
Felicidad - happiness
Feligreses - parishioners
Feliz - happy
Fenómeno - phenomenon
Feriado - holiday
Feroz - ferocious, fierce
Ferrocarril - railroad, railway
Festejo - celebration
Festival - festival
Fiel - faithful, loyal
Fiesta - party
Filosofía - philosophy
Fin - end
Finanzas - finances
Finca - farm, ranch
Fino/a - fine, excellent, thin

Fisgón - snooper, nosy
Flaco - thin, skinny
Flauta - flute
Flecha - arrow
Flor - flower
Florería - flower shop, florist
Fluido/a - flowing, fluent
Flujo - flow
Folclórico - Folkloric
Follaje - foliage
Fondo - bottom
Forma - form
Fornido/a - well-built, burly
Fortalecimiento - strengthening
Foto - photo
Fotografía - photograph
Fotógrafo/a - photographer
Franqueado - open
Frase - phrase
Frecuentemente - frequently
Freno - brake
Frente - front, in front, forehead
Fresa - strawberry
Fresco - fresh
Frijoles - beans
Fritangas - junk food, greasy food
Frívolo/a - frivolous
Frontera - border, frontier
Fruta - fruit
Frutal - fruit, fruit-bearing; fruit tree
Fuego - fire
Fuente - spring
Fuerte - strong
Fuerza - strength
Función - function
Funcionario/a - civil worker
Fundación - foundation

Fundamental - fundamental
Fútbol - soccer
Futbolista - soccer player
Futuro - future

G

Gallo - rooster
Gancho - hook
Garaje - garage
Gasto - expense
Gastronomía - gastronomy
Gato - cat
General - general
Género - gender, genre, class, kind
Generosidad - generosity
Generación - generation
Generoso/a - generous
Genialidad - genius, brilliant
Gente - people
Geometría - geometry
Gerente - manager
Gesto - gesture
Gigantesco/a - gigantic, huge
Gimnasio - gymnasium
Gira - tour
Giro - turn, turn of phrase, draft
Gloria - glory
Glúteos - buttocks
Gobernador/a - governor
Gobernante - ruling, governing
Gobierno - government
Golondrina - swallow (bird); tern
Golosinas - sweets
Golpe - a blow, knock, punch
Gordo/a - fat

Grabadora - tape recorder

Gracias - thank you

Grada - harrow, step

Grado - grade, school year

Grande - big

Gratuito/a - gratuitous, unwarranted

Grave - grave, very ill, serious

Gravidez - Pregnancy

Griego - Greek

Grosero/a - rude, nasty

Grupo - group

Guantes - gloves

Guantera - glove compartment

Guapo/a - handsome, lovely, beautiful

Guarda - security guard

Guardería - nursery, day-care center

Güero - blonde, light-skinned

Guerra - war

Guía - directory, guidebook; guide, leader

Guión - screenplay

Guionista - script writer

Guitarra - guitar

Gusano - worm

Gustoso - willingly

H

Habilidoso/a - skillful, clever

Habitación - room, bedroom

Hablante - speaker

Hada - fairy

Halcón - hawk, falcon

Hamburguesa - hamburger

Hampa - underworld

Hasta - even; until, up to, as far as

Hebreo - Hebrew

Hecho/a - made, done

Helado - ice cream, chilly, cold

Henequén - sisal hemp

Herida - injury, wound

Hermano/a - brother/sister

Hermoso/a - beautiful

Héroe/heroína - hero

Hermosura - beauty, loveliness

Herramienta - tool

Hidrante - hydrant

Hielo - ice

Hígado - liver

Hijo/a - son/ daughter

Híjole - Wow! Good grief!

Hilo - thread

Himno Nacional - National Anthem

Historia - history

Hogar - home

Hoja - leaf, sheet

Hola - hello, hi

Hombre - man

Homogéneo/a - homogeneous

Hongo - fungus; mushroom

Hora - hour

Horario - schedule, timetable

Horror - horror, dread

Horroroso/a - horrifying, terrifying

Hotel - hotel

Hoy - today

Hoyo - hole

Huarache - huarache sandal

Huerta - orchard

Huevo - egg

Hueso - bone

Humano/a - human

Humildad - humility

Humo - smoke

Hundimiento - collapse, subsidence, sinking

I

Identidad - identity

Identificación - identificación

Idioma - language

Iglesia - church

Igualdad - equality

Iluminación - lighting

Ilusión - illusion

Ilustrado - illustrated

Imagen - image

Imaginación - imagination

Impaciente - impatient

Imperio - empire

Imponente - imposing, impressive

Impredecible - unpredictable

Imprenta - printing, press, print

Imprescindible - essential, indispensable

Impresora - printer

Impresionados - impressed

Imprevisto - unexpected, unforeseen

Impuestos - taxes

Impulso - impulse

Inaugural - inaugural, opening

Incendio - fire

Incertidumbre - uncertainty, suspense

Inclinación - inclination

Incluso - even

Indicador - gauge, dial, meter

Indudable - unquestionable, beyond doubt
Inestabilidad - instability, unsteadiness
Inferior - inferior, lower
Infinito - infinitely, vastly
Influencia - influence
Información - information
Informática - computer science
Infracción - infringement
Ingeniero/a - engineer
Ingenuo - naïve
Inglés - English
Ingrato - ungrateful
Ingreso - entrance, entry
Iniciativa - initiative
Inicio - beginning, initiation, start
Ininterrumpido/a - uninterrupted, continuous
Injusto - unfair, unjust
Inmenso/a - immense, vast
Inmortal - immortal
Innegable - undeniable
Innovación - innovation
Insatisfacción - insatisfaction
Inserción - insertion
Inservible - useless
Instituto - institute
Instrumento - instrument
Integración - integration
Integridad - integrity, honesty
Inteligencia - intelligence
Inteligente - intelligent
Intención - intention
Intensivo/a - intensive
Interamericana - Interamerican
Interés - interest
Interesante - interesting
Interjección - interjection
Intermedio - intermission

Intérprete - interpreter
Intervención - intervention
Intimamente - intimately
Íntimo/a - intímate, close
Intolerancia - intolerance
Investigación - investigation, inquiry
Inyección - injection, shot
Irrupción - irruption
Isla - island
Islote - small island
Istmo - isthmus
Itinerario - itinerary
Izquierda - left

J

Jabón - soap
Jamás - never
Jarabe - syrup
Jardín - garden
Jaula - cage
Jazmines - jasmine
Jefe - chief, head, leader,
Jesuita - jesuit
Jolgorio - merrymaking, fun
Joyas - jewels
Joven - young
Judío - Jewish
Judo - judo
Juego - game
Juez - judge
Jugador/a - player
Juguete - toy
Jugo - juice
Junto/a - joined, united
Juntos - together
Jurídico/a - legal
Justamente - precisely, exactly
Justo - just, justly; right

K

Karate - karate
Kilo - Kilogram
Kiosco - Kiosk

L

Labio - lip
Laboral - working, laboring, occupational
Laboratorio - laboratory
Labrado/a - cultivated, tilled
Lado - side, close by, nearby
Ladrón - robber, thief, burglar
Lago - lake
Laico/a - lay, secular
Lámpara de mano - flashlight
Lancha - boat, launch, powerboat
Langosta - lobster
Lápiz - pencil
Largo - long
Lástima - compassion, pity
Lavabo - wash basin, sink
Lavadora - washing machine
Lavandería - laundry
Lebrel - greyhound
Lección - lesson
Leche - milk
Lechuga - lettuce
Lectura - reading
Legalidad - legality, lawfulness
Legalización - legalization
Legumbres - vegetables
Leído - well-read

Lejano/a - remote, distant, far away
Lejos - far. far away, distant
Lema - motto, slogan
Lengua - tongue, language
Lenguaje - language, speech
Lentamente - slowly
Lente - lens
Lentes - glasses
Lento - slow
León - lion
Letra - letter
Ley -law, authority
Libélula - dragonfly
Libertad - freedom
Libre - free
Librería - bookstore
Libro - book
Licencia - license
Licenciatura - college/Bachelor degree
Liderazgo - leadership
Ligado/a - linked, connected
Ligero/a - light, lightweight
Lima - lime
Limitado - limited
Limón - lemon
Limonada - lemonade
Limosna - alms, charity
Limpieza - cleanliness, tidiness
Limpio/a - clean
Línea - line
Lingüística - linguistics
Líquido - liquid, fluid
Lirio - iris
Lista - list, clever girl
Literario/a - literary
Literatura - literature
Llaga - sore, wound
Llamada - call

Llamas - flames
Llanta - tire
Llave - key
Llegada - arrival
Lleno - full, filled, crowded
Lluvia - rain, rainfall
Loco/a - crazy
Locuaz - talkative
Locutor - announcer
Logo - logo
Logro - achievement, attainment
Loza - pottery
Lucha - struggle, fight, wrestling
Luego - later
Lugar - place
Lumbre - fire
Luminoso/a - luminous, shining
Luna - moon
Lunes - Monday

M

Macabro/a - macabre
Maceta - flowerpot
Machete - machete
Machista - male chauvinist
Madre - mother
Madrina - godmother, bridesmaid
Maestría - mastery, skill
Maestro /a - teacher, master, masterly, skilled
Magisterio - teaching, Teacher's
Association
Magnífica - magnificent
Magnitud - magnitude
Mago/a - magician
Maíz - corn
Majestad - majesty
Maleta - suitcase, bag

Maletero - trunk
Malo/a - bad
Maltratados - abused
Manatí - manatee
Mandado - supplies
Mandato - order command, mandate
Mandioca - manioc, cassava
Mando - leader, person in charge, commandant
Manejo - driving, handling, use
Mango - hilt, handle, mango
Manguera - fire hose
Mano - hand, brother (in México)
Manta - blanket, coarse, cotton fabric
Mantel - tablecloth
Mantequilla - butter
Manzana - apple
Mañana - morning, tomorrow
Maquillaje - makeup
Mar - sea, ocean
Maraca - maraca
Maravilla - marvel, wonderfully
Marca - mark, brand
Marfil - ivory
Marido - husband
Mariposa - butterfly
Mármol - marble
Marzo - March
Más - more
Masa - mass, volume
Masaje - massage
Máscara - mask
Matemáticas - mathematics
Materia - subject, matter
Mayor - bigger, larger, greater, older
Mayoría - majority

Mecánico - mechanic

Mediante - through, by means of

Medias - pantyhose, socks

Medicina - medicine

Médico - doctor

Medieval - medieval

Medida/o - measure

Mejilla - cheek

Mejor - best

Melocotón - peach

Melón - melon, cantaloupe

Menor - smaller, lesser, younger

Menos - less

Mensaje - message

Mentira - lie

Mentón - chin

Menudo - small, type of food in Mexico

Mercado - market

Mercancía - merchandise, goods

Merced - gift, favor, grace

Meridional - southern

Merienda - afternoon snack, night time snack (in Mexico City)

Mes - month

Mesa - table

Mesero/a - waiter/waitress

Meseta - plateau, tableland

Meta - goal, objective

Metralleta - submachine gun

Mezcla - mixture

Mezclilla - denim

Mezquino - mean, cheap

Mezquita - mosque

Microonda - microwave

Miedo - fear, apprehension

Miembro - member

Migración - migration

Migrante - migrant

Mil - a thousand

Milagro - miracle

Milla - mile

Millonario/a - millionaire

Ministro/a - minister, secretary

Minuto - minute

Misa - mass

Miserable - miserable, wretched

Misión - mission

Misionero/a - missionary

Mismo/a - same

Misterio - mystery

Mitad - half

Mochila - backpack

Moda - fashion

Modales - manners

Modalidad - kind, type

Modelo - model

Módem - modem

Modernización - modernization

Moderno/a - modern

Modesto - modest

Modistos - tailors, fashion designers

Mole - spicy sauce made with chilies; mass, bulk

Monarquía - monarchy

Moneda - coin

Monje - monk

Monja - nun

Monolingüe - monolingual

Monstruos - monsters

Montaje - assembly, montage

Montés - wild

Monumento - monument

Morbo - morbid curiosity

Morfema - Morpheme

Moro - Moorish; Muslim

Mortal - mortal

Motivo - motive

Mosca - fly

Mostaza - mustard

Mudanza - change, move

Mudo/a - silent, mute

Mueble - piece of furniture

Mueblería - furniture store

Muerte - death

Muestra - sample, sign

Mugre - dirt, filth

Mujer - woman

Muletas - crutches

Multa - fine

Múltiple - multiple

Multitud - crowd, multitude

Mundo - world

Mundial - world, worldwide

Muñeca - wrist, doll

Musical - musical

Músico - musician

Muslo - thigh

Musulmán - Muslim

Muy - very

N

Naciente - newfound, growing, rising

Nacimiento - birth

Nacional - national

Nada - nothing

Nadie - no one

Nanotecnología - Nano technology

Naranja - orange

Nariz - nose

Natación - swimming

Natal - native country, hometown

Nave - ship

Navegación - navigation

Navidad - Christmas

Neblina - light fog, mist

Nebulosa - nebula, misty, cloudy

Necesidad - need, necessity

Negocio - business

Neoclásico/a - neoclassical

Neologismo - neologism

Nervios - nerves

Niebla - fog, mist

Nieto/a - grandson, granddaughter

Ninguno/a - none, nobody

Niñería - childishness

Nivel - level, height

Noche - night

Nombre - name

Noreste - northeastern

Normal - normal

Norte - north

Noticias - news

Noticiero - television news

Notorio - notorious

Novedad - newness, novelty

Novela - novel, soap opera

Novio/a - boyfriend, fiancé, groom/ girlfriend, fiancée, bride

Noviembre - November

Nudillo - knuckle

Nuestro/a - our

Nuevo/a - new

Número - number

Nunca - never

Nutria - otter

O

Obediencia - obedience

Obesidad - obesity

Obituario - obituary

Obligatorio/a - mandatory, required

Obra - work

Obrero/a - worker, laborer

Obsoleto - obsolete

Obstante - nevertheless, however

Occidente - west

Ocio - free time, leisure

Octubre - October

Oculista - oculist, ophthalmologist

Ocupada - occupied

Oferta - offer, sale

Oficina - office

Ofrenda - offering

Ojalá - I hope, God willing, May God granted

Ojo - eye

Olor - smell, odor

Ombligo - belly button

Operador/a - operator

Oportunidad - opportunity

Óptimo/a - optimum, optimal

Orden - order

Ordenada - orderly

Oreja - ear

Orgulloso/a - proud

Oriente - east

Orilla - edge

Oro - gold

Oscuro/a - dark

Ostra - oyster

Otro/a - other

Oveja - sheep

P

Paciencia - patience

Paciente - patient

Padre - father

Padres - parents

Página - page

País - country

Paisaje - view, landscape

Pájaro - bird

Palabra - word

Palacio - palace

Palanca - lever

Pálido/a - pale

Palomitas - popcorn

Pan - bread

Panadería - bakery

Panadero - baker

Panorama - panorama, view

Pantalla - screen, monitor

Pantorrilla - calf

Panza - belly, paunch

Paño - cloth

Pañuelo - handkerchief

Papa - potato, Pope

Papel - paper

Para - for

Parabrisas - windshields

Parachoques - bumper

Paradigma - paradigm

Paraguas - umbrella

Parecido/a - similar, alike

Pared - wall

Pareja - couple, pair

Parlanchín/a - chatty, talkative

Parque - park

Párrafo - paragraph

Párroco - parish priest

Parte - part

Particularmente - particularly

Partida - departure

Partido - game

Pasaporte - passport

Pasatiempo - hobby

Paseo - walk, stroll

Pasillo - corridor

Pasión - passion

Pastel - pastel, cake

Pastilla - pill, tablet, tablet, lozenge

Pasto - pasture

Pastor - shepherd
Pata - paw, female duck, leg of things, animals and even people
Paté - pâté
Patente - patent
Paterno - parental
Patria - native land
Patrón - boss
Pauta - rule, guideline
Pavo - turkey
Paz - peace, peacefulness
Peatón - pedestrian
Pecho - chest
Pedal - pedal
Pedazo - piece, bit, chunk
Peine - comb
Película - movie
Pelo - hair
Peluca - wig
Pena - punishment, penalty, sorrow
Pensador/a - thinker
Pensamiento - thought
Pensión - pension
Peor - worse
Pepino - cucumber
Pequeño/a - small
Percepción - perception
Perdido/a - lost
Perdón - I'm sorry
Peregrino - pilgrim
Perfectamente - perfectly
Periódico - newspaper
Periodista - journalist
Perlas - pearls
Peligro - danger
Peligroso/a- dangerous
Pelota - ball
Pera - pear
Pérdida - loss
Perejil - parsley
Perífrasis - periphrases
Periódico - newspaper

Periodista - journalist
Pero - but
Perro - dog
Pesado/a - heavy
Persona - person
Personaje - character
Persuadido - persuaded
Pertenencia - membership
Pertinente - pertinent
Pesado/a - heavy
Pesca - fishing
Pescadería - fish shop
Pescado - fish
Pescuezo - neck
Pesero - minibus
Pestaña - eyelash
Petate - mat
Petróleo - oil, petroleum
Pie - foot
Piedra - stone
Piel - skin
Pierna - leg
Pieza - piece, part, room
Pijama - pajama
Pilón - basin, added for free, extra
Piloto - pilot
Pimienta - pepper
Pintor - painter
Piragua - canoe
Pirata - bootleg, pirated, pirate
Piratería - privacy, bootlegging
Piscina - pool
Pisco - Alcoholic beverage from Chile and Peru
Piso - floor
Pizarrón - blackboard, chalkboard
Pizca - pinch
Plana - page
Plano - map
Planta - plant

Plástico - plastic
Plátano - banana
Plática - chat, talk
Platillos - cymbals, dishes, saucer
Plato - plate, dish
Playa - beach
Playeras - t-shirts
Plomada - plummet
Plomero/a - plumber
Pluma –pen; feather
Pluralidad - plurality
Población - population, town, village
Poblado/a - inhabited, populated
Poblador/a - settler
Pobre - poor
Pobreza - poverty
Poco - little
Poderosa - powerful
Poema - poem
Poeta - poet
Policía - police
Policiaco/a - police
Polímero - polymer
Político - political
Polo - pole
Pollera - chicken coop, typical dress from Colombia
Pollo - chicken
Porcentaje - percentage
Por favor - please
Por qué - why
Porque - because
Portafolio - briefcase; portfolio
Portero/a - goalkeeper, bellman
Posada - inn, advent celebration in México
Posgrado - Grad. School
Posible - possible
Posición - position

Posteriormente - later, after

Postre - dessert

Potestad - authority, jurisdiction

Pozo - well

Precavido - cautious

Precio - price

Precioso/a - beautiful, precious, lovely

Precoz - precocious

Predominantemente - predominantly

Pregunta - question

Premio - prize, reward

Prenda - piece of clothing

Prensa - press

Preocupado - worried

Preparación - preparation

Preparatoria - high school

Preponderante - preponderant, predominant

Preposición - preposition

Presentación - presentation

Presidente -president

Presidido - prison

Presión - pressure

Prestigio - prestige

Primera - first

Princesa - princess

Príncipe - prince

Principio - beginning

Prioridad - priority

Prisa - hurry

Privado/a - private

Problema - problem

Procedencia - origin, source

Proceso - process

Productor - producer

Profesión - profession

Profesor/a - professor

Programador/a - programmer

Progreso/a - progress

Prolijo - long winded; neat, meticulous

Promoción - promotion

Pronombre - pronoun

Propina - tip

Propio/a - own

Propuesta - proposal

Prosperidad - prosperity

Provecho - benefit

Proverbio - proverb

Provincia - province

Prueba - test, proof

Psicoanálisis - psychoanalysis

Psicología - psychology

Psicológico - psychological

Psiquiatra - psychiatrist

Publicación - publication

Público - public

Pueblo - town

Puente - bridge

Puerco - dirty, filthy, pig

Pulseras - bracelets

Puerta - door

Pues - since, because, for

Pucho - end of a cigarette

Punta - tip, end

Punto - dot, point

Pupitre - desk

Q

Quebrantos - break, breaking

Quena - flute, Peruvian reed flute

Querido/a - dear

Queso - cheese

Quién - who

Quietud - tranquility

Química - chemistry

Quizá - perhaps, maybe

R

Rábano - radish

Rabia - rabies, rage, anger

Raíz - root

Ramo - branch

Rana - frog

Ranura - groove, slot

Rápido/a - fast

Rasgo - stroke (of a pen)

Ratero - thief

Rato - time, while

Ratón - mouse

Rayo - ray, beam

Rayos X - X-rays

Raza - race

Razón - reason, motive

Reacción - reaction

Realidad - reality

Realización - realization

Recado - message

Recámara - bedroom

Recepción - reception

Recepcionista - receptionist

Recibo - receipt

Reciente - recent

Recientemente - recently

Reclusorio - federal prison

Recolector - colector

Recreación - re-creation

Rectangular - rectangular

Rector/a - president of a college/university

Recuerdo - memory, souvenir

Recurso - resource

Red - net, network

Reducción - reduction, decrease

Reflejo - reflection

Reformas - reforms

Refrán - saying

Refrigerio - refreshments
Regadera - watering can, shower
Regalo - gift, present
Región - region
Regional - regional
Registro - register
Regla - rule, norm
Reino - kingdom, realm
Reja - bars, grating, fence
Relaciones - relations
Relajado/a - relaxed, loose
Relativo/a - relative
Reloj - clock, watch
Remedio - remedy, cure
Remitente - return address
Remo - paddle, oar; rowing
Renacentista - a person from the Renaissance
Renta - rent
Reportero/a - reporter
Represión - repression
Reprensión - reprimand
Representante - representative
Repugnante - disgusting
Resbaladizo/a - slippery
Resentimiento - resentment
Reses - cattle
Reservado/a - reserved, reticent
Residuo - residue
Resorte - spring
Respaldo - back
Respectivamente - respectively
Respeto - respect, consideration
Respuesta - response, answer, reply

Restaurantes - restaurants
Resto - rest, remainder
Resultado - result
Retraído/a - retracted
Retraso - delay
Retrato - depiction, portrayal
Revancha - revenge
Reverso - reverse
Revisor/a - corrector, inspector
Revista - magazine, journal
Revolucionario - revolutionary
Rey - King
Ribera - bank, shore, riverside
Rico/a - rich, delicious, delightful
Riesgo - risk
Rincón - corner, nook
Rines - wheels
Riñón - kidney
Río - river
Riqueza - wealth, riches
Risa - laughter, laugh
Ritmo - rhythm
Rodilla - knee
Ron - rum
Ropa - clothing
Rostro - face
Rubio/a - blonde
Rueda - wheel
Ruido - noise, sound
Ruina - ruin, devastated, downfall

S

Sábana _ sheet
Sabio - wise
Sabor - flavor, taste
Sabroso/a - tasty, delicious

Saco - bag, sack, jacket
Sacudida - shake, jolt
Sal - salt
Sala - living room
Salario - salary
Salchicha - sausage
Salida - departure
Salud - health, cheers
Saludable - healthful
Salvavidas - lifeguard
Sandía - watermelon
Sangre - blood
Santuario - Shrine, Sanctuary
Sarcástica/o - sarcastic
Sartén - pan
Saxofón - saxophone
Secretario/a - secretary
Secreto - secret
Sede - seat, headquarters
Seguido - continued
Seguidor - follower, fan (fan of someone or something)
Según - according
Segundo/a - second
Seguramente - surely
Seguridad - security
Seguro - insurance
Seguro/a - safe, sure, certainly, definitely
Sellados - sealed
Selva - jungle, forest
Semáforo - traffic light
Semana - week
Sembrado - cultivated field
Semejante - similar
Semestre - semester
Sencillo - simple
Sentidos- senses, directions, meanings,
Sentimiento - feeling, emotion
Seña - sign, signal

Señal- sign
Septiembre - September
Serio/a - serious
Serranía - mountainous area
Servicio - service
Servidumbre - servitude
Servilleta - napkin
Sesión - session
Seso - brain
Sibilante - sibilant
Siempre - always
Siglo - century
Siguiente - following, next
Silencio - silence
Silla - chair
Símbolos - symbols
Simpático/a - nice, friendly
Simplemente - simply
Sinagoga - synagogue
Sin - without
Sin embargo - however, nevertheless
Sinceridad - sincerity
Sinfonía - symphony
Sino - destiny, but
Sinónimo - synonymous
Sintáctico/a - syntactic, syntactical
Sinuosas - winding
Siquiera - at least
Sirena - mermaid; siren
Sirviente/a - servant, maid
Sistema - system
Sitio - place, site
Sobre - envelope, packet, on, on top of, over, above, about
Sobrepeso - excess weight
Sobresaliente - protruding, projecting, excellent

Sobrino/a - nephew, niece
Social - social
Sociedad - society
Socio - partner, member
Socorro - aid, help
Soga - rope, noose
Sol - sun
Solamente - only, just
Soldado - soldier
Soledad - loneliness, solitude
Solicitud - solicitude, concern, application
Solo - only
Soltero/a - single
Sombrero - hat
Sonido - sound
Sopa - soup
Soprano - soprano
Sorpresa - surprise
Sótano - basement
Submarinismo - scuba diving
Subsiguiente - subsequent
Subterráneos - underground, passage, tunnel
Sucio/a - dirty, filthy
Sueldo - salary, wages
Suelo - ground
Suerte - luck
Suéter - sweater
Suficiente - enough
Sugerencia - suggestion
Sujeto/a - secure, fastened, subject, guy
Suizo/a - Swiss
Sumamente - extremely, exceedingly
Superior - superior
Supermercado - supermarket
Sureste - southeast
Suroeste - southwest

Suscripción - subscription
Suspiro - sigh
Susto - fright, scare

T

Tablero –dashboard
Tabloide - tabloid
Tacón - heel
Tacto - touch, feel, tact
Taller - the shop, workshop
También - also
Tambor - drum
Tanque - tank, reservoir
Tanto - so much, so many
Taquilla - ticket counter
Tarde - late, afternoon
Tarea - homework
Tarjeta - card
Tarjeta de crédito - credit card
Taxi - taxi
Taxista - taxi driver
Taza - cup
Teatro - theater
Teclado - keyboard
Técnica - technique, skill
Tecnología - technology
Tejones - badgers
Telar - loom
Tele - TV
Teléfono - telephone
Telenovela - soap opera
Tema - theme, topic, subject
Temor - fear
Temperamento - temperament
Templo: temple, church
Temporada - season, time

Temporal - temporal, long period of time that rains continuously
Temprano - early
Tendencia - tendency, inclination
Tenedor - fork
Tenis - tennis, sneakers
Tentación - temptation
Tequila - Tequila
Tercera - third
Tercio - a third
Termómetro - thermometer
Ternera - calf, veal
Terraza - terrace, veranda, deck
Terremoto - earthquake
Territorio - territory
Tesis - thesis
Testigo - witness
Textil - textile
Tez - skin
Tía - aunt
Tianguis - Farmers markets
Tiempo - time
Tienda - store
Tierra - land, earth
Tigre - tiger
Timbre - ring, stamp
Tímido/a - timid, shy
Tintorería - dry cleaner's
Tío - uncle
Tipo - type, subject, guy
Tiraje - printing
Tirantes - suspenders
Título - title
Tiza - chalk
Toalla - towel
Tobillo - ankle
Tocador - dressing table
Todavía - still, yet
Todos - all
Tomates - tomatoes

Tono - dial tone, voice tone
Tonto/a - silly, fool
Tonterías - nonsense
Torno - lathe
Toro - bull
Toronja - grapefruit
Torpe - awkward, clumsy
Torre - tower
Tortillas - tortillas
Tos - cough
Trabajador/a - worker, labor
Traductor/a - translator
Tragedia - tragedy
Trago - drink
Traje - suit
Tranquilo/a - calm, relaxed
Transcurso - course, progression
Transparente - transparent
Transporte - transport
Tranvía - streetcar
Traste - fret
Tratado - treaty
Tratamiento - treatment
Travieso/a - mischievous, naughty, playful, menage
Tren - train
Tribu - tribe
Trilogía - trilogy
Trípode - tripod
Triunfo - triumph, victory
Trompeta - trumpet
Trueno - thunder
Tú - you
Turista - tourist
Turística - touristic
Turno - turn

U

Ubicación - location, position
Ubicado - located
Últimamente - lately
Último/a - last, final
Único - only, unique
Unidad - unity
Uniformidad - uniformity
Unión - union
Unísono - unison
Universidad - university
Uña - toe nail, nail
Urbe - large city, metropolis
Uso - the use
Útil - useful, helpful
Utilización - utilization, use
Uva - grape

V

Vaca - cow
Vacación - vacation
Vacío - vacant
Validez - validity
Valioso/a - valuable, precious
Valle - valley
Valor - courage, value, worth, importance
Vanguardia - vanguard
Vaqueros/as - jeans, cowboys, cowgirls
Variedad - variety
Varios/as - various, several
Vaso - glass
Vasco - Basque
Vecindad - vicinity
Vecino/a - neighbor
Vegetación - vegetation
Vehemente - vehement

Vejez - old age, golden years
Velada - show
Velocidad - velocity
Veloz - rapid
Venado - deer
Vendedor/a - salesperson
Venerable - venerable
Venta - sale
Ventaja - advantage
Ventanilla - window, ticket window
Verano - summer
Verbal - verbal
Verbo - verb
Verborrea - verbiage
Verdad - truth, true
Verdadera - true
Verde - green
Verdulería - vegetable store
Verdura - vegetable
Vereda - path, trail
Versatilidad - versatility
Verso - verse
Vestido - dress
Vez - time
Viaje - trip
Videograbadora - VCR
Viejo/a - old person
Viento - wind
Vientre - belly
Vigente - valid, in force
Villa - town, village
Vinagre - vinegar
Vínculo - tie, link, bond
Vino - wine
Violación - violation, offense
Violencia - violence
Violín - violin
Virtudes - virtues
Visitante - visiting or visitor
Vista - view, sight

Vitrina - show case, display cabinet, case
Viudo/a - widower, widow
Vocablo - word, term
Vocacional - vocational
Volante - steering wheel
Voleibol – volleyball
Voluntad - will
Voluntario - volunteer
Voto - vote
Voz - voice
Vuelta - return

Y

Ya – already
Yo - I
Yugo - yoke

Z

Zanahoria - carrot
Zapatos - shoes
Zócalo - central plaza, baseboard
Zona - zone, district, area
Zorro - fox

Made in the USA
Middletown, DE
31 August 2020

17861227R00261